FOCUS ON THE FAMILY®

10-minute devotions to ignite the faith of
parents & teens

joe**white**

TYNDALE

Tyndale House Publishers, Inc.
Wheaton, Illinois

A Focus on the Family book.
Published by Tyndale House Publishers, Wheaton, Illinois.

Focus on the Family books are available at special quantity discounts when purchased in bulk
by corporations, organizations, churches, or groups. Special imprints, messages, and excerpts
can be produced to meet your needs. For more information, contact: Resource Sales Group,
Focus on the Family, 8605 Explorer Drive, Colorado Springs, CO 80920; or phone (800)
932-9123.

Library of Congress Cataloging-in-Publication Data
White, Joe, 1948-
  Fuel : 10-minute devotions to ignite the faith of parents and teens / Joe White.
     p. cm.
"A Focus on the Family book."
  ISBN 1-58997-121-3
 1. Christian teenagers—Religious life. 2. Christian teenagers—Conduct of life. 3. Christian
life—Biblical teaching. I. Title.
  BV4531.3.W48 2003
  248.8'3—dc21

                                                          2003008854

Editor: Betsy L. Holt & Mick Silva
Cover Design: Kurt Birky
Cover Copy: Joy Olson
Cover Photo: Photodisc
Interior Design: Kurt Birky & Angie Barnes

Printed in the United States of America.
04 05 06 07 08/10 9 8 7 6 5 4 3

contents

To my daddy.
You showed me how a busy dad gets it done.

Special thanks to Will Cunningham, Elizabeth Jones, my mom,
and the Kanakuk staff for their invaluable contributions to this book.

introduction
family devotional time

This book is written for families: adults and teens in the *critical years* from 11-18.

These are the years when the hormones peak.

These are the years when media begins marketing sex and hollow philosophies to minors.

These are the years when political correctness tells teenagers that God is irrelevant and science has all the answers.

These are the years of peer pressure when even the strongest young Christians will be pushed to the breaking point.

> *"On TV sporting events, bikini-clad females are used to sell beer, and a nude man and woman kissing in the shower MTV-style are used to sell a wet-dry electric shaver. Ask a 19-year-old boy and girl who walk shamefully away from an abortion clinic if they bought the shaver or bought the sex."*[1]

Unfortunately, this is also the time when many families stop having devotions together. Folks, these are *not* the years to taper off. If anything, you should be turning up the heat. There's no better time to teach your son or daughter about God than during these years. And you'll be rewarded for doing it. You can have fantastic discussions with your child, and you'll rejoice as you watch your teenager make good decisions and learn to develop a godly lifestyle.

In fact, family devotional time is not an option. God commands moms and dads to teach their children about Him.

> *These words, which I am commanding you today, shall be on your heart. You shall teach them diligently to your sons and shall talk of them when you sit in your house and when you walk by the way and when you lie down and when you rise up.* —Deuteronomy 6:6-7

The Bible doesn't say, "Teach your kids *about* God's Word." It says, *"Teach them God's Word."* Then you can help them apply it to their daily lives. God didn't issue this command to Sunday school teachers and educators. He gave it to ordinary parents like you and me.

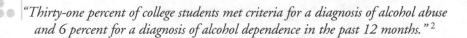

"Thirty-one percent of college students met criteria for a diagnosis of alcohol abuse and 6 percent for a diagnosis of alcohol dependence in the past 12 months." [2]

"In 1970, 5 percent of 15-year-old girls had sex; in 1972, 20 percent of 15-year-old boys said they had sex. In 1997, 45 percent of boys and 38 percent of girls said they have had intercourse in their teen years." [3]

Does having an intentional devotion time with your teenager pay off? Does it work? You'll know when your son or daughter hits college. You'll get another report card when you see how your grandkids are raised. As a counselor of teens, I've heard hundreds of horror stories about drug addictions, alcohol-related accidents, date rape, unwanted pregnancies, abortions, and eating disorders—and more from kids whose parents didn't spend consistent time with them.

"According to some statistics, sixty percent of all high-school Christian kids in America abandon their faith sometime during their college days." [4]

On the flip side, after working with kids at our Christian sports camps in Missouri and Colorado, I've also seen thousands of kids with strong character and an even stronger faith, raised by parents who've guided their spiritual paths.

Open my eyes, [Lord,] that I may behold wonderful things from Your law.
—Psalm 119:18

The devotionals in this book are designed to help your kids earn straight A's on their life report cards. Each devotion brings God's Word to life—and the results are *guaranteed.* Says who? Not me. *God* guarantees these family devotional times.

How blessed is the man [child, mom, dad]
who does not walk in the counsel of the wicked,
nor stand in the path of sinners, nor sit in the seat of scoffers!
But his delight is in the law of the Lord,
and in His law he meditates day and night.
He will be like a tree firmly planted by streams of water,
which yields its fruit in its season, and its leaf does not wither;
and in whatever he does, he prospers.—Psalm 1:1-3

We are in a battle for the hearts and minds of American teens. This devotional book is intended to help you win that battle.

Start today. Then when it's time to leave home, you will be sure the gift has been received—the one that never gets outdated and will join your family together forever.

Every family will do the devotions differently, but here are some suggestions that helped ours get the most out of it:

1. Ask someone to open in prayer.
2. Read the Scripture passage.
3. Discuss what you hear God saying in the passage.
4. Read the devotional amplification and discuss each question.
5. If appropriate, make each other accountable to the devotional's challenge.
6. Close with prayer.

Some tips:

a) Alternate which family members lead the reading and discussion each day.
b) Strive for equal discussion time for each family member.
c) Encourage encouragement! Find the good in each person's response. In our house, criticisms or put-downs cost the critic a quarter, which was then put into the family charity fund.

matthew

It's fitting that the gospel account according to Matthew should lead the 27 books of the New Testament writings. Matthew records more of Jesus' teachings than any other book in the Bible. And Matthew knew Jesus personally as "King of the Jews"—the Messiah, and the fulfillment of all Old Testament prophecies about "the One who is to come." In reading and understanding this book, we encounter the Savior's fundamental plan for life the way it was designed to be lived.

The Night that Was

the WORD | Matthew 1:20-23

"But when he had considered this, behold, an angel of the Lord appeared to him in a dream, saying, 'Joseph, son of David, do not be afraid to take Mary as your wife; for the Child who has been conceived in her is of the Holy Spirit. She will bear a Son; and you shall call His name Jesus, for He will save His people from their sins.' Now all this took place to fulfill what was spoken by the Lord through the prophet: 'Behold, the virgin shall be with child and shall bear a Son, and they shall call His name Immanuel,' which translated means, 'God with us.'"

the Message

There will never be another night like it.

Two young people, singled out by the Lord, were picked to become parents of the Messiah. God chose Mary for her purity and dedication to Him. Purity mattered to God then, and purity matters to God today. God chose Joseph because he was a righteous man. Righteous living mattered to God then, and righteous living matters to God today.

Jesus' parents were righteous, and His conception was pure. The Bible tells us He was conceived by the Holy Spirit. Many people such as the late Joseph Smith, the founder of Mormonism, believe that's just a story—there's no way Mary was a virgin.[1] But that's the human version of "truth." God is powerful. If God can turn a crawling caterpillar into a graceful butterfly, if He can create the universe with a word, then He can easily conceive a life inside a virgin's womb.

Baby Jesus, growing in Mary's womb, would transform "the law into grace" as He gave His followers forgiveness from sin and the hope of eternity. This baby would allow our biggest failures to lead to God's biggest acts of mercy. This baby demonstrated, once and for all time, that God's heart overflows with love toward His people.

Discussion Starters:

• Is that night significant to you? Why or why not?
•• Why does God value righteousness and purity?
••• How does God turn our sinfulness into righteousness?

Lifeline:

How can you show God's love to one another?

Gifts to the Manger Child

the WORD | Matthew 2:9-11

"After hearing the king, they went their way; and the star, which they had seen in the east, went on before them until it came and stood over the place where the Child was. When they saw the star, they rejoiced exceedingly with great joy. After coming into the house they saw the Child with Mary His mother; and they fell to the ground and worshiped Him. Then, opening their treasures, they presented to Him gifts of gold, frankincense, and myrrh."

the Message

We aren't much different from the wise men of Jesus' time. Like them, we have gifts to offer our Savior.

The apostle Paul wrote of some. In Romans 12:1-2, he urged us to give our bodies to Jesus as a holy sacrifice. Paul also said that we shouldn't let the world mold our minds, but instead to allow Christ to make us more like Him.

Keeping our bodies and minds pure are gifts to Jesus.

In Matthew 25:31-40, Jesus also spoke of gifts. He promised that when we give our time or money to the poor, the lonely, the hurt, or the downtrodden, we are actually giving gifts to Him. When you befriend an unpopular student from your high school, for example, sponsor a needy child, or even comfort your brothers or sisters when they're hurting, your love reveals Christ in you.

Our love for others is a gift to Christ.

Gift giving is easy. Your trip to the manger begins each day when you decide to say no to premarital sex or refuse to look at a trashy magazine. Your purity is a gift. You also give to Jesus when you consider the needy people around you. A smile and a kind word, your money, a missions trip are a few gifts you can offer the Savior. You may not have frankincense and myrrh, but you do have a gift to offer the Messiah that's even greater—your love.

Discussion Starters:

How can you keep your mind pure for Jesus? Your body?

What did Jesus mean when He said, "When you give it to the least of these, you give it to me" (see Matthew 25:40)?

What is the greatest gift God has given you?

Lifeline:

Discuss what manger gifts you (individually or as a family) can give to Christ.

Perspective

the **WORD** | Matthew 2:16-18

"Then when Herod saw that he had been tricked by the magi, he became very enraged, and sent and slew all the male children who were in Bethlehem and all its vicinity, from two years old and under, according to the time which he had determined from the magi. Then what had been spoken through Jeremiah the prophet was fulfilled: 'A voice was heard in Ramah, weeping and great mourning, Rachel weeping for her children; and she refused to be comforted, because they were no more.'"

the **Message**

In northwest Arkansas beneath the Ozark Mountains lies a beautiful wilderness cave with millions of pristine crystal formations. My boys and I love to visit and explore that cave. The utter darkness of it is foreboding and cold, but when we turn on our cave lights, the underground treasure chest comes alive.

Darkness and light cannot coexist. The rays of light beaming into the cave's darkness immediately eliminate its blackness.

That's how it was with the light of Christ. His life chased away the darkness of sin and corruption among His followers in Israel. But King Herod, with his black heart, couldn't stand the thought of Jesus, the pure ray of light, coming into the world. Herod tried to destroy the baby Messiah and ended up murdering countless innocent babies. But Jesus' light prevailed—and it always will.

When you carry your Bible to school, when you refuse to join the party scene, when you avoid ungodly movies, and when your actions match your words of faith, you are a witness for Christ. As they did with Jesus, the people who live in darkness will try to put out your light. They'll laugh at you, gossip about you, and belittle you.

When it happens, continue to love those people as Christ did. As a witness for Jesus, you'll be rewarded with eternal light—heaven, where no darkness exists.

Discussion Starters:

• How have you represented Christ in your school? At work?

•• Have you ever been put down or ridiculed for representing Jesus? If so, how?

••• Which biblical people were mistreated because of their faith? How did they respond to their "persecutors"?

Lifeline:

Discuss how your family can bring Christ's light to your neighborhood.

Obedience

"Then Jesus arrived from Galilee at the Jordan coming to John, to be baptized by him. But John tried to prevent Him, saying, 'I have need to be baptized by You, and do You come to me?' But Jesus answering said to him, 'Permit it at this time; for in this way it is fitting for us to fulfill all righteousness.' Then he permitted Him."

the *Message*

I was pretty sure my happy-go-lucky son Cooper would have a tough time keeping his foot off the accelerator of his "slightly used" Ford Explorer during his beginning months as a new driver. Sure enough, to his dismay, one of his first views in the rearview mirror was the flashing red lights of a police car.

Cooper called me immediately.

"Hey, Dad, uh, guess what I just got?" His voice sounded sheepish.

"Hmmm." (I was almost scared to ask.) "Tell me." I chuckled nervously.

"Uh, well, I sorta got a speeding ticket. I'll give you back my license as soon as I get home. I'm sorry, Dad," Cooper said, sighing.

We had prearranged a deal that his first ticket would cost him his license for a month. His second would cost him six months, etc. As crazy and fun and outgoing as he is, I appreciated his obedience that day. I knew it would kill him to give up his driving privileges, but his cooperation meant so much to me. It makes our relationship honest, open, and fun.

Jesus was a *perfect* Son. He was perfectly obedient.

"Why in the world," you might ask about today's Scripture passage, "is Jesus, the perfect man, getting baptized?"

Because, as a Jewish boy, Jesus had been asked by God to "fulfill all righteousness" (verse 15). Similarly, Jesus observed the Passover even though He was the Passover Lamb. He was obedient to Mary and Joseph even though He created them. He gave Himself up for sacrifice on a Roman cross even though He had never sinned.

No wonder His Dad said proudly at Jesus' baptism, "This is My beloved Son, in whom I am well-pleased" (Matthew 3:17).

Discussion Starters:

• Why is obedience sometimes seen as a harsh or distasteful word?

•• Why is it hard to be obedient to authority figures (like Mom and Dad)?

Lifeline:

How can your family create an environment where obedience is more palatable?

"It's Tempting, but I'll Pass"

"Again, the devil took Him to a very high mountain and showed Him all the kingdoms of the world and their glory; and he said to Him, 'All these things I will give You, if You fall down and worship me.' Then Jesus said to him, 'Go, Satan! For it is written, "You shall worship the Lord your God, and serve Him only."'"

the *Message*

Justin, a high school sophomore in Memphis, is nervous about the party at Jennifer's house. He's deciding if he should smoke a joint with his friends before the party. Satan whispers, "It would be better to feel relaxed from the marijuana than to act tense and uncool without it."

Sarah is working the grocery store checkout line when a customer accidentally gives her an extra $20. Satan reminds Sarah, "You're in charge of the money. No one will know if you pocket it."

Eric, an eighth grader in San Diego, notices a *Playboy* magazine on the counter at a surf shop. Satan knows that Eric's curiosity for girls has been getting the best of him lately. Satan nudges Eric, "Go ahead. It's what any normal, red-blooded male would do."

Janelle, a 16-year-old beauty from Boston, is chatting with her friends at lunchtime. They want her to date Todd, the cute basketball player. Janelle has always wanted to go out with someone like him but isn't sure it's the best idea. Satan tells her, "So what if Todd has a bad reputation with girls? All your friends say you'd look great as a couple."

Temptation. Deception. Satan's the master of them both. He always tries to give us the things we think we want now—without giving us a clue of the consequences we'll face later.

Jesus knew that, so He dealt with Satan in the only surefire way available. Jesus didn't argue; He didn't rationalize; He didn't play around. Jesus simply put the arrow of Scripture right through Satan's heart—and knocked the devil right off his feet.

Discussion Starters:

* How are you being tempted this week?
** What Scripture verse can you memorize to help you the next time you're tempted?
*** Why does Satan flee when we toss Scripture at him?

Lifeline:

Family devotions build an arsenal your family can use to overcome temptation.

Fishers of Men

the **WORD** | *Matthew 4:18-19*

"Now as Jesus was walking by the Sea of Galilee, He saw two brothers, Simon who was called Peter, and Andrew his brother, casting a net into the sea; for they were fishermen. And He said to them, 'Follow Me, and I will make you fishers of men.'"

the **Message**

My gran'ma was 100 years old when the curtain between life on earth and eternal life with Jesus was raised and her new heavenly theater became her home. I always called her "Pardner" because she let me know in clear terms that she wasn't old enough to be my gran'ma.

Pardner taught me to fish when I was a young lad. We caught more fish together in my growing-up days than I could even begin to count. During the last few years of Pardner's life she was confined to a wheelchair, but her big, caring smile and the twinkle of love in her pretty brown eyes never dimmed. Just before her 100th birthday, I took her fishing, and she caught a beautiful rainbow trout in the Ozark mountain lake in front of my house.

Her 100th birthday party was the greatest, as I'm sure you can imagine. As I walked in the door to wish her happy birthday, her eyes caught mine, and she never looked away until I knelt by her side.

"Joe Boy," she said sincerely, "take me fishing."

"Aw, Pardner, I can't take you fishing today," I responded lovingly. "This is your 100th birthday, and everybody is here to see you."

Her eyes narrowed in gran'ma-style sternness as she said, "Joe Boy, if you love me, you'll take me fishing."

When Jesus spoke to Peter and Andrew in today's passage, He invited them to go fishing, too. But His call was to a different kind of fishing—"fishing" for the souls of men and women, boys and girls.

Discussion Starters:

• What do you think the disciples thought of Jesus' invitation as they stood on the shore of the Sea of Galilee?

•• Their trade was fishing. Yours might be basketball, school, cheerleading, band, work, home, or family. How would Jesus tell you to witness for Him in your trade?

••• When Jesus wants to take you "fishing for men," what does He want you to do?

Lifeline:

Make a list of people you can "fish" for, then follow up and keep one another accountable.

Radical Forgiveness

the WORD | Matthew 5:22-24

"But I say to you that everyone who is angry with his brother shall be guilty before the court; and whoever says to his brother, 'You good-for-nothing,' shall be guilty before the supreme court; and whoever says, 'You fool,' shall be guilty enough to go into the fiery hell. Therefore if you are presenting your offering at the altar, and there remember that your brother has something against you, leave your offering there before the altar and go; first be reconciled to your brother, and then come and present your offering."

the Message

Jesus demands radical forgiveness. But forgiveness is not easy.

Mr. Jefferson knows that full well. His son Alonzo was murdered by a teenaged gang member during a drive-by shooting. Mr. Jefferson was devastated, but then he decided to adopt the gang member and bring him into his home. The teenager who took Alonzo's life is now treated with all the honor Mr. Jefferson gave his own deceased son. That's radical forgiveness.

My close friend "Ad" Coors also knows forgiveness. His father was murdered in cold blood. It took a lot of courage for Ad to visit the prison and release his bitterness toward the man who robbed him of many wonderful years with his father. Ad forgave the man, which was a monumental accomplishment. But Ad went even further and actually apologized to the man for holding that bitterness against him. That's radical forgiveness.

Many of us may not have experienced such severe wrongdoings, but regardless of the circumstances, it's always difficult to forgive. We like to hold on to our hurt and let others know how much they have wronged us. It takes humility and devotion to God for us to release our bitterness.

Jesus knew that. That's why He talked so much about the need to forgive. When we know God, it's much easier to do, because we remember that we've been forgiven, too. And when we know God, we remember that all things "work together for good to those who love God, to those who are called according to His purpose" (Romans 8:28).

Is there someone you need to forgive today?

Discussion Starters:

* Why did Jesus command us to forgive others (especially family members) before we come to God in worship, prayer, or offering?

** Do you need to seek reconciliation with someone? How will reconciliation be reached?

Lifeline:

How well do you forgive each other in your family? How can you do it better?

Integrity

the **WORD** | Matthew 5:34-37

"But I say to you, make no oath at all, either by heaven, for it is the throne of God, or by the earth, for it is the footstool of His feet, or by Jerusalem, for it is the city of the great King. Nor shall you make an oath by your head, for you cannot make one hair white or black. But let your statement be, 'Yes, yes' or 'No, no'; anything beyond these is of evil."

the **Message**

My oldest brother, Bob, at 6'3" tall and with 210 pounds of solid muscle, is a man's man to the core of his heart. He's a successful dentist, avid bird dog trainer, and skilled outdoorsman. He's one of my heroes.

Thirty years ago, Bob married the first girl he ever loved. He said yes to the preacher on that wedding day and gave his word that he'd give Mary Evelyn his life, *no matter what*. Two summers ago, Mary Evelyn's kidneys quit. Her blood was poisoning her (according to the charts) almost to the point of death. She needed a donor kidney immediately to stay alive. No kidney that matched her biological chemistry was available. Immediately, Bob volunteered his. He was tested for compatibility and, amazingly enough, his matched perfectly.

Soon after, the doctors opened up Bob from his belly button to his backbone, took three ribs and the kidney, placed the kidney into his bride's abdomen, and hooked up the tubes and vessels. The next day, Mary Evelyn was alive and well. Now she feels like a million bucks. Bob feels pain every day, but he just smiles and shrugs it off as a small expression of love for his "wife of a lifetime."

When Jesus said, "Let your yes be a yes," He meant, "Keep your word." Unfortunately, it's easy to see that our culture doesn't often hold to its promises. Politicians say "I promise" and then forget those promises, magazines feature celebrities who've gotten yet another divorce, and so-called best friends will quickly forget their commitment to friendship if someone more exciting comes along. It makes you wonder if anyone values commitment anymore.

But Brother Bob showed me that followers of Jesus keep their word.

Discussion Starters:

* When is it hardest for you to keep a commitment? Why?
** Why is a person's yes the most important word in his or her life?
*** How can you become a more reliable person?

Lifeline:

Make honesty the only policy in your home!

Humility

"Beware of practicing your righteousness before men to be noticed by them; otherwise you have no reward with your Father who is in heaven.... But when you give to the poor do not let your left hand know what your right hand is doing so that your giving will be in secret; and your Father who sees what is done in secret will reward you."

the Message

How many times have you heard people boasting like this?

"I give 15 percent of my paycheck to the Lord's work." "I'm fasting and praying today." "I support that ministry, too." "I go to church every Sunday." "I would never do a thing like that."

Those words remind me of the way an NFL receiver looks when he catches a great pass and goes strutting into the end zone like a peacock courting his girlfriend. A while back, when the NCAA began to enforce stiffer penalties for such ego flaunting, Notre Dame coach Lou Holtz glibly said to his players, "When you get into the end zone, act like you've been there before."

Humility. Discreetness. Secret giving. Silent offering. These are the kinds of qualities that get God's attention and please Him deeply. Jesus makes it clear that when you do something special, God wants all the glory. If you take the glory, there's none left for Him. (He'll get His chance to return the glory to you when you meet Him at heaven's gate.) Heaven will be the final awards ceremony! That's where the rewards, honors, and glory will really matter.

Next time you get a chance to take the credit for something God has honored you with, have some fun and discreetly let Him or someone else get the glory. Be careful, it may become habit-forming!

Discussion Starters:

* Why is it hard to give the glory to God?
** What did Jesus mean by saying that hypocrites already "have their reward in full" (verse 2)?
*** Why is humility such an attractive quality?
**** Who is the most humble person you know? Why?

Lifeline:

Discuss ways in which your family can encourage humility at home.

Treasures

"Do not store up for yourselves treasures on earth, where moth and rust destroy, and where thieves break in and steal. But store up for yourselves treasures in heaven, where neither moth nor rust destroys, and where thieves do not break in or steal; for where your treasure is, there your heart will be also."

the **Message**

I remember one of my greatest days of all time. I got to do what I absolutely *treasure* the most. First, I had the whole day off. I cooked blueberry cinnamon muffins for Brady and chocolate chocolate chip muffins for Cooper. (Yes, I ate one of each.) After a fantastic breakfast devotional together, we went to our little country church and sang those old hymns I used to sing with my daddy when I was a pip-squeak. After church, my boys and I played catch with the football and hit golf balls. Then I was lucky to get phone calls from Jamie and Courtney, who were in college at the time. And if that wasn't enough, I was fortunate enough to hold my precious wife's hand as we prayed together before bed.

I treasure those times with my God, my wife, and my kids. You can burn down my house, steal my car, and take everything I own (except my dog), but leave my treasures and life will still be a "10" for me.

God says it's dangerous to treasure the wrong things. Last night, a dear family friend told me a sad story. My friend said that his 18-year-old daughter, Shauna, is dating a troubled guy. Shauna treasures her popularity and wants to be loved, so she's begun compromising her beliefs for her boyfriend. He's pressuring her into drinking and partying. Now she's confused, depressed, and feels as if her whole world is falling apart.

It's easy to treasure popularity, expensive toys, power and position, houses, careers, sex, and cars. But Jesus tells us to treasure eternal things.

And most of all, God says, "Treasure Me."

Discussion Starters:

• What things do you treasure? Is your heart in the right place?
 •• Why is it so hard to treasure what really matters more than the stuff that clutters our lives?
 ••• What do you really want to treasure more today? How can you do that?

Lifeline:

Talk through how your family can better treasure the things that matter most.

Monkey See, Monkey Do

the **WORD** | Matthew 6:22-24, 33

"The eye is the lamp of the body; so then if your eye is clear, your whole body will be full of light. But if your eye is bad, your whole body will be full of darkness. If then the light that is in you is darkness, how great is the darkness! No one can serve two masters; for either he will hate the one and love the other, or he will be devoted to one and despise the other. You cannot serve God and wealth.... But seek first His kingdom and His righteousness, and all these things will be added to you."

the *Message*

What you see is what you get.

It's true. Your eyes are windows into your mind and heart. What you see, what you choose to put into your mind each day, will have a profound impact on you. Are you too materialistic for your own good? Are you being selective enough in choosing magazines and TV programs? What kinds of movies do you watch? It's hard to keep your eyes on Jesus and not on money or the world. It's difficult to stay sexually pure and drug- and alcohol-free. But it's even harder when you let the culture constantly parade money, sex, and alcohol in front of your eyes.

Temptation is everywhere. A reviewer for *Rolling Stone* magazine remarked that after only a few hours of watching MTV, he had seen more than 100 women scantily clad and portrayed like the seductive models who grace the cover of *Cosmopolitan* magazine.[2] The soaps and sitcoms aren't much better. *USA Today* reported that a survey of more than 500,000 fourth graders said "TV prompts them the most" to try drugs and alcohol.[3] It isn't any wonder when you consider that the average TV viewer will see 100,000 beer commercials by age 18[4] and 14,000 sexual references *per year*.[5]

The apostle Paul, knowing where true peace and happiness lie, said, "Set your mind on the things above, not on the things that are on earth" (Colossians 3:2). Place your eyes on God, and all good things will be given to you.

Discussion Starters:

Why does Jesus talk so much about the eyes?

Are you trying to serve two masters? Explain.

How can your family create a healthy media environment?

Lifeline:

Have each person set goals to help him or her develop eyes for God.

Log Eye

the WORD | Matthew 7:1, 3, 5

"Do not judge so that you will not be judged.... Why do you look at the speck that is in your brother's eye, but do not notice the log that is in your own eye? ...You hypocrite, first take the log out of your own eye, and then you will see clearly to take the speck out of your brother's eye."

the Message

According to Paul Aldrich, Christian recording artist and comedian, old "Log Eye" is a funny ol' critter. He roams in every home, every school hallway, every church, every business, every human mind. He's a weird-looking dude because he has a magnifying glass in front of one eye, a big, bowed-up log in the other eye, and a sharp, pointy finger always showing somebody else's faults. The first word out of his mouth is always "You."

I fight with Log Eye in my own mind every day. The big chump! He makes me so critical of my wife and kids that I want to take the log out and hit him with it! One time when one of my boys was young, I was "rantin' and ravin'" about something he had done when my sweet wife, Debbie Jo, stopped me dead in my tracks.

"Honey," she said to me, "your son sees himself in your eyes." Oooo, that hurt. But she was right. I was so bent on criticizing my son, I forgot the damage I could cause to him. Log Eye was ruling my life that day!

God instructs parents to teach godly principles and to correct bad behavior, but He never intended our *focus* to be critical or judgmental. Our first priority is to love God and then love others (see Matthew 22:37-40).

With that in mind, for *all* members of the family, the motto I like is:

"Catch each other in the act of doing something *good* and tell 'em about it."

Discussion Starters:

Why is it so dangerous to be judgmental?

What is a blind spot? Why are logs so hard to see?

Why is it sometimes easier to be critical rather than loving?

How can your family kick ol' Log Eye out of the family circle?

Lifeline:

Say something affirming to your family today.

Legitimacy

the **WORD** | Matthew 7:21-23

"Not everyone who says to Me, 'Lord, Lord,' will enter the kingdom of heaven, but he who does the will of My Father who is in heaven will enter. Many will say to Me on that day, 'Lord, Lord, did we not prophesy in Your name, and in Your name cast out demons, and in Your name perform many miracles?' And then I will declare to them, 'I never knew you; depart from Me, you who practice lawlessness.'"

the **Message**

Imagine what we'd all look like if we were completely transparent and could see the inside of other people's hearts. What if others could see the inside of *your* heart?

No baloney, no excuses, no hoopla, just truth. What would people see in you?

Unlike us, the Lord looks *only* at our hearts (see 1 Samuel 16:7). Many Christians are dedicated and sincere in their faith. But many of them run around churches and Christian homes calling themselves "Christians" when they've never given their hearts to Him. In this passage, Jesus was talking to those halfhearted souls. Are you one of them?

The chronicler expresses God's focus this way: "For the eyes of the Lord move to and fro throughout the earth that He may strongly support those whose heart is completely His" (2 Chronicles 16:9).

I believe that once we're truly His, we're always truly His. But if we have lawless, rebellious, or dishonest hearts, we have to wonder where our hearts truly lie.

The apostle Paul urged us to search our hearts. He said, "Test yourselves to see if you are in the faith; examine yourselves!" (2 Corinthians 13:5). Do you consider anything in your life to be more important than God? Are you only a "Sunday Christian"? If so, give Him your whole heart. Then you'll have a faith that is, as people say, "the real thing."

Discussion Starters:

• What does it mean to do the will of the Lord?
    •• What do you think Jesus meant when He said, "I never knew you"?
  ••• Are you giving God your whole heart?

Lifeline:

Discuss specific ways to help one another put God first in your hearts.

That Special Touch

the WORD | Matthew 8:1-3

"When Jesus came down from the mountain, large crowds followed Him. And a leper came to Him and bowed down before Him, and said, 'Lord, if You are willing, You can make me clean.' Jesus stretched out His hand and touched him, saying, 'I am willing; be cleansed.' And immediately his leprosy was cleansed."

the Message

Cathy hardly ever went out. In fact, the boys in our high school didn't even notice her. As a little girl, Cathy had battled a rare illness that left her neck and mouth grossly distorted. Even though Cathy was as sweet as any girl in my school, no boy would ask her for a date because of her strangely disfigured features...that is, until her senior prom.

David was the president of our student council and was about as nice a guy as I've ever met. He not only asked Cathy to the prom, but he also took her there and treated her like a queen. Cathy looked stunningly beautiful in her blue dress lined with white lace.

That prom night was significant for another reason as well. Alfonse, a quiet but sincere country boy, was also at the prom, and he noticed Cathy's previously hidden beauty. Alfonse took a special interest in Cathy after that dance, and they developed a wonderful relationship. Eventually, Alfonse asked for her hand in marriage.

Imagine the good we could do if we all reached out with hands of love and compassion! David, the boy who asked Cathy to the prom, demonstrated Christ's loving touch when he looked beyond Cathy's appearance, beyond what other kids might think of him, and asked her to the dance. Christ was able to work through David, beautifully fulfilling Cathy's need for love and attention.

The miracle that happened with David, Cathy, and Alfonse always reminds me of the story of Jesus and the leper. Jesus, with unfathomable compassion, reached out His hand in love. He risked disease and rejection from society and touched the disfigured leper right in front of everyone. While others backed away and turned their heads in disgust, Jesus reached His hand straight into the heart of the man's greatest need.

Discussion Starters:

* What would be a modern equivalent to Jesus' touching a leper with compassion?
** Are you in need of Jesus' loving touch? Explain.
*** Do you know someone who needs your hand of compassion? If so, who? How can you help him or her?

Lifeline:

Discuss how your family can both receive and give Jesus' healing love.

Sufficient Faith

the **WORD** | Matthew 8:23-26

"When He got into the boat, His disciples followed Him. And behold, there arose a great storm on the sea, so that the boat was being covered with the waves; but Jesus Himself was asleep. And they came to Him and woke Him, saying, 'Save us, Lord; we are perishing!' He said to them, 'Why are you afraid, you men of little faith?' Then He got up and rebuked the winds and the sea, and it became perfectly calm."

the **Message**

My friend Shannon is an actress in Hollywood. She is talented, beautiful, capable, sought after...and poor. She has read dozens of scripts from wooing directors and producers, but to this date in her young career, she has not accepted one. Every script has suggestive romance. Every script has crude language. And every time, she says the same thing—"No thanks. I'll wait for a script my conscience can live with."

My dear friend Shannon has faith that God will meet her needs.

God *will* meet your needs. But so often we struggle to believe it.

Even the disciples struggled with their faith. All day long in the boat, before the big storm, the disciples had heard Jesus deliver the greatest sermon on faith ever preached. But when the clouds came in and the rain poured down, they floundered. Had they really listened to their teacher?

"Save us, Lord; we are perishing!" they cried (verse 25).

We read the Bible and wonder, *How could the disciples forget Jesus' words so soon?* But how do *you* deal with life's storms?

You haven't had a date in months. You could lower your standards.

Your weight lifting program for football training has gone flat. Several guys have a higher benchpress max. You could take steroids.

Algebra is becoming impossible. The tests are killers. That girl sitting next to you always gets it right. Just one look at her paper would help.

There will always be storms, but your God is bigger than the storms in your life. Is your faith big enough?

Discussion Starters:

* What is testing your faith today?
* Where is Jesus in your boat?
* Why is it so hard to believe that Jesus can silence and calm our storms?
* How can you find peace and serenity in the midst of your storm right now?

Lifeline:

In the storms, remember, "God will supply all your needs..." (Philippians 4:19).

True Friends

the WORD | Matthew 9:2

"And they brought to Him a paralytic lying on a bed. Seeing their faith, Jesus said to the paralytic, 'Take courage, son; your sins are forgiven.'"

the Message

Have you ever thought about the paralytic's friends?

His friends knew him. They knew he needed help, and they knew he needed the Savior. They went out of their way, went to work, and took their friend to the only place he could get the help he desperately needed. They were true friends.

I'm sure you've learned that not everyone is a true friend, though. Some so-called friends help friends sneak out of the house at night. Other "friends" buy beer and drugs so friends can party. Some "friends" take friends to suggestive movies. And many supposed "friends" push their girlfriends or boyfriends to have sex. These wanna-be friends are dangerous. I know—almost all the mistakes my teenage friends make are due to their "friends" who have led them in the wrong direction.

That's not the case with Andy, Justin, Chris, Brady, Skippy, Jared, and Isaac, though. These high school juniors are star athletes, so drinking and partying aren't even options for them. They know that drugs and alcohol are completely uncool, and they remind each other of that at their weekly Bible study. They encourage each other to keep off drugs, to be sexually pure, and to be moral leaders in their school.

Want to be a true friend? Build others up. Encourage your friends to do the right thing. And let your friendship reveal Christ's unconditional love.

That's what real friendship is all about.

Discussion Starters:

* What's the difference between a "friend" and a true friend?
* Who are your true friends? Why do you consider them to be true friends?
* To *have* a true friend, you need to *be* a true friend. Describe the kind of friend you'd like to be.
* In what ways is Jesus a friend to you?

Lifeline:

How can you be true friends to another? How can you encourage true friendships?

Just a Touch

the WORD | Matthew 9:20-22

"And a woman who had been suffering from a hemorrhage for twelve years, came up behind Him and touched the fringe of His cloak; for she was saying to herself, 'If I only touch His garment, I will get well.' But Jesus turning and seeing her said, 'Daughter, take courage; your faith has made you well.' At once the woman was made well."

the Message

Jesus loves it when His children reach out to Him in faith.

Just look at how He responded to the thief on the cross (Luke 23). This criminal hung next to Jesus, dying. In the final breath of his futile life, the thief looked to the Savior nailed on the cross beside him and squeaked out a tiny plea for mercy. Immediately, Jesus promised him life in heaven.

Peter, one of Jesus' reckless disciples, also called out to Him in faith. Peter and the other disciples had watched Jesus walk on the Sea of Galilee. Eager to follow in his Master's footsteps (literally), Peter impulsively stepped out of the boat to walk on the sea. But his fear caught up with him, and he began to sink. Peter cried desperately, "Lord, save me!" (Matthew 14:30). In a heartbeat, Jesus' hand was there, and Peter's life was spared.

The hemorrhaging woman had great faith in Jesus' power as well. After 12 years of continuous bleeding, the woman realized she needed a touch from Jesus. She approached Him in a crowd and, amidst the pushing and shoving, reached out in faith and touched not Him but His garment! Jesus responded to her hopefulness and courage, and her faith was rewarded.

What about you? Are you sinking in despair? Do you have faith that Jesus can help you?

Your coach hasn't noticed you in weeks. Your close friend has cancer. You cringe every time you look in the mirror. Your girlfriend just called it quits. Your bleeding just won't stop, and you need a Savior.

Christ is your ultimate problem solver, and He's ready to rescue you. All it takes is a tiny prayer and a speck of faith because He's only an arm's reach away. He'll be there. Count on it.

Discussion Starters:

* What is faith? Why is faith so important to God?
    ** Can you relate to any of the biblical people in today's devotional? If so, how?
        *** How can you touch His garment when your heart's bleeding?

Lifeline:

Discuss a situation in which your family must reach out to Jesus in faith.

Sodom and Gomorrah, Dallas and San Francisco

the WORD | Matthew 10:11, 14-15

"And whatever city or village you enter, inquire who is worthy in it, and stay at his house until you leave that city.... Whoever does not receive you, nor heed your words, as you go out of that house or that city, shake the dust off your feet. Truly I say to you, it will be more tolerable for the land of Sodom and Gomorrah in the day of judgment than for that city."

the Message

It's a sunny Thursday afternoon. School has just ended, and Cindy and Rebecca are racing out the door to the parking lot. They hop into Rebecca's Jeep, and Cindy pops in the newest CD. Jamming down the road, singing, they drive to the mall, where Cindy sees this sweater she "has to have." She doesn't have cash, but—not to worry—she can always charge it to Mom and Dad's platinum card. Cindy's just got to have a new outfit for her date on Friday with Brian. It's a *necessity.*

Maybe you aren't accustomed to the lifestyle Cindy and Rebecca enjoy, but chances are you know someone who is. We live in a rich country. Americans have it all. Some of our "poor" would be among the rich in other lands. The things we take for granted, like indoor plumbing and electricity, are luxuries in other countries.

And as spoiled as we are, we still want more. That's why we trade in our cars, rack up debt, move to bigger houses, hit the mall, and upgrade everything. Yet, with all our blessings, our music, TV shows, books, and movies continue to blaspheme God.

God has sent us a steady stream of His disciples for 400 years. We have churches on almost every corner and Bibles all over the house. But God is quickly being taken out of our schools, courtrooms, and businesses. If God leveled Sodom and Gomorrah in a flash, what will become of America if we don't heed God's Word? America's blessings will mean nothing if the hearts of its people are still sinful.

Discussion Starters:

• Would the disciples have to "shake the dust off
   their feet" if they came to your house today?
•• How can your family remain humble and live lives pleasing to God?

Lifeline:

Building a godly home is the best way to begin rebuilding America (or any nation).

the **WORD** | Matthew 10:28, 32

"Do not fear those who kill the body but are unable to kill the soul; but rather fear Him who is able to destroy both soul and body in hell.... Therefore everyone who confesses Me before men I will also confess him before My Father who is in heaven."

the **Message**

The secret had slipped out. It was the mid 1970s, during the days of fierce Russian Communism and the ruthless suppression of Christianity. A group of more than 100 Christians was singing hymns and worshiping God in an "underground" church when the service was abruptly interrupted by KGB soldiers equipped with automatic guns.

The congregation immediately became deathly silent as the guards demanded that all true followers of Jesus Christ stand up. Those not willing to confess Christ were free to leave. With fear and trepidation, a few dozen devout believers stood on their feet, knowing the next sound they'd probably hear would be gunshots snuffing out their final breath. The rest desperately fled from the building.

When the scuffling ended and the room was silent, one of the KGB gunmen spoke up. "All right," he said, "we've also converted to Christianity, and we just wanted to know who the true Christians were. Now let's have a real worship service together." The worship that night was powerful.

No, we don't live in the old USSR, and the United States isn't communist, but this "one nation under God" can be awfully cruel to Christians sometimes. Speaking up or saying no in high school often brings on heavy persecution. The evolutionists will sneer, the popular crowd will gossip, the partyers will laugh, and sometimes your friends will leave you. Standing up for Jesus is not easy.

But He defended you. He subjected Himself to ridicule, persecution, and even death—all for you, because He loves you. Is your love for Him strong enough to stand?

Discussion Starters:

* If you lived in a communist country and were convicted of being a Christian, what evidence would the witnesses bring up to convict you?
** If you were one of the Russian worshipers that day, would you have stood or fled the scene?
*** Have you ever been persecuted for your faith? If so, how did you persevere through it? Was your faith strengthened? Why or why not?

Lifeline:

Pray together that God will enable your family to stand up for Jesus.

Is He God, or What?

"Now when John, while imprisoned, heard of the works of Christ, he sent word by his disciples and said to Him, 'Are You the Expected One, or shall we look for someone else?' Jesus answered and said to them, 'Go and report to John what you hear and see.'"

the *Message*

"I and the Father are one" (John 10:30).
"I am the good shepherd" (John 10:11).
"I am the true vine" (John 15:1).
"I am the way" (John 14: 6).

Make no mistake about it—whatever the world thinks about Jesus, He was convinced He was God. Call Him crazy; call Him delirious; call Him a liar; but don't call Him a good man, a prophet, a great moral teacher, or any other title of human significance, because either He was God or He was the most misleading person who ever lived.

John the Baptist, another man with a definite mission from God, had given his life to proclaiming the coming of Christ. Sitting in his prison cell, he wanted to make sure he was sold out for the right person. In so many words, Jesus told John's disciples to tell him the same thing He'd tell you the next time you ask. "I do things that only God can do. I'm the fulfillment of all messianic prophecy. I have power that no mere man could ever have. Yes, John, when you see Me, you've seen the Father."

If Jesus was anything less than God, His sacrifice on the cross could never have paid for your sins. At the same time, He had to become a man and identify with your sinfulness so that He could literally die for those sins. As God, He had the holiness and authority; as man, He had the empathy and the humanity.

John was convinced. Are you?

Discussion Starters:

* Why did God have to become a man?
** What did He mean when He said, "I and the Father are one"?

Lifeline:

What defense could you give to the claim that Jesus was just a great moral teacher?

The Light Burden

"Come to Me, all who are weary and heavy laden, and I will give you rest. Take My yoke upon you and learn from Me, for I am gentle and humble in heart, and you will find rest for your souls. For My yoke is easy and My burden is light."

the Message

The night before my college football team played the University of Oklahoma in a major New Year's Eve bowl bash, we went to a professional ice hockey game to ease our nerves and forget the tension of the upcoming duel on the field. The hockey game was brutal. The hitting, checking, and fighting made our game of football seem more like Nintendo. We moaned, groaned, and empathized with the physical punishment each player dealt to his opponent. We left the arena, relieved to be putting on our football gear the next day and playing such a comparatively tame sport!

My buddy Shane plays goalie for his high school hockey team. It's no small task. The goalie takes the heat with every play. The frozen puck slams into his face mask at speeds up to 100 mph, and every opponent longs to shove him away from the goal so his teammates can score into the net. But Shane plays the game fearlessly because in hockey, the goalie is protected by his teammates at all costs. In one critical game, a crazed opponent bashed into Shane with both fists. Immediately, Shane's teammates leaped on the intruder with protective vengeance. The goalie's burden of protecting the goal is light. He has no fear of the opposing players because at all times, his teammates are ready, willing, and able to defend him.

As a Christian, you are the goalie. The pressure of life is intense. You may be weary and burdened by the demands around you. The opponents—peer pressure, guilt, perfectionism, failure, and lust—are constantly before you, desiring to eliminate you from the game. But thanks to our caring, self-sacrificing, protective Savior, Jesus Christ, the game is fun! We know that Jesus will respond immediately to our prayers. He'll overpower the enemy as we look to Him in faith and let Him intercede for our daily needs.

Discussion Starters:

* What burden have you been carrying this week?
  ** How can you give it to Jesus?
    *** How has Jesus taken up your burdens in the past?

Lifeline:

Pray about each other's burdens today, and give the load to Christ.

The Lord of the Sabbath

"At that time Jesus went through the grainfields on the Sabbath, and His disciples became hungry and began to pick the heads of grain and eat. But when the Pharisees saw this, they said to Him, 'Look, Your disciples do what is not lawful to do on a Sabbath.' ...[And Jesus said,] 'Have you not read in the Law, that on the Sabbath the priests in the temple break the Sabbath and are innocent? But I say to you that something greater than the temple is here.... For the Son of Man is Lord of the Sabbath.'"

the **Message**

Until the time Jesus came, the word *law* was a stumbling block for everyone who lived according to it. It meant keeping tons of nitpicky rules, and many people who lived by it were judgmental and hypocritical.

Jesus changed all that. He said that it's not just sinful to murder, but it's also sinful to hate a guy enough to want to kill him.

It's not only sinful to fornicate, commit adultery, and practice homosexuality, but it's also sinful to entertain sexual thoughts about anyone except your spouse. It's not just sinful to talk in a derogatory manner behind your parents' or children's backs, but it's also sinful to harbor unresolved bitterness in your heart.

The letter of the law didn't matter so much to Jesus. He cared about the spirit of the law. Your motives. Your thoughts. What's in your heart.

In Scripture, Jesus is referred to as "the Christ" (John 11:27), "the Word" (John 1:1), the co-creator of the universe (Colossians 1), and the "Lord of the Sabbath" (Matthew 12:8). As you love Him and worship Him in all things, you are keeping the law. The name of the game on the Sabbath (as well as the other six days of the week) is not to keep from breaking a sweat, but to think of Him, worship Him, live for Him, and love Him.

On Sundays, we're supposed to focus on God and remember His command to rest one day a week. But whatever we do, our *hearts* matter most to God. If we're truly devoted to Him, we'll try to stay pure, represent Christ, be reconciled with our families, and honor Him in all we do.

Discussion Starters:

• What is one way in which you frequently lose track of God's words?
•• God's law is to simply, sincerely love Him. Does knowing that bring you freedom?

Lifeline:

How can your family honor Christ better this next Sabbath?

It's All or Nothing

the WORD | Matthew 12:25, 30

"And knowing their thoughts Jesus said to them, 'Any kingdom divided against itself is laid waste; and any city or house divided against itself will not stand.... He who is not with Me is against Me; and he who does not gather with Me scatters.'"

the Message

Sonya follows Christ and tries to spend time praying and reading the Bible each day. She wants her life to reflect her love for God and other people. Ted, on the other hand, is defiant and rebellious. He cusses up a storm and uses Christ's name in vain—all the time. Crystal and Tony are in a completely different group. They're not living for God, but they're not out to get Him, either. They party a little and go to church a little, too. They believe in God, but they don't want to be associated with Him.

Jesus didn't mince words when He said, "He who is not with Me is against Me" (verse 30). Jesus' half brother James put it this way: "Whoever wishes to be a friend of the world makes himself an enemy of God" (James 4:4). For decades, I've heard stories of kids and adults who cop out on God by saying, "I'm not doing anything that bad. I'm just not ready to commit my life to Christ." In case after case, it was only a matter of time before each person was reeling in emotional pain because her "friendship with the world" had led her into some disaster.

No one *wants* to be a drug addict, but one little joint doesn't look all that bad. No one *wants* to be a hopeless alcoholic, but one little beer looks pretty harmless. No one *wants* to be a porn addict, but that *Cosmopolitan* magazine doesn't look that dangerous. One joint, one beer, or one flip through a questionable magazine can start you on a path toward a bunch of bad habits, though.

Jesus knew what He was talking about when He warned, in effect, "Either you love me with your whole heart or you don't love me at all." Our Lord is demanding. He wants all of you. Have you made that total commitment?

Discussion Starters:

• Why does Satan like to see us walk down the middle of the road, morally speaking?
•• Are you facing any compromising circumstances this week? Explain.
••• How can you love Jesus with your whole heart? What things do you need to change so you can do that?

Lifeline:

Discuss and reflect on Revelation 3:15-16. What significance does this have for your family?

His Family Matters

"And stretching out His hand toward His disciples, He said, 'Behold My mother and My brothers! For whoever does the will of My Father who is in heaven, he is My brother and sister and mother.'"

the *Message*

I'll never forget the sting of rejection I felt that day as a shy and insecure seven-year-old. It was after one of Elvis Presley's small concerts during his early performance days, before he hit the big time. Presley had given me his autograph earlier, but I'd lost it somewhere in the crowd. He must have remembered my nervous and embarrassed face the second time around because he said, annoyed, "Hey, kid, didn't I already do this once tonight?" After I fumbled a torn piece of paper and a pencil into his hands, he reluctantly scribbled "Elvis Presley" a second time. I ducked my head in complete embarrassment and scurried off to find my bike and pedal home.

Some people collect Elvis albums like diamonds and even call him the "King of Rock and Roll." To each his own, I guess, but I'd rather invest my money and soul in the real King—Jesus Christ. Christ gave me a longer lasting autograph than Elvis did. Christ's words are written "on the tablet of my heart" because He died for me, and through His Spirit, He lives in me (see 2 Corinthians 3).

But even better, Jesus actually calls me family! As I choose to follow Him, He chooses me to be His son. First John 3:1 says, "See how great a love the Father has bestowed on us, that we would be called children of God; and such we are." I'm part of His family because He loves me so much. As His child, I even share in His heavenly inheritance. Now, that's love! Some people would do anything for my old Elvis autograph, but I'd trade in the rock 'n' roll king's paper for the almighty King's eternal riches and love any day.

He has invited you to be His child, too. Have you joined His family?

Discussion Starters:

* What does it mean to be invited into God's family?
  ** Why does He call His obedient followers "family"?
*** What do you see when you picture your heavenly Father?
**** How do you feel knowing you are part of God's divine family?

Lifeline:

Since you are members of God's family, how should you act toward each other?

Heartfelt Growth

the **WORD** | Matthew 13:3-8

"And He spoke…to them in parables, saying, 'Behold, the sower went out to sow; and as he sowed, some seeds fell beside the road, and the birds came and ate them up. Others fell on the rocky places, where they did not have much soil; and immediately they sprang up, because they had no depth of soil. But when the sun had risen, they were scorched; and because they had no root, they withered away. Others fell among the thorns, and the thorns came up and choked them out. And others fell on the good soil and yielded a crop, some a hundredfold, some sixty, and some thirty.' "

the **Message**

I had just spent an exciting week snowboarding in the Rockies with my five best friends—my wife and four kids. As we sat in the Denver International Airport, waiting for our flight home, a petite seven-year-old girl and her daddy caught my eye. The girl's long, brown ponytail bobbed up and down each time she caught the small, red, bouncy ball her daddy tossed her way. For several minutes, I watched them giggle together as they played catch. With each bounce of the ball, he sowed another seed of love in her heart. With each assuring word and positive glance, her tiny heart expanded as she smiled back at her daddy.

After they left, I thought, *What will happen to her when she's 16, 17, and 18?* I looked over at my own daughters, ages 18 and 21, and wondered, *Will she and her dad still be friends? What decisions will she make? What kind of friends will she run with? Will she make her parents proud?* As a father, I could see that the little girl's daddy had sown seeds of love and planted them with high expectations that someday a fulfilled, happy, productive woman would grow from those innocent days of childhood.

I hoped that love would take root. That was my desire for the little girl, and that is Jesus' desire for us. He hopes that the thorns—temptations—of work and school won't choke the growth in our hearts. He has faith that bad attitudes, bitterness, and jealousy won't harden our hearts. Jesus has sown seeds from the fruit of His Spirit—love, joy, peace, patience, kindness, goodness, faithfulness, gentleness, and self-control—into the hearts of His children. If we spend time with the Sower, Jesus, His seeds *will* take root.

Discussion Starters:

- How have God's seeds grown in your heart this year? Be specific.
  - Have any thorns crept into your life? If so, how can you uproot them?

Lifeline:

Family time with God creates deep and fertile soil.

Weeds and Flowers

"Jesus presented another parable to them, saying, 'The kingdom of heaven may be compared to a man who sowed good seed in his field. But while his men were sleeping, his enemy came and sowed tares among the wheat, and went away. But when the wheat sprouted and bore grain, then the tares became evident also.... [So the landowner said], "Allow both to grow together until the harvest; and in the time of the harvest I will say to the reapers, 'First gather up the tares and bind them in bundles to burn them up; but gather the wheat into my barn.'"'"

the *Message*

As a kid, I dreaded certain Saturdays. My brothers and I would trudge out to the yard to begin our least favorite chore—weeding. Weeding out the Bermuda grass from the flower gardens that surrounded our Texas home was no small task. Bermuda grass is tough as all get-out, and its long, gnarly roots grab the soil. We would pull and complain, dig and grumble for hours on Saturday mornings in the spring and fall. The flowers that grew after we weeded were beautiful, and I loved cutting a handful of them for my mom, but I couldn't get rid of those weeds fast enough. Weeds are such a big pain that they can make beautiful flowerbeds a chore!

Weeds and tares are like rotten habits, bad TV shows, sick music, and bitter thoughts. Once they plant themselves in your heart, it's hard to pull them out. I'm ashamed to tell you I can *still* remember the lyrics from some of the foul songs that I listened to in junior high. Those weeds are brutal, and they're often deeply buried in your heart. The worst part of all is that they choke out your wheat.

What's your wheat? Reading and memorizing Scripture, spending time with family and uplifting friends, praying, volunteering your time, doing family devotionals...all those things can be the wheat—the good—in your life. And when you weed out the tares from the wheat, the result is rich and enduring! My mom had me memorize some of the Sermon on the Mount when I was nine, and do you know what? I still remember those verses!

When Christ comes, the tares go into the fire, and the wheat becomes a bouquet of flowers that is presented to God.

If He came today, what would *your* "crop" look like?

Discussion Starters:

* Describe the wheat in your life today.
    ** What tares or weeds have lodged themselves in your mind?
  *** What kind of bouquet do you want to present to God?

Lifeline:

How can your family encourage spiritual weeding?

The Best of the Best and the Worst of the Worst

the WORD | Matthew 13:44, 47-50

"The kingdom of heaven is like a treasure hidden in the field, which a man found and hid again; and from joy over it he goes and sells all that he has and buys that field.... Again, the kingdom of heaven is like a dragnet cast into the sea, and gathering fish of every kind; and when it was filled, they drew it up on the beach; and they sat down and gathered the good fish into containers, but the bad they threw away. So it will be at the end of the age; the angels will come forth and take out the wicked from among the righteous, and will throw them into the furnace of fire; in that place there will be weeping and gnashing of teeth."

the Message

My son Brady stood past the half-court line, ready to make the three-point, tie-breaking shot. This was Brady's sophomore year, and he'd been sitting on the varsity bench most of the season. But Brady was ready. He had practiced the shot millions of times. Brady fired the ball through the air, and the ball swished through the net just as the buzzer sounded. The crowd went wild! Brady felt as if he were perched on the front row of heaven as the mob embraced him. It was the thrill of victory! The best of the best!

During his bitterly disappointing junior year, he missed the same last-second shot five times in game after game. Each time, Brady's miss cost his team the game. He felt personally responsible for each defeat and spent most of the season perched on the bench of despair. It was the agony of defeat! The worst of the worst!

What do you think is the best thing the world has to offer? What's worth your sacrifice and patience? A BMW convertible? An Ivy League scholarship? Making it to the NFL? Being voted homecoming queen?

On the flip side, what's your worst nightmare? A broken heart? Public humiliation? A tragic car wreck? Flunking out of school?

Nothing on earth, no matter how seemingly wonderful, will compare to the treasure of heaven. And the worst nightmare on earth will pale in comparison to a second spent in hell. Jesus always shot it straight. He told us what to expect based on how we respond to His offer of salvation.

Discussion Starters:

• Why did Jesus compare heaven to a treasure?

•• Why did Jesus say that in hell there will be "weeping and gnashing of teeth" (verse 50)?

Lifeline:

Discuss what you picture heaven to be like and why. (We'll learn more in the book of Revelation.)

A Promise Is a Promise

the WORD | Matthew 14:6-10

"But when Herod's birthday came, the daughter of Herodias danced before them and pleased Herod, so much that he promised with an oath to give her whatever she asked. Having been prompted by her mother, she said, 'Give me here on a platter the head of John the Baptist.' Although he was grieved, the king commanded it to be given because of his oaths, and because of his dinner guests. He sent and had John beheaded in the prison."

the Message

Have you ever had a friend who always called you at the last minute to cancel plans? A friend who stood you up? A friend who backed out on an offer to help? A friend who said one thing and then did another?

Not many people weigh their words these days.

In the movie *Hook*, Robin Williams played a Wall Street businessman who was also a preoccupied father. He was so busy working that he left no time for family. During a trip with his son, Williams said to the boy, "When we get back, I'll go to all the rest of your ball games. I promise. My word is my bond."

His son had already seen too many broken promises and replied with disgust, "Yeah—junk bonds."

Like the busy businessman, King Herod also spoke thoughtlessly. Swayed by the moment and his guests, Herod rashly promised to give Herodias's daughter whatever she asked. Later, the king "was grieved" to realize that keeping his promise would mean beheading John the Baptist (verses 9-10). He probably would've given anything to take back his promise.

What about you? How dependable are your promises? Do you always think before you give your word? Do you count the cost before you sign your name to an agreement? Are you someone who follows through?

Your word is the key that will open the door to every important relationship you'll ever have. If you're trusted, you will be able to talk openly with people, and they will listen. If you break your word, everything you say will be suspect and insignificant to others. By simply watching what you say and then standing by those words, you will become a trustworthy, dependable, credible friend.

Discussion Starters:

* Has there been a time when you gave your word flippantly, without thinking about it first?
  ** What can you do to remind yourself to think about what you're promising the next time you're in that situation?

Lifeline:

Think of a situation in which you could forgive someone who has made a flippant promise.

The Storm of Rejection

the WORD | Matthew 14:25, 27-31

"And in the fourth watch of the night He came to them, walking on the sea.... But immediately Jesus spoke to them, saying, 'Take courage, it is I; do not be afraid.' Peter said to Him, 'Lord, if it is You, command me to come to You on the water.' And He said, 'Come!' And Peter got out of the boat, and walked on the water and came toward Jesus. But seeing the wind, he became frightened, and beginning to sink, he cried out, 'Lord, save me!' Immediately Jesus stretched out His hand and took hold of him, and said to him, 'You of little faith, why did you doubt?' "

the Message

It's been decades, but I can still remember the pain of rejection I felt as a fifth grader. I was playing out in front of our house, and my "buddies" were inside my neighbor's house, watching a football game on TV. The door was locked, so I knocked to be let in.

"There's no one home," one of the giggly voices inside called out.

I naively responded, "What do you mean? I can see you in there."

The voice turned cutting and cruel. "Go away. Can't you take a hint?"

Rejection. It cuts like a knife. During junior high and high school, it's probably the worst kind of pain. I can almost laugh today when I think about my first girlfriend, Jenny, back in seventh grade, but it wasn't funny then! We "went out" (whatever that meant) for a few months. One day, Jenny told her best friend to tell me that she liked my best friend better than me. Getting dumped by Jenny cut me to the quick.

I'm sure the disciple Peter could relate to my need for love. He denied Jesus three times, undoubtedly to gain others' approval. He tried to walk on the water, perhaps to gain Jesus' and the disciples' acceptance.

Like Peter, I often feel I'm "outside the boat," trying to build friendships and dreams. The wind and waves of rejection and difficulty seem overpowering. My faith weakens, and I get discouraged. Then I remember Peter's plight, look to my Savior, and pray Peter's prayer:

"Lord, help. I'm sinking. I'm lonely, hurting. Please take my hand."

The same hand that reached out to Peter will pull you to safety when the waves of life threaten to drown you. Jesus will always be there, lifting you up with His amazing forgiveness and love. And He won't let go.

Discussion Starters:

• How can you relate to Peter today? When did you last pray his prayer?
•• How does Jesus calm your waves and bring you peace?

Lifeline:

Discuss some times when you felt rejected or alone and thank God for getting you through them.

A Matter of the Heart

"You hypocrites, rightly did Isaiah prophesy of you: 'This people honors Me with their lips, but their heart is far away from Me. But in vain do they worship Me, teaching as doctrines the precepts of men.'"

the **Message**

Steve was a little arrogant. The night before his 16th birthday (and the day before he was to take his driving test), he called Tanya up for a date. "Hey, how'd you like to go to the school dance with me on Friday? I'll pick you up in my brand-new, fully-loaded, high-rise truck," he said. Tanya agreed, and Steve hung up smugly, anticipating the 100 percent he'd receive on his test and the look of admiration on Tanya's face when he came to get her.

Steve's birthday came, and his mother drove him to the DMV. Steve got behind the wheel, nodded to the instructor, and pulled forward. Or, he tried to. The poor guy put the car in reverse instead of first gear and backed into the car behind him. Steve had had so much confidence in his new truck that he hadn't practiced driving enough. His red-faced instructor promptly drew a big, fat "F" across Steve's test, forcing Steve to ride home with his mother and, worse, to ask Tanya if *she* could drive them to the dance.

As Steve learned, who's in the driver's seat is more important than the type of car you drive. The driver makes the judgment calls, acts and reacts, and directs the vehicle. Likewise, your heart is the driver of your life. It is the volitional center where life makes up its mind. Your heart tells you to say yes when things are right and no when situations are wrong. That's why Jesus wants to occupy your heart. He can direct you when other people and things lead you in a dozen different directions. When Jesus is in your heart, in your driver's seat, you'll always travel on the right road.

Discussion Starters:

* How will having a Christ-centered heart help you pass life's tests?
•• What was Dale Carnegie urging when he said, "Flattery is from the teeth out. Sincerity is from the heart out"?[6]
••• Why do you think the heart is so significant?
•••• Who is the most sincere, Christ-centered person you know? Why?

Lifeline:

Rather than image and appearances, how do you emphasize the importance of a sincere heart?

Multiplication

the WORD | Matthew 15:32, 34

"And Jesus called His disciples to Him, and said, 'I feel compassion for the people, because they have remained with Me now three days and have nothing to eat; and I do not want to send them away hungry, for they might faint on the way.' ...And Jesus said to them, 'How many loaves do you have?' And they said, 'Seven, and a few small fish.'"

the Message

I always loved multiplication tables as a kid. I remember setting up a chalkboard with multiplication tables written on it, trying to prepare for tests. What I really liked about multiplication, though, was that the numbers increased so much faster than they did with addition.

That's one of the things I love about Jesus, too. Jesus is a multiplier.

Give Him a talent and He makes a career.

Give Him a date and He builds a friendship.

Give Him a need and He fills it completely.

Give Him a family and He creates a home.

Jesus sees to people's needs. After preaching to the multitudes, He knew they were hungry. The food was scarce, but Jesus, the multiplier, filled their empty stomachs and empty hearts—and had leftovers!

Sadly, not everyone allows Jesus to bring her fulfillment. Yesterday I learned that a young friend of mine, "Angie," died from a drug overdose. She was a popular cheerleader and class officer. She seemed to have everything—except happiness. To numb her pain, Angie turned to alcohol. She started drinking in junior high, and by high school she was an alcoholic. Soon Angie turned to drugs. I wish she had turned to Jesus.

Jesus can fill you with true happiness and peace. If you look to Him, He will multiply love and joy in your life—no matter how hopeless the conditions appear, no matter how great the need may be.

Discussion Starters:

* What do you hunger for today? How can Jesus fill that need?

** What was Angie's first mistake? How can you learn from her?

Lifeline:

Discuss how Jesus has been the great multiplier and great fulfiller in your family.

It's All About Faith

"But He replied to them, 'When it is evening, you say, "It will be fair weather, for the sky is red." And in the morning, "There will be a storm today, for the sky is red and threatening." Do you know how to discern the appearance of the sky, but cannot discern the signs of the times? An evil and adulterous generation seeks after a sign; and a sign will not be given it, except the sign of Jonah.' And He left them and went away."

the Message

Do you believe the sun will come up tomorrow morning? Do you believe your bed won't collapse tonight when you climb into it? Do you believe you'll find enough to eat tomorrow? Do you believe your car will start the next time you turn the key? Do you believe your house will be there when you return from a family trip?

Do you believe that God loves you? Are you convinced He knows and guides your future?

Belief. Faith. The writer of Hebrews described it like this: "Now faith is the assurance of things hoped for, the conviction of things not seen" (11:1). Everyone has faith. Lots of it. Each day, we place our faith in people, places, and things we believe in—even though we never know what the future holds.

So why is it so hard to place our faith in Christ? Even though we haven't seen Him face-to-face, Jesus has proved—through His unconditional love for us—that He can be trusted. If you need to have God constantly prove His abilities, your trust is shallow and your love for Him is weak. Next time you pray, instead of commanding God, "Lord, show me that You're here," say to Him, "Lord, I'm so thankful You're always with me."

Faith means "**F**ather, **A**ll **I**n **T**hy **H**ands." Jesus loves it when we give our belief and trust to Him—and we *should*, whether or not we see one of His mighty deeds.

Discussion Starters:

* How have you put your faith in God the Father and Son?
* Why does God value our faith so highly?
* Could God show us great signs each day if He wanted to? Why doesn't He?
* What makes it hard for you to trust God?

Lifeline:

Remind each other of the little (and big) ways in which God shows Himself in your home.

I Call It As I See It

"He said to them, 'But who do you say that I am?' Simon Peter answered, 'You are the Christ, the Son of the living God.' And Jesus said to him, 'Blessed are you, Simon Barjona, because flesh and blood did not reveal this to you, but My Father who is in heaven.'"

the **Message**

"I think so." "Uh, I'm not sure, but …" "Well, I sorta guess that you're the..." "I'm thinkin' I might be able to..." "One of these days I'm gonna do that, but..." "Well, maybe..."

In the hills, we call it "hum-hawing" around. Others call it "copping out."

The University of Texas versus Texas A&M baseball game was hot, and the rivalry was intense. The count on the batter was three balls and two strikes, a full count. The pitcher wound up and greased a fastball across the inside corner of the plate. The ball stung the catcher's mitt with fire. The umpire gazed intently at the plate and said absolutely nothing. The catcher jumped up and screamed, "What is it ump? Is it a ball or a strike?"

The seasoned old umpire glared right into the catcher's eyes and quietly responded, "It ain't nothin' 'til I call it, boy."

Peter also called it as he saw it. He said, in effect, "Yes, You're the Messiah, plain and simple. You're the One the Old Testament prophets spoke of for 1,500 years. You're the Anointed One. You're God in the flesh."

As I counsel teens, college kids, and adults who are either in trouble, under stress, or despairing, I often see that they're afraid to call it as they see it. They're scared to admit:

"It's pornography, so I shouldn't look at it."

"He's God, so I shouldn't say words that are derogatory to His name."

"My body is a temple of the Holy Spirit, so I shouldn't drink like I do."

"It may be rated PG, but it doesn't glorify Christ."

"It's a lie, so I shouldn't say it."

It takes a real man or woman to call a spade a spade—to say, "No, that's not what I should do." Peter was such a man.

Discussion Starters:

* Who do you say that Jesus is? What does that answer mean to you?
** Why do you think we respect people who shoot straight?
*** When are you most tempted to "cop out"?

Lifeline:

Pray together that God will give you strength to call it as you see it this week.

In Whose Opinion?

the WORD | Matthew 17:1-2, 5

"Six days later Jesus took with Him Peter and James and John his brother, and led them up on a high mountain by themselves. And He was transfigured before them; and His face shone like the sun, and His garments became as white as light.... And behold, a voice out of the cloud said, 'This is My beloved Son, with whom I am well-pleased; listen to Him!' "

the Message

Next Christmas or Easter, go check out the grocery store magazine stand. Chances are, it'll have masses of magazines doing their traditional feature about the mysteries of Jesus of Nazareth. Usually the content is watered down and liberal, written by people who don't know Jesus at all. They mention that Jesus is a literary figure who's been the main focus of humankind for centuries. But you and I know that Jesus is much more than that. I wonder why they don't quote those who knew Him best.

Why don't they quote from God Himself, who said, "This is My beloved Son, with whom I am well-pleased" (verse 5)? Or they could talk of Peter, who proclaimed, "You are the Christ, the Son of the living God" (Matthew 16:16). Even those who crucified Him posted a sign above His head which read, "This Is Jesus the King of the Jews" (Matthew 27:37).

How well do you know Him? Who is He in your life? Your Friend? Father? Almighty Lord? Guide? Comforter? How important is He to you? If you don't know Christ, your faith is only religion—a bunch of beliefs and rules. But when He's close to your heart, your faith becomes something much deeper. It becomes a *relationship* with a holy and loving God.

Next time you want to read more about Jesus, pick up the Bible. It's packed with people who knew Him intimately. They all attested to the fact that He was God in the flesh, the second Person of the triune Godhead, the Living Word, Immanuel, God with us.

Discussion Starters:

• What was the significance of the transfiguration?
•• Why does our culture tend to belittle the deity of Jesus?
••• How can you best discern the truth about Jesus?
•••• How would you respond if a friend vehemently denied that Jesus is Lord?

Lifeline:

How well do you know Christ? How can you help your family know Him better?

Faith that Moves Things

"And He said to them, 'Because of the littleness of your faith; for truly I say to you, if you have faith the size of a mustard seed, you will say to this mountain, "Move from here to there," and it will move; and nothing will be impossible to you.'"

the **Message**

Christina has a faith that could move mountains. She also has an illness that could easily put her in valleys of despair. Most of the time, she's sick in bed with a fever, the flu, insomnia, or migraines. Often, Christina is so ill that she doesn't answer the phone. She has to live with her parents so someone can take care of her all the time. She had to quit a successful job. She's in financial disaster. But she has the joy of Christ. During those times when Christina can't leave the house, talk on the phone, or see her friends, she talks to God. Sometimes she'll spend literally all day praying. And her life reflects her powerful relationship with Christ.

Last week, Christina told me that she needed $2,500 to pay doctor bills and buy groceries. She couldn't go out and work for the money, so she prayed. A few days later, an anonymous letter appeared in the mailbox. It contained a check for $2,000. The other $500 came through anonymous mail during the rest of the week.

Christina's faith made the impossible a reality. She prayed that God would provide for her needs. More importantly, though, she believed that God could do what she asked.

Jesus told us that all we need is faith the size of a mustard seed for Him to work in our lives. Have you seen a mustard seed lately? It's a tiny little thing—about the size of a grain of sand. If you have just *that much faith*, Christ will move the obstacles, leap over the challenges, and meet your every need. That's His promise.

Discussion Starters:

 • What does the tiny size of a mustard seed reveal about faith?
 •• What limitations does the world put on you? Are you facing a challenge that seems impossible to handle? Explain.
 ••• Name someone you know who has great faith. Why is his or her faith so big?
 •••• What does today's verse tell you about the power of God?

Lifeline:

God plants the seeds of faith. A strong family keeps them watered with encouragement.

Do You Trust Him?

the **WORD** | Matthew 18:3-4

"And [He] said, 'Truly I say to you, unless you are converted and become like children, you will not enter the kingdom of heaven. Whoever then humbles himself as this child, he is the greatest in the kingdom of heaven.'"

the Message

My college football coach and his seven-year-old son, Lee, came to our sports camp one summer to help lead our staff. Shortly after they arrived, Coach Utley, Lee, and one of the campers, Chad, went water skiing. Coach drove the ski boat while Chad, a 220-pound football player, skied behind. But soon after Chad got up on the slalom (single) ski, he lost control. Chad crossed the wake—the wave path behind the boat—too quickly and leaned hard on the tow rope. The boat flipped instantly, throwing Coach and Lee into the cold waters. Coach swam desperately around the boat to find Lee. He panicked—the little fellow was nowhere to be found. Several minutes passed. In final desperation, Coach ducked under the overturned boat and found Lee treading water and breathing in the air pocket created by the "turtled" boat.

"I knew you'd be here, Daddy," were Lee's first words. He never doubted for a second that his daddy would rescue him.

Little kids have great faith! They believe in people with all their hearts. They trust their parents, teachers, and God. Their love is pure and wholehearted. Children find joy in little things. They don't worry much about the next day of school or what they're going to have for lunch. They believe that those things will be provided for them.

Jesus knew what He was talking about when He said we should become like little children. He's more impressed with the simple love of a child than with the theological doctrines and doubts of an adult. Jesus wants us to let go of our worries and skepticism. He wants us to quit saying, "Prove it, God!" and start declaring, "I believe it, God!"

Discussion Starters:

• Why do we lose our childlike faith as we grow up?
•• Why does Jesus want us to have the faith of a child?
••• How can we have faith when we haven't seen Him yet with our own eyes?

Lifeline:

Discuss a situation in which your family needs to have childlike faith.

They're Everywhere

the WORD | Matthew 18:20

"For where two or three have gathered together in My name, I am there in their midst."

the Message

You can find them in the most amazing and unusual places. They're in adobe huts in Mexico, igloos in Alaska, prison cells in Siberia, Amazon villages in South America, and in homes across this nation. What are they? Groups of believers gathered together in twos, threes, and fours to worship in the name of Christ. It might seem odd or even impossible to have such a small body of worshipers, but Jesus promised that it only takes you and one other person to have Christ in your midst.

He's with your family right now.

As you read Scripture, pray, and talk about Jesus, you might as well put one more place setting at the table for Him. Maybe you can't see Him, and maybe He seems quiet, but Christ is with you just the same. Through His Holy Spirit, Jesus keeps you coming back to devotions time and again. He helps you understand God's Word as it is read. He gives meaning and purpose to your discussion. He even helps you to remember and apply His instructions and promises to your life.

How would your life change if you never once forgot that Christ is with you? How would your family devotions improve? Would you let your mind wander during prayer? Would you look over at your brother and think about getting back at him? Would you find more meaning in reading the Bible?

Next time you pray with a friend or family member, seeking the Lord's presence, praising Him, and asking for answers, keep in mind that He's already there. He's listening, and He's nearer than you think. But don't take my word for it—take His.

Discussion Starters:

* What would you call a gathering of believers? A church? A Bible study? Explain.
** Christ is here in your family worship time. How does that affect you?
*** How can you include Him more in your discussion?
**** When are you most aware of Christ's presence? Why?

Lifeline:

How should you treat one another, knowing that Jesus is watching and listening?

Adam and Who?

"And He answered and said, 'Have you not read that He who created them from the beginning made them male and female, and said, "For this reason a man shall leave his father and mother and be joined to his wife, and the two shall become one flesh"? So they are no longer two, but one flesh. What therefore God has joined together, let no man separate.'"

the *Message*

"And I now pronounce you husband and...husband?"

Wait a minute. Doesn't that seem a little strange? It does to me—especially when I consider that the most valuable expression of God's craftsmanship was His creation of Adam and Eve. The two were made "in God's own image." Adam and Eve were designed distinctly male and female for an incredible marriage relationship built to last a lifetime. Sexual intimacy was God's gift for the husband and wife to enjoy with each other and nobody else, for their entire lifetime. In that way, marriage is set apart from every other relationship.

I know it's different from what you hear in the media, but God didn't make the first couple Adam and Steve. Nor did He create one-night stands. There is no provision in the Bible for homosexual relationships, premarital sexual relationships, or extramarital sexual relationships. The Bible repeatedly says that all sex outside of marriage is dead wrong.

A lot of people will tell you otherwise, though. *Time* magazine recently reported that since we evolved from apes and apes are unfaithful, it's okay for us to be unfaithful, too![7] Nothing could be further from the truth. Married partners should save their affection for each other. Unwed people should save their affection for their future spouses.

My friend Davis recently married. He and his wife, Sarah, waited to have sex until they married. They'll tell you it was hard. Their hormones often felt out of control. But on their wedding night, Davis and Sarah were able to love freely, without comparing themselves or each other to past sweethearts. Now it's easier for them to be vulnerable with one another because they built trust and respect by not pushing any God-given boundaries.

Wait to give yourself to your spouse. It will be well worth it.

Discussion Starters:

• Why did God invent marriage?   •• Why is it so hard to remain sexually pure?
••• Why did God tell us to wait for sex until we're married?

Lifeline:

How can your family promote abstinence and healthy dating?

I'll Give You All My Heart (Almost)

the WORD | Matthew 19:20-22

"The young man said to Him, 'All [your commandments] I have kept; what am I still lacking?' Jesus said to him, 'If you wish to be complete, go and sell your possessions and give to the poor, and you will have treasure in heaven; and come, follow Me.' But when the young man heard this statement, he went away grieving; for he was one who owned much property."

the Message

Girls, imagine the finest boy you ever laid eyes on. He's cute, smart, funny, popular—and he's in love with you. Sound good? Well, let's say he asks you to marry him (after you've dated for a while). He promises to be absolutely faithful to you...364 days out of the year. On his bended knee, the guy then says he loves you with *almost* all his heart—but he has this small crush on Jenny, whom he wants to save his affection for just one day out of the year. What would you say? Would you marry him? Or what flavor of pie would you smash in his face?

Guys, how about you? The gorgeous babe you've secretly liked since kindergarten suddenly decides she wants to share *almost* all her life with you. She tells you that she'll be loyal most of the time, but she says she can't promise that you'll always be her number one man. She's got a thing for guys with blond hair, and yours is brown. But she claims she still loves you. How would you respond? Would you give her a wedding band? (If you say yes, we'd better talk!)

I'm sure you would never make a lifelong commitment to someone who was even a tiny bit wishy-washy about you. Jesus is the same way. He saw through to the rich young man's heart and knew he wasn't totally sold on Him. We might read this scripture and think, *That's pretty harsh. The young man did almost everything right, and Jesus still turned him away.* But if we wouldn't accept anything less than complete commitment from someone, why should He?

Jesus knows exactly what keeps us from loving Him fully. He realized the rich young man loved money more than he loved Him.

What's keeping *you* from making a total commitment to Christ?

Discussion Starters:

• What things are getting in the way of your relationship with Christ?
•• Why did the young man walk away?   ••• Why does God want all of our hearts?

Lifeline:

Encourage one another to make a sincere, total commitment to God.

Premeditated Sacrifice

the WORD | Matthew 20:18-19

"Behold, we are going up to Jerusalem; and the Son of Man will be delivered to the chief priests and scribes, and they will condemn Him to death, and will hand Him over to the Gentiles to mock and scourge and crucify Him, and on the third day He will be raised up."

the Message

Little Lori Ann was 14 when she slipped into the back row of our rowdy, fun, and growing youth group. The patch over her eye immediately gave away her condition when I saw her precious, innocent face. Lori had facial cancer. Doctors had removed her eye to try to save her life. But her illness was growing—and fatal. Over the next two years, the cancer spread throughout her face and neck. Amazingly, as she walked steadily toward death, Lori's faith grew stronger. She and I became close and talked as a father and daughter would about death, heaven, and Christ's provision for eternal life. Lori grew to love her Savior.

The week before her death, her doctor came into her room and told her that they had done all they could. The medicines weren't working. Soon the tumors would take over. With the faith of an 80-year-old saint, Lori looked at her doctor and bravely said, "I appreciate all you've done, but don't worry, I won't die when the medicine runs out— I'll die when Jesus takes me home."

As I stood by her hospital bed, I realized that Lori was facing her death the same way Jesus faced His...with courage, grace, and dignity. In fact, Lori's last words before she closed her eyes for the last time were to her unsaved mom. Lori softly whispered, "Mom, I hope some day you'll know Jesus like I do."

Lori was able to face pain and death without fear because she knew God's plan for her eternal life. Christ knowingly endured incredible suffering because He knew God was in control as well. Do you?

Discussion Starters:

• If Jesus knew when and how He'd die, why didn't He change the plan and run?
    •• What do you think His disciples thought
        when He told them the fate that was ahead of Him?
    ••• How can a 16-year-old like my friend Lori have such great faith?

Lifeline:

How can your trials make you a better witness for Christ?

When in Doubt, Serve

"It is not this way among you, but whoever wishes to become great among you shall be your servant, and whoever wishes to be first among you shall be your slave; just as the Son of Man did not come to be served, but to serve, and to give His life a ransom for many."

the *Message*

How often do you sit around the house and just "veg" with nothing to do? What do you do when you come home from school or work? Watch a little TV? Plug in your Walkman? Skim the newspaper? Lounge on the couch? Do you want to make life at home really fun and dynamic and surprising—anything but boring? Then adopt Jesus' motto. He always said, in effect, "When in doubt, *serve*."

Seriously! It probably sounds backward to you because our society likes to indulge. We treat ourselves to movies, dessert, and reclining chairs. When we're bored, we usually sit. But Jesus told us how to best spend our time when He said, "Do you wanna be great or be fulfilled? Then serve!"

We have fun with the "serving motto" at my house. Our family found that serving others brings harmony to our home, brings smiles to faces, and kicks life in the funny bone. Whose job is it to wash the dishes? Mine. Who's supposed to take out the trash? Me! Who tries to do whatever needs doin'? Me! Why waste all that time and energy arguing about who's supposed to do what? It's much easier to serve.

If your family has trouble letting go of grudges, arguing, or having touchy feelings, I suggest you adopt the "when in doubt, serve" philosophy. If each person joyfully serves one another with Christ's love, in 30 days there will be peace. Servanthood will wave the magic wand of love—Christ's love—throughout your home.

Is someone in your house hurting? Rub his shoulders or send some encouraging words his way. Is your mom tired? Fold her laundry or put gas in her car. People appreciate even the smallest things you do for them.

Jesus hit the nail right on the head! Do you wanna be the best you can ever be? Become an expert in other people's needs, find joy in meeting those needs, and that's exactly what you'll become!

Discussion Starters:

* Why is the greatness/serving paradox so true?
** What would Jesus say about the present state of servanthood in your house?
*** What is one new way that you could be a servant to your family?

Lifeline:

Let serving begin with you!

Mangers, Donkeys, and Crosses

" 'Say to the daughter of Zion, "Behold your King is coming to you, gentle, and mounted on a donkey, even on a colt, the foal of a beast of burden." ' And the disciples went and did just as Jesus had instructed them, and brought the donkey and the colt, and laid their coats on them; and He sat on the coats."

the *Message*

He could have ridden a chariot into town...that's how the self-proclaimed gods of the Roman military made their arrival. He could have forced His followers to carry Him in a sedan chair. That's how Egyptian, Syrian, and Babylonian kings made their slaves carry them atop their shoulders. So what was this divine King doing on a donkey, a lowly beast of burden?

Jesus rode a donkey in fulfillment of prophecy (see Zechariah 9:9) and because He never intended to elevate Himself. He came to earth as a man to identify with your hurts and forgive your sins, not to bring Himself worldly glory.

My friend Andy lost his granddad to cancer yesterday. Jesus hurts for Andy. He knows how Andy feels because He saw the pain of the sick and diseased as well (see Matthew 8). Sandi lost her dad to alcoholism, and the next week her brother was killed in a drunk driving accident. Jesus sheds tears with Sandi. He's been there. He knows the pain of losing a dearly loved one. When His close friend Lazarus died (before Christ raised him from the dead), "Jesus wept," too (John 11:35).

Jesus even understands our temptations. Billy is torn, struggling like crazy because his friends are turning to pot and alcohol. He wants to be true to his parents and his personal convictions, but now he's losing his friends.

Jesus sighs deeply. He felt the same pain as Judas walked out on Him and turned his back after years of friendship (see Matthew 26).

Jesus chose to be all man while being all God. He wanted to know firsthand how you feel. He wanted to participate in and understand your pain. So He came from a manger to a donkey to a Roman cross.

Next time you wonder, *Does anybody know how I feel?* you can bet your last penny that Somebody knows. Jesus, the One who loves you most, also understands you best. He knows, and He cares.

Discussion Starters:

• What does it mean to you that Jesus shared in your humanity?
•• How do you think Jesus understands your pain right now?

Lifeline:

How can your family better empathize with one another's trials?

Kids Say the Greatest Things

the WORD | Matthew 21:15-16

"But when the chief priests and the scribes saw the wonderful things that He had done and the children who were shouting in the temple, 'Hosanna to the Son of David,' they became indignant and said to Him, 'Do You hear what these children are saying?' And Jesus said to them, 'Yes; have you never read, "Out of the mouth of infants and nursing babies You have prepared praise for Yourself"?' "

the Message

Dan Roberts, my country music songwriter buddy, absolutely loves his four-year-old son. The other day, Dan and his son, J. D., were saying how much they loved each other, and their comparisons grew more profound each time they spoke.

"Dad, I love you more than a car," J. D. said, his eyes big.

"J. D., I love you more than an 18-wheeler," Dan responded proudly.

J. D. knew just how to top that. He gleefully said, "Dad, I love you more than all the tables in McDonald's!"

Now, to a four-year-old, that's all the love imaginable. Kids just tell it like it is, don't they? We grown-ups get so stiff, prideful, and arrogant that we sometimes forget to say honest, simple things like "God is so good" and "Jesus loves me, this I know, 'cuz the Bible tells me so." Children embrace God's truth and His love, while adults usually reason their faith away. Kids could teach adults a thing or two by their trusting example.

Next Sunday at church, watch the four-year-olds' Sunday school class. Chances are, they'll come out of class proudly carrying an "I love Jesus" card or wearing a big heart with a cross in the middle.

Or take note of your younger brother or sister (or other little kids you know). Watch how easily they fold their hands to pray. Notice how quickly they accept that God loves them.

Kids aren't complicated. They don't argue over issues of faith. They believe God is good because it's in the Bible. They want to know Jesus, and they readily ask Him into their hearts. Kids are the best living examples of faith. That's why Jesus said, "Let the little children come to Me, for theirs is the kingdom of heaven" (see Matthew 19).

Discussion Starters:

• Why did Jesus place such value on children?

•• How can we be mature and responsible and still have a childlike faith?

Lifeline:

Write several positive childlike characteristics and pray for help for your family to trust God.

Once Upon a Rock

the **WORD** | *Matthew 21:42-43*

"Jesus said to them, 'Did you never read in the Scriptures, "The stone which the builders rejected, this became the chief corner stone; this came about from the LORD, and it is marvelous in our eyes"? Therefore I say to you, the kingdom of God will be taken away from you and given to a people, producing the fruit of it.' "

the **Message**

Ever notice that when you give your life over to God, things can get much easier? Often when you start tithing your money, your finances work themselves out. When you let go of a hurtful friendship, God will usually bring a better friend along. And when leaders place the nations they are guiding in the hands of God, God usually responds with blessings as well.

That's what happened in the United States. The nation was founded by serious Christians. America's early leaders sowed the teachings of God into its schools, laws, and cities because their faith was so important to them. And the nation was blessed because of it.

The first president, George Washington, wanted to glorify God as he led the nation. Washington said reverently, "O most glorious God in Jesus Christ, my merciful and loving Father, let me live according to those holy rules which Thou hast this day prescribed in Thy Holy Word."[8]

Alexander Hamilton, known as "the ratifier of the Constitution," signed the Constitution and then said, "I now offer you the outline of the plan they have suggested. Let an association be formed to be denominated 'The Christian Constitutional Society', its object to be first: The support of the Christian religion. Second: The support of the United States."[9]

America was built on strong Christian principles, and as a result, God blessed her with more prosperity than any other nation in the history of the world. But now her federal government, media, and educational system are systematically and purposefully snuffing God out of the people's daily lives. America's soaring crime rate, divorce rate, and sexually transmitted disease rate stand testimony to the way the nation has willfully turned its back on Him.

Through prayer and the democratic process, you can make a difference in the world. What are you doing to help turn your country to God?

Discussion Starters:

* What are some of the good things about your nation?
  ** How can you help turn the anti-God trend in your nation?

Lifeline:

How can your family be an example in your community?

Wedding Clothes

the WORD | Matthew 22:11-14

"But when the king came in to look over the dinner guests, he saw a man there who was not dressed in wedding clothes, and he said to him, 'Friend, how did you come in here without wedding clothes?' And the man was speechless. Then the king said to the servants, 'Bind him hand and foot, and throw him into the outer darkness; in that place there will be weeping and gnashing of teeth.' For many are called, but few are chosen."

the Message

I love weddings. I always get a 50-yard-line seat (the best view) as the pastor—the guy lucky enough to help the bride and bridegroom "tie the knot." I've done $50,000 weddings and $50 weddings. As long as you can say "I do" and stand by it for about 50 years, it doesn't really matter what the price tag is. But no matter how much is spent, the most incredible moment is the second the bride enters the chamber adorned with delicate white lace. Guys, as you stand there waiting, it will make you faint in awe if you're not prepared. There is simply nothing on earth like a bride adorned for her husband.

Earthly weddings are beautiful and magical, but God's wedding feast will be even more special. In that union of God's children (the bride) to Jesus Christ (the bridegroom), God's true believers will adorn themselves with spiritual wedding clothes. The love, faith, and righteousness that we clothe ourselves in each day will shine brilliantly in heaven.

Just as earthly brides spend hours preparing for their husbands, so should Christ's children take the time to be ready for their awesome meeting with Him. Is there someone for whom you need to have more compassion? Are you being patient enough with your brother or sister? Does your head swell with every A you receive or each relationship you have?

On the fantastic day when you meet Jesus face-to-face, you'll be blown away by His glory and majesty. But God makes it clear that the only ones welcome into His home are those clothed in Jesus' righteousness.

Would you be dressed appropriately for your Bridegroom if you saw Him today?

Discussion Starters:

* What is God's criterion for His wedding guests?
** Why does God compare our union with His Son to a wedding feast?
*** Are you dressed for the occasion? Why or why not?

Lifeline:

What would your wedding clothes look like if you met Him face-to-face right now?

Give It to Whom?

"[The Pharisees asked,] 'Tell us then, what do You think? Is it lawful to give a poll-tax to Caesar, or not?' But Jesus perceived their malice, and said, 'Why are you testing Me, you hypocrites? Show Me the coin used for the poll-tax.' And they brought Him a denarius. And He said to them, 'Whose likeness and inscription is this?' They said to Him, 'Caesar's.' Then He said to them, 'Then render to Caesar the things that are Caesar's; and to God the things that are God's.' "

the *Message*

Adolf Eichmann, a German officer serving under Adolf Hitler, was responsible for the extermination of several million Jewish citizens in World War II. He was apprehended, then tried and convicted in Jerusalem in 1961. There, Eichmann pleaded his alibi. He said, "I never did anything, great or small, without obtaining in advance express instructions from my superiors. I was in the iron grip of orders." Eichmann, maintaining his innocence, repeated, "I had to obey the rules of war and my flag."[10]

He rendered to Hitler and ended up killing countless innocent people.

Maybe Eichmann was following Hitler's orders, but there is always a higher law that rules when issues of right and wrong are at stake.

As a young person living in a society which has become more hostile to God, you, too, will have to decide where your loyalties lie. For instance, many schools now forbid organized prayer meetings on campus. Other schools teach only evolution and won't hear of presenting creationism. What will you do when you're confronted with situations like these? Where will you place your loyalties?

There are times when we must follow the law and "render to Caesar," but God is our ultimate authority. No matter what the cost, we're supposed to stand up for Him and His Word. This calls for submission and courage. Do you have the strength of character to render yourself to God when He asks you for obedience?

Discussion Starters:

* How can you apply Jesus' parable to your life?
** How can you discern when it's appropriate to submit to God rather than the law?
*** Describe a time in your life when you should have obeyed God but instead rendered your loyalty to Caesar (meaning, the government, the world, etc.).

Lifeline:

How can you better obey God's authority in your life?

I'm Third

the WORD | Matthew 22:35-39

"One of them, a lawyer, asked Him a question, testing Him, 'Teacher, which is the great commandment in the Law?' And He said to him, '"You shall love the Lord your God with all your heart, and with all your soul, and with all your mind." This is the great and foremost commandment. The second is like it, "You shall love your neighbor as yourself." ' "

the Message

Plain and simple, it's the key to happiness. You want to enjoy life? Put God first. You wanna enjoy it greatly? Put others second. You wanna enjoy it fully? Put yourself third. At our sports camps, we call it "I'm Third." It's our motto.

Johnny Ferrier was a longtime family friend. This pilot bravely chose to guide his crippled Air National Guard jet into a backyard garden in the center of a heavily populated suburb, where he stayed with the plane and died on impact. Johnny could have bailed out to save himself, but he knew that leaving the plane unguided could have resulted in the death of many innocent civilians. To his last breath, he lived placing himself third.

God is the best! He rules. And when you let Him rule your priorities, you place Him first. If you're wondering whether you need to adjust your priorities, take this quick test. Ask yourself, "Where do I spend my money? What takes up most of my time?" How you answer those questions will show you if you're putting other things or people before God.

You place others second by loving them, serving them, and putting their needs ahead of your own. Look at the people around you. How well do you serve your family? Do you consider their needs, too?

How can you put yourself third? By loving yourself—treating your body as a temple of the Holy Spirit, not using alcohol or drugs, and not filling your eyes and ears with impure sights and sounds. God commanded us to love others as we love *ourselves*. Low self-esteem isn't for children of God. Love yourself the way God commands you to love others.

Jesus. **O**thers. **Y**ourself. That formula spells "joy." And if you follow the two greatest commandments, that's what you'll have.

Discussion Starters:

* How will you put God first in your life today?
** What are some specific ways you can practice "I'm Third" throughout this week?

Lifeline:

An "I'm Third" home is a great place to live.

Lead, Don't Mislead

the **WORD** | Matthew 23:1-3

"Then Jesus spoke to the crowds and to His disciples, saying: 'The scribes and the Pharisees have seated themselves in the chair of Moses; therefore all that they tell you, do and observe, but do not do according to their deeds; for they say things and do not do them.'"

the **Message**

Governor Spencer endorses abortion and then says she's tough on crime.

Dan boasts of his football skills as he buys beer for his underage brother.

Mr. Owens tells his daughter not to cheat while he cheats on his taxes.

Jana scolds her son for talking back, while she regularly belittles her husband.

Bobby, student council president at his Christian high school, pushes his girlfriend to sleep with him.

Samantha parties on Saturday and carries her Bible to church on Sunday.

Hypocrisy...it's the antithesis of leadership. It confuses, misleads, and destroys.

Brad showed up at my door, heartbroken. His high school youth leader, the one who led him to Christ, had turned his back on God. Brad couldn't understand how someone who always appeared so on track with God could become involved in drugs. "Is Christianity just a big joke?" Brad asked.

True leadership is consistent. You must be able to trust the one you follow. Jesus was a true leader, an example for others. His actions always mirrored His words, and He condemned those who said one thing and then did another.

But Jesus also forgave those inconsistencies, our tendencies toward hypocrisy and judgmentalism. Have you confessed yours?

Discussion Starters:

• Whom do you lead? Who follows your example?

•• How can you demonstrate consistent leadership?

••• Who are you following? What kind of a leader is he or she? Explain.

•••• Why was Christ the best example of a leader?

Lifeline:

Forgive each other's inconsistencies and strive to be faithful as a Christlike example.

House Painting

"Woe to you, scribes and Pharisees, hypocrites! For you clean the outside of the cup and of the dish, but inside they are full of robbery and self-indulgence. You blind Pharisee, first clean the inside of the cup and of the dish, so that the outside of it may become clean also…. You are like whitewashed tombs which on the outside appear beautiful, but inside they are full of dead men's bones and all uncleanness. So you, too, outwardly appear righteous to men, but inwardly you are full of hypocrisy and lawlessness."

the Message

My brothers and I were always *so* excited to do yard work. (As if!) But when Dad said, "Do it, boys," we were left with no choice. So we would tell our friends we'd play baseball later and work to make our house shine like new. We mowed the grass, weeded the flowerbed, painted the house, and watered the trees. It was hard work, but when we were done, our house looked great—on the outside.

Even more important, though, was to ensure our house was clean *inside*. It was everybody's job to make our home a happy place to live, a place that honored God. We worked, sweated, and spent time cleaning up that Texas home. Now, the inside view didn't always look as good as the outside view. But God knew we were working on it. And fortunately, He isn't nearly as concerned about the kind of grass growing in the front yard or the shade of paint on the door as He is about the reasons for our arguments or the thoughts in our hearts.

Cleaning up the inside of your home is a daily job. How do you clean it? By praying consistently and truly forgiving those who've let you down. By saying "I'm sorry" and deciding to follow Christ more diligently tomorrow.

Jesus was telling the Pharisees to clean *their* thoughts and insides, but He also meant it for me and you and your family, too. Are you painting the walls of your heart with faithfulness and weeding the bitterness out of your mind?

Discussion Starters:

• What can you do today to help beautify the outside of your home? The inside?

•• How clean is your house on the inside? Are you focusing too much on the yard?

Lifeline:

Ask God to show your family the areas in your lives that need more housecleaning.

Follow the (Right) Leader

the WORD | Matthew 24:23-25

"Then if anyone says to you, 'Behold, here is the Christ,' or 'There He is,' do not believe him. For false Christs and false prophets will arise and will show great signs and wonders, so as to mislead, if possible, even the elect. Behold, I have told you in advance."

the Message

Follow the wrong crowd to a party and you're liable to get into serious trouble with alcohol or drugs. Follow the wrong boy or girl on a date and you might get incredibly hurt. Follow the wrong spiritual leader and you just might wind up in hell.

Almost 10 million misled Mormons follow the lead of the late Joseph Smith. This man, who grew up in a Christian home, believed that all denominations of the Christian faith are wrong and that God would set up the only true Christian denomination through him.[11] Joseph Smith taught that God was once a man who progressed to be a God and that "man is co-equal to God himself."[12] That's certainly not what the Bible says.

Charles Taze Russell began the Jehovah's Witnesses in 1870. Today two million people align themselves with this cult. It denies every cardinal belief of traditional Christianity, including the doctrine of the Trinity, the divinity of Jesus Christ, His bodily resurrection, salvation by grace, and the eternal punishment of the wicked.[13]

The New Age movement is even more prevalent. Its philosophy includes reading palms and tarot cards, consulting psychics, doing Eastern meditation, and channeling with crystals (basically, spirit possession). Horoscopes are also part of the growing New Age movement—millions of people read them in the newspaper each day.

The Bible warns against cultic beliefs and practices for a reason. The beliefs are not only completely opposed to the principles Jesus taught, but they are also extremely enticing. Many people will start out "dabbling" in cultic ideology and end up full-fledged cult members—often without realizing what they've done. There are an estimated 700 to 5,000 false religions in America to watch out for. Don't follow any of them. Let only the real Jesus of the Bible lead you. Your eternity depends on it!

Discussion Starters:

* What is a cult? What are the characteristics of a cult?
  ** What should you do when you encounter false christs or cult members?

Lifeline:

How can you help one another to distinguish between false christs and the real Christ?

Daddy's Home!

the **WORD** | Matthew 24:30-31

"And then the sign of the Son of Man will appear in the sky, and then all the tribes of the earth will mourn, and they will see the Son of Man coming on the clouds of the sky with power and great glory. And He will send forth His angels with a great trumpet and they will gather together His elect from the four winds, from one end of the sky to the other."

the *Message*

It's my job to travel and recruit Christian athletes for our sports camps. I love sports and working with students, but I hate leaving home. Chuck Swindoll says, "Happiness is seeing anything but home in the rearview mirror of my car"—and I agree. Unfortunately, however, I'm on the road 40-50 days a year.

Now, there's nothing special about the White house, but the people in it—my wife and kids—are the strongest magnets I've ever known. I'll drive a million miles if that's what it takes to be home when my kids wake up in the morning. When they were small, sometimes after I'd been gone a week or two, I'd be greeted with "DADDY'S HOME" and "WELCOME HOME, DAD" banners and posters strung all over the house. Back then, I would bring home little gifts for all the kids.

"Dad, what did you bwing me?" little Cooper would always ask.

"I brought you...me!" I'd reply, grinning.

"I know dat, Dad, but what did you *really* bwing me?"

I'd smile, bend down, and pull out from behind my back a small present. Cooper would excitedly throw his little arms around my neck.

After one particularly long trip, I arrived home late one night and found one of my little girls asleep with her blanket by the front door. She didn't want me to miss her. I joyfully picked her up and carried her to her room, cuddling her to my chest.

My homecomings are a blast. But they're nothing compared to what Jesus' return to earth will be like. Scripture says that the Lord will return with power and glory. Trumpets will announce His arrival; angels will gather His children. And we will be joyfully united with Him as He takes us to our heavenly home.

Discussion Starters:

* Do you know that Jesus will include you when He returns to earth?
** Why do you think He's coming back someday?
*** What can you do to be as ready as possible for His return?

Lifeline:

Help your family get ready for Jesus' homecoming!

The Second Coming

the WORD | Matthew 24:36-39

"But of that day and hour no one knows, not even the angels of heaven, nor the Son, but the Father alone. For the coming of the Son of Man will be just like the days of Noah. For as in those days before the flood they were eating and drinking, marrying and giving in marriage, until the day that Noah entered the ark, and they did not understand until the flood came and took them all away; so will the coming of the Son of Man be."

the Message

Scripture is clear and history stands witness that Jesus Christ came once to planet earth as a lamb to be sacrificed for our sins. Scripture is equally clear that He will return again. Literally hundreds of passages in the Old and New Testaments state this. When will His return be? No one except God knows. Will it be soon? We hope so, because when He does come back, all murder, abuse, crime, and sorrow will cease for His followers.

There are many indications that Christ's return could be soon.

According to the books of Daniel, Isaiah, and Revelation, the nation of Israel will be intact when He returns. That was impossible from A.D. 67, when Israel was destroyed, until May 14, 1948, when Israel was restored as a nation. Today, the tiny, turbulent country is poised for His return.

According to Revelation 13:17, a world leader will emerge who will control all world purchasing through one system. Only those people who have this leader's approval (the mark of the beast) will be allowed to buy or sell. The World Wide Web, scanners, and electronic banking have only recently made such a system feasible.

There's more. Revelation 9:16 states that a 200-million-man army will come from the land east of Israel (India, Japan, China). This was impossible until recently. Today, China boasts of an army of 200 million.[14]

Although Christ gave a ton of references to His second coming, He was discreet about the details to ensure that "no man knows the hour" (see verse 36). But He spoke about His return with certainty to give us hope and to encourage us to live for His coming every day of our lives.

Discussion Starters:

* If Jesus were returning today, would you live differently? If so, how?
** What do you picture when you hear the phrase "Daddy's coming home"?
*** What will you say when you first meet Jesus face-to-face?

Lifeline:

What other signs does the Bible give that point to the time Jesus will return?

Eternal Investments

the WORD | Matthew 25:14-16, 19-20

"For it is just like a man about to go on a journey, who called his own slaves and entrusted his possessions to them. To one he gave five talents, to another, two, and to another, one, each according to his own ability; and he went on his journey. Immediately the one who had received the five talents went and traded with them, and gained five more talents.... Now after a long time the master of those slaves came and settled accounts with them. The one who had received the five talents came up and brought five more talents, saying, 'Master, you entrusted five talents to me. See, I have gained five more talents.'"

the Message

Who you are is God's gift to you. What you do with it is your gift to God.

On September 19, 1967, Jim Abbott was born with only one hand. When he was in grade school, he didn't stand a chance when baseball season came around and all his friends went out to play catch and hit the ball. But Jim had a dream and the courage to back up his dream. He later pitched for the USA Olympic team and helped win them the gold medal. As a New York Yankee, he stunned the world by being the first one-handed pitcher to throw a no-hitter in a professional baseball game.'[15]

Ludwig van Beethoven, the great composer, became hearing impaired. But his deafness didn't keep him from writing music. He wrote some of his best compositions—music that broke with tradition and made history—*after* he turned completely deaf. Beethoven is universally recognized as one of the most brilliant composers who ever lived.

The pages of history are literally packed with men and women who the world said "had no talent," "didn't stand a chance," and "could never make it." But instead of believing that they'd never go anywhere in life, these "untalented" people invested and used their God-given gifts every day until their dreams came true. And that's what Jesus wants us to do—use our talents for His glory.

Discussion Starters:

* What is your dream? What talents did God give you that can help you achieve that dream?
** How can a weakness actually help you realize your dream?
*** What is the greatest gift God has given you? How can you invest this gift to its fullest?

Lifeline:

Encourage one another to reach your dreams!

Have You Done It for Them?

"Then the King will say to those on His right [the sheep], 'Come, you who are blessed of My Father, inherit the kingdom prepared for you from the foundation of the world. For I was hungry, and you gave Me something to eat; I was thirsty, and you gave Me something to drink; I was a stranger, and you invited Me in; naked, and you clothed Me; I was sick, and you visited Me; I was in prison, and you came to Me.' ...[Then] the King will...say to them, 'Truly I say to you, to the extent that you did it to one of these brothers of Mine, even the least of them, you did it to Me.'"

the Message

Poor people starve. Most rich people throw food away.

Elderly people lie in their hospital beds or nursing homes and wish for attention. Young people waste an average of three to five hours a day in front of their TV set, video games, or CD player.

Mentally and physically challenged people long for the opportunity to have a friend in school. The athletes, whiz kids, and popular people pass them by in the hallways without even a hello or a smile.

Fortunately, lots of Christians reach out to the less fortunate and sacrifice to give to the poor. In this passage, Jesus was clear that if you love Him, you'll do just that...you'll take your time, your talents, and your possessions and give them away. If you do, you're what He calls a "sheep," and He is well pleased with you. If you don't, you're a "goat," and your faith is questionable (see Matthew 25: 41-46).

A few years ago when our kids were all at home, we had a piggy bank at our breakfast table. In order to get breakfast every morning, each family member had to bring a coin to put in the bank, which we used to sponsor urban kids to Kanakuk-Kanakomo Kamps. Whenever *anyone* in the house made any money, no matter how much or how little, the first portion always went to some work God was doing around the world.

You don't need to be ashamed of your blessings. But you do need to share them. It'll show God where your heart is and where you stand with Him. How much of your time and resources do you give to His children?

Discussion Starters:

* What are some ways you can give back to Jesus?
** Who are some less fortunate people you know who would benefit if you shared your time, heart, and resources?
*** Who gets the most when you give? Why?

Lifeline:

Giving is often a trademark of legitimate faith!

Dedication or Desertion?

the WORD | Matthew 26:7, 12-16

"A woman came to Him with an alabaster vial of very costly perfume, and she poured it on His head as He reclined at the table.... [And Jesus said,] 'When she poured this perfume on My body, she did it to prepare Me for burial. Truly I say to you, wherever this gospel is preached in the whole world, what this woman has done will also be spoken of in memory of her.' Then one of the twelve, named Judas Iscariot, went to the chief priests and said, 'What are you willing to give me to betray Him to you?' And they weighed out thirty pieces of silver to him. From then on he began looking for a good opportunity to betray Jesus."

the Message

Scholars suggest the vial of perfume could have been the poor woman's most valued possession. Perhaps she had been saving it since her 18th birthday, planning to give this treasured gift to the man who would be her husband. But whatever the woman's aspirations, it's obvious she admired the Savior and would sacrifice any of her possessions to show her family and friends that she was a devoted follower.

Two thousand years haven't erased the story of her great dedication.

Judas Iscariot walked with the Savior for three wonderful years. He watched this God-man heal outdoor hospitals full of people with debilitating diseases. He saw the Messiah reach out and touch the hearts of the poor and lonely, value children as heavenly treasures, and elevate women to their proper place of dignity and honor. Judas walked with Jesus as He introduced grace to this world and literally brought God's mercy from heaven, showing the almighty Creator's amazing love for His children. Yet Judas couldn't resist the bribe and sold his soul for a bag of silver.

Two thousand years haven't erased the story of his great desertion.

You, too, have been exposed to the Savior. You also have seen His love and mercy. How are you going to respond? You will either embrace Him or betray Him by your choices and actions. Will you sacrifice for Jesus, or will you be swayed by money and the moment and lose the best Friend you've ever had? What story will you leave behind?

Discussion Starters:

• What would you give Jesus if He came to your home today? Why?

•• It's easier to deny Jesus than to sacrifice for Him. What things in your life (or in the culture) deny Jesus? In what ways do you sacrifice for Him?

••• Practically speaking, how can you live in a way that honors Him today?

Lifeline:

Honor Jesus by honoring your family.

The Blood Covenant

"While they were eating, Jesus took some bread, and after a blessing, He broke it and gave it to the disciples, and said, 'Take, eat; this is My body.' And when He had taken a cup and given thanks, He gave it to them, saying, 'Drink from it, all of you; for this is My blood of the covenant, which is poured out for many for forgiveness of sins.'"

the *Message*

"I promise." "Let's shake on it." "I guarantee it!" "Trust me."

Jesus didn't have to say all those things to seal His covenant with us. He simply held up the loaf of bread, ripped it in half, and in so many words said, "Friends, tomorrow they're going to do this to My body. Eat this, and remember Me." He poured out the wine and affirmed, "My blood will pour out for you until My heart bleeds to death. It's proof positive that I love you. I came for this purpose. Drink this and remember My love for you."

Jesus' death created an even stronger covenant with His children. He, being a man, made a blood covenant promise with God on behalf of all men. And He, being God, the Creator of all people, was able to forgive you and me when He took the nails in His wrists and died so that you and God could be bonded forever.

We break our word as easily as chefs crack eggshells in restaurants on Sunday mornings.

But Jesus keeps His. The term He used, "covenant," means a promise, and biblical blood covenants are never, ever broken. Period. On the day of the cross, Jesus sealed a friendship between God's kids and Himself that makes Communion the most important banquet you'll ever attend. The Bible calls it, in effect, a covenant meal. Discover now in your family discussion the full impact of this "commitment feast" between you and God.

Discussion Starters:

* What did Jesus mean when He said, "This cup...is the new covenant in My blood" (Luke 22:20)?
** How does His pledge give you freedom?
*** Why was the shedding of blood necessary in this covenant between God and man?
**** Why is it important to take Communion regularly?

Lifeline:

Write your family commitment to God and dedicate your love for Him.

The Night Sorrow
Mastered the Master

the WORD | Matthew 26:36, 38-39, 42

"Then Jesus came with them to a place called Gethsemane, and said to His disciples, 'Sit here while I go over there and pray.' ...Then He said to them, 'My soul is deeply grieved, to the point of death; remain here and keep watch with Me.' And He went a little beyond them, and fell on His face and prayed, saying, 'My Father, if it is possible, let this cup pass from Me; yet not as I will, but as You will.' ...He went away again a second time and prayed, saying, 'My Father, if this cannot pass away unless I drink it, Your will be done.'"

the Message

I cried pools of tears when my older daughter left home for a college far, far away. I missed her beyond description. Her genes are half me! I poured all that I had into her for 18 years. We were best friends and mutual admirers. I have more sweet memories of her than I can count.

Jesus also felt deep sorrow. He knew the night before His crucifixion that a torturous death awaited Him. I've often wondered which part of the ordeal He dreaded the most. The flogging? The public ridicule? The fists in His face? The crown of thorns? The grueling walk to Golgotha? The crucifixion?

As the father to my four best friends (outside of my wife), I know that one of life's greatest agonies is being separated from those you deeply love. I believe that as Jesus agonized in the Garden of Gethsemane, His greatest anxiety was knowing that in a few short hours His close bond with His Father would be ruthlessly—even if only for a short while—broken. As He looked ahead to the next day, He could see Himself becoming the curse of sin. His holy Father would turn His head and for the first time ever, Jesus would be fatherless—desperately alone—and the thought crushed Him.

Jesus' grief was deep, but His obedience to the Father ran deeper. Even under terrible sorrow and anxiety, Jesus was able to say, "Not My will, but Yours be done."

Discussion Starters:

• Teens, describe the importance of having a close relationship with your parents (even if you don't always feel like it). Parents, describe your love for your kids.
•• How do you think Jesus was feeling that night in Gethsemane?
••• How does Jesus' statement to His Dad, "Your will be done," inspire you today?

Lifeline:

Parents, be careful in giving commands; teens, make sure you respond with obedience.

A Distant Follower

the **WORD** | Matthew 26:58, 69-74

"But Peter was following Him at a distance as far as the courtyard of the high priest, and entered in, and sat down with the officers to see the outcome.... Now Peter was sitting outside in the courtyard, and a servant-girl came to him and said, 'You too were with Jesus the Galilean.' But he denied it before them all, saying, 'I do not know what you are talking about.' When he had gone out to the gateway, another servant-girl saw him and said to those who were there, 'This man was with Jesus of Nazareth.' And again he denied it with an oath, 'I do not know the man.' A little later the bystanders came up and said to Peter, 'Surely you too are one of them; for even the way you talk gives you away.' Then he began to curse and swear, 'I do not know the man!' And immediately a rooster crowed."

the Message

The pressure was as intense as it gets. Peter's hero was being whipped, stripped, spit upon, and beaten like a rabid wolf. The trial was merciless, and the Roman cross awaited Him. The Jewish leaders were in a rage. Peter saw his own impending death flash before him. He had followed Jesus for three life-changing years. Peter had hungrily sunk his teeth into every word He spoke. Now, afraid and timid, Peter followed at a distance. The distance made him question. The distance made him curse. The distance made him forget that Jesus could overcome any obstacle.

The distance made him deny the One he loved most.

Your eighth-grade friends like heavy metal music. Your best friend slips a pack of cigarettes into your backpack. That gorgeous cheerleader with the bad rep wants you to ask her out. Everybody cusses, so why can't you? You haven't been invited to a party in weeks because you're a "Jesus freak." The popular kids are asking you for take-home test answers. You look pretty weird carrying a Coke at a keg party.

Pressure. Peter felt it, and every teenager alive feels it. Sometimes it gets too hot to handle during those turbulent growing-up years. When you desire to have a close relationship with Jesus and you live with a constant awareness of His presence in your life, it's easier to do the right thing. But when you follow Him at a distance, denying Him is as natural as breathing.

Discussion Starters:

• Why do you think Peter denied Jesus? From fear? Embarrassment?
   •• Why do distant followers fall?
      ••• What temptations cause you to fall?

Lifeline:

How can your family follow Him more closely?

The Sacrifice

the WORD | Matthew 27:15, 21-22, 26

"Now at the feast the governor was accustomed to release for the people any one prisoner whom they wanted.... But the governor said to them, 'Which of the two do you want me to release for you?' And they said, 'Barabbas.' Pilate said to them, 'Then what shall I do with Jesus who is called Christ?' They all said, 'Crucify Him!' ...Then he released Barabbas for them; but after having Jesus scourged, he handed Him over to be crucified."

the Message

Within a matter of minutes, the run-down New York apartment building went up in flames. Firemen rushed to the scene, futilely shooting water into the mountain of fire and smoke. The crowd looked on in horror as Sharon, one of the residents, stood by and called out in fear, "My baby, my baby! Someone save my baby!" In a burst of great courage, Fireman John leaned his tall ladder into the inferno on the second story balcony, scurried to the top, and disappeared into the smoke. The astonished crowd cheered wildly as John reappeared with Sharon's baby in his arms, wrapped safely in her nursery blankets. The building collapsed just as John pitched the baby into the soft safety net outstretched below. Overcome with emotional gratitude for the stranger and his dying act of heroic sacrifice, Sharon cried wild, happy tears as she cuddled her child to her breast.

Seventeen years later, Alisa, a tall, sober, teenage girl, stands next to a granite tombstone. She stares intently at the hand-hewn figure carved into the stone—a fireman with a baby in his arms. As she places fresh-cut flowers next to the grave, a passerby asks, "Are those for your father?"

Alisa tenderly wipes the tears from her cheeks with the back of her hand, swallows the lump in her throat, and replies, "No, I never knew him, but he's my friend. See, this man died for me."

And another man—Jesus—died for *you*.

Discussion Starters:

* How do you think Barabbas felt as he walked away from prison?
  ** How do you feel as you read these stories? How does the story of Barabbas affect you?

Lifeline:

As we sacrifice for each other, we more fully appreciate Jesus' sacrifice for us.

An R-Rated Death

| Matthew 27:28-31

"They stripped Him and put a scarlet robe on Him. And after twisting together a crown of thorns, they put it on His head, and a reed in His right hand; and they knelt down before Him and mocked Him, saying, 'Hail, King of the Jews!' They spat on Him, and took the reed and began to beat Him on the head. After they had mocked Him, they took the scarlet robe off Him and put His own garments back on Him, and led Him away to crucify Him."

the Message

It looks too easy when you see it in the movies and on carved statues in churches. But if the Crucifixion were pictured accurately, Hollywood wouldn't be able to film it, and many Christians would not feel right buying a ticket to watch the horrible human sacrifice. The statue would be far too graphic to place in our churches.

No, it isn't a Hollywood blockbuster, and it didn't look like the romanticized pictures that hang on museum walls. The Roman cross and the scourging that led up to it were the cruelest human torture imaginable.

He endured it for you. He loved you that much.

He knew we'd end up in hell if He didn't die for us. It was too much for Jesus to imagine His precious children hurting, so He allowed Himself to suffer through it so that by believing in and receiving Him, we might never know the pain of hell.

Read Isaiah's words as he prophesied about Jesus' death 1,500 years before it took place: "But He was pierced through for our transgressions, He was crushed for our iniquities; the chastening for our well-being fell upon Him, and by His scourging we are healed" (Isaiah 53:5).

Imagine standing on a platform in front of your entire school while your friends and enemies shout insults at you and other people kick and punch you until all your strength is gone. That would be awful.

But what Jesus went through was far worse.

Next time you read about His death in the Bible, let the words sink in. Christ was humiliated, physically and emotionally stripped naked, beaten mercilessly, and *nailed* to a cross. And He endured it all for you.

Discussion Starters:

• Why do we so often ignore or glamorize Jesus' death on the cross?
•• What does Jesus' sacrifice reveal about His relationship with His children?

Lifeline:

How can your family learn to be more appreciative of Jesus' sacrifice?

Grounds for Resurrection

"Now on the next day…the chief priests and the Pharisees gathered together with Pilate, and said, 'Sir, we remember that when He was still alive that deceiver said, "After three days I am to rise again." Therefore, give orders for the grave to be made secure until the third day, otherwise His disciples may come and steal Him away and say to the people, "He has risen from the dead," and the last deception will be worse than the first.' Pilate said to them, 'You have a guard; go, make it as secure as you know how.' And they went and made the grave secure."

the **Message**

Jesus' physical resurrection gives the greatest evidence that He is "God in the flesh." No *other* religious leader in history was resurrected. Because He rose from the dead, your faith is as real as the food in your cupboard. But critics say it was a hoax, so how do we know it's historical fact?

- *The Roman guards*—Jesus' tomb was guarded by Roman sentries. Roman soldiers were highly trained and able to defend their ground against many times their number of enemies. If they retreated, slept on the job, or defected, they'd be subject to gruesome execution.[16]

- *The Roman seal*—Josh McDowell says, "Considering in like manner the securing of Jesus' tomb, the Roman seal affixed thereon was meant to prevent any attempted vandalizing of the sepulchre. Anyone trying to move the stone from the tomb's entrance would have broken the seal and thus incurred the wrath of Roman law."[17] If you were caught breaking the seal, you might have been crucified yourself.

- *The stone*—In keeping with Jewish tradition, a one- to two-ton rock was rolled up against the tomb entrance. One man could never move the stone by himself. But eye-witness accounts documented in the Gospels say the rock was completely removed.[18]

- *The appearances*—The Gospel of John and 1 Corinthians document Jesus appearing to the apostles and 500 others.

No one could have stolen Jesus' body. No one could've broken into the tomb. The only way Jesus could have left His grave was if He'd supernatually risen from the dead. And we have evidence to prove He did.

Discussion Starters:

- Do you need "proofs" like these historical facts to believe in the Resurrection? Explain.
  - Why is the Resurrection so important?

Lifeline:

Christians can look forward to eternal life together in heaven because Jesus is risen.

The Great Commission

the WORD | Matthew 28:16-20

"But the eleven disciples proceeded to Galilee, to the mountain which Jesus had designated. When they saw Him, they worshiped Him; but some were doubtful. And Jesus came up and spoke to them, saying, 'All authority has been given to Me in heaven and on earth. Go therefore and make disciples of all the nations, baptizing them in the name of the Father and the Son and the Holy Spirit, teaching them to observe all that I commanded you; and lo, I am with you always, even to the end of the age.'"

the Message

Imagine you have a million dollars for yourself and a million dollars to give away to a friend who is penniless. Now picture your friend opening the suitcase to discover all that money inside. Wouldn't it be amazing to see the look of happiness and astonishment on his face? Wouldn't that be a fun and rewarding thing to do?

Now envision this: You're standing with a friend you've witnessed to at the gates of eternity. Heaven is on the right, and hell is on the left. You both joyfully run through heaven's gates, praising God. Imagine how grateful your friend would be to you for leading her to eternal salvation and telling her about having a relationship with Jesus Christ.

Doesn't one scenario strike you as much more fulfilling, important, and lasting than the other? Folks, Jesus admonishes us to understand and hold on to our faith, to live the Christian life to its fullest, and to talk about Him everywhere we go!

When I accepted Christ into my heart as a 17-year old, my first prayer was about how to share it with my brother and my best friend, Wade. Being nervous about this new adventure and scared of rejection, I prayed and prayed. Well, God answered those prayers. He had prepared both of them to hear what I wanted to say. They were open, ready, and eager to know Him, too.

Witnessing to my loved ones was one of the best events of my life. I challenge you to be Christ's messenger to an unbeliever. The experience is more valuable than all the money in the world.

Discussion Starters:

* Read verses 18-20 again. What do they say to you?
** Whom do you know who needs Jesus? How might you help that person?

Lifeline:

Home is the best place to encourage one another in carrying out the Great Commission.

mark

Less than 40 years (and perhaps as few as 20) passed between Jesus' crucifixion and the writing of Mark's inspired Gospel. It is the first known written record of Jesus' life, death, and resurrection. John Mark was a companion of both Paul and Peter. This straight-to-the-point book provides a wonderful description of the Messiah's wonderful acts.

Mark moves quickly through Jesus' amazing life with intense and captivating action. The word *immediately* is used over 40 times as Mark attempts to motivate the Gentiles in Rome and throughout the world to understand Jesus that they might believe. By the end of his account, Mark proves that Jesus is the One who came to save the world.

The Messenger

"As it is written in Isaiah the prophet: 'Behold, I send My messenger ahead of You, who will prepare Your way; the voice of one crying in the wilderness, "Make ready the way of the LORD, make His paths straight."' John the Baptist appeared in the wilderness preaching a baptism of repentance for the forgiveness of sins."

the **Message**

Listen, my children, and you shall hear
Of the midnight ride of Paul Revere,
On the eighteenth of April, in Seventy-five;
Hardly a man is now alive
Who remembers that famous day and year.

He said to his friend, "If the British march
By land or sea from the town tonight,
Hang a lantern aloft in the belfry arch
Of the North Church tower as a signal light…"

I still recall this Henry Wadsworth Longfellow poem from high school. Paul Revere is an American hero who will never be forgotten—a messenger who risked his life to warn his fellow colonists that the British were coming. I can almost hear the American officers speaking with words of faith and assurance: "We can depend on Paul Revere."

Longtime friend Michael W. Smith used to be an opening act "preparing the way" for Amy Grant at her electrifying concerts. When Smitty's own career took him to the top of the charts, he chose promising but unknown groups like dc Talk and Jars of Clay to lead the way and open for him.

Imagine being chosen by God to "open" for Jesus. It was John the Baptist's job to prepare the people for what was to come. Paul Revere thought the British were big news. John the Baptist was announcing news about God's only Son, coming as a man to die for our sins.

Heed John's message. The next time Jesus appears, there won't be a warning.

Discussion Starters:

* In what ways are you as a Christian like John the Baptist?
** What character qualities does God expect from Jesus' modern-day messengers?
*** Paul Revere warned of the attacking British.
How can you warn people of Satan's attacks?

Lifeline:

Consider how you can be a "John the Baptist" in your own home.

Eager Fishermen

the WORD | Mark 1:16-18

"As [Jesus] was going along by the Sea of Galilee, He saw Simon and Andrew, the brother of Simon, casting a net in the sea; for they were fishermen. And Jesus said to them, 'Follow Me, and I will make you become fishers of men.' Immediately they left their nets and followed Him."

the Message

My next-door neighbor Gary Smalley told me a story about a guy who was ice fishing with his golden retriever. Scattered across the ice were many little huts, each containing a fisherman or two, a fire for warmth, and a hole drilled into the ice from which to catch the fish. The guy with the dog caught a huge fish, but as he pulled the "whopper" up to the surface, the line broke. He tried to grab the fish with his hands, but he missed. The dog then tried to grab the fish with his mouth, lost his balance, fell into the hole, and disappeared beneath the ice.

The fisherman was crushed. The dog had been his best fishing buddy. Now what would he do? But he only had to grieve for about 60 seconds. That's when he heard the guy in the next fishing hut screaming because a dog had popped up out of his hole in the ice and into his hut!

Gary tells me the story is true, but it sounds a little fishy to me! Anyway, I like eager fishermen because it's the guys who really work hard who have the most fun—and usually catch the most fish!

My son Cooper and I used to pray for his seven best school friends every single night. Every Thursday morning, he brought them to our house for doughnuts and a Bible study. Some of them didn't know Christ personally. But Cooper was a persistent fisherman, eager to "catch" his friends for God.

My 16-year-old friend Missy led three of her Iowa friends to Christ one day last fall. She would dive through the ice to catch more friends for God!

Eager fishermen can be found in all age groups, different churches, all 50 states, and most nations. If you enjoy a good challenge, why don't you join us today?

Discussion Starters:

* What does "fishing for men" mean?
** Do you think the "fishing for men" invitation was primarily for Peter and Andrew, who were fishermen? Or is it for everyone? Explain.
*** As a family, focus on one person and have each identify a positive quality and how Jesus might put it to good use.

Lifeline:

Be an eager fisherman wherever God takes you.

Carrying Friends to Jesus

the **WORD** | Mark 2:3-5

"And they came, bringing to [Jesus] a paralytic, carried by four men. Being unable to get to Him because of the crowd, they removed the roof above Him; and when they had dug an opening, they let down the pallet on which the paralytic was lying. And Jesus seeing their faith said to the paralytic, 'Son, your sins are forgiven.'"

the **Message**

Larry is a helicopter mechanic for the Ohio Highway Patrol. He has been a Christian for many years and has walked with God with a peace in his heart that only a true Christian understands. He works on helicopters for a particular highway patrolman who didn't know Jesus…in the least. For over a year, Larry prayed for him and invited him to church—to no avail.

Finally, Larry invited the officer to a Promise Keepers event in Pittsburgh where I was speaking. During the event, the patrolman gave his heart to Christ, and he has never been the same. His "spiritual paralysis" was healed, and his sins were forgiven. He's now a happy man. (But watch out if you see a helicopter overhead; he *still* might give you a speeding ticket!)

Adam is 15 and is the best athlete in our school. Coming from the streets of New Orleans, he had a hard childhood. As a kid, he was kicked out of school more than once for his behavior. But every week his friends bring him to my house for a sophomore Bible study. I'm confident that he will meet Jesus soon. He, too, will never be the same.

Across America and around the world, caring friends still bring their spiritually paralyzed peers to Jesus the same way the guys in Capernaum lowered their friend through the roof when Jesus came to town.

By the way, Jesus is visiting your town today. Whom do you know who might need directions—or a personal escort—to see Him?

Discussion Starters:

* Friends take friends to rock concerts. Friends take friends to football games. Why do relatively few friends bring friends to Jesus?
** How many friends of yours can you think of who need to know Jesus today?
*** Over the next year, what steps can you take to help your friends see Jesus more clearly?

Lifeline:

When a friend is hurting, let him or her see Jesus in you.

Forgiveness—The Ultimate Family Gift

the WORD | Mark 2:8-9

"Immediately Jesus, aware in His spirit that they were reasoning that way within themselves, said to them, 'Why are you reasoning about these things in your hearts? Which is easier, to say to the paralytic, "Your sins are forgiven"; or to say, "Get up, and pick up your pallet and walk"?' "

the Message

Bob is a flying ace. Twice he has been awarded the prestigious navy "Top Gun" distinction as the hottest F-16 pilot in the sky. His love for flying is surpassed only by his love for God and his endearment for his wife, Debbie, and their three precious children, who revere him not only as Dad, but as their hero and best friend as well.

Bob's quest to raise a model family underwent a foundation-shaking earthquake this year when his oldest daughter, Heather—unmarried and barely out of high school—brought a baby girl home from the hospital for Daddy to help her raise and support. Bob's emotional Richter scale catapulted to a record level.

Bob and Debbie had raised their girls with high morals and Christian convictions. They trained the girls in the way of the Lord, pouring their time, talents, and gifts into the girls' hearts. Heather was a wonderful child who loved to please her mom and dad. But she let herself fall into a relationship that culminated in sin which affected not only herself, but also her entire family.

Bob had a number of choices. He could kick his little girl out of the house; he could demand she get an abortion; or he could assure her that his love was unconditional and his forgiveness certain, in spite of the pain he felt.

The grace Bob has received from God not only saved his soul, but it also guides his lifestyle with the precision he uses to guide his F-16. Consequently, his choice was obvious. Any option but the last one would create a second mistake bigger than the first. Heather knows she will always be Daddy's little girl and has learned the value of her father's—and her Father's—love.

Discussion Starters:

* Why do you think Bob's relationship with Jesus made his decision obvious?
** How does Jesus' sacrifice on your behalf motivate you to serve your family members today?
*** Why do we hold grudges in the home? Is there anyone you need to forgive today?

Lifeline:

God gives so much forgiveness—there's always enough to pass to friends and family.

New Wine

"No one sews a patch of unshrunk cloth on an old garment; otherwise the patch pulls away from it, the new from the old, and a worse tear results. No one puts new wine into old wineskins; otherwise the wine will burst the skins, and the wine is lost and the skins as well; but one puts new wine into fresh wineskins."

the Message

Larry King Live has become the most watched daily interview program in television history. Although Larry does not profess to be a Christian, he is very open to interviewing Christians in the public sector. One night Larry was in the Texas State Penitentiary on death row interviewing Karla Faye Tucker, a strikingly beautiful young lady in her mid-30s. She was awaiting execution for being an accomplice to a murder more than 14 years earlier. The murder was too gruesome for words, yet the mind-altering drugs she was on had left her in a state where, for a long time, she had felt no remorse. Indeed, her inner spirit was dead.

Then, with no explanation other than God's mercy, Karla Faye Tucker was completely transformed in that Houston prison by the Spirit of Christ. He came into her heart, granted her complete forgiveness, and gave her new life. Since that time, she had turned into an effective minister on death row, where she loved and served her fellow inmates each day. Her warmth, sincerity, and genuine love for Christ blew away Larry King and his viewing audience.

Karla Faye Tucker was not a *better* person after she accepted Jesus into her heart; she was a *new* person. She had a new mind and a new heart.

Becoming a Christian is not simply a matter of raising your hand, walking the aisle, getting baptized, or going to church (although those are all indications of a changed heart). Becoming a Christian is new wine in a new wineskin—everything old is left behind. When people see the new you, they see Jesus. You love Him, live for Him, and with time even become willing to die for Him. Without Christ, we're all on "death row." But with the pardon and release of Jesus, we are paroled from the prison of sin and find precious freedom—for eternity.

Discussion Starters:

* What did Jesus mean when He said that new wine needs to be put in new wineskins?
  ** What problems might you expect to encounter if you put your faith in Jesus yet continue to live like a non-Christian?
*** How does sinful living damage the cause of Christ when you call yourself a Christian?

Lifeline:

The acid test of true Christianity is how you treat family.

Divided Kingdom

the **WORD** | Mark 3:24-25

"If a kingdom is divided against itself, that kingdom cannot stand. If a house is divided against itself, that house will not be able to stand."

the Message

It was extremely difficult to upset Jesus. He was the epitome of self-control and coolness under stress. This day, however, the religious leaders kicked over the beehive. In frustration and perhaps envy, they charged that Jesus' power came from Satan. Jesus told them that their refusal to acknowledge the Holy Spirit would be their eternal regret (verses 28-29). And as He pointed out their faulty logic, His defense was that a house divided against itself can never stand.

In other words, Jesus was saying that Satan would not be casting out his own demons (verse 22). That would be like a military general suddenly turning around and shooting his own men.

Satan will pull out all the stops in an attempt to divide your house. The most powerful institution on earth is the family, a home united in love and devoted to Christ. So Satan tries to divide your house by whispering in your ear: "Your parents aren't being fair!" "Your little brother stole your flashlight. Get even." "Your big sister called you a liar behind your back."

And while he's working on you, he's also trying to get your parents to turn against each other. His list of accusations goes on and on for a lifetime. If you don't watch out, you begin to believe him. Then a wedge of strife forms between you and someone else. If allowed to remain, the wedge becomes bitterness, anger, fighting, and, eventually, a divided house.

The best way to keep this from happening is to stop listening to Satan and tune in to God's voice instead. God says to forgive, be patient, and stop judging one another. It's the voice of reason that will keep your house united forever.

Discussion Starters:

• What are some recent temptations that have threatened to divide your family?
•• Do you forgive others as Christ forgave you?
••• What are three things you can do this week to better unite your family?

Lifeline:

Unite your family at all costs.

Nothing Like Real Family

"Answering them, [Jesus] said, 'Who are My mother and My brothers?' Looking around at those who were sitting around Him, He said, 'Behold My mother and My brothers! For whoever does the will of God, he is My brother and sister and mother.'"

the **Message**

All we can see of the universe is that it contains millions of galaxies containing too many stars to count. They are all God's. He created them with a word…and that's just the known universe. The things beyond that we can't see are His as well.

All the people who ever lived on earth will one day bow down to God. He oversees the angels who joyfully give Him their worship. Everything that people consider important—such as gold, silver, and precious stones—is owned by God.

With all God has, what else could He ever want? God wants a family! He wants to bestow love and receive love. God wants sons and daughters to whom He can be a father. Each of His millions of children are even more special and unique to Him than you are to your parents. He knows about all your proudest moments in sports, music, and other achievements—as well as your innermost thoughts and fears. He rejoices when you do well. He hurts when you hurt. Jesus prays specifically for you, that you will find your way home to your heavenly Father.

Jesus came to earth to show us more about what God is like. Jesus' "family" consists of anyone willing to love Him, accept Him, and live for Him. He is eager for you to invite Him into your heart. And the second you do, welcome to the family!

Just remember that grateful kids honor and obey parents who give love so generously. Only fools take that kind of love for granted.

Discussion Starters:

* How would you describe the fatherhood of God?
** How does it make you feel when you think of yourself as an actual member of God's family?
*** Why should good kids want to honor and obey their parents?

Lifeline:

Gratitude is shown by obedience.

Little Bitty Seeds

"Behold, the sower went out to sow; as he was sowing, some seed fell beside the road, and the birds came and ate it up. Other seed fell on the rocky ground where it did not have much soil; and immediately it sprang up because it had no depth of soil. And after the sun had risen, it was scorched; and because it had no root, it withered away. Other seed fell among the thorns, and the thorns came up and choked it, and it yielded no crop. Other seeds fell into the good soil, and as they grew up and increased, they yielded a crop and produced thirty, sixty, and a hundredfold."

the **Message**

Have you seen them? They're everywhere. There are more of them than people to count them—as many as snowflakes in a blizzard.

What are they? God's "seeds."

Our nation is blessed with more "seeds" than any nation that has ever existed. Almost every hotel room in America has a Bible in a drawer. Thousands upon thousands of TV and radio stations across the country spread the seeds, around the clock, on invisible airwaves. Seeds are scattered throughout the Internet. Seeds are spread in churches on almost every street corner (in 453 denominations, by last count).

This is not to say that all the seeds are taking root. In Hollywood, for example, the seeds of God's Word seem to run up against a lot of rocky, shallow, and thorny soil. Studios create far more R-rated movies containing profanity and/or pornography than clean films.

Seeds don't grow so well in our public schools anymore either. Public prayer was removed in 1962, the Ten Commandments in 1980, and Bibles in 1982.

Seeds don't produce well on television. Most mentions of God you'll hear are as profanities or as an object of ridicule.

So where do God's seeds grow these days? In hearts. In homes. They grow whenever someone pushes the world aside and says, "God, You are my God. You're the God of my home. You're welcome here."

With that in mind, why not commit to letting God's seeds produce a harvest in your life?

Discussion Starters:

• Why does God compare His Word to seeds? (See Mark 4:13-20.)

•• How can your heart be like a garden that produces fruit for God?

••• How can you make your *home* such a garden?

Lifeline:

Let's make our homes the most fruitful gardens in all creation.

A Speck of Faith

the WORD | Mark 4:30-32

"How shall we picture the kingdom of God, or by what parable shall we present it? It is like a mustard seed, which, when sown upon the soil, though it is smaller than all the seeds that are upon the soil, yet when it is sown, it grows up and becomes larger than all the garden plants and forms large branches; so that the birds of the air can nest under its shade."

the Message

My friend Neal Jeffery stuttered badly in high school. He was quarterback on his football team, but a receiver had to call the plays in the huddle. At the line of scrimmage, the fullback had to call the snap count for him. But Neal was a strong Christian with faith that God would bless him. Not only did he go on to play quarterback in college, but in the NFL as well. And not only did he learn to speak clearly, but he also became the most motivational Bible teacher that I know today. A high school kid who stutters may seem like an insignificant nobody to some people. But stir in a speck of faith and watch the mustard seed grow.

Debbie-Jo grew up without a father in her house. Although her mother struggled to hold the fragile family together, her brothers had numerous problems with the law. Drugs and alcohol were literally all around Debbie-Jo. Neither her family nor her friends read the Bible, prayed, or went to church. You can almost finish the story, can't you? A bad reputation in high school, perhaps? Rebellion against God? Broken home of her own?

Hardly, because she found a mustard seed of faith. She went to a Christian camp and accepted Jesus into her heart at age 15. The mustard seed grew. She now teaches a Bible study for 50 ladies, has raised four terrific Christian kids, and has been married for 25 wonderful years. I should know. She's married to me!

You may be the youngest, the smallest, the least popular, or the poorest. It makes no difference to God. Stir in a mustard seed of faith, and He'll bless you and use you beyond your wildest dreams.

Discussion Starters:

* Why is a tiny speck of faith such a powerful thing?
* Describe how your faith has been growing lately. Is it shooting up like a mustard seed, or does it need a bit of your personal attention to increase its growth?
* How can you cultivate the mustard seed within you until it becomes a giant, productive tree for God?

Lifeline:

Home is where faith is planted.

Faith During the Storm

the WORD | Mark 4:37-40

"And there arose a fierce gale of wind, and the waves were breaking over the boat so much that the boat was already filling up. Jesus Himself was in the stern, asleep on the cushion; and they woke Him and said to Him, 'Teacher, do You not care that we are perishing?' And He got up and rebuked the wind and said to the sea, 'Hush, be still.' And the wind died down and it became perfectly calm. And He said to them, 'Why are you afraid? How is it that you have no faith?'"

the Message

My young friend Jana is an inspiration to me. She has been sick for eight years and has had six major surgeries. Every two weeks, she spends six hours getting a transfusion that leaves her even sicker for a day or two. One such transfusion was improperly disinfected, leaving her with a gruesome two-year bout with hepatitis. And on top of her physical struggles, she underwent a horrendous personal trauma.

Yet through all her pain, Jana loves God and serves Him faithfully. She never blames Him or gripes about her circumstances.

One day, she told me the secret of her amazing faithfulness: "I see my life as a fight. I can either fight God, or I can fight to make good out of it. I have chosen the latter. I consider the pain I face very small in comparison to the great things God is going to do with my life. My emotions make me mad or sad or depressed, but I have to override my emotions and stop and think, 'What is truth?' The truth is that my life is His. He's a faithful Father, and I can always say, 'I love You, God.'"

The disciples in the boat with Jesus could have learned something from Jana. Storms don't destroy a Christian's faith; they test and strengthen it. Thank you, Jana, for showing us that no matter how big the storm we encounter, Jesus Himself is always in the boat with us.

Discussion Starters:

* Recall a recent storm in your life. How did you react?
** Why is having "faith during the storm" so important for us?
*** What storms are you facing now where you need Jesus' help to "be still" and find peace?

Lifeline:

Think of someone who was faithful recently and let the person know you noticed.

A Gentle Touch

"A woman who had had a hemorrhage for twelve years...came up in the crowd behind [Jesus] and touched His cloak. For she thought, 'If I just touch His garments, I will get well.' Immediately...she felt in her body that she was healed of her affliction. Immediately Jesus, perceiving in Himself that the power proceeding from Him had gone forth, turned around in the crowd and said, 'Who touched My garments?'... The woman fearing and trembling, aware of what had happened to her, came and fell down before Him and told Him the whole truth. And He said to her, 'Daughter, your faith has made you well; go in peace and be healed of your affliction.'"

the *Message*

When I was little, my mom used to read me fascinating fairy tales about cows jumping over the moon, ladies cutting off the tails of blind mice, talking spiders, old women who lived in shoes, and other wild antics. When you think about them, it sort of makes you wonder what those guys were smoking down in Mother Goose land!

One fairy tale I'll never forget was about a princess who had such sensitive skin she could detect a pea underneath her—even when it was placed beneath 20 mattresses. *Wow, that's pretty sensitive,* I thought. *Oh well, it's just another fairy tale.*

But when I got older, I discovered a similar story in real life that pertained to the central figure of all human history, Jesus Christ. He was surrounded by a mob pressing in all around Him when one woman intentionally touched His garment with great faith. Instantly, Jesus sensed her touch among all those who were frantically seeking His attention.

I'm impressed with people who have sensitive spirits. I'm more amazed that God Himself listens and responds to a little pip-squeak like me whenever I approach Him with sincere faith.

The Princess and the Pea is a clever story, but it's a figment of someone's wild imagination.

The Savior and the Woman's Touch is a true story that will bless us beyond our wildest dreams—if we just have enough faith to believe it.

Discussion Starters:

• What made that one woman's touch different from that of all the other people who were jostling against Jesus that day?

•• How can you tell whether faith is sincere?

••• What hurts are you feeling today that need the sensitive attention of Jesus?

Lifeline:

Pray as a family every day for the needs and hurts that require a Savior's gentle touch.

Only Believe

"While [Jesus] was still speaking, they came from the house of the synagogue official, saying, 'Your daughter has died; why trouble the Teacher anymore?' But Jesus, overhearing what was being spoken, said to the synagogue official, 'Do not be afraid any longer, only believe.'"

the **Message**

Three best friends began gymnastics training at a very young age. All three succeeded in the sport, and the performance of their tiny bodies won them many medals at the meets they attended. In junior high, boys began to be attracted to these girls in their slim-fitting jeans and short cheerleader skirts. Life confirmed what gymnastics had taught them: "Skinny is better." After seeing the airbrushed models in their teen magazines, the three began to watch their diets carefully, eating only salads, fruits, and small portions of other foods. By the time they were in high school, they were bingeing, purging, and suffering the full effects of anorexia.

The disease came upon them like a whirlwind and left their emotions frazzled like a Florida hurricane. Depression and confusion became their daily companions.

But the three joined together and sought God's healing touch. They went to Christian counselors, prayed with their parents, and sought God diligently in Scripture and private prayer. As each entered college, God began the process of healing. They discovered a book titled *The Weigh Down Diet* that taught them how to seek God with all their hearts. They learned how to eat healthfully, and today all three are healing and finding the freedom that only the Savior can provide.

As these young women prepare their hearts for a lifetime of Christian ministry, they will tell you that Jesus is still the same miraculous healer He was 2,000 years ago. No disease is too much for His healing touch—not even death! (See Mark 5:35-43 for further proof.) Whenever you're facing a struggle beyond your control, remember His words of comfort: "Do not be afraid any longer, only believe."

Discussion Starters:

• Do you have a need that enables you to relate to these three girls in any way? If so, what is it?

•• How can your family better support one another whenever one of you needs Jesus' healing touch?

••• "Do not be afraid any longer, only believe." How do those reassuring words speak to your heart today?

Lifeline:

Christ sometimes uses afflictions to bring us to our knees and unite around the cross. When healing comes, remain there long enough to give Him the glory.

A Christian at Home

"Jesus...came into His hometown; and His disciples followed Him. When the Sabbath came, He began to teach in the synagogue; and the many listeners were astonished, saying, 'Where did this man get these things, and what is this wisdom given to Him, and such miracles as these performed by His hands? Is not this the carpenter, the son of Mary...?' And they took offense at Him. Jesus said to them, 'A prophet is not without honor except in his hometown and among his own relatives and in his own household.'"

the Message

The summer of my junior year in high school I became a Christian. It was the most wonderful night of my life! I couldn't wait to tell my best friend, Wade. Both of us needed the change Christ would make in our friendship and in our lives. Telling Wade couldn't have gone better! The real test was when I went home. It was difficult telling my older brother about my new relationship with Christ because he knew all my weaknesses. He knew my many failures. And I couldn't say much when he asked, "Who are you to tell me how to live?"

But I plugged along as best I could. My failures and inconsistencies continue to this day, but I continue to deal with them, thanks to the grace of God. And while it's hardest to be a witness at home, I've discovered it's well worth the effort! I'll never forget the night years later when that same brother's son was very sick. God allowed me to be with the brother I loved so much as he bowed his head and asked Jesus to come into his heart.

When you start looking closely, you see testimonies to God in unexpected ways, even at home. For example, my wife witnesses to me through her daily acts of kindness. My kids witness to me when they are obedient at times when they would rather do things their way. I witness to them whenever I serve them.

Home may be a difficult mission field, but it is the best place on earth to let your light shine for God.

Discussion Starters:

• Why was it hard for Jesus to be effective in His hometown? Was it because of anything He did?

•• What is the biggest challenge you face in trying to live out the Christian life at home?

••• How can your family support you as you try to be a better witness at home?

Lifeline:

A family that is quick to forgive and slow to judge creates an atmosphere where witnessing is easy.

Abundance

the WORD | Mark 6:41-44

"[Jesus] took the five loaves and the two fish, and looking up toward heaven, He blessed the food and broke the loaves and He kept giving them to the disciples to set before them; and He divided up the two fish among them all. They all ate and were satisfied, and they picked up twelve full baskets of the broken pieces, and also of the fish. There were five thousand men who ate the loaves."

the Message

Each summer thousands of kids from around the world come to our Christian sports camps to have the time of their lives. Many more can't get in each year because the camps are full. Why the abundance? All I know is that we try to glorify God and His Word the best we know how.

I love my wife more than words can describe. I can't contain my love for her. My four kids and I share a mutual respect that is indescribable. Yes, we've had crazy conflicts and have even approached "gang warfare" at times, but our love saw us through. Why the abundance of good things in my life? Again, it is God's amazing provision.

When I think about God, I am overcome with gratitude. His love overawes me. He not only puts up with me, but He also supports me as my dad, my best friend, and my guide. I can't comprehend the degree of His love. Why does He care so much? Same reason.

On days when I seek fulfillment on a worldly level, I find my plate half empty and become selfish, irritable, and impatient—with God, my family, and myself. But when I keep in touch with God, I always have much more than enough.

Jesus fed the 5,000 (plus women and children) and had baskets of leftovers. Similarly, He provides His children with confidence, peace, and fulfillment in abundance. And as we reflect His love toward one another, we discover an abundance of that as well.

Discussion Starters:

• How do you tap into God's abundance for you each day?
•• Other than God, what sources have you tried in attempting to meet your needs? What happened in each case?
••• In 25 words or less, what would you say is the secret of an abundant life?

Lifeline:

If Christ can feed over 5,000 people with a few loaves of bread and a couple of fish, think what He can do with a family totally yielded to Him.

the **WORD** | Mark 7:6-8

"And [Jesus] said to them, 'Rightly did Isaiah prophesy of you hypocrites, as it is written: "This people honors Me with their lips, but their heart is far away from Me. But in vain do they worship Me, teaching as doctrines the precepts of men." Neglecting the commandment of God, you hold to the tradition of men.'"

the **Message**

In the past 25 years, 35 million babies have been killed in America—legally. If you and I oppose this practice, we are accused of being old-fashioned, narrow-minded, and worse.

According to recent statistics, the average homosexual male will have 300 sexual partners in his lifetime and will live to be only 41, due mostly to the proliferation of AIDS in the gay population. After celebrating her lesbian lifestyle on television, Ellen DeGeneres received the coveted Entertainer of the Year award. Those who despair at the growing gay movement or oppose gay marriages and parenthood have been labeled "homophobic hatemongers."

In Alabama it's illegal to pray in public schools—under any circumstances. You can read books that slander God. You can get a condom at the school health clinic. But you can't pray. To oppose this situation makes you an "ultra-right-wing fundamentalist."

You could face ridicule in science class if you say you believe God created the universe in six days.

High schoolers put people down for not drinking at parties, for saying no to a joint, or for valuing virginity. They support the philosophy, "If it feels good, do it!"

All these things attempt to sweep God out of public life. The question to ask is: "Is it tradition, or is it truth?" Popular, self-centered traditions won't get you to heaven—and they don't usually do you a lot of good here, either.

But God has a tradition that's worth looking into. It's called truth. And it will set you free.

Discussion Starters:

• What are some traditions that oppose your understanding of truth?
•• How do you respond when faced with a "new tradition" you don't agree with? Do you speak up and risk potential ridicule? Or do you tend to remain silent?
••• Since truth never changes, can it ever become old-fashioned? Or is it always new? Explain.

Lifeline:

How can you spread truth to the people around you this week?

The Sign of Signs

the WORD | Mark 8:11-12

"The Pharisees came out and began to argue with [Jesus], seeking from Him a sign from heaven, to test Him. Sighing deeply in His spirit, He said, 'Why does this generation seek for a sign? Truly I say to you, no sign will be given to this generation.'"

the Message

Dr. George Wald, Harvard graduate, Nobel Prize winner in physics, and devout evolutionist, said: "There are only two possible explanations as to how life arose: Spontaneous generation arising to evolution or a supernatural creative act of God…there is no other possibility. Spontaneous generation was scientifically disproved 120 years ago by Louis Pasteur and others, but that just leaves us with only one other possibility…that life came as a supernatural act of creation by God, but I can't accept that philosophy because I do not want to believe in God. Therefore, I choose to believe in that which I know is scientifically impossible, spontaneous generation leading to evolution" ("Origin/Life and Evolution," *Scientific American,* 1978).

Every living cell is a miraculous sign from God. When I saw my precious wife give birth to the utter miracle of my youngest son, Cooper, indescribable awe came over me. I can't come close to comprehending how many miraculous events combined to give that baby life.

Every morning when I cook pancakes for my children, I thank God for the miracles that sit at our table. Every time a butterfly or bluebird flies past, I acknowledge yet another sign from God. The same is true when I speak to teenagers around the country and see their sadness turn to joy, their confusion turn to peace, and their guilt and shame washed away by God's forgiving grace.

But the ultimate sign, to me, is the one that was erected on Calvary, where "God's little boy" hung as a public human sacrifice to buy my redemption. That's the only sign I will ever need.

Discussion Starters:

* Why do people continue to demand signs from God?
** What signs have you seen lately that awed you?
*** What impression are you giving people who see you as a sign of what God does?

Lifeline:

If you wonder where God is, keep looking. How many miracles has He filled your home with?

Who Do You Say that I Am?

the WORD | Mark 8:27-29

"Jesus…questioned His disciples, saying to them, 'Who do people say that I am?' They told Him, saying, 'John the Baptist; and others say Elijah; but others, one of the prophets.' And He continued by questioning them, 'But who do you say that I am?' Peter answered and said to Him, 'You are the Christ.'"

the Message

As our family traveled from Denver to our vacation destination in Steamboat Springs, Colorado, our last driving hurdle was Rabbit Ears Pass. At 9,425 feet, snow-covered Rabbit Ears is the site of the Continental Divide. Snow that melts on the east side of Rabbit Ears eventually winds up in the Atlantic Ocean. Snow that melts on the west side ends up in the Pacific Ocean.

Peter's statement to Jesus, "You are the Christ," is like a spiritual Continental Divide. People who agree with Peter are in one group. All others are in the other.

The Muslims say Muhammad is the way to God. The Mormons say it's Joseph Smith's teaching. Jehovah's Witnesses say Jesus' sacrifice wasn't enough to bring us to God for eternity. Each group's beliefs differ from what the Bible says about Jesus. So what does the Bible say?

• Jesus is the fulfillment of all Old Testament prophecy about the Messiah (Hebrews 1:1-4; 1 Peter 1:10-12).
• Jesus is the only way to God (John 14:6).
• Jesus is fully God (John 1:1; Colossians 2:9).
• Jesus is the complete atonement for our sin (Romans 5:11).
• The Bible is God's complete Word to us (2 Timothy 3:14-17).

Who do you say Jesus is? Peter answered correctly, and upon that belief Jesus built His church and His eternal family.

Discussion Starters:

• How would you respond if a six-year-old asked, "Who is Jesus?"
•• How is "the Christ" different from "Christ"?
••• When Jesus said, "No one comes to the Father but through Me," what do you think He meant? Explain.

Lifeline:

To believe Jesus is to love Him. To love Him is to follow. To follow Him is to obey. To obey Him is to walk with Him forever.

Whom Do You Listen To?

the WORD | Mark 9:2-3, 7

"Jesus took with Him Peter and James and John, and brought them up on a high mountain by themselves. And He was transfigured before them; and His garments became radiant and exceedingly white, as no launderer on earth can whiten them....Then a cloud formed, overshadowing them, and a voice came out of the cloud, 'This is My beloved Son, listen to Him!'"

the Message

"What's right for you may not be right for me." "There are many ways to find God." "It may be pornography to you, but it's art to me." "You may call it profanity, but I call it freedom of speech." "It's not a moral issue; we simply have different opinions." "C'mon, one little drink won't hurt you." "Don't worry. Safe sex is fine."

Voices are all around us and give us a lot of mixed messages these days. It's easy to get confused and begin to question our beliefs. Who are you going to listen to?

Fortunately, God makes things clear for anyone who is willing to listen. He gave all authority to His Son. Jesus' message was very clear, and God made sure Jesus' words were written down.

Practically everyone has a book containing Jesus' words (a Bible). And when the other voices start to get loud and confusing, those words are welcome and reassuring. Here are just a few statements (from Jesus and others) to help get you through difficult times.

- "You [Jesus] have words of eternal life" (John 6:68).
- "If you love Me, you will keep My commandments" (John 14:15).
- "He who overcomes will inherit these things, and I will be his God and he will be My son" (Revelation 21:7).
- "Do you not know that your body is a temple of the Holy Spirit...? For you have been bought with a price: therefore glorify God in your body" (1 Corinthians 6:19-20).
- "If you ask the Father for anything in My name, He will give it to you.... Ask and you will receive, so that your joy may be made full" (John 16:23-24).

Discussion Starters:

· What "voices of the world" have you heard lately that contradict what Jesus has said?
·· When you receive conflicting messages, how do you determine what is the truth?
··· How can your family help each other listen to the right voices?

Lifeline:

Hold each other accountable to keep ungodly voices out of the home.

From the Beginning

the WORD | Mark 10:6-8

"But from the beginning of creation, God made them male and female. For this reason a man shall leave his father and mother, and the two shall become one flesh; so they are no longer two, but one flesh."

the Message

How long have people been on the earth? Who or what caused us to be here? Whose idea is marriage anyway?

You have questions? Jesus has answers! Take a look at today's passage, straight from the mouth of the One who was there to witness the beginning of creation—unlike scientists and psychologists.

How long have people been on the earth? "From the beginning." (The difference between this concept and Darwin's theory is vast.)

Who or what caused us to be here? "God made them male and female." Humankind was created by a supernatural God. Even Darwin conceded in *The Origin of Species*, "To suppose that the human eye…could have been formed by natural selection seems, I freely confess, absurd in the highest degree."

Whose idea is marriage? God's. It was His institution and He stands squarely behind it with as much intimate love and authority for us as for Adam and Eve. Evolutionary psychologists try to make us believe that because the monkeys we evolved from were unfaithful to their mates, it's understandable if we are, too. To quote my friends from Indiana, "Hogwash."

A quick look at American culture may suggest there aren't any rules for marriage. But while the rulebook for sex, marriage, and gender orientation may be ignored, it hasn't been tossed out completely.

Discussion Starters:

* Which of these three questions would be of most interest to your closest friends? Why?
  ** What does "from the beginning" mean in terms of Genesis 1 and the Creation account?
  *** If you were putting a price tag on marriage, what would it be? What, if anything, is more important? To what extent will you go to protect it?

Lifeline:

Only a creative God could build something as priceless and unique as a marriage relationship.

The Eye of the Needle

"Jesus...said to them, 'Children, how hard it is to enter the kingdom of God! It is easier for a camel to go through the eye of a needle than for a rich man to enter the kingdom of God.' They were even more astonished and said to Him, 'Then who can be saved?' Looking at them, Jesus said, 'With people it is impossible, but not with God; for all things are possible with God.' "

the **Message**

I belong to an organization that helps support thousands of poverty-stricken children in Haiti. When I visit to personally hug our many "adopted" kids there, I'm amazed at their smiles! I'm blown away by their sense of appreciation! I'm taken aback by their pure love for Jesus! He's just about all they've got. They get one shirt to wear to school (every day for a whole year)! They wash it and wear it with pride. Even the poorest of Americans are rich by Haiti's standards.

We are so abundantly blessed in America. One of our fastest-growing industries is the rental of mini-storage buildings. Our houses can't hold all we possess. Yet Jesus makes it clear that money and things in excess can hinder a person from coming to God. Rather than putting our faith in possessions, we must be willing to hunger for Him like the Haitian kids do. We must be willing to make Him number one, *numero uno*, in everything.

Ancient Middle Eastern villages had giant wooden gates that welcomed guests during the day but could be closed at night for protection. Beside the large gate in the huge stone wall was a smaller entrance called "The Needle's Eye" because only one person at a time could pass through. For a camel to enter, it had to first be unloaded and then squeeze through on its knees.

One camel, on his knees, unloaded. No excess baggage could get through the wall.

Our Haitian kids and others like them have a single bowl of beans and rice to eat each day. I'm guessing you have more. If so, are you hoarding your possessions or counting your blessings?

Discussion Starters:

* What point do you think Jesus was trying to make with His illustration of the camel and the eye of the needle?
** Why do excessive wealth and possessions keep people from God?
*** What actions can your family take to be more aware of what Jesus is trying to teach in this passage?

Lifeline:

Families that give together, stay together.

Humility in the Highest

the WORD | Mark 11:7-10

"They brought the colt to Jesus and put their coats on it; and He sat on it. And many spread their coats in the road, and others spread leafy branches which they had cut from the fields. Those who went in front and those who followed were shouting: 'Hosanna! Blessed is He who comes in the name of the Lord; blessed is the coming kingdom of our father David; hosanna in the highest!' "

the Message

Never has there been, nor will there ever be, a parade as significant as when Jesus rode into Jerusalem on a donkey across the garments and branches scattered by thrilled people. Daniel had designated the time for this event 600 years earlier (Daniel 9:24-27). Zechariah had foretold that the Messiah would ride in on the colt of a donkey (Zechariah 9:9). All the Macy's Christmas parades and Tournament of Roses New Year's parades and Mardi Gras parades combined can't approach the historical magnitude of this parade we now call Palm Sunday.

It was a day when Jesus was publicly acknowledged as the King of all mankind, the Messiah and Savior of the world. The example He set on that day, however, drops me to my knees. God rode in His "Parade of Roses" on a donkey. The humility astounds me. He had led a life of humility, of course, but even His "big day" was low-key in light of how other human leaders would have chosen to celebrate. The apostle Paul explains the mind-set of Jesus in Philippians 2:6-7: "Although He existed in the form of God, [Jesus] did not regard equality with God a thing to be grasped, but emptied Himself, taking the form of a bond-servant."

This story makes me want to pick up the dishtowel and dry the dishes for my wife tonight. It makes me want to write my mom and dad a thank-you note, then get a broom and sweep out their carport. It makes me want to apologize for all I've done wrong and let other people have their way a lot more often.

Someday the humble will be exalted and the proud will be brought down. And as we begin to understand and apply this valuable lesson, there's no place like home.

Discussion Starters:

• What do you imagine Jesus was thinking as He rode into Jerusalem on the donkey, knowing that many of the people who were praising Him would soon turn against Him?

•• How can you lay *your* coat before Jesus (symbolically)?

••• How does Jesus' life of exemplary humility affect the way you will live this week?

Lifeline:

From now on, mount your pride on the saddle of a donkey.

The Root of Bitterness

the **WORD** | Mark 11:25-26

the WORD | Mark 11:25-26

"Whenever you stand praying, forgive, if you have anything against anyone, so that your Father who is in heaven will also forgive you your transgressions. But if you do not forgive, neither will your Father who is in heaven forgive your transgressions."

the Message

A first-grade teacher read her students just the first part of many old sayings to see what they would come up with. Just before the conclusion she would ask her students to fill in the rest. Their answers (taken from *Priceless Proverbs*, Price Stern Sloan Publishers) are classic:

"Better [to] be safe than...punch a fifth grader."
"Never underestimate the power of...termites."
"Don't bite the hand that...looks dirty."
"A penny saved is...not much."
"Two's company, three's...the Musketeers."
"Children should be seen and not...spanked or grounded."
"If at first you don't succeed...get new batteries."

No proverb is more reliable and life shaping than Jesus' statement "Forgive...so that your Father...will also forgive you." Have you ever wondered why He spoke so frankly on this subject? It's because forgiveness is much more important than we may realize.

Forgiveness heals! Forgiveness is the glue that will restore broken relationships with parents, brothers, sisters, and friends. It restores joy and peace. It heals your relationship with God. No pharmacy, hospital, or doctor can beat the healing power of forgiveness.

Bitterness kills! If you don't forgive, you're left with a killer. It kills your relationships. It kills inner joy and peace. Worst of all, it kills your daily fellowship with God.

Forgiveness or bitterness? The choice shouldn't be that hard.

Discussion Starters:

- Why does God put so much emphasis on forgiveness?
  - What should you do if you try to forgive someone but find it hard to do so?
  - Whom do you need to forgive today? Are you willing to do so before the sun goes down? (See Ephesians 4:26-27.)

Lifeline:

Forgiving hearts create happy homes.

Render to Caesar

"They came and said to [Jesus], 'Teacher,…is it lawful to pay a poll-tax to Caesar, or not? Shall we pay or shall we not pay?' But He, knowing their hypocrisy, said to them, 'Why are you testing Me? Bring Me a denarius to look at.' They brought one. And He said to them, 'Whose likeness and inscription is this?' And they said to Him, 'Caesar's.' And Jesus said to them, 'Render to Caesar the things that are Caesar's, and to God the things that are God's.' And they were amazed at Him."

the *Message*

As I sped down Interstate 70 (doing 70 mph) one beautiful November morning, a speed zone sign swept by me in a blur. It was a 40 mph construction zone with no workers around. Well, almost no workers. The one guy there had a white car with flashing lights on top. His job was simple: catch nuts like me who don't pay attention to warning signs. Within seconds those irritating little lights were flashing in my rearview mirror. I'd rather see a dentist approaching with a drill in his hand than a highway patrolman in hot pursuit of my billfold.

But, I have to "Render to Caesar."

The law says you must be 17 to attend an R-rated movie and 21 to buy alcohol: "Render to Caesar."

Each April 15, the IRS takes a chunk of our yearly income: "Render to Caesar."

In spite of my complaining, I don't mind paying taxes. We live in the best country in the world, and I'm glad our highways have good men patrolling them. The blessings are worth it. "Rendering to Caesar" is an important part of making it happen. And every time I begin to gripe, I am reminded of the even more important part of the command: "Render to God the things that are God's." When I do that, I find I have little, if anything, to complain about.

Discussion Starters:

* What, if anything, are you expected to "render" to the government? What should you render to your father? Your mother? Your teachers?
** Why is it important to render to others with a positive attitude?
*** Which forms of giving/spending do you suppose give the most joy to God?

Lifeline:

Mom and Dad have God-given authority. Kids will receive theirs in due time.

False Christs

"See to it that no one misleads you. Many will come in My name, saying, 'I am He!' and will mislead many.... If anyone says to you, 'Behold, here is the Christ'; or, 'Behold, He is there'; do not believe him; for false Christs and false prophets will arise, and will show signs and wonders, in order to lead astray, if possible, the elect."

the *Message*

You're headed for Fun City when you reach a fork in the road. You know one road goes to Fun City, the other to Liarsville, but which is which? Two men are at the fork: one *always* tells the truth, one *always* lies. But again, you don't know which is which. Both know the right way, but you can only ask *one* question. What question would you ask? (The answer is at the bottom of the page.)

It's easy to be misled. Sometimes drinking seems as cool as the beer commercials say. Maybe the right perfume will make us irresistible. Maybe we should overlook certain character issues to date the popular person. Maybe we'll be the exception of those who face horrible consequences from drugs, sex, and so forth.

Most of us must deal with temptations to indulge in momentary sin. But when the deception is spiritual, the dangers are even worse. I've seen many high school and college students—even entire families—get wooed into cults. Many appear harmless, even loving. But some teach working your way to heaven. Others say Jesus wasn't truly God. Some believe God is everything, both good and evil. They're not only inaccurate, they're also dead wrong.

It's one thing to fall into a sin that can cost you your life yet is covered by the forgiveness of Christ. It is far worse to be misled in a way that will cost you your eternal life.

Discussion Starters:

* What was the most deceptive thing you've heard or seen lately? Where did it come from?
** How would you define a "false Christ"?
*** How can you differentiate truth from clever lies?

Lifeline:

Strong families discern truth together.

[Answer: Ask either man "What will he say is the way to Fun City?" and then take the other way.]

The Winning Team

the **WORD** | Mark 13:8, 13, 33

"For nation will rise up against nation, and kingdom against kingdom; there will be earthquakes in various places; there will also be famines. These things are merely the beginning of birth pangs.... You will be hated by all because of My name, but the one who endures to the end, he will be saved.... Take heed, keep on the alert; for you do not know when the appointed time will come."

the Message

It will be years before sports fans forget the upset win of the young Arizona Wildcats over the number-one University of North Carolina Tarheels in the 1997 college basketball national championship. Or how about the USA ice hockey team upset of the mighty Russians in the 1980 winter Olympics? And who can forget 16-year-old Kerri Strug vaulting to a gold medal for the 1996 USA gymnastic team in spite of a badly sprained ankle? These heroes all had one thing in common: They really wanted to win.

According to today's passage, Jesus is coming back—perhaps very soon. He said He would come back during a time of war. More people died in wars during the twentieth century than in all the previous centuries combined.

Jesus said the gospel of the kingdom would be preached to the whole world (Mark 13:10). Each day approximately 186,000 people around the world come to Christ. I sat beside evangelist Franklin Graham recently and asked him when he thought this prophecy would be fulfilled. He said, "It has been done."

Jesus said that false Christs would arise (Mark 13:22). Today there are 1,800 cults in America with over 20 million followers.

Jesus said there would be a push toward supernatural phenomena. Ouija boards, Dungeons and Dragons, séances, witchcraft, psychics, and so on have worldwide followings.

Jesus said Christians would be persecuted for their faith. If you think it's bad bringing up Jesus, the Bible, or other Christian teachings in class, there are places on earth where you might be *killed* for it.

But Jesus also said that if you want with your whole heart to overcome and be on His winning side, you *will*! And the rewards will be beyond belief.

Discussion Starters:

• Which of Jesus' "signs of His coming" have you observed recently?
•• What did Jesus mean when He said to "keep on the alert"?
••• How can your family better pull together as a team to defeat the enemy of this world?

Lifeline:

Individuals often lose tough contests. But a team—united, focused, and full of heart—is almost impossible to defeat.

FUAGNEM

"While [Jesus] was in Bethany at the home of Simon the leper, and reclining at the table, there came a woman with an alabaster vial of very costly perfume of pure nard; and she broke the vial and poured it over His head."

the **Message**

FUAGNEM isn't a word you'll find in Webster's unabridged dictionary or read about in *USA Today*. It's a word we use at Kanakuk Kamps that stands for "Fired Up And Going Nuts Every Minute." In other words, it means, "giving it everything you've got all the time."

The woman with the perfume was definitely a FUAGNEM girl. Chances are, she had been saving that expensive perfume her whole life. Maybe she was expecting to use it as a dowry for her husband. Perhaps she was adding a few drops with each passing birthday. For a poor Bethany peasant girl, the perfume was no doubt her most valuable possession. Yet without hesitating, she gave it all to the one she had trusted for her salvation.

Before John Elway led the Denver Broncos to the historic upset of the world champion Green Bay Packers in Super Bowl XXXII, he told an ESPN commentator that he would give every penny he'd ever made in the NFL (certainly millions of dollars) for just one Super Bowl ring. His team got fired up by Elway's FUAGNEM commitment, and Green Bay didn't know what hit them.

Prior to his sophomore high school football season, I asked my son Cooper if he thought he would start on the varsity team (a rare feat in our tough 3A-4A league). He responded with utter conviction, "Either I'm going to get a concussion or blood clot and die, or I'm going to start on defense this year."

The lady with the perfume went down in biblical history the day she gave it all to Jesus. John Elway won his Super Bowl ring. And yes, my sophomore son made the starting team and was even named Defensive Player of the Week in the second round of the state playoffs.

Don't you think it's about time *you* became a little FUAGNEM?

Discussion Starters:

• Why are so few people unwilling to "give it all" to Jesus?

•• What do *you* tend to hold back from being a "give it all" Christian?

••• Why is it so hard to have a FUAGNEM attitude when it comes to faith in Christ?

Lifeline:

If Jesus were visiting your house today, what prized possession would you give Him?

Betrayal

"As they were reclining at the table and eating, Jesus said, 'Truly I say to you that one of you will betray Me—one who is eating with Me.' They began to be grieved and to say to Him one by one, 'Surely not I?' And He said to them, 'It is one of the twelve, one who dips with Me in the bowl. For the Son of Man is to go just as it is written of Him; but woe to that man by whom the Son of Man is betrayed! It would have been good for that man if he had not been born.'"

the **Message**

It's easy to point an accusing finger at Judas, that betrayer, liar, and thief. We would never do anything to betray our Lord and Savior. Or would we?

Maybe you're a senior at a party with a cross around your neck and a can of beer in your hand. A ninth grader thinks you look cool and takes his first drink. Three years later he's a full-blown alcoholic.

Maybe you have a date with Sally, whose character is as beautiful as her physical features. You take her to the hottest movie in town—R-rated but not supposed to be "that bad." To your shock, various actors take God's name in vain, undress, and have sex. You're aroused and Sally is embarrassed.

Maybe other girls are trashing a new girl because the guys have been noticing her. Without thinking, you join in and land a couple of terrific insults that get a good response from the group. Maybe crude jokes and four-letter words are flying around school like sand in a desert windstorm. Before long it seems natural for them to come from *your* mouth as well.

Maybe you forget to study for a big test, but you just happen to sit next to straight-A Debbie, whose answers are as plain as day. Isn't it better to sneak a peek than go home and face your parents with an F?

I have to confess, I've betrayed Jesus too many times to count. I'm humbled beyond words that, when I ask, He forgives me and forgets about it. It's a humbling experience to confess your sins, but not nearly as bad as not confessing. If you don't believe me, just ask Judas.

Discussion Starters:

* Why is it so easy to judge *other* people's sins?
** In what ways do people your age betray Jesus?
*** Can you think of a time when *you* betrayed Jesus and found forgiveness? If so, share it with someone who might need to hear.

Lifeline:

Following Jesus will get you to heaven. Following Judas will get you to the end of your rope.

Don't Leave Me, Daddy

the WORD | Mark 14:35-36

"[Jesus] went a little beyond them, and fell to the ground and began to pray that if it were possible, the hour might pass Him by. And He was saying, 'Abba! Father! All things are possible for You; remove this cup from Me; yet not what I will, but what You will.'"

the Message

Any time one of my four kids asks me to do something with him or her, the event goes on my "top 10" list of that day or week.

"Hey, Dad, let's go get an ice cream cone at Baskin Robbins." That's a top 10.

"Hey, Dad, let's go throw the football together." That's a top 10.

"Hey, Dad, will you take me shopping? I need a new dress for the sorority dance." I received this top 10 call when Courtney was a sophomore in college. I was ecstatic. We met in Dallas at the Galleria Mall, where I looked for dresses with her for five straight hours. It was fantastic! And in addition, I saw a picture that day in the men's waiting area that would become one of the most cherished pictures of my life.

I was looking through *Sports Illustrated*'s "Pictures of the Year" edition and found a photo of "Mr. Basketball," Michael Jordan. He wasn't shooting a three-pointer or dunking the ball with the graceful acrobatics that set him apart as the greatest player in NBA history. He was lying on the floor, clutching a basketball in his arms and bawling his eyes out.

M. J. had just won his fourth NBA championship with the Bulls. So why the tears and utter despair? It was Father's Day and his daddy wasn't around to see the game. His father had been tragically murdered three years before.

Jesus was grieved beyond imagination in the Garden of Gethsemane. He could hardly bear the thought of going through the excruciating torment of death by crucifixion without His Daddy beside Him. The worst part of any sin is that it separates us from God. When Christ bore our sins on the cross, they separated Him from His Father for the first and last time in all eternity. But Jesus made that sacrifice so that we, too, could come to the Father. After what He did for us, is anything He expects of us too great a sacrifice to make in return?

Discussion Starters:

* Why did God have to turn His head when Jesus died?
** Why did God create the parent-child bond to be so strong?
*** What burdens can you help someone in your family carry this week?

Lifeline:

Parents and their children share a bond that can withstand any burden.

Is Jesus the Christ?

the **WORD** | Mark 14:61-62

"Again the high priest was questioning [Jesus], and saying to Him, 'Are You the Christ, the Son of the Blessed One?' And Jesus said, 'I am; and you shall see the Son of Man sitting at the right hand of Power, and coming with the clouds of heaven.'"

the Message

"I am the way, and the truth, and the life; no one comes to the Father but through Me" (John 14:6).

"I am the vine, you are the branches;…apart from Me you can do nothing" (John 15:5).

"He who has seen Me has seen the Father" (John 14:9).

"I and the Father are one" (John 10:30).

Make no mistake about it, Jesus was very sure about who He was. He was in no way insecure about His identity. "I am the Christ." "I am the only way to God." "I am God in the flesh."

Some people attempt to limit His significance by calling Him "a great moral teacher," "a very good man," "one of many prophets," or "a special messenger from heaven." But such claims are inaccurate and/or incomplete in light of biblical eyewitness accounts of Jesus and the claims He made about Himself.

Jesus knew He was God and said so. For that, the Jews accused Him of blasphemy, and He was willing to die for His claim.

The apostle Paul clearly confirms Jesus' claim to deity throughout the epistles. Here are just a couple of examples:

• "He is the image of the invisible God, the firstborn of all creation" (Colossians 1:15).

• "For in Him all the fullness of Deity dwells in bodily form" (Colossians 2:9).

God created heaven and hell. He created the world we live in and the universe around us. He created you in His likeness. Only someone with that kind of power has the credentials to become sin on your behalf so that you can face Him someday without shame, without guilt, and wholly adequate to spend eternity in His kingdom.

Is Jesus the Christ? I think you have your answer.

Discussion Starters:

* How can you be sure that Jesus was actually God in the flesh?

•• Why is this significant to you as you face eternity?

••• What are some other Bible verses you can think of that emphasize the importance of Jesus?

Lifeline:

"He is no fool who gives what he cannot keep to gain what he cannot lose" (Jim Elliot).

Barabbas and Telemachus

the WORD | Mark 15:11-15

"But the chief priests stirred up the crowd to ask [Pilate] to release Barabbas for them instead. Answering again, Pilate was saying to them, 'Then what shall I do with Him whom you call the King of the Jews?' They shouted back, 'Crucify Him!' But Pilate said to them, 'Why, what evil has He done?' But they shouted all the more, 'Crucify Him!' Wishing to satisfy the crowd, Pilate released Barabbas for them, and after having Jesus scourged, he handed Him over to be crucified."

the Message

In his wonderful book *Loving God*, Chuck Colson tells of a monk named Telemachus who lived faithfully and reverently during the final years of the tyrannical Roman Empire. One day he unexpectedly heard the voice of God within his spirit telling him to go to Rome.

As Telemachus strolled into the huge city, a strange inner directive guided him into the Roman Colosseum. He could hear the cheers of the people and the roaring of animals as the Romans, thirsty for thrills, pitted gladiators against one another or against wild beasts. The fighting was bitter and bloody. All encounters ended in death. Telemachus couldn't believe what he saw!

Spontaneously he stood up and screamed, "In the name of Christ, forbear!"

No one heard. He ran to the barrier, jumped across it onto the sandy Colosseum floor, and again addressed the Roman leaders at the top of his lungs, "In the name of Christ, forbear!" The crowd began to laugh and jeer at this puny figure who seemed so out of place among the warriors around him. One of the gladiators knocked Telemachus to the dirt. He again stood to his feet and cried, "In the name of Christ, forbear!" Another huge gladiator turned to the monk and slashed him across the chest with a fatal blow of his sword. With his last breath, Telemachus cried, "In the name of Christ, forbear."

The crowd became silent. One by one they filed from the stadium. Never again would the Colosseum host Rome's deadliest games. Telemachus's unwarranted death unified the people in opposition to this ruthless practice. Thousands of gladiators were spared by the courage of one simple man.

Discussion Starters:

* How does Telemachus remind you of Jesus?
** How does Barabbas's unexpected good fortune remind you of what Christ did for you?
*** What did Jesus mean when He said, "Greater love has no one than this, that one lay down his life for his friends" (John 15:13)?

Lifeline:

Love is truly genuine when it's strong enough to die for.

Reverence

"Those passing by were hurling abuse at [Jesus].... In the same way the chief priests also, along with the scribes, were mocking Him among themselves.... Those who were crucified with Him were also insulting Him."

the *Message*

I recently heard a terrific story from my friend Coach Bill McCartney. In 1994 Coach planned to take his Colorado Buffaloes football team to the national championship. All that stood in the way was Michigan, the Wolverines. Now, Coach had been studying Haggai 2 and believe it or not, he sensed God saying that He would do two things. First, He would use Coach to "shake the nations" (verse 7). Second, He would bless Coach on the 24th day of the ninth month (verses 10, 18). The upcoming game just happened to be on September 24.

McCartney had previously coached at Michigan for 13 years and made many friends. The night before the game, he was praying with 10 couples, all Michigan fans. Coach explained that he believed God told him he would win the next day (and as good Michigan fans, they were probably fairly skeptical).

The next day, Michigan led the whole game. In the final minute they were up 26 to 20. The 100,000 people in the stands were falling all over themselves. Colorado finally got the ball on their own 30 but had only six seconds to go 70 yards. As a hushed silence spread through the crowd, someone screamed, "Hey, McCartney, where's your God now?"

Down. Set. Hike! Quarterback Kordell Stewart dropped back and threw—no, chucked—the ball as far as his arm would send it. A Michigan defender tipped it...right into the hands of the Colorado receiver, Mike Westbrook, standing in the end zone. Time up. Final score: Colorado 27, Michigan 26!

When the players accepted the ESPY Award for Play of the Year, they held the trophy above their heads and gave the glory to Jesus Christ.

We can mock God, but our empty words do not diminish His glory in the least. How much better it is for us to offer God our reverence, and to receive His love, mercy, forgiveness, and peace in return.

Discussion Starters:

* What is the difference between reverence and ridicule?
** How do you feel when people ridicule you? How do you suppose a perfect, all-powerful God feels when people ridicule Him?
*** What are some ways people mock God today?

Lifeline:

When you say "Jesus," you've said it all!

Who Tore the Veil?

the WORD | Mark 15:37-39

"Jesus uttered a loud cry, and breathed His last. And the veil of the temple was torn in two from top to bottom. When the centurion, who was standing right in front of Him, saw the way He breathed His last, he said, 'Truly this man was the Son of God!' "

the Message

A group of scholars has calculated that it would have taken numerous teams of horses pulling in opposite directions to tear the veil of the temple in half. The purpose of the veil was to keep everyone out of the Holy of Holies, a small room containing the Ark of the Covenant (which held the tablets with the Ten Commandments, a jar of manna, and Aaron's staff that had miraculously budded and produced ripe almonds [Numbers 17]). Only the high priest could enter the Holy of Holies, and then only once a year to offer a blood sacrifice for the sins of the people. It would be immediate death for anyone else who attempted to see what was behind the veil.

But the moment Jesus died, in an instant, the separating veil was torn in two, "from top to bottom." Only God could have done that.

God was now approachable. The Holy of Holies was open for business, accepting all comers. No more sacrifices were required. The high priest was no longer needed to access God's presence. At that very moment in history, we received a permanent invitation to come to God for rest, advice, mercy, grace, or anything else we need from a loving Father. (See Hebrews 10:19-22.)

As an earthquake shook the ground beneath the Roman centurion, so his proclamation shakes my occasionally hard heart into a state of tenderness. I can echo his statement made almost 2,000 years ago: "Truly this man [is] the Son of God!" And thanks to what Jesus did for me, now I'm a child of God as well.

Discussion Starters:

- How do you feel, way down inside, about what Jesus did for you on the cross?
- How well do you think you could communicate with God if the veil had not been torn and the Holy of Holies were still a place for yearly sacrifices? Explain.
- Now that you can come to God with confidence through personal prayer, do you make the most of the opportunities you have? Why or why not?

Lifeline:

A family that prays together stays together.

Did Jesus Really Die?

"Joseph [of Arimathea] bought a linen cloth, took [Jesus] down, wrapped Him in the linen cloth and laid Him in a tomb which had been hewn out in the rock; and he rolled a stone against the entrance of the tomb."

the Message

We love to talk about the resurrection of Jesus and the new life it makes possible for us. It's a glorious story with angels, the rolled-away stone, fresh hopes, and new beginnings. Yet what makes the Resurrection so significant is that Jesus had been executed by crucifixion—the most painful and humiliating way the Roman Empire knew to kill a person.

Make no mistake: The cross was a punishment that led to certain death. The victim remained hanging until his shoulders dislocated and his lungs collapsed. To ensure the death of Jesus, a Roman soldier thrust a spear into His side. The separated blood and water which poured out is a medical sign of death.

According to Roman custom, two coroners would confirm the death of a crucified victim before signing the death certificate. A mistake could result in their own deaths. The same was true of the centurion who reported Jesus' death to Pilate. And you can bet that Jesus' Jewish opponents were going to make sure He was out for good.

Numerous doubters have proposed theories to explain away history's greatest miracle. One example is the "swoon theory," suggesting that Jesus really didn't die, but just lost a lot of blood, "swooned" (fainted), and was revived in the coolness of the tomb. The proponents of this theory want us to believe that after Jesus was beaten, nailed to a cross, speared, and deprived of food and water for three days, He just recovered. In that condition, He somehow unwrapped His grave clothes, pushed aside a two-ton stone, and escaped the Roman guards.

But then He then appeared to His disciples for 40 days and they actually believed Him to be the risen Lord of life. Could anything be more preposterous?

It's one or the other, but for me, it's much easier to believe that Jesus died and rose again as the loving and merciful Lord and Savior I know He is.

Discussion Starters:

Why did Jesus have to die?

Why do so many critics try to explain away Jesus' resurrection?

The degree of Jesus' love for us is reflected in His willingness to die for us. How does that make you feel?

Lifeline:

Jesus wore the crown of thorns so that you and I can wear the crown of life.

20/20 Vision

the WORD | Mark 16:5-7

"Entering the tomb, [the women] saw a young man sitting at the right, wearing a white robe; and they were amazed. And he said to them, 'Do not be amazed; you are looking for Jesus the Nazarene, who has been crucified. He has risen; He is not here; behold, here is the place where they laid Him. But go, tell His disciples and Peter, "He is going ahead of you to Galilee; there you will see Him, just as He told you." ' "

the Message

An Easter edition of *Time* magazine ran a cover story entitled "Rethinking the Resurrection." The story reported on an assortment of liberal theologians and other current "experts" who expressed their doubts concerning the plausibility of Jesus' resurrection.

Any reasonable attorney in a court of law would first interview eyewitnesses of the event and let them testify, wouldn't they? Well, not *Time* magazine. They quoted none of them.

Did the resurrection of Christ really occur? Eyewitnesses say yes. On the day of the Crucifixion, Jesus' disciples had been utter cowards, literally running for their lives (Matthew 26:56). When they thought Jesus was dead, they weren't eager to line up and face the same punishment He had received. But after they saw Jesus alive, they were infused with new hope and strength. They committed to Him with tremendous courage—so much so that 10 of them eventually died martyrs' deaths for what they believed. Peter wrote, "We were eyewitnesses of His majesty" (2 Peter 1:16). And John confirmed that after the resurrected Jesus had spoken with the disciples and shown them His hands and His side, they rejoiced (John 20:20).

The next time someone questions Jesus' resurrection, get a Bible and turn to the book of John. Think about the people who were closest to Jesus and died for what they saw as eyewitnesses to the event. You'll see a lot clearer with John 20:20 vision.

Discussion Starters:

- Why do unbelievers continue to scoff at Jesus' resurrection—even after 2,000 years?
  - It has been said that many a man has died for a lie when he thought it was the truth, but only a crazy man would die for a lie when he knows it's a lie. Does the to-the-death commitment of the disciples give credence to the Resurrection account?
    - What does Jesus' resurrection mean to you on a personal level?

Lifeline:

Jesus is alive, and so are you! Live the life He makes possible for you today.

luke

Luke, the "beloved physician," contributed this accurate, historical document in his effort to reach the Greek culture—the Gentiles—with the good news of God's saving grace. Luke is noted for his attention to detail and his concern for the hurting, the brokenhearted, and the lost. In this Gospel, Luke made it clear that Christ was born to save true believers from all the world's nations—Jesus didn't die just to save the Jewish people. The Gospel of Luke is also unique because while Luke recognized Christ's deity, he emphasized Christ's humanity—showing us His compassion and empathy for us in our earthly struggles.

Old Men and Rivers

the **WORD** | Luke 1:7, 11, 13, 18-19

"But [Zacharias and Elizabeth] had no child, because Elizabeth was barren, and they were both advanced in years....And an angel of the Lord appeared to him, standing to the right of the altar of incense....But the angel said to him, 'Do not be afraid, Zacharias, for your petition has been heard, and your wife Elizabeth will bear you a son, and you will give him the name John [the Baptist].' ...Zacharias said to the angel, 'How will I know this for certain? For I am an old man, and my wife is advanced in years.' The angel answered and said to him, 'I am Gabriel, who stands in the presence of God, and I have been sent to speak to you and to bring you this good news.'"

the **Message**

Some people are late bloomers.

My father started kayaking at 70 years old. He liked it so much, he couldn't keep it to himself. Dad made his kids all try it. "We Whites get our feet wet together," he said.

So we took the plunge. Most of us have become decent at the sport. Still, we marvel how Dad can still paddle circles around us.

In '88, Dad kayaked the Grand Canyon. He made it through in two weeks with a bunch of yuppies half his age. When he finished, they hoisted him up on their shoulders and marched him around like a king.

Old men like Dad aren't supposed to do that stuff. Old men sit in rocking chairs, snoozing with their feet up and their newspapers spread across wide expanses of cotton pajamas. Old men order oatmeal in restaurants and drink Milk of Magnesia. Old men play Scrabble.

But Dad's no ordinary man.

In some ways, my dad reminds me of Zacharias, who, in the twilight of his life, fathered the prophet John the Baptist. In Zacharias's case, however, God chose him to be John's father and did it through His power.

If you're facing formidable circumstances, don't stress. As He did with Zacharias's situation, God can easily turn your impossibility into a reality.

Discussion Starters:

• When did you last face an impossibility? How did God work through it?
•• What does Scripture say about impossible situations (see Matthew 19:26)?

Lifeline:

Have each family member describe a time in which God helped him or her overcome hopeless circumstances.

Sign of the Times

the **WORD** | Luke 1:34-38

"Mary said to the angel, 'How can this be, since I am a virgin?' The angel answered and said to her, 'The Holy Spirit will come upon you, and the power of the Most High will overshadow you; and for that reason the holy Child shall be called the Son of God. And behold, even your relative Elizabeth has also conceived a son in her old age; and she who was called barren is now in her sixth month. For nothing will be impossible with God.' And Mary said, 'Behold, the bondslave of the Lord; may it be done to me according to your word.' And the angel departed from her."

the *Message*

"Live a little," said the bright billboard.

Our local Dairy Queen meant no harm when it erected the thing 15 years ago. The message was intended to say, "Come in. Get out of the heat. Forget your diet." Problem was, the sign was located next to a cemetery.

Folks depend on signs for direction in life where to go, what to do, whom to believe. Sometimes people depend on signs too much. Zacharias did, as we saw in the preceding devotional.

The angel Gabriel said to him, "Your wife Elizabeth is going to have a baby."

Zacharias answered, "How do I know you're not pulling my leg? Elizabeth and I are old!"

It wasn't enough to be chatting with an angel. He wanted proof to convince him that two old people could still be parents. Zacharias was preoccupied with signs, so Gabriel gave him one—muteness.

Not so with Mary, the mother of Jesus. Sure, she didn't know how she'd conceive a child. She said to Gabriel, "But...I'm a virgin." When Gabriel explained that Jesus would be conceived by the Holy Spirit, though, she yielded. It didn't matter to Mary that no one might believe her—she believed the angel of the Lord. She simply said, "If God says so, then okay."

God's word wasn't enough for Zacharias. He wanted a sign. But after Mary understood what was to happen in her, she believed God's word. She didn't need a sign.

Sometimes we're just supposed to take things—especially God's promises to us—on faith.

Discussion Starters:

* Zacharias's questioning seemed so innocent. Why was Mary given God's approval while he was struck mute?
** This story proves God will have His way. Have you been resisting God?
*** How might you be blessed if you quit resisting?

Lifeline:

Pray for your family to submit (like Mary) to God and His will for your life.

Engaged and Pregnant

the WORD | Luke 2:4-5

"Joseph also went up from Galilee, from the city of Nazareth, to Judea, to the city of David which is called Bethlehem, because he was of the house and family of David, in order to register along with Mary, who was engaged to him, and was with child."

the Message

Engaged and with child. That sounds like an oxymoron if I've ever heard one. If you're a little taken aback by Mary's condition, think how Joseph felt. Understandably, he wanted to send her away for nine months so she—and probably, he—wouldn't be publicly embarrassed. But God said, "The baby is Mine. Marry her and raise that child as if He were your own" (see Matthew 1).

Joseph swallowed his pride and did exactly what God commanded.

Mary and Joseph most likely were subject to a bunch of gossip, rumors, and accusations. But they trusted and obeyed God. The Lord had told them it was necessary that Jesus be born of a virgin. Prophets had proclaimed that the Messiah's mother would be a virgin, which would make God the Father of His Son—in every sense of the word.

A couple of things come to mind when I think about the virgin birth. First, virginity was important then, and virginity is important now. Sex was meant for marriage back then, and sex is still meant only for marriage. Second, the fact that Mary was a virgin shows just how powerful God is. Just as God created Eve from Adam's rib, so He created a tiny baby in Mary's womb.

The miracle child of Bethlehem is still the miracle child. God is still omnipotent. And if He could create a child in a virgin womb, He can turn your life around.

There's just one catch. You, like Joseph and Mary, must be obedient and let God do things His way.

Discussion Starters:

• Why was it important for Mary to be a virgin?

•• Could you have been as obedient to God as Mary and Joseph were? How do you think they dealt with the scorn and humiliation they undoubtedly faced?

••• In what ways do you need God to work a miracle in your life today? Do you believe He can do it? Why or why not?

Lifeline:

A miraculous God can build a miraculous family. How can your family be more obedient to God and allow Him to build you up together?

Nameless in Nazareth

the WORD | Luke 2:21

"And when eight days had passed, before His circumcision, His name was then called Jesus, the name given by the angel before He was conceived in the womb."

the Message

You may not realize this, but God once went a week without a name.

Look for yourself. It's there.

God without a name. Here's the ruler of the universe, lying around in diapers with all the relatives calling Him "the baby." Like the rest of the boys in the neighborhood, God had to wait eight days for His name. Then when His parents, following Jewish custom, named Him at His circumcision, they gave Him the most popular name in Israel.

"Jesus." It was every mom's choice back then. They'd have called him "Justin" or "Jeremy" if He were born today. There were probably 50 others with His name around town. I can just imagine roll call in the synagogue.

"Abram?" *"Here."* "Benjamin?" *"Here."* "Eli?" *"Here."*

"Jesus?" *"Uh, do you mean the one from Jericho? Or the weaver's son? Or the one whose mom said she was a virgin?"*

"Now, class..." the rabbi would say, attempting to stop the laughter.

Think he was embarrassed growing up with a common name? I think that's how He planned it. And I think that's what Luke intended to capture for us in chapter 2. Jesus came into this world just like you and me. He cried, sucked His thumb, wet His bed, and slowly grew to manhood. That's part of why I love Him. He spent some time on my level before He died for me.

I suppose it's all right that Jesus began His life on earth without a name. In the end, He had a slew of them: Wonderful Counselor, Prince of Peace, Lamb of God, Holy One, The Christ, Alpha and Omega, The Almighty, King of Kings, Lord of Lords.

He's not such a no-name kid from Nazareth anymore.

Discussion Starters:

• Ever been made fun of for your name? Why do you think that's so common?

•• What does your own name mean? (Parents should take the time to find this out in advance.) What is one way you can live up to your name?

Lifeline:

Although it was common, the name Jesus means "savior."

Repent!

the **WORD** | Luke 3:3

"And he came into all the district around the Jordan preaching a baptism of repentance for the forgiveness of sins."

the **Message**

Copernicus, founder of modern astronomy, put scientists and clergy in an uproar when he said the earth circled the sun. Einstein developed the theory of relativity. Susan B. Anthony led the movement which gave women the right to vote. Michael Jordan led his team to several national titles and is regarded as one of the best basketball players of all time.

These men and women have all shaped our lives in some way. We recognize their names, and in some cases, read about them in school. But when it comes to salvation, your name and your accomplishments are not enough. You've got to repent and accept Christ to enter heaven.

In a loud voice, John the Baptist told his audience those same things. He said, "It's not enough to call yourself a Jew! Your name and heritage alone won't get you into heaven! You've got to turn from your wickedness before the wrath of God comes upon you!"

Those are fighting words. They're also *impossible* words. Who of us is good enough to gain eternal life? Not me. Nevertheless, John roared on. "Repent and be baptized!" he shouted.

It wasn't popular, but he preached it. He was showing the world its need for a Savior, paving the way for Jesus to come and die for those of us who just can't seem to be perfect.

Jesus is coming back some day. He'll leave His awesome home up in heaven and come to interrupt our lives. The thing is, He won't care what a big shot you are. It won't matter if you're smart, rich, funny, or popular. Jesus will only be impressed with eternal things. He'll stride right up to Michael Jordan (or whoever happens to be MVP of the universe at the time) and say, "Nice jump shot. But did you repent?"

Discussion Starters:

• What do repentance and baptism have to do with salvation?
•• Is repentance a one-time thing? Why or why not?

Lifeline:

Make a list of things you've done that you're ashamed of. Then, confess the list to God, ask His forgiveness, and destroy the list.

Canoe Trips in May

| Luke 3:23-24

"When He began His ministry, Jesus Himself was about thirty years of age, being, as was supposed, the son of Joseph, the son of Eli, the son of Matthat, the son of Levi, the son of Melchi, the son of Jannai, the son of Joseph."

the Message

"Nathan...David...Jesse...Obed...Boaz...Sala...Nashon...zzZZZ...zzZZZZ...zzZZZZ..."

I'll bet you've skipped over the genealogies of the Bible. Why read a bunch of names? Well, part of the reason the scribes kept all that in the Bible was to trace the Messiah's family line. Lineage—family—is important.

One May, I went down the Buffalo River in northwest Arkansas on a father and son "experiment." The men and boys were pumped. But the women weren't.

"It's too cold. They're only four years old." The moms were worried before we plunged into the first rapid, even though we vowed each life jacket would stay on until we returned. "Can't you wait until July when the water's lower?" they pleaded.

Well, this time the moms were right. Our first evening out was spent drying out Batman sleeping bags. But when the stars appeared and our boys were finally asleep, the fathers began to do something that would have shocked psychologists.

We began to talk.

Chuck confided that he expected too much from his son, Treven.

"It's driving both of us crazy," he concluded.

But the next morning, when Chuck capsized in whitewater and Treven was pulled under the canoe, Chuck wasn't so concerned with his son's IQ or batting average. He was groping wildly for a tiny hand beneath the waters. When he finally pulled the shivering child to his chest, a new relationship formed before my eyes.

I thank God for Luke's cumbersome river of names—and for canoe trips in May. They always remind me of what's important.

Discussion Starters:

- Give five reasons why your family is important to you.
  - Why are family times significant? What's your favorite family tradition?

Lifeline:

Starting new family traditions is easy. Think of one you'd like to begin.

Master of the Moment

"Jesus, full of the Holy Spirit, returned from the Jordan and was led around by the Spirit in the wilderness for forty days, being tempted by the devil. And He ate nothing during those days, and when they had ended, He became hungry. And the devil said to Him, 'If You are the Son of God, tell this stone to become bread.' And Jesus answered him, 'It is written, "Man shall not live on bread alone."' ...When the devil had finished every temptation, he left Him until an opportune time."

the **Message**

Diets come and go in the White house (*my* White house, that is). Jogging regimens begin, then come to a standstill. New Year's resolutions turn to faint memories by Valentine's Day.

Jesus understands. He was tempted to break His diet (and give in to the devil) once. It was a "slimmer than slim" fast in the desert of the Dead Sea region. He went there to get wisdom. He had some important decisions to make and didn't want anything interfering.

After 40 foodless days and nights, the devil offered the Lord a stone sandwich.

"Here," he said. "Have a bite. A month and a half is bound to make a man hungry."

But Jesus didn't budge. His resolution didn't become a faint memory because He knows a thing or two that you and I don't. He knows the power of the moment. He understands the way it can defeat our promises. He realizes the devil never takes a day off and that Satan can pinpoint just when we're ready to give up—pouncing on our moments of weakness.

Jesus must have been thin as a rail that morning when He looked the devil in the eye and told him to get lost. The devil slinked away, defeated. And Jesus, with His mind made up, marched straight back to Galilee and chose His disciples.

Satan may be the master of temptation...but Jesus can help us master those weak moments. With Him, we *can* make our goals a reality.

Discussion Starters:

* What resolution is hardest for you to follow through on?
** How does Satan usually tempt you?
*** How can God's Word help you say no to Satan when you're tempted?

Lifeline:

Write out a way you can reach an important resolution. Then pray that God would help you when you're tempted to give up.

Close to Home

"And all were speaking well of Him, and wondering at the gracious words which were falling from His lips; and they were saying, 'Is this not Joseph's son?' And He said to them, 'No doubt you will quote this proverb to Me, "Physician, heal yourself! Whatever we heard was done at Capernaum, do here in your hometown as well."' And He said, 'Truly I say to you, no prophet is welcome in his hometown.'"

the *Message*

Jon, a former programs director at Kanakuk Kamp, was bringing his sweetheart home from college to meet his folks. The two had gotten out of the car and were walking up the sidewalk when a sudden panic seized Jon.

Without explanation, he'd completely blanked out on his girlfriend's name.

Fifty feet stretched between Jon and disaster as He stopped to tie his shoe, scrolling mentally through the alphabet, hoping to land on the correct initial. No luck. They continued toward the door. He tried picturing her signature at the bottom of notes she'd written. Nothing.

Desperate, Jon asked if she thought it might be better to wait until another night.

"It's fine, Jon. Why? Is something wrong?"

"I just wanted to be sure you're ready to meet my folks," he said.

When they finally reached the porch, Jon had an epiphany. He asked to see her driver's license. "My dad doesn't believe you and my mom have the same birthday. I need to prove it," he explained. He glanced at her license and sighed in relief.

Anne Marie. How could I forget?

Has familiarity ever caused you amnesia? This case may be a bit extreme, but we've all experienced a time when we couldn't remember something so familiar to us that it made us crazy. Sometimes, that's how it is with Jesus. Many Christians know Jesus, but we still forget.

Are you too familiar with Jesus to remember Him?

Discussion Starters:

• Why do you think it was so hard for the people of Nazareth to accept Jesus?

•• Why might it be difficult for some churchgoers to really know Him?

••• What does it mean to "know Jesus"? How can you improve your friendship with Him?

Lifeline:

How different would our prayers be if we always realized our Friend was present?

Bootfish and the Believer

the WORD | Luke 5:4-7

"When He had finished speaking, He said to Simon, 'Put out into the deep water and let down your nets for a catch.' Simon answered and said, 'Master, we worked hard all night and caught nothing, but I will do as you say and let down the nets.' When they had done this, they enclosed a great quantity of fish, and their nets began to break; so they signaled to their partners in the other boat.... And they came and filled both of the boats, so that they began to sink."

the Message

The back of the menu at the Reservoir Cafe in Deckers, Colorado, reads, "If ya want whiskerfish, go to Walsenburg." My friend Barry, who was about to dine there, considered the advice, then looked at his young waiter. "You're not going to believe this," said Barry, "but I caught a seven pound cutthroat at Spinney Lake today. Want to know how I caught him?"

The boy nodded, his mouth hanging open. Barry went on. "I had just fallen in the inlet at Spinney. My waders (fishing pants) were almost filled with ice cold water. I was shouting, and all the fellas on the shore were laughing at me. So do ya know what I decided to do?"

"No, sir. What's that?" asked the boy.

"Pray," said Barry. "I said, 'Lord, I've been out here since five o'clock this morning, and I haven't caught a thing. I'd be ever so thankful if You'd treat me like You did Peter on the Sea of Galilee and give me one big, fat fish that I can tell my friends about back home.'

"Well," Barry continued, "I walked about five feet, saw a huge cutthroat caught in the shallows, kicked him up onto the grass, put him in my net, and walked off. But then I threw him back in the river."

"Yeah, right," mumbled the young waiter. "So what'll it be, sir?"

"Nothing, thanks," said my friend as he closed the menu and smiled. "I think I'll go to Walsenburg for the whiskerfish."

Why do folks have such a hard time believing God blesses His children? God is the great gift-giver. And if you don't believe me or Barry, look in the Word. Simon Peter has an even better fishing story than Barry.

Discussion Starters:

* When were you surprised by one of God's blessings?
    ** The book of John tells us 153 fish were caught that morning (21:11).
    *** When God gives so extravagantly, what does that tell us about Him?
        **** What kind of attitude should we have toward Him?

Lifeline:

Keep tabs on God's blessings today. Share your findings at family devotions tomorrow.

A Chilling Proposal

the WORD | Luke 5:18-20

"And some men were carrying on a bed a man who was paralyzed; and they were trying to bring him in and to set him down in front of Him. But not finding any way to bring him in because of the crowd, they went up on the roof and let him down through the tiles with his stretcher into the middle of the crowd, in front of Jesus. Seeing their faith, He said, 'Friend, your sins are forgiven you.'"

the Message

Kris loved Diane enough to freeze his backside off. Literally.

With a sign in one hand and a spool of twine in the other, he carefully climbed the ski lift pole at Breckenridge, Colorado. Wind whipped his naked face. Snow collected inside his jacket and melted, tracing two wet paths down Kris's legs, soaking his socks. Pneumonia was a distinct possibility.

At the top, Kris wrestled the sign onto cold steel and squinted toward the top of the mountain. Kris tied one last knot and threw a prayer toward heaven. "Dear God, thanks for Diane," he shouted to the wind. "Please let her say yes. And please let this marriage last!" Then he came down from the sky, took his three other signs, hung them on three other poles, and waited for morning.

At noon the following day, Diane took a fairy-tale ski-lift ride. With that trademark sparkle in her eyes, she read the words: "Little Mo...you're sooper dooper...will you be... Mrs. Cooper?"

And Diane said yes!

Since then, I have often thought that any other fool would've found a safer way to ask for a woman's hand in marriage. My friend Kris, though, is not just "any other fool." He was and still is a fool for Diane.

Sometimes the greatest love is one that's willing to play the fool. The paralytic's friends had that kind of love for him. They were willing to climb the building where Jesus was preaching and lower their friend through the roof. They loved him so much and wanted him healed—physically and spiritually—so much that they were willing to look silly. Jesus looked at their foolish love and rewarded them for being faithful.

Oh Lord of the sky, snow, and wind, let our love for You be foolish.

Discussion Starters:

* What was so amazing about the men's love for their paralyzed friend?
** What are you willing to do to see your friends come to Jesus?

Lifeline:

Have each person write down the name of one pre-Christian friend. Then pray for those friends, and think of one way to show Jesus' love to them.

The Right-Handed Man

the WORD | Luke 6:6

"On another Sabbath He entered the synagogue and was teaching; and there was a man there whose right hand was withered."

the Message

Doctors notice things. You can go see them for a sprained ankle and leave with allergy medicine. They spend about 10 minutes checking you and about 15 minutes asking you questions. Doctors are thorough. They don't want to miss anything.

Luke was a doctor. More than any other New Testament writer, he chronicled the details of disease. Men with withered right hands in other Gospels might as well have taken a number and stood in line for sympathy. (Notice that the books of Matthew and Mark don't note which hand was deformed as Luke does.) But Doctor Luke eyed the patient and said, "Aha! Now, that man's *right hand* is withered!"

Okay, so it's a minor detail. But if it was *your* hand being operated on, wouldn't you want the doctor to know the difference?

God notices the details of our lives even more. Nothing slips by the Great Physician. To God, I'm not just the man in Branson who's having a good or bad day. To Him I'm Joe White, husband, father of four, financer of two college students, director of seven camps, manager of a thousand employees, zookeeper of countless pets, man prone to exhaustion...and coincidentally a right-handed, beloved member of His kingdom.

God knows what makes us happy and why we get miffed. We can't do anything, say anything, or think anything without His knowledge (see Psalm 139). Growing up is often tough. Sometimes we can't even comprehend ourselves. But God can, and when you pray to Him, He'll understand what you need—even before you ask.

That thought is comforting to me. It makes me happy to know that some day when God calls me up from the dugout, He'll know which side of the plate I like to bat on.

Discussion Starters:

* What things would you like to be known for in your family? Why?
  ** How can it change your prayer life to realize that God knows about all your needs?
* *** What does it do for your self-esteem to know that God cares about the details of your life?

Lifeline:

Take some time to praise one significant characteristic of another family member.

Two Hearts?

"The good man out of the good treasure of his heart brings forth what is good; and the evil man out of the evil treasure brings forth what is evil; for his mouth speaks from that which fills his heart."

the *Message*

Pay attention and read closely, 'cause I'm going to tell you something you probably didn't hear in biology class.... Did you know you have two hearts? You do! Your first heart pumps blood. If it quits, your body dies. But the "heart" the Bible talks about the most is your personality, your spirit. If it quits, your soul dies.

Your heart reflects who you are, what your character is. It's your decision-making, emotional side. If your heart and thoughts are centered on Christ, your actions and words will reveal Him living in you. If your heart is focused on junk, your actions and words will show it, too. Make no mistake about it: Every TV show, movie, magazine, and CD you see and hear programs your heart. Even the kinds of friends you associate with will have a deep impact on you.

Ally, a young friend of mine, tells me that she stopped buying fashion magazines at the grocery store last year. "I used to spend hours reading them," she says, "but then I realized that I always felt bad about myself afterward. I thought my clothes were too ugly and my body was too fat. I got so obsessed with myself, I couldn't even focus on God."

The kind of stuff you put in your heart will determine who you become.

If you feed your body only junk food and candy, you'll eventually get sick. Your hair will lose its shine, your teeth will rot, and you'll get tired more quickly. The same principle applies to your heart. If you feed it rotten entertainment and expose it to friends who are bad influences, your heart will get spiritually sick.

Take some time to evaluate whether your heart is getting enough spiritual nourishment. It's important—what you put in it will either draw you close to God or take you far from Him.

Discussion Starters:

* How well is your heart getting fed these days? Explain.
    ** Why is it so important to consider what you put in your heart?
  *** Why does the Bible talk so much about the heart?

Lifeline:

Evaluate whether your hearts are getting enough spiritual nourishment.

Long-Distance Love

the WORD | Luke 7:2-3, 6-7, 9

"And a centurion's slave, who was highly regarded by him, was sick and about to die. When he heard about Jesus, he sent some Jewish elders asking Him to come and save the life of his slave.... Now Jesus started on His way with them; and when He was not far from the house, the centurion sent friends, saying to Him, 'Lord, do not trouble Yourself further, for I am not worthy for You to come under my roof; for this reason I did not even consider myself worthy to come to You, but just say the word, and my servant will be healed.' ...Now when Jesus heard this, He marveled at him, and turned and said to the crowd that was following Him, 'I say to you, not even in Israel have I found such great faith.'"

the Message

Every year at Christmastime, Will and Cindy save all their Christmas cards and put them in a basket. They keep the basket on a shelf next to the dining room table, and each night at dinner, they select a card and pray for the person or people who sent it.

"Dear God, help Johnny in his dental practice in Oregon."

"Lord, comfort Ted and Ginger as they make their move from Boise."

It didn't take too long for word to get out concerning Will and Cindy's basket. Now people send them Christmas cards throughout the year just so they can be on the prayer list.

Do you see what's happened here?

Prayer is effective whether it is long distance or as close as a touch. Jesus prayed for people no matter where they were, and the results were amazing! Jesus didn't even have to touch the centurion's slave to heal him. The Lord just prayed for him—long distance (see verse 10).

Prayer is powerful. One July, Will was sent another Christmas card. It was in the heat of summer, when all us Ozark people are nothing more than muffins in an oven. Will opened the letter and read, "Just praying that God relieves you of this heat. Love, Todd— in cool Colorado." Will told me that at that moment, a breeze blew across his face. And he said he may be mistaken, but he thought he could smell just a hint of pine in it.

Prayer across the plains. It's long-distance love, and it works!

Discussion Starters:

* Why did the centurion's faith get results?
** When and how has Jesus most powerfully answered your prayers?

Lifeline:

Make a family prayer basket and lift your friends and relatives up in prayer.

Move Over, Saint Mary

the WORD | Luke 7:20-23

"When the men came to Him, they said, 'John the Baptist has sent us to You to ask, "Are You the Expected One, or do we look for someone else?"' At that very time He cured many people of diseases and afflictions and evil spirits; and He gave sight to many who were blind. And He answered... 'Go and report to John what you have seen and heard: the blind receive sight, the lame walk, the lepers are cleansed, and the deaf hear, the dead are raised, up the poor have the gospel preached to them. Blessed is he who does not take offense at Me.'"

the Message

A youth pastor friend pulled into the gas station for one last stop. "I don't need a map," he informed the attendant. "I've been there a half dozen times before."

He paid up, hopped back in the van full of a dozen teenagers, and drove on. Dave parked and led his group up the mountainside. They were pumped. In July there's no better place for sledding than St. Mary's Glacier. But the hike is long, and the heat that day was brutal. After three hours hiking around trying to find the glacier, the teens demanded an explanation.

"Dave! I thought we were gonna go sledding!" one boy complained.

"Where's the snow, Dave?" asked another. "You need snow to sled."

Dave turned red. "I'm sure we came the right way. It's got to be here."

"Look!" said a girl in the back of the crowd. She pointed way below to a tiny patch of white on a distant ridge. Dave's heart sank as he realized his mistake and the mob dog piled him.

Fortunately, Dave and his group found other snow that day and ended up having a blast. But after hearing Dave's story, I couldn't help but wonder, *How could a youth leader miss something as big as a glacier?*

In the same way, we as Christians fail to recognize our Lord. We often look right past Jesus, the most important Person in our lives. We can't identify His voice. Or His direction. Or His love. We say we know Him, and then we don't notice Him and His work in our lives.

Can you recognize Jesus, or do you constantly stumble over Him?

Discussion Starters:

- Why was John anxious to confirm Jesus' identity?
  - What do you think Jesus meant in verse 23?

Lifeline:

What things has God been doing in your life that you might have missed?

Tuning Out

the **WORD** | Luke 8:4, 8-10

"When a large crowd was coming together, and those from the various cities were journeying to Him, He spoke by way of a parable.... As He said these things, He would call out, 'He who has ears to hear, let him hear.' His disciples began questioning Him as to what this parable meant. And He said, 'To you it has been granted to know the mysteries of the kingdom of God, but to the rest it is in parables, so that seeing they may not see, and hearing they may not understand.'"

the *Message*

As a young man, Arthur was devastated when a short stint of navy navigation ruined his hearing. Eventually he grew bitter. Often, he cursed the cannons that had blasted him into near silence. He'd never again hear a bluebird, a tractor, or the sounds of farm life without his hearing aids. In time, though, Arthur grew to love his hearing aids because he found power in them.

Slowly, Arthur began to abuse that power. If Martha, his wife of 43 years, wanted him to help can fruit, he'd simply turn the dial down on his hearing aids and tune her out. If she needed eggs fetched, he'd casually reach behind his ear, pretend to scratch his head, and *presto!* Martha was gone. If Arthur didn't feel the urge to help that day, well, the dial was always close at hand. But Martha wasn't fooled.

Fortunately for Arthur and his marriage, his ways came to a smoking halt one hot August night. Martha had just asked Arthur to help with the dishes when she heard sirens. She looked out the kitchen window and saw an ominous glow. Martha looked at Arthur in his easy chair, acting oblivious to her request. Casually, she walked over to him and knelt down.

"Arthur?" she asked, mouthing the words without a sound.

Arthur turned his volume up just a hair.

"Arthur?" she mouthed again.

When she finally got his full attention, Arthur's eyes grew round and wild. That's because Martha leaned close to her husband's cheek and shouted, "In case you're interested, Arthur, *the barn is on fire!*"

"He who has ears to hear, let him hear!"

Discussion Starters:

* What did Jesus mean when He said, "Seeing they may not see, and hearing they may not understand" (verse 10)?
** How can you know when God is trying to tell you something?
*** Do you ever tune Him out? How?

Lifeline:

As a family, how can you help each other better listen to God?

A Time for Music

the WORD | Luke 8:42-45, 47-48

"But as He went, the crowds were pressing against Him. And a woman who had a hemorrhage for twelve years, and could not be healed by anyone, came up behind Him and touched the fringe of His cloak, and immediately her hemorrhage stopped. And Jesus said, 'Who is the one who touched Me?' ...When the woman saw that she had not escaped notice, she came trembling and fell down before Him, and declared in the presence of all the people the reason why she had touched Him, and how she had been immediately healed. And He said to her, 'Daughter, your faith has made you well; go in peace.'"

the Message

Often God's timing surprises us. Winn would tell you he's found that to be true.

Winn's guitar was his prized possession—one might even say he was obsessed with his talent. He loved that guitar more than anything except his wife, Sarah. One August, the insurance premium came due on Sarah's Corvette. For days, Winn prayed for a way to pay the debt, but nothing came. Winn dreaded the inevitable solution.

"Winn," Sarah suggested, "your guitar would cover the bill."

Winn fought it, but he knew Sarah was right. They sold the guitar and settled the account.

After a long winter, something wonderful happened. Winn's obsession faded. And in the spring, after Sarah's Corvette was pummeled by a hailstorm, she decided not to use the insurance money to fix her car, but instead took the check to a guitar shop and bought Winn the best guitar there.

When he asked her why she'd done it, Sarah told a beaming Winn, "I believe God says the time has come again for music in our home."

As Winn found, God's timing is unexpected.

I'll bet the hemorrhaging woman would agree. She'd been bleeding for 12 years, but as soon as she touched Jesus, *poof!* her illness was gone.

Why didn't He heal her before? we might wonder.

We don't know the answer. But we do know the Lord always has a plan and a reason for His ways—and His timing is perfect.

Discussion Starters:

- At first, what did you think of God's timing with the hemorrhaging woman? How did everything work out for the best?
- How do you usually respond to "lousy timing" in your life?

Lifeline:

Pray the Lord's Prayer together. When you reach the part about "Thy will be done," consider what this means concerning His timing in your life.

Big Things...Small Packages

the WORD | Luke 9:46-48

"An argument started among them as to which of them might be the greatest. But Jesus, knowing what they were thinking in their heart, took a child and stood him by His side, and said to them, 'Whoever receives this child in My name receives Me, and whoever receives Me receives Him who sent Me; for the one who is least among all of you, this is the one who is great.'"

the Message

My friend Lyle is sick! He once talked a friend of mine, Bill, into getting on a bull. He did some smooth talking. Bill had never ridden anything fiercer than a 10-speed. Nonetheless, Bill stood in the arena and watched as Lyle brought the animals out, preparing to stomp out Bill's tongue.

"Dear God," Bill prayed in a whimper, "don't let me get that one with the broken horn. Or that one in the middle who looks like he could cough up bigger things than me."

Then Lyle chuckled and called for a little, tiny bull way back in the corner.

"This one oughta do," said Lyle as Bill climbed aboard. "Puny little thing like this can't be too tough."

"They don't come any punier than this," smiled Bill, relieved enough now to poke fun.

"Careful, though. Big things come in small packages," said Lyle, smiling, and slapping the little bull on the rump.

The gate opened and six seconds later, Bill was on his back, rubbing his head and picking mud from his teeth. Come to find out, the little bull was named Thunderbolt, star of the movie *My Heroes Have Always Been Cowboys*. He snorted once and trotted back to the pen.

"Why don't *small* things ever come in small packages?" Bill groaned.

I think Jesus got a chuckle out of that. Like Bill, His disciples also had a hard time believing those who were small and unassuming—"the least of these"—could be great. Jesus had to bring over a little child so the disciples would get it. Bill had to be thrown from a puny bull. But the point was made: Those who appear weak or small are often the strongest and greatest—in the bullring and in the kingdom of God.

Discussion Starters:

• Why were the disciples arguing over who was greatest among them?

•• What types of things do you argue about in your family?

••• What did Jesus mean by, "Whoever is least among you is greatest" (see verse 48)?

Lifeline:

Discuss what things make a person "great" in your family.

Revenge of the Flattened Parakeet

the **WORD** | Luke 10:25-27

"And a lawyer stood up and put Him to the test, saying, 'Teacher, what shall I do to inherit eternal life?' And He said to him, 'What is written in the Law? How does it read to you?' And he answered, 'You shall love the Lord your God with all your heart, and with all your soul, and with all your strength, and with all your mind; and your neighbor as yourself.'"

the **Message**

Ty knew the Golden Rule. But when it came to practical jokes he chose to ignore it—especially when one of his friends was getting married. It seems Ty had played one too many wedding tricks on pals who preceded him in matrimony. Ty had done it all: written "Save me" in white polish on the bottoms of the bridegroom's shoes (for the congregation to read when the couple knelt at the altar), fired cap guns during solemn vows, stuck a melted candy bar down the groom's pants while the couple kissed, and so on.

So when Ty's turn came to tie the knot, there was a long line ready to retaliate. On the morning of his wedding, his friends "did unto him as he had done unto them." They pretended to throw him a "handyman shower."

"You shouldn't have," said Ty to his grinning groomsmen. In the end, he wished they wouldn't have. Instead of tools, Ty got some interesting pets. A short list of the gifts he opened that day: a rabbit, a squirrel, a cat, and a mouse. All of them stiff. And from the best man, Ty got a paper-thin parakeet, too flat to hold a tune.

Now, I don't mean to imply that practical jokes are sinful. My point is simply this: Love other people the way you want to be loved. If you don't want people to gossip about you, stop broadcasting your friends' stories to the entire school. If you want to be heard, listen first.

What you do for others is as powerful as what you don't do. If you would follow God's greatest commandment, decide how you want your family and friends to treat you and love them that way first.

Discussion Starters:

* There are active and inactive components of God's command. In other words, proper love involves doing and not doing. Give examples of both.
** Who is your neighbor?
*** Is there anything you do to others that you wouldn't want done to you?

Lifeline:

Keep one another accountable for changing the way you treat others.

Beef Jerky from Heaven

the **WORD** | Luke 10:30, 33-34, 36-37

"Jesus replied and said, 'A man was going down from Jerusalem to Jericho, and fell among robbers, and they stripped him and beat him, and went away leaving him half dead.... [A priest and a Levite passed the man by without helping him.] But a Samaritan...felt compassion, and came to him and bandaged up his wounds, pouring oil and wine on them; and he put him on his own beast, and brought him to an inn and took care of him.... Which of these three do you think proved to be a neighbor to the man who fell into the robbers' hands?' And he said, 'The one who showed mercy toward him.' Then Jesus said to him, 'Go and do the same.'"

the *Message*

It was raining when Dennis slowed to pick up the old hitchhiker on I-35 (though picking up hitchhikers is not usually a good idea).

"Wow, Den! He's dirty as tar," said a buddy from the backseat as they drew near. "What if he pulls something funny? Let's go—I'm starving. I'd kill for some jerky."

Dennis listened but still braked his Buick to a halt. Dennis's friends jeered as the wet, old man ran to catch his ride. "Wouldn't it be funny to burn rubber right when he got to the door?"

"Yeah! Yeah! Fling gravel everywhere. C'mon, Den, we're hungry. This geezer will probably want us to drive clear across the state."

"Shhh," Dennis said. The door opened, the backseat got quiet, and the old man climbed inside, wringing wet and very grateful.

"Lawd, it's a soggy day in paradise," said the handsome old man, offering something to the guys. "Any you boys want a piece o' jerky?"

"Yes, sir," said Dennis. "We were just saying how nice that'd be, weren't we, guys?" Dennis grinned and looked at his red-faced friends. Then he got back on the road and took the man as far as he needed to go.

As Dennis discovered, being a "Good Samaritan" takes time and patience. It also takes guts. Your friends might laugh at you. Other people won't understand. But Jesus calls us to show mercy, regardless of how dirty, poor, or unattractive they are.

Discussion Starters:

- Why didn't the "holy men" help the man in Luke 10:30-37?
  - What compelled the Samaritan to help the man?
    - How can you serve others this week?

Lifeline:

Take 15 minutes of your time today or tomorrow to help someone.

"Godda Skrate"

the **WORD** | Luke 11:1-4

"It happened that while Jesus was praying in a certain place, after He had finished, one of His disciples said to Him, 'Lord, teach us to pray just as John also taught his disciples.' And He said to them, 'When you pray, say: "Father, hallowed be Your name. Your kingdom come. Give us each day our daily bread. And forgive us our sins, for we ourselves also forgive everyone who is indebted to us. And lead us not into temptation." ' "

the **Message**

Do you ever wonder if God laughs when kids pray? I think He might. After all, some of what they say is pretty funny. One father told me of a conversation he had with his five-year-old, Ashley, the other day.

"Dad?" Ashley asked.

"Yeah, pumpkin?"

"Who's Howard?"

"Howard who?"

"Daaad! You know...the Howard-be-Thy-name, Howard. That's who."

How could God not laugh at that?

Ed told me of a prayer his nephew Timmy prayed during the debate over abortion laws in the beginning of Bill Clinton's presidency.

"Dear God," Timmy said, "thank You for this day. Thank You for Mommy and Daddy and Uncle Jim and Aunt Carolyn and all my friends at school. And God, please ... please don't let Bill Clinton get an abortion."

Okay. That one probably brings a tear as well as a smile. At any rate, here's the point: "Godda skrate" and "Godda skood" (that's five-year-old talk for "God is great" and "God is good"), no matter how anyone prays it.

It doesn't matter so much what your prayers sound like.... God cares more about having you come to Him honestly and regularly, with love and honor. And He always hears you.

Have you come to Him lately?

Discussion Starters:

* The disciples had probably prayed all their lives. So why did they suddenly come to Jesus, asking Him to teach them how to pray?

    ** Some say the Lord's Prayer is a how-to model. What does it teach us about the practice of prayer?

  *** Why does God want His people to pray?

Lifeline:

Set aside a time each day to pray together individually and/or as a family.

More Light!

the WORD | Luke 11:34-36

"The eye is the lamp of your body; when your eye is clear, your whole body also is full of light; but when it is bad, your body also is full of darkness. Then watch out that the light in you is not darkness. If therefore your whole body is full of light, with no dark part in it, it will be wholly illumined, as when the lamp illumines you with its rays."

the Message

Some kids think of running away at least once in their lives. Bonnie did when she was eight. From her point of view, the problem started with spinach.

"I'm not gonna eat it!" said Bonnie.

"You most certainly are!" her mother stated.

"I'll run away if you make me!"

"I'll help you pack," said Bonnie's father. And up the stairs they went to find the suitcase. Ten minutes later, Bonnie's parents continued the reverse psychology at the front door.

"It might be kind of scary out there, Bonnie's father warned. "And it's cold and dark. But if you've got to go, you've got to go."

"I'm not afraid!" said Bonnie, hungry for independence, and not for spinach. With suitcase in hand, she crept to the edge of the porch, stopping where the light from inside the house ended.

"I want more light!" she demanded.

Her father switched on the porch lamp, and Bonnie ventured out into the yard, where once again the light melted into the shadows.

"More light!" she said again.

"That's all there is," said Bonnie's father.

For a brief moment, the suitcase heavy in her hand, Bonnie considered. Then she shrugged her shoulders, came back inside, and ate some cold spinach.

I'm leery of the darkness too. It blots out God's light and leads us in the wrong direction. Next time you encounter it, turn back toward the light.

Discussion Starters:

• How does darkness enter a person or a family?

•• How can we get rid of darkness and bring more light to our lives?

Lifeline:

Jesus brings light into the darkest of situations.

Treasures

the WORD | Luke 12:15-16, 19-21

"Then He said to them, 'Beware, and be on your guard against every form of greed; for not even when one has an abundance does his life consist of his possessions.' And He told them a parable, saying, 'The land of a rich man was very productive.... [And the man said to his soul], "Soul, you have many goods laid up for many years to come; take your ease, eat, drink and be merry." But God said to him, "You fool! This very night your soul is required of you; and now who will own what you have prepared?" So is the man who stores up treasure for himself, and is not rich toward God.'"

the Message

In our Ozark mountain hometown each Friday night, our friends and neighbors pack the grandstands like sardines in a tin can to cheer wildly for the heroes of the gridiron (that's hard-core football talk for "football field"), the Branson Pirates. My son, for better or for worse, is an outside linebacker who would rather run into a stadium wall than open his English book. He tells me the loud and rather obnoxious football crowd gives him tremendous energy that he discharges with every leather-cracking tackle.

I love watching my son play. But I'm still a little puzzled by his team name. People cheering for the *Pirates?* It seems odd to scream and yell for a name that represents a team of thieves, murderers, and rebels.

Pirates were greedy guys. Those swashbucklers were known to do anything to get treasure. They blew up and raided ships, robbed people blind, and invaded homes to obtain and hoard their fortunes. Gold, jewelry, diamonds, silver, rubies, and pearls filled their chests of sordid gain.

We desire treasures, too. A lot of us place too much value on popularity, athletic skill, sex appeal, fast cars, trendy clothes, or money.

Jesus said, "Where your treasure is, there your heart will be also" (Luke 12:34). If anything is more important to us than God, it's a problem. If you're unwilling to talk about Jesus with others, that's a problem. If you think about something other than Him too much or it becomes a source of pride, it's a problem.

Store your treasures in heaven. That's where you'll find real wealth.

Discussion Starters:

* According to the parable, what is the definition of greed? Can a person be financially wealthy but not greedy? Explain.
** What does it mean to be "rich toward God"?

Lifeline:

Decide upon the richest couple you know—people who seem to be "rich toward God." Then invite them over for dinner and ask what their secret is.

On Cat's Feet

the WORD | Luke 12:36, 40, 46, 35

"Be like men who are waiting for their master when he returns from the wedding feast, so that they may immediately open the door to him when he comes and knocks.... You too, be ready; for the Son of Man is coming at an hour that you do not expect.... The master of [a disobedient] slave will come on a day when he does not expect him and at an hour he does not know, and will cut him in pieces, and assign him a place with the unbelievers.... Be dressed in readiness, and keep your lamps lit."

the Message

Catherine was a tenured, experienced schoolteacher—until she had her own kids. Now she's a stay-at-home mom. Her kids sure don't get away with anything, though. Catherine already knows every trick in the book.

Most teachers are like that—goof-proof, eagle-eyed, always waiting for trouble to materialize, and hoping to catch students causing problems. Catherine was *exactly* like that. She told me a story that proves my point.

"Edward, one of my students, was a good kid," she assured me. But he had a sweet tooth that made him a thief.

Every day when Catherine went to turn in attendance, Edward would sneak to the top drawer of her desk, steal her breath mints, and pass them out to the class. Then, somehow he'd always hear her and be back at his desk before she discovered him.

"I finally caught him red-handed one day," Catherine told me. "You should've seen his face."

"How'd you do it?" I asked. "Didn't he hear you coming?"

"It was nothing special," she said, smiling. "I just took off my shoes."

Edward got lazy and overly confident. He took it for granted that he'd be able to detect his teacher's footsteps. And he was caught unawares.

Jesus similarly warns us to be ready for His return. We won't hear footsteps, and we don't know when He's coming back, so we'd better live all the time in a way that glorifies Him—and not just when we think someone's looking.

Our souls are too important to play games with the Teacher.

Discussion Starters:

• Why do you suppose people do bad things while Jesus is away?

•• Is it possible to do good in His absence—for the wrong reasons? Why?

••• If you knew Jesus were coming back tomorrow, would you live differently? If so, how?

Lifeline:

Determine as a family to live every day as if He's returning tomorrow.

Hail to the Band-Aid

"And there was a woman who for eighteen years had had a sickness caused by a spirit; and she was bent double, and could not straighten up at all. When Jesus saw her, He called her over and said to her, 'Woman, you are freed from your sickness.' And He laid His hands on her; and immediately she was made erect again and began glorifying God."

the **Message**

Band-Aids fascinate me. They do! I mean, who could have guessed that Band-Aids would end up being so important, effective, and necessary? Since Earl Dickson invented the first Band-Aid in 1921, millions of people have used them. I know—I've used them countless times on myself and my kids. Even now, a tiny bandage stares at me from my index finger. The funny thing is, I've forgotten why it's there.

But looking at it reminds me of how often we take healing for granted.

I read recently that initial sales of the Band-Aid were so low the product was almost canceled.[1] Isn't it odd how sometimes we reject the things that are intended for our own good?

Jesus understands such rejection. His healing was severely criticized (see Luke 13:14-17). You would think that healing someone who had been sick for *18 years* would have caused the people to throw Jesus a party, close down the town, and celebrate the miracle. But the synagogue official got legalistic on Jesus. He didn't care that the woman was healed from a life of pain.

We often take the Lord's healing for granted, too—even His spiritual healing. Why don't we tell our friends and fellow church members when God has released us from a sinful habit? Why don't we proclaim it from the rooftops when Christ heals our hearts and eases our suffering? And why don't we ask Him for healing more often? God is still as powerful as He was in biblical times. He *can* heal your heart and body.

Fortunately, the story will change someday. Men and women will reach for the Savior. People will bring their hurts to God. Jesus will bind up every wound and dry every tear (see Revelation 21). And all of heaven will say thank you to the great and glorious Healer.

Discussion Starters:

* Why did the synagogue official in verse 14 respond the way he did?
** How did the woman respond to her own healing?
*** Tell about a time when you've seen God heal.

Lifeline:

Develop the habit of praying for family and friends who are sick. Then watch for God to work.

A Tight Spot

the WORD | Luke 13:24

"Strive to enter through the narrow door; for many, I tell you, will seek to enter and will not be able."

the Message

Near Cricket Creek in southwest Missouri is a mud cave. It's full of thick, red, sloppy mud—the kind that never, ever comes out of your mother's carpet if you're unfortunate enough to bring it in on your shoes.

In that cave, there's a narrow tunnel that leads from one room to the next—"the birth canal." It's about the size of a chubby sixth grader.

A long time ago (when I was in sixth grade myself), some friends and I explored that mud cave. Harry, one of the boys, thought he was a real explorer. He entered the cave, bragging loudly to the other guys about his earlier adventures in other caves.

"This cave ain't nothin'," Harry boasted, walking behind me. "I'm bored. The other caves were tons better. I hope we meet a bobcat or a bear or a badger or somethin'. Did I tell you I fought off a snake the last time I went cavin'?—" He stopped, his eyes wide.

We had just reached the birth canal. Embarrassed, Harry knew it'd be no picnic trying to squeeze himself through that tunnel. Well, we pulled while Harry squawked, squirmed, and rearranged himself. When we were done, a more humble Harry came out of the birth canal. And that was the last we heard about Harry's more exciting, previous adventures.

I like to tell that story because it makes me think about the way we become born again as Christians. When Jesus said the path to eternal life is through the narrow door, He wasn't kidding. Sometimes it's a little painful, kind of a tight squeeze. Some people want to go an easier way and try to get around it, but there's only one correct route.

In the cave, to get from one room to the other you have to go through the birth canal. In life, to get from death to eternal salvation you must enter through the narrow door—and the only way to do that is to accept Jesus Christ as your Lord and Savior.

Discussion Starters:

• What is the "narrow door" that Jesus spoke of in verse 24?
   •• How do you enter through that door?
   ••• Have you walked through that door yet?

Lifeline:

How can your family introduce people to Christ?

They'll Be Watching You

the WORD | Luke 14:1

"It happened that when He went into the house of one of the leaders of the Pharisees on the Sabbath to eat bread, they were watching Him closely."

the Message

St. Francis of Assisi said, "Witness always. Use words when necessary."

Did you know you can be an evangelist for Christ without ever opening your mouth? It's true. Why? Because people who don't know Christ are more likely to notice His love when they see it *demonstrated.*

Every day I look around and see people showing God's love through their actions. I see staff workers at Kanakuk tying little boys' shoes and making them laugh. I see friends drying friends' tears, teenagers taking the time to smile at and greet the elderly, and parents leaving work early to see their kids' games and recitals. Those acts of kindness are remembered because love is powerful. Loving people through your actions melts boundaries, brings forgiveness, builds trust and credibility, and reveals Jesus Christ.

Like it or not, the unbelieving world is watching you closely. They see your bowed head in restaurants, your breaking of bread with others, your joyful conversation and encouragement, your hugs and handshakes, your extra-large tip for the worn-out waitress. They'll call you a hypocrite if you cut people off on the road or roll your eyes at the slow cashier in the grocery store. If your actions don't line up with what you profess, if you aren't consistent, your words will be meaningless.

If you love Jesus, you must be accountable for your actions. It's not always easy to live as a witness for Christ, but it's important. Your loving actions could cause someone to desire a relationship with the most loving One of all—Jesus.

Discussion Starters:

• What can you do at work, school, or home to be a witness for Christ?
 •• Have you ever damaged your witness by something you've done? How can you resolve this?
 ••• What's the difference between loving others through our actions and trying to earn salvation?
 •••• The spoken message is important, too. When and how should words be used in expressing our faith?

Lifeline:

Discuss together how each one of you will aim to show Christ's love. Then during your next devotional time, describe your results.

The Fattened Ruffles Bag

the WORD | Luke 15:11-14, 20-24

"And He said, 'A man had two sons. The younger of them said to his father, "Father, give me the share of the estate that falls to me." ...And not many days later, the younger son gathered everything together and went on a journey into a distant country, and there he squandered his estate with loose living. Now when he had spent everything... he began to be impoverished.... So he got up and came to his father.... And the son said to him, "Father, I have sinned against heaven and in your sight; I am no longer worthy to be called your son." But the father said to his slaves,... "Bring the fattened calf, kill it, and let us eat and celebrate; for this son of mine was dead and has come to life again; he was lost and has been found."'"

the Message

The problem with prodigals today is that none of them wants to leave. They want their inheritance, and they want to keep their bedroom, too. They want all the benefits of the "distant country" right there in the den—with the TV, the CD player, and a big bowl of potato chips. They want cash, no curfews, and maid service.

Parents of these prodigals contribute to the problem. They're not like the father in Jesus' parable who let his son walk away so he'd grow up. Today's parents sigh and fill the potato chip bowl again. They nag, scold, and plead for change. But they don't draw any lines. And in failing to do so, they don't prepare their kids for the distant country of adulthood.

Friends of mine recently told their prodigal, Sherry, to "hit the road." When Sherry smirked at them, they sent her out, duffel bag in hand, with no clue where to go. She went to the library and lasted about 12 hours.

Sherry returned that night with a humble attitude; a smile instead of a smirk; and a "sir," a "ma'am," and a "please." She realized that the life of a prodigal is not all it's cracked up to be.

"Praise God!" said her parents. "Our daughter has come home! Quick! Go fetch the fattened Ruffles bag." And they celebrated long into the night.

Discussion Starters:

• How can parents prepare their kids for the distant country of adult life?
  •• Why are rules and discipline important?

Lifeline:

Ultimately, every child must move away from home. Use this story as an opportunity to talk about what skills kids need to learn for adulthood.

Big Brother Is Watching You

the WORD | Luke 15:25, 28-30

"Now his older son was in the field, and when he came and approached the house, he heard music and dancing.... He became angry and was not willing to go in; and his father came out and began pleading with him. But he answered and said to his father, 'Look! For so many years I have been serving you and I have never neglected a command of yours; and yet you have never given me a young goat, so that I might celebrate with my friends; but when this son of yours came, who has devoured your wealth with prostitutes, you killed the fattened calf for him.'"

the Message

On a beautiful stretch of land near my hometown, the Brown brothers battle a constant war with each other. Both are wealthy. Both live in fabulous mansions. It seems they should both be happy. But they aren't. Why? Because neither brother wants the other to be happy.

The older brother, Jim, built his house first. It was huge, with wall-length windows and a fountain in front. But soon after, the younger brother, Joe, struck it rich and built an even bigger—and more lavish—home. Jim added a wing to his house; Joe put a pool in the backyard. Jim poured a tennis court; Joe installed a top-of-the-line entertainment system.

This game Jim and Joe play has gone on for years. It's all very entertaining to the neighbors. But I can't recall even a single time when I've driven by and seen either one of them enjoying that "stuff."

The prodigal's brother also struggled with being competitive. He couldn't look past himself to rejoice in his sibling's warm welcome. He thought he deserved much more than his wayward brother.

We are all like the prodigal son who ran from his father, but we are also like his older brother. We, too, struggle with envy and bitterness. I challenge you to release your jealousy and give it to God. When you do, I can guarantee that it won't matter as much who's wearing what or which neighbor has more money. By His grace, God will enable you to become more content with what you have.

Discussion Starters:

• Why was the brother's response (in Jesus' parable) so sad?
•• How are you most like that older brother?
••• We're never told, but what do you think might have become of the older brother? Why?

Lifeline:

Rather than focus on what you don't have, be thankful for God's blessings. Write a list together of the things for which your family is most grateful.

It's the Little Things
that Make the Difference

the **WORD** | Luke 16:10-12

"He who is faithful in a very little thing is faithful also in much; and he who is unrighteous in a very little thing is unrighteous also in much. Therefore if you have not been faithful in the use of unrighteous wealth, who will entrust the true riches to you? And if you have not been faithful in the use of that which is another's, who will give you that which is your own?"

the **Message**

Before Joseph Lister pioneered sanitary operating conditions in the nineteenth century, as many as 90 percent of some hospitals' patients died after surgery. When he first presented his views on germs, Lister's fellow doctors laughed at him.[2]

"You're kidding," they scoffed. "Germs are too tiny to cause infection!"

But Lister remained faithful to his theories. He pressed on, telling anyone who would listen that "it's the little things that can make the difference." Soon surgeons began to employ his methods of cleanliness. Before long, they reported fewer infections and higher survival rates.

I believe that's how it works in life as well. When we pay attention to the seemingly trivial parts of our friendship with God—like tithing, praising Him, praying regularly, and studying His Word—the other things always seem to fall into place.

God wants to be Lord over your whole life. He wants you to follow Him through to the last detail. How you handle the small stuff reveals your character. That little white lie does matter to God. Taking that dollar from your friend is a big deal.

At the same time, the good things we do for Him—no matter how small—are significant, too. That kind word is noticed by Jesus. Your feeble prayers for your unsaved friend *always* matter. The offering you give from your small allowance is a lot.

Jesus made a good point when He said, "Why should I trust you with eternal things when I can't trust you with worldly details?" (see verse 11).

You can take a chance and ignore the little things. But if you ask me, that's bad medicine.

Discussion Starters:

* Describe a time when you were faithful with a little and the Lord gave you a lot.
** What will you do to be more faithful with the small things?

Lifeline:

What little things can you improve in your relationship with God?

Serving in God's Court

the **WORD** | Luke 16:22

"Now the poor man died and was carried away by the angels to Abraham's bosom; and the rich man also died and was buried."

the **Message**

A friend of mine promises this story is true.

Carolyn and her seven-year-old daughter, Stephanie, were walking down a steep hill to a tennis court one early autumn evening. Suddenly, Carolyn caught her toe on the root of an elm and tumbled forward.

Stephanie was too small to support her mother's weight and too young to find help alone, so the two of them huddled in the chilly evening and prayed for somebody to come along. As they prayed, they heard voices. They looked up and saw two men dressed for tennis, carrying rackets. When the men saw Carolyn, they rushed to her aid. One of them got Carolyn to an emergency room, while the other called her husband.

During the ride to the hospital, Carolyn learned from her rescuer that he and his friend belonged to her church's singles' group. The next Sunday when Carolyn tried to hunt them down for a proper "thank you," no one in the church seemed to know who she was talking about, which was rather unusual for the small-town church.

To this day, their identities remain a mystery.

Now, I know you can't believe everything you hear, but God works in strange ways—and maybe sometimes He uses angels. After all, the Bible is full of them. God sent angels to speak His messages (Luke 1), to reveal things (Genesis 31), and to protect and help people (Matthew 4). Even today's Scripture says angels carried the poor man into heaven.

With what the Bible says about angels, I'm inclined to believe there were two angels, ready to play tennis that day, sent to help Carolyn.

Discussion Starters:

* Jesus said He could call upon a multitude of angels to help Him (see Matthew 26). Do you think God uses them to protect us today? Explain.
** Why wasn't God more specific about angels in the New Testament?
*** What do you know of angels? Who were some other angels in the Bible?

Lifeline:

Thank You, Lord, for sending Your angels to help us in times of need!

Can You Take the Heat?

the WORD | Luke 17:29-30

"But on the day that Lot went out from Sodom it rained fire and brimstone from heaven and destroyed them all. It will be just the same on the day that the Son of Man is revealed."

the Message

Kyle and Sharon had saved a long time to build a house. When it was finally done, the place was beautiful—big, airy windows; rich wooden floors; French doors; and a big, long redwood deck that wrapped around the house. They'd been in it no more than six months when their son, Stephen, came in from the yard one day covered with seed ticks.

"Here," Sharon said, grabbing a rag. "Let me wipe those nasty things off you."

When she was finished, Sharon lit the rag on fire and let it burn until she was sure the ticks were gone. Then she stomped on the rag and threw it in the trashcan, thinking the fire was out.

It wasn't.

A few minutes later, Sharon and Kyle smelled smoke. And it wasn't coming from the oven. Their dream home burst into flames, and the fire began to consume everything in sight. The heat was incredible.

They called me, and I helped battle the flames and move furniture until my skin was red, my hair was singed, and our efforts were halted by the danger at hand. In the end, it was a total loss.

Since then, Kyle and Sharon have rebuilt their home. Still, every time I drive down their road, I can't help but remember that devastating fire and the terror, pain, and loss it brought. As awful as it was, though, I believe that fire was only a glimpse of what hell will be like.

I know it's unpopular today to speak of fire and brimstone. I'm not comfortable with the way some preachers use it to scare folks, but I don't believe we should ignore it, either. Jesus talked about hell a lot. Obviously He thought it was important. Do you?

Discussion Starters:

• Why do you think many people are reluctant to admit God will one day punish sin?
  •• Hell is real, and sin is serious. What do *you* think about God's coming judgment of sin? Does it scare you? Will you be ready? Explain.
    ••• How can you convey the truth of God's judgment without sounding judgmental yourself?

Lifeline:

Together, thank God for His forgiveness and for saving you from hell.

Bugging Daddy

the **WORD** | Luke 18:1, 7-8

"Now He was telling them a parable to show that at all times they ought to pray and not to lose heart.... [And Jesus said,] 'Now, will not God bring about justice for His elect who cry to Him day and night, and will He delay long over them? I tell you that He will bring about justice for them quickly. However, when the Son of Man comes, will He find faith on the earth?'"

the Message

Kids have the gift of persistence. They know exactly how to wear down their parents until their folks buckle and give in.

My friend Will could tell you about that. One summer day, his three year-old, Wesley, bugged him 47 times for a Coke.

"I was painting the bedroom when I heard the refrigerator door open," Will told me. "I knew something was up when I saw Wes coming down the hallway with his hands behind his back. He had deliberately disobeyed me. Believe me, when he saw the look in my eyes, he knew he was history. I was serious when I told him, "No pop before dinner."

"And?" I asked.

"Well, the little guy thought fast," said Will. "He pulled that bottle of Coke from behind his back and said, 'Happy birthday, Daddy!' But I didn't let him get away with that. My birthday was still a month away.

"So," Will continued his story, "I took that Coke and started chugging, just to show him I meant business when I said no. But then—" Will cleared his throat, "—well, then he sorta gave me that cute grin of his and said, 'It's my birthday, too.'" Will looked sheepish. "So I gave him the last sip," he said, shrugging his shoulders.

Okay, Wesley was being devious. But he was persistent—he didn't give up, and eventually his dad granted his request.

Similarly, Jesus told us in Luke to be persistent with our heavenly Father. If you have a request, don't stop asking. Have faith—your heavenly Father loves you more than your earthly father ever could. If you're persistent, God *will* answer.

Discussion Starters:

- Why does God want us to pray "at all times"?
  - Have you ever lost heart over a prayer request? When? How can you keep from getting discouraged in your prayer life?

Lifeline:

Pray persistently as a family for those requests that haven't been answered right away. Then wait and watch for God's hand to work.

Good Doggies

the WORD | Luke 18:18-19

"A ruler questioned Him, saying, 'Good Teacher, what shall I do to inherit eternal life?' And Jesus said to him, 'Why do you call Me good? No one is good except God alone.'"

the Message

Next time you hear someone calling his dog, listen to the choice of words. Often the person will say, "Here, Spot! Come here, Spot! Yeah. That's a good doggie!"

A "good" doggie? There's no such thing as a good doggie. Why, if I committed one-tenth of the crimes ol' Spot does on the neighbors' lawns, or stayed out all night, or chewed a hole in my wife's favorite sweater, you'd be hard pressed to find somebody who'd call me "good."

Last Christmas, I visited a neighborhood manger scene, complete with hay, glittering angels, and kids dressed like wise men. It was peaceful. But in the midst of it all, I started thinking about the fact that we all need a Savior—even those cute kids. *I'm so thankful Jesus was born and came to die for our sins,* I thought. Just then, the "good" doggies of Kanakuk Hill arrived suddenly, disturbing the peace and interrupting my thoughts.

At least one dog in the 15-member pack was not in the Christmas spirit, because a nasty fight began. It took 10 minutes to separate the combatants and a good deal longer to calm the kids. When it was all over, I heard one dog owner who had the audacity to call his animal a "good doggie." *If good doggies ruin the neighborhood manger scene and cause a fight, I don't want to know what bad doggies do,* I thought.

Jesus was also careful in using the word *good.* When the ruler addressed Him as "good Teacher," Jesus pointed out that only God is good. He said, in effect, "You must know I'm God since you're calling *Me* good. Everyone else is sinful."

It's easy to misuse the word. Often we'll say people are good if they stay out of trouble and are nice to be around. But no matter how good we think they are, they're still sinful inside—still in need of a Savior.

Discussion Starters:

* Jesus seemed to disagree at first with the man's assessment of His "goodness." But what was His real point?
** Why is it not enough to call Jesus a "good teacher"?
*** Do you strive to be a good Christian? Where does your goodness come from?

Lifeline:

Discuss the difference between believing Jesus is a "good teacher" and following Him as your "good Master."

The Stones

the WORD | Luke 19:37-40

"As soon as He was approaching, near the descent of the Mount of Olives, the whole crowd of the disciples began to praise God joyfully with a loud voice for all the miracles which they had seen, shouting: 'Blessed is the King who comes in the name of the Lord; peace in heaven and glory in the highest!' Some of the Pharisees in the crowd said to Him, 'Teacher, rebuke Your disciples.' But Jesus answered, 'I tell you, if these become silent, the stones will cry out!' "

the Message

If you haven't already noticed, cave exploring is one of my favorite things to do. And near Branson, Missouri, there is a cave worth visiting. The original concept behind Talking Rocks Cavern was this: Let the rocks speak for themselves, and the beauty of nature will tell its own story.

When the cave was first opened, you could press a button and listen to a deep, booming voice describe the world of stalactites and the influence of a trillion drops of water on a boulder. Now the tour is led by guides.

I miss the old days when you could hear the rocks talk.

Nature reveals God's awesome handiwork and power. With all we do, our work doesn't even come close to His. We construct buildings; God creates mountains. We build speedy cars; God pours fast-moving rivers. We paint pictures of flowers; God fills the earth with wildflower meadows.

God cares for all of His creation—especially for His people (see Matthew 6). But we've become, as C. S. Lewis stated, "the silent planet." We've become a largely praiseless people, afraid of vocal worship. How often do you say, "Lord, You've done a great job" or "You're amazing, God!"?

I think we usually get too caught up in what we've done and dismiss what God does for us. The Pharisees were like that. They didn't want swarms of people praising Jesus. But Jesus said that even if the Pharisees stopped the people from giving thanks to God, He would still be glorified through nature (see verse 40).

There will come a time when *all* of God's creation praises and glorifies Him. Until then, I challenge you to exercise those God-given vocal cords. Spiritual laryngitis is unhealthy for your soul.

Discussion Starters:

* Why did the Pharisees want to silence the people's praise?

** Have you ever been too timid to praise God? Why?

*** How can you be more vocal about your love for God?

Lifeline:

Read Psalm 33 together, then discuss one thing for which you can each thank God.

The Robbery of Religion

the **WORD** | Luke 19:45-47

"Jesus entered the temple and began to drive out those who were selling, saying to them, 'It is written, "And My house shall be a house of prayer," but you have made it a robbers' den.' And He was teaching daily in the temple; but the chief priests and the scribes and the leading men among the people were trying to destroy Him."

the Message

Until you've experienced it, you can't imagine what it's like to be robbed.

"It's shocking," a friend of mine said. "You come home expecting your house to be just as you left it. Instead, you find that someone sneaked inside and threw your things all over the place. When you discover that some of your most prized possessions are missing—like a graduation ring or the tennis racket you used to win your high school state championship—well, it makes you just want to sit down and cry."

Robbery is like that. It takes away that for which someone has poured out sweat and effort. It takes without a second thought or even a backward glance at the trouble it has caused. It takes and walks away.

Legalistic religion is like that, too. It takes the free gift of salvation, for which Jesus poured out blood, and puts a price on it. It claims that grace isn't enough—that you have to work your way to heaven. Religion takes the peace of a believer and replaces that peace with guilt. It takes and walks away.

Rule-based religion made Jesus mad. He couldn't stand the legalistic Pharisees telling people (step by step) how they could be saved. He got furious when He saw the hypocrisy in the Jewish temple—so mad, in fact, that He grabbed a whip and drove the "robbers" out of His presence. Religion made Jesus angry because it robs people of intimacy with God. Fortunately, true Christianity, which focuses on having a relationship with the Lord, recovers the stolen goods.

And it's a relationship that can never be taken away.

Discussion Starters:

* In biblical times, men sold sacrificial animals for an enormous price, right there in the temple. Why did this anger Jesus?
    ** It's disturbing to see our Lord so angry. Yet what does this passage reveal about God's view of "religion" as opposed to a "relationship"?
  *** Are there other times when anger is appropriate? When?

Lifeline:

When something is free, you might wonder if the product is inferior or damaged. How could this mentality affect your view of God's grace?

The Flip of a Coin

the WORD | Luke 20:21-25

"They questioned Him, saying, 'Teacher, we know that You speak and teach correctly, and You are not partial to any but teach the way of God in truth. Is it lawful for us to pay taxes to Caesar, or not?' But He detected their trickery and said to them, 'Show me a denarius. Whose likeness and inscription does it have?' They said, 'Caesar's.' And He said to them, 'Then render to Caesar the things that are Caesar's, and to God the things that are God's.'"

the Message

"Heads, you win. Tails, you lose."

Jesus grew up during a time when people believed major decisions should be made by the gods. Consequently, they devised tons of methods by which they could persuade the gods to give a definite yes or no.

That's how the coin toss got started.[3] With the flip of a silver piece, great tracts of land were bought, criminals were indicted, marriage partners were chosen, and crops were planted. The people revered the gods (and Julius Caesar, whose head appeared on all the money in the land) so much that they were willing to stake their futures on whichever way a coin landed in the sand.

So when the Pharisees asked Jesus whether it was lawful for them to give back to Caesar, their question was a loaded gun.

Jesus didn't flinch, though. I love the way my Lord answered those weasels who tried to trick Him into making some negative statement about the law. He simply said, "By all means, pay the man! His head's on the coin, isn't it?" But then, with a little twist they hadn't counted on, Jesus said to them, "But whatever has God's picture on it belongs to God." In one swoop, Jesus affirmed both the government's leadership and God's authority.

I believe Jesus would offer the same advice to twenty-first-century people. He'd say, "If you want to be good citizens, don't cheat on your taxes. And if you want to be on good terms with God, give to Him the things that bear His image—namely, your life, your soul, yourself."

Discussion Starters:

- How were the Pharisees trying to manipulate Jesus?
  - What was Jesus' attitude toward authority? What is your attitude?
    - What does it mean to bear the image of God?

Lifeline:

Make a list of some leaders in your community. Then, as a family, decide how you can honor God's command to submit to those leaders and render the appropriate things back to them. For example, police officers enforce the speed limit. You can honor God and your local officers by not speeding.

They Say...

the **WORD** | Luke 20:27, 36-38

"Now there came to Him some of the Sadducees (who say that there is no resurrection)....
[And Jesus said, 'The sons of this age cannot] die anymore, because they are like angels, and
are sons of God, being sons of the resurrection. But that the dead are raised, even Moses
showed.... Now He is not the God of the dead but of the living; for all live to Him.' "

the Message

It's funny how we live our lives by what "they" say without even knowing who "they"
are or how "they" got their information. Nevertheless, for successful living, it's important for you to know a few of these "theysayisms." For instance...

"They say you should wait 30 minutes after eating before you get back in the pool."
(What would happen if you got back in after 29?)

"They say you should drink eight glasses of water a day." (Why not nine?)

"They say a swallowed piece of gum takes seven years to digest." (How do they
know that?)

"They say more people die every year in automobile accidents than in airplane
crashes." (This last one does nothing to comfort me, especially since I know that when
my plane lands, I have to take the freeway home during rush hour. Besides, it's no wonder more people die every year in automobile accidents. Who can afford to fly?)

As it is, we treat this information like gospel, don't we? We live and breathe and
make decisions as if "they" wrote the book on life.

It's hard to overlook what "they" say, especially when you're growing up. But while
what your friends say is important, what God says is *truth*.

Next time you're confronted with what "they" say, remember what Jesus did under
peer pressure. Whenever He was presented with a "theysayism," He always responded
with a "Word-of-Godism." And when He did, "they" usually had very little to say in
return.

Discussion Starters:

• Like the Sadducees, there are many in this world who will urge you
to live according to some code besides the Bible. How will knowing
the Bible help you resist their advice?

•• One of the clearest modern examples of a faulty theysayism is this: They say,
"Everyone is doing it." Why is this wrong? How could you answer this statement with Scripture?

Lifeline:

Discuss your favorite "Word-of-Godism" with your family.

Eight Seconds

the WORD | Luke 21:1-4

"And He looked up and saw the rich putting their gifts into the treasury. And He saw a poor widow putting in two small copper coins. And He said, 'Truly I say to you, this poor widow put in more than all of them; for they all out of their surplus put into the offering; but she out of her poverty put in all that she had to live on.'"

the Message

Lyle's been the best in America in his sport more than once. He makes his living on the back of a snorting beast. He goes to work in jeans and steps in piles of manure at the office. He eats power lunches with tobacco-spitting cowboys. He pays his entry fees with the money he earned shoeing horses. He gets on. He rides. He falls. He lands on his head. The next time he rides, he's wearing a neck brace. This time he stays on. Sometimes he works all night and comes home poor and dirty. His wife, Kathy, and his daughter, Sasha, adore him. Lyle loves riding bulls, but he loves Jesus more. Lyle lives life eight seconds at a time.

Sometimes success is measured in small increments. The widow in Jesus' parable gave her "all" even though she had only a few meager coins. My friend Lyle, as a professional bull rider, gives his all in the ring, even if only for a few seconds at a time. If each one of us gave of ourselves and loved God with the widow's and Lyle's intensity, we'd all be closer to Him.

Love God with 100 percent of your heart. Although it's important to give to Him and spend time with Him, God doesn't measure our faithfulness in quantity. He cares more about the level of devotion, the quality of our relationship with Him. Sometimes small things are the greatest measuring sticks of our inner character.

Discussion Starters:

• Why was the widow's gift of two small copper coins so significant?
•• What are some various ways Christians can give their all for Christ?
••• How can you give 100 percent to God?

Lifeline:

Have each person write "100" on a slip of paper. Then carry it around for a few days as a reminder to give God your all, in everything you do.

Doug and the Volcano

"[He said,] 'There will be great earthquakes, and in various places plagues and famines; and there will be terrors and great signs from heaven. But before all these things, they will lay their hands on you and will persecute you, delivering you to the synagogues and prisons, bringing you before kings and governors for My name's sake.... But you will be betrayed even by parents and brothers and relatives and friends, and they will put some of you to death.... Yet not a hair of your head will perish. By your endurance you will gain your lives.'"

the *Message*

Being a camp director, I hear some wild stories. But Doug's volcano story was the strangest—so crazy that at first I thought it was a hoax.

"You're kidding," I said to Amy, who was waving her hands frantically, telling me the news. "Doug was in a volcano? The same Doug who used to be a Kanakuk counselor in cabin 13? No way."

But it was true. Several other Kanakukers were with him, too, singing and praising God on top of Mount Merapi on a clear summer's day in 1992.

They'd been told it was safe.

"The mountain hasn't erupted in 16 years," said some of the locals.

So with confidence, Doug and his friends neared the rim and sat on the rocks to worship God. Suddenly, the mountain gurgled and spewed hot lava everywhere. It was probably the shortest worship service in history.

"It's sorta hard to keep singing 'Kumbaya' when you're running for your life. Anyway, it's nice to still have all my hair," Doug told me when we finally talked. He paused and touched the scar on his head, then added, "I believe God has more plans for me on earth."

I believe that, too. And I believe that some time in life, we all will go through our own fiery ordeals. We'll be tested, tried, and persecuted. But don't fear it. God assures, "Not a hair of your head will perish" (verse 18).

Someday, the things Jesus predicted will come to pass. Are you ready for your own Mount Merapi?

Discussion Starters:

- What fiery ordeals has the Lord already seen you through?
  - What fears do you have about the end times?
    - Scripture says that during the end times, not a hair on our heads will perish. It also says that some of us will die. In what sense is each of these statements true?

Lifeline:

Jesus said that in the end times some family members will betray one another. Make a pact that such betrayal will never happen in your family. Write it down and sign it. Perhaps you can even display it in your home.

Not Me!

" 'But behold, the hand of the one betraying Me is with Mine on the table. For indeed, the Son of Man is going as it has been determined; but woe to that man by whom He is betrayed!' And they began to discuss among themselves which one of them it might be who was going to do this thing."

the Message

On a hill about 300 yards from Kanakuk Kamp sits a residential treatment center for teenagers. It's so close that I could probably take a bow and shoot an arrow to its doorstep. But I wouldn't. Some of those kids can't have anything that sharp. They are troubled kids—the kind parents usually have in mind when they say, "No kid of *mine* will ever act like that." Parenthood, however, has a way of changing our thinking.

Vince and Marie really believed their daughter Tiffany was an angel. So when Tiffany's first-grade teacher called them in for a conference, they were stunned. Tiffany had been bullying the other kids? Never!

"The other kids must have been really mean to her. Tiffany would never start a fight," her parents protested.

The teacher just shook her head.

It's easy to think like Vince and Marie. Often, we don't want to accept responsibility. We say, "I would never do such a thing. Not me." We reason, *The preacher is speaking to that guy over in pew 47. He's not looking in my direction. Sure, I'm a sinner, but look at the Smiths. They're worse.*

We don't like to admit that we (or our kids, friends, or family) are capable of sin because it's uncomfortable. But we are very capable.

Look at Judas. I'm sure he never wanted (in the beginning, at least) to betray Jesus. Well, I don't want to turn my back on God, either. But I have this haunting feeling that if I'd been in Judas's shoes way back then, I might have done the same thing he did.

So instead of arrows, I shoot prayers at that little center on the hill. I know that in spite of my own daily betrayals, God looks at me and says, "There's Joe White. I'm proud he's a kid of Mine"—and I am so thankful.

Discussion Starters:

• Judas wasn't the only disciple who turned on Jesus. Who else did? Why?

•• Jesus knew who was going to betray Him, but He still broke bread with the traitor. What does that say about Him?

••• What is one way *you* have betrayed Jesus? How have you experienced His forgiveness?

Lifeline:

Thank the Lord that He loves you, even when you betray Him.

Living Tombstone

"And He withdrew from them about a stone's throw, and He knelt down and began to pray, saying, 'Father, if You are willing, remove this cup from Me; yet not My will, but Yours be done.'"

the *Message*

If Jesus had wanted something inscribed on His tombstone, I'll bet it would have been, "He did His Father's will."

What do you want written on yours someday? It's helpful to think about the message you want to leave to the world and then try to live in a manner consistent with that. My gran'ma took this idea of living with the "end" in mind to an unusual level.

Sixty years ago, Gran'ma bought a marker for her own grave. She got it for a good price and has taken it with her on countless moves. To my knowledge, she has never regretted the extra weight.

It's a sturdy stone—like the lady whose name is already on it. It's gone with her so many places that the stone has become chipped and flecked with rain.

I believe my grandmother's habit of carrying death around like a suitcase is noble. It makes her appreciate life more fully, breathe more deeply, kiss more babies, and plant more flowers.

Sometimes when I look at Gran'ma's stone, I wonder what we'll write there in that little space left purposely blank beneath her name. She hasn't told us yet what *she* wants it to say. But whatever it is, I know she will have lived up to it.

Somewhere out there is a stone that will bear *your* name one day. What will be written on that piece of granite? For what do you want to be remembered? Will people say that you, like Jesus, did your Father's will?

Discussion Starters:

• How did Jesus' willingness to do His Father's will influence everything He did?

•• How did Jesus feel about His upcoming crucifixion?

••• As He wept in the Garden of Gethsemane, what do you think Jesus wanted us most to remember about His life and ministry? Why?

Lifeline:

Discuss: What's the one thing you'd like others to remember about you? About your family?

Roll Call at the Top of the World

"And [the thief] was saying, 'Jesus, remember me when You come in Your kingdom!' And He said to him, 'Truly I say to you, today you shall be with Me in Paradise.'"

the Message

Joey is a fierce competitor. As a former member of Athletes in Action, he has played hard all his life. He has won frequently, lost graciously, and always, always given 100 percent in everything he does.

That's why he got up at 3:00 A.M. with 15 other men and boys one day to climb one of Colorado's tallest, toughest peaks. With his hands in his pockets and his breath puffing white, Joey gazed at the renowned Diamond Face on the east side of Longs Peak.

The mountain is a jewel in the crown of creation, with rock that changes colors as the day goes by and a surface as smooth as ice. That's why they call it Diamond Face.

It's beautiful at the top. But it costs a lot to get there. Men have died on that face—slipped clean off the top, like snow from a high church steeple. For a thousand feet they are black, falling specks against a hard background. Then they are gone.

It was exactly the kind of challenge Joey likes.

I'd love to tell you that Joey conquered Longs, but he didn't. An hour into the 12-hour trek, Craig, one of the boys, got sick. Joey stayed with Craig, and he accomplished something far greater than reaching the peak. He led Craig to Christ!

Joey's name is on the registration sheet anyway, rolled up in a metal canister at the top of Longs Peak. His friends signed him in, knowing full well he probably would've beaten them all to the top. But since Joey stayed behind, Craig's name is on a more important roll—heaven's.

Someday, Craig will be with Christ in paradise, thanks to Jesus and to Joey.

Discussion Starters:

- The thief on the cross never did anything to earn eternal life. What does that tell you about salvation?
  - Jesus said, "*Today* you shall be with Me in Paradise" (verse 43, emphasis added). What does that reveal about the passage from death to life?

Lifeline:

If you're a Christian, write your name in the margin next to today's verse. It'll remind you that your name is on the roll in heaven.

A Grave Matter

the WORD | Luke 24:2-6

"And they found the stone rolled away from the tomb, but when they entered, they did not find the body of the Lord Jesus. While they were perplexed about this, behold, two men suddenly stood near them in dazzling clothing; and as the women were terrified and bowed their faces to the ground, the men said to them, 'Why do you seek the living One among the dead? He is not here, but He has risen.'"

the Message

One night, two old bums wandered into a graveyard and got separated. Unaware that his friend had fallen into an open grave, the first bum, Fred, found his way out the other side. He had just given Charlie up for lost when he heard a noise.

"Helllp!" came Charlie's mournful voice. "Helllp! It's cold down here."

Fred went stumbling back, searching the bushes, poking around in the tall grass. He heard the voice again coming from a nearby hole in the ground.

"Sounds like Charlie over thar," Fred mumbled as he ran to the lip of the grave. "Charlie? That you?"

"Helllp!" said the pitiful voice. "Helllp! It's coooold down here."

Unfortunately, Fred, being a man of some honor—but few brains—made a sad miscalculation. "If dead folks cain talk, then I'm leavin'!"

Fred turned on his heel and heard the cry again. "Helllp! It's coooold down here!"

"O' course it's cold down there!" said Fred, peering into the darkness. "Ya done kicked all yer dirt off!"

It's a silly story, but it illustrates a good point. Fred was right—it's ridiculous to look for the living among the dead. That's precisely why the women who visited Jesus' grave were so stunned. They didn't expect Him to be up and at it. He was supposed to be in His tomb, resting in peace.

Fortunately for us, Jesus isn't dead. His resurrection transformed history and count-less lives. How has your life changed since "He has risen"?

Discussion Starters:

* Why is Jesus' resurrection so important to the Christian faith?
** Why do you think it's so hard for people to believe in the Resurrection?
*** Will we have bodies when we're resurrected? (Read the rest of Luke 24.)

Lifeline:

Visit a graveyard and thank God that one day you'll be with Him in heaven.

A Date with Pain

the WORD | Luke 24:46

"And He said to them, 'Thus it is written, that the Christ would suffer and rise again from the dead the third day.' "

the Message

"A little rain never hurt anyone," Will's dad used to say. So Will took that advice to heart and to an extreme. In one naïve move, he lumped all elements of weather together in that "nonhurtful" category and went headlong into life with his magical raincoat on.

Fog? "No problem," Will would say. "Just turn the fog lights on and drive a little faster. We'll be out of it soon."

Tornado watch? "Super day for a kite!"

As one might guess, problems were bound to arise for Will. Take, for instance, his first date with Cindy. The weatherman couldn't have given a more thorough prescription for disaster. It was snowing. Will was lovestruck. He drove too fast on an icy bridge and lost control. His truck skidded into oncoming traffic and collided with a semi.

Will and Cindy's first date lasted a little longer than he had planned. It took six weeks for them to (partially) recuperate from the terrible accident and even longer to finish the physical therapy. But, according to Will, all that pain was worth it. When he and Cindy finally left the hospital, they'd developed a special—if unique—relationship. And after that, Cindy had no choice but to marry the guy.

Now and then, I see the two lovers in my hometown. He's the one with the grin and the T-shirt on in January. She's the one on his arm, shaking her head and happily providing the warmth her husband needs.

If you talk to Will, he'll tell you the awful pain of that accident was worth it because that's what brought him close to Cindy. I think Jesus would say the same thing about His pain on the cross—that it was terrible, but necessary. Because He suffered, we now have eternal life and are in a never-ending relationship with Him.

Sometimes pain is good for the soul. Wouldn't you agree?

Discussion Starters:

• Whose idea was it for Jesus to endure the pain of the cross?

•• How could a Father allow such suffering in His Son's life?

••• What tremendous good came from all that pain?

•••• Describe a time when God brought something good from your pain.

Lifeline:

Thank God for the suffering He's allowing you to experience. How can you cling to Him now?

john

Perhaps the most valuable and insightful book in the New Testament is the Gospel of John. Why? Because the New Testament is all about Jesus, and John knew the Lord's heart better than anyone.

Many great leaders in the Bible had one loyal friend or servant who was called by God for an important mission. Nebuchadnezzar had Daniel. David had Jonathan. And of all Jesus' followers, John was the most intimately connected to the Lord. John saw Jesus as who He really was—Son of God, Lord, Messiah, and loving Bridegroom of all sincere believers.

One with Whom?

the WORD | John 1:1-4

"In the beginning was the Word, and the Word was with God, and the Word was God. He was in the beginning with God. All things came into being through Him, and apart from Him nothing came into being that has come into being. In Him was life, and the life was the Light of men."

the Message

People smile when Keith comes to town. Once a stellar wide receiver in the NFL, Keith now works with youth and celebrates every minute of it. His home base is Denton, Texas, but he spends a lot of time at the growing Church of Katmandu, a third world, poverty stricken church at the base of 29,000-foot Mount Everest in the Himalayas. When he goes, he takes deflated soccer balls, footballs, and basketballs—and a hand pump.

On a 26-hour flight there, Keith sat next to Rob. They started talking, and Rob mentioned he was heading for Mount Everest to become "one with the mountain."

Keith chuckled. "One with the mountain?"

"Yeah," the climber said, "the mountain and I will be united. It'll be an awesome feeling."

Keith pondered this for a while. *How do you become one with a pile of rocks?*

After a few hours, Keith looked at Rob carefully and asked, "How would you like to become one with the God who made that mountain? It's possible if you know His Son, Jesus."

Rob smiled. "One with God? Hmmm... Is it possible?" he wondered aloud.

It is possible. There is no greater "oneness" than knowing the God of the universe. When you're in a relationship with Christ, His Spirit lives in you. It's one of the best things about being a Christian because it enables us to know intimately the God who created everything.

How well do you know the Lord? Does His Spirit live in you?

Discussion Starters:

• Who is "the Word" in this scripture?

•• Where was Jesus when the universe was created? Why did He come to earth?

••• How is it possible to become "one with God" (see John 14:20)?

Lifeline:

Do you (individually *and* as a family) live as if Jesus' Spirit is in you?

Taking a Dip

the WORD | John 1: 31-33

" 'I did not recognize Him, but so that He might be manifested to Israel, I came baptizing in water.' John testified saying, 'I have seen the Spirit descending as a dove out of heaven, and He remained upon Him. I did not recognize Him, but He who sent me to baptize in water said to me, "He upon whom you see the Spirit descending and remaining upon Him, this is the One who baptizes in the Holy Spirit." ' "

the Message

Mrs. Cecily Simmons is 86 years old and still runs her kitchen as if she were a "young pup." Every holiday, the smells of pies cooking, cookies baking, and turkeys roasting permeate her house. But the rest of the year, she likes to can. And every summer, Cecily makes jars and jars of pickles to give her friends and neighbors.

"Picklin'" (as Cecily likes to call it) is such a big job that she's started to hire neighborhood kids to help with the process. Together, Cecily and her helpers will pick cucumbers; slice 'em; soak 'em in salt, dill, and vinegar; and can 'em. After it's all done, she'll drop off the finished product on people's doorsteps—and her pickles are so good that you'd never remember they came from her dinky little garden out back.

They're totally transformed from the original cucumbers. They smell different, taste different, and even look different.

Baptism is supposed to work the same way. The word *baptism* comes from the Greek word *baptizo*, which means "to place into." Baptism in water symbolizes the change that occurs in your heart when you accept Christ. But baptism in the Holy Spirit is what *actually happens* when you become a Christian. Christ's Spirit lives in you and influences your decisions, your thoughts, and your actions. When you commit your life to Him, you start out looking like yourself and (hopefully) end up looking and acting more like Jesus. Your life progressively changes.

Cecily's pickles can't claim to be cucumbers after she's done with them—and you shouldn't aim to be the same person after Christ enters your heart. Have you invited Him into yours?

Discussion Starters:

* How is baptism in water like being baptized into Christ?
   ** What properties or characteristics of Christ are we supposed to take on when we become believers?

Lifeline:

How can we help each other be more like Christ today?

Disciples

the WORD | John 1:40-43

"One of the two who heard John speak and followed Him, was Andrew, Simon Peter's brother. He found first his own brother Simon and said to him, 'We have found the Messiah' (which translated means Christ). He brought him to Jesus. Jesus looked at him and said, 'You are Simon the son of John; you shall be called Cephas' (which is translated Peter). The next day He purposed to go into Galilee, and He found Philip. And Jesus said to him, 'Follow Me.'"

the Message

"I just can't get my act together."

"I'm totally addicted to drugs."

"I need peace. I've got ulcers, and I'm having anxiety attacks."

"I'm doing stuff I never, ever thought I'd do."

"I can't sleep at night."

For 20 years, I've counseled thousands of hurting teenagers and adults. One of the things I've found is that almost all the people who get caught up in sin and, as a result, get badly hurt have decided not to follow anyone. They rebel, stop listening to their parents or to wise counsel, and make up their own rules. In the process, they quit following God.

The best decision you can make is to become a disciple of Christ—to follow Him, learn from Him, and model your life after Him. Trying to live by following someone or something other than Christ is like trying to find a contact lens in the dark. It's difficult, risky (because you might make a mess of it), and eternally unsuccessful. You need Christ to light your way through life.

The happiest people I know are followers—disciplined learners, that is—of Christ and His teachings. For three intense years, 12 men followed Jesus practically everywhere He went. They attended every lecture, heard every parable, and witnessed every healing. Jesus taught His disciples by word and example, and eventually they changed the world.

You can, too. Are you a disciple of Christ?

Discussion Starters:

• What do the words *discipline* and *disciple* have in common?

•• What do you think Jesus was looking for when He picked His disciples?

••• What kind of disciple are you? Explain your answer.

•••• How well do you know your Leader?

Lifeline:

Who is the most devoted disciple of Christ you know? Why? What qualities make that person an obvious follower of Christ?

Oinos

"And both Jesus and His disciples were invited to the wedding. When the wine ran out, the mother of Jesus said to Him, 'They have no wine.' ...Now there were six stone waterpots set there for the Jewish custom of purification, containing twenty or thirty gallons each.... And He said to them, 'Draw some out now and take it to the head-waiter.' So they took it to him. When the headwaiter tasted the water which had become wine, and did not know where it came from (but the servants who had drawn the water knew), the headwaiter called the bridegroom, and said to him, 'Every man serves the good wine first, and when the people have drunk freely, then he serves the poorer wine; but you have kept the good wine until now.'"

the Message

When is alcohol bad for you? How much is too much? If Jesus turned water into wine, is today's wine okay to drink?

The Bible is clear that certain things are harmful to the body and a sin to indulge in. But would Jesus make something that God wouldn't like?

The New Testament was written in the colorful Greek language. The original meaning of each word makes these questions about alcohol easy to understand. *Wine* in the English language comes from one of two Greek words. *Oinos* (the kind of wine Jesus made) is a word for purified grape juice that was 1 to 2 percent alcohol. *Oinos* was always diluted by 20 times its amount with pure juice or water. *Shekar*, on the other hand, is a word for strong drink. It's roughly 3 percent to 12 percent alcohol. Getting drunk with *shekar* is condemned in the Bible. All American beer (5 percent), wine (more than 12 percent), and hard liquor (20 to over 30 percent) are made of *shekar*.

Shekar is the most destructive drug in America. It's responsible for more deaths, abuses, and broken homes than any other substance.[1] Proverbs sounds the warning: "Do not look on the wine when it is red, when it sparkles in the cup, when it goes down smoothly; at the last it bites like a serpent, and stings like a viper" (Proverbs 23:31-32).

Don't let the sting of alcohol destroy you!

Discussion Starters:

- What are the dangers of alcohol?
  - Why are people so attracted to strong drink?
  - Why is getting drunk a sin?

Lifeline:

Alcohol can lead to a lot of trouble for many people. What should your family policy toward alcohol be?

Righteous Anger

the WORD | John 2:14-17

"And He found in the temple those who were selling oxen and sheep and doves, and the money changers seated at their tables. And He made a scourge of cords, and drove them all out of the temple, with the sheep and the oxen; and He poured out the coins of the money changers and overturned their tables; and to those who were selling the doves He said, 'Take these things away; stop making My Father's house a place of business.' His disciples remembered that it was written, 'Zeal for Your house will consume me.' "

the Message

Typically, our anger as humans is sinful. But when God's reputation is at stake, anger is right and just. And in our society, His name is put down everywhere. If you're a Christian, you should be frustrated, angry, and upset that your Best Friend, Master, and Leader is so often belittled and blasphemed. I'm sure mad, especially at Hollywood. I have made the decision that I won't watch a movie or TV show that takes God's name in vain. Unfortunately, almost all movies and TV programs do it—repeatedly. So at my house, we are very careful about what shows and movies we choose to watch.

But God's name isn't just demeaned in the entertainment industry. At school and work, people take His name in vain repeatedly as well. How often do you hear, "Oh, my God!" or "Jesus Christ!" from your friends or coworkers? Don't excuse those remarks. That's not just the way people talk nowadays. Those comments are hurtful to God, the One who created you.

That's why Jesus got mad in the temple. The money changers made the temple into a shopping mall, cheapening God and His house of worship. Everyone who loves God should get angry when His name is cheapened. Jesus said we're to love our enemies and pray for those who persecute us (see Matthew 5:44). But we're also supposed to love God with everything we've got (see Mark 12:30). When we love Him, we'll live for Him. And when we live for Him, we'll do anything to protect His name.

Do you take a stand when you see people tear down God's reputation, or do you stand quietly by and let others drag His name through the mud?

Discussion Starters:

• What's the difference between having righteous anger (like Jesus') and just plain getting mad? When is it wrong to get mad?
•• Why is it wrong to take His name in vain (see Exodus 20:7)?

Lifeline:

Discuss what you can say in response to people who put down God.

Pecking at the Shell

the **WORD** | *John 3:1-3*

"Now there was a man of the Pharisees, named Nicodemus, a ruler of the Jews; this man came to Jesus by night and said to Him, 'Rabbi, we know that You have come from God as a teacher; for no one can do these signs that You do unless God is with him.' Jesus answered and said to him, 'Truly, truly, I say to you, unless one is born again, he cannot see the kingdom of God.'"

the **Message**

When my daughter Jamie was growing up, we raised geese, rabbits, squirrels, raccoons, dogs, deer, possums, and any other stray animal that found its way (or was brought by Jamie) to our door.

One spring, I was incubating some duck eggs and made an awful mistake. It takes a baby duck 28 days to hatch, and the last two to three days, he's busy pecking out of his shell. Although the ducks struggle during this time, the process helps them become strong enough to survive once they're out in the world. Well, I felt so sorry for one of the toiling little ducklings that I "helped" him out of his shell the day after he'd pecked a hole in the egg. He died that night. The other ducklings struggled on their own and were free of their eggshells by the third day. They all survived.

God's timing exists for a reason—for baby ducks and for baby Christians. Just as I hurt the duck by forcing an early hatching, so we can wound our friends or family by trying to "make" them ready to be born again. When you're witnessing to someone, the Holy Spirit must be leading you or your friend will never cross the line to eternal life. Why? Because God needs to work in her heart first. What you say will usually confirm what God is already doing inside her soul.

How do you know when the time is right for someone to be born again? Observe. Is your friend "pecking at his shell," asking questions, becoming curious about Jesus? Is he interested in spiritual things?

It's important that we witness to others about Christ. But we also must remember that we can't do anything without God's power and wisdom. God says it's "not by might nor by power, but by My Spirit [and in My time]" that miracles will happen (Zechariah 4:6). Wait on Him.

Discussion Starters:

• What does it mean to be born again?
  •• Why did Nicodemus (a very religious man) need to be born again?
    ••• Why do we need to depend on God's timing for others to be born again?
      •••• In what ways do we try to "open the shell" too soon?

Lifeline:

Pray for Christ to work in the hearts of your pre-Christian friends.

The Greatest Verse

the WORD | John 3:16

"For God so loved the world that He gave His only begotten Son, that whoever believes in Him shall not perish, but have eternal life."

the Message

For God...(the greatest lover)
so loved...(the greatest love)
the world...(the greatest need)
that He gave...(the greatest gift)
His only begotten Son...(the greatest life)
that whoever ...(the greatest offer)
believes in Him...(the greatest faith)
shall not perish...(the greatest death)
but have eternal life...(the greatest place)

Probably the most memorized verse in the Bible, but as with all familiar things, sometimes we just mumble the words and forget that the meaning is life-or-death significant. In one powerful sentence, John 3:16 affirms that God loves you, and He sent Jesus to die for you so you can live with Him forever in heaven. It describes the whole New Testament—and possibly your future—in a nutshell. Amazing!

Discussion Starters:

* Why do some people call John 3:16 the greatest verse in the Bible? What does it mean to you?

** What does the word *whoever* mean?

*** What does the word *believe* mean in this verse?

**** What do you think it will be like to have eternal life?

Lifeline:

First, memorize John 3:16. Then practice saying it to one another, but explain the verse in words that an unbeliever would understand. This will help prepare you to discuss it (and God's message of salvation) with your friends who don't know Him.

Auction Over!

the WORD | John 3:33-36

"He who has received His testimony has set his seal to this, that God is true. For He whom God has sent speaks the words of God; for He gives the Spirit without measure. The Father loves the Son and has given all things into His hand. He who believes in the Son has eternal life; but he who does not obey the Son will not see life, but the wrath of God abides on him."

the Message

Bradford Fowler, an upstate New York man, was exceedingly rich. His 100-acre estate was worth millions. He owned houses, land, antiques, and cattle. But although on the outside he had it all, he was unhappy on the inside. His wife, Kate, was getting older, and they were childless. Bradford's only wish was to have a son who could carry on the family legacy.

Almost miraculously, Kate became pregnant in her later years, and she gave birth to a baby boy. Although Benjamin was born severely retarded, Bradford loved him whole-heartedly. He took his son everywhere he could and taught Benjamin everything possible.

When Benjamin turned five, Kate died. Grief-stricken, Bradford drew even closer to his special son. But soon after Benjamin's 13th birthday, his birth defects cost him his life, and he passed away almost as suddenly as he was born. Bradford died six months later, brokenhearted.

With no family left to inherit his riches, Bradford had requested in his will that his possessions be put up for auction. So one blustery November day, hundreds of wealthy bidders gathered to buy the Fowler family's riches. The first item offered was a painting of Benjamin. No one bid. Instead, the people waited like vultures for the riches. Finally, the poor housemaid who had helped raise Benjamin offered five dollars for the picture and easily took the bid. To everyone's shock, the auctioneer ripped a handwritten will from the back of the picture. In it, Bradford had written, "To the one who thinks enough of my son to buy this painting, I give my entire estate."

"Auction over!" the auctioneer shouted. And the greedy crowd walked away, stunned and dismayed.

Discussion Starters:

- How was that auction like God's offer to us?
  - What exactly does God offer?
  - Who will be disappointed when the "auction" is over?

Lifeline:

Does your family value one another as much as Bradford valued his son?

God's Thirst Quencher

"There came a woman of Samaria to draw water. Jesus said to her, 'Give Me a drink.' Therefore the Samaritan woman said to Him, 'How is it that You, being a Jew, ask me for a drink since I am a Samaritan woman?' (For Jews have no dealings with Samaritans.) Jesus answered and said to her, 'If you knew the gift of God, and who it is who says to you, "Give Me a drink," you would have asked Him, and He would have given you living water.'... [Then Jesus said], 'Everyone who drinks of this water will thirst again; but whoever drinks of the water that I will give him shall never thirst; but the water that I will give him will become in him a well of water springing up to eternal life.'"

the *Message*

Thirst-quenching drinks are everywhere. Coke, Gatorade, Quick Kick, Canadian Coolers, Dr Pepper, and Snapple are just a few of hundreds on the market. These drinks are so popular that advertisers spend a ton of money on drink product commercials every year. Gatorade paid legendary basketball player Michael Jordan millions just to call him "Mike" in its new product promoting commercial. Pepsi paid Jordan just as much to drink Pepsi in front of a TV camera.

Fluids are popular because they're necessary for survival. In fact, as I've mentioned before, we need eight glasses of water every day to keep ourselves hydrated! But while we need drinks to stay alive, nothing we drink can permanently quench our thirst.

Jesus' living water is the exception.

His water will quench your thirst for meaning and purpose in life. As He told the Samaritan woman at the well, you'll never thirst again when you continue to trust Jesus and live for Him.

Unfortunately, there are as many cults and God-seeking religions as there are soft drinks. Millions of people, thirsty for God, flock to false religions every day. Even more try to quench their thirst through other people and things. They fill their desert-dry souls with friends, sports, fashion, love, parties, and work—hoping to find satisfaction.

But unless they drink from Jesus' well, they will all die with parched lips.

Discussion Starters:

* Why did Jesus call Himself "living water"?
** Why do sincere followers of Christ never thirst for another drink?
*** How can someone get a drink of living water?

Lifeline:

How has Jesus quenched your family's thirst with His living water? Discuss.

The Arrival

the WORD | John 4:25-26, 42

"The woman said to Him, 'I know that Messiah is coming (He who is called Christ); when that One comes, He will declare all things to us.' Jesus said to her, 'I who speak to you am He.' ... [The woman left and told others about Christ's arrival] and they [said] to the woman, 'It is no longer because of what you said that we believe, for we have heard for ourselves and know that this One is indeed the Savior of the world.' "

the Message

Imagine that your hero was coming to your hometown and staying at your house. You would probably spend weeks preparing for his or her arrival. What would you do to get ready for this person? Make up the best bedroom? Cook the best food? Clean the house from top to bottom?

Once you did that, you'd have to decide where you would take your hero. How would you entertain this person? What would you say?

Think about the impact your hero's visit would have on your life. You'd probably talk about the event until your friends turned purple.

That's how excited the Old Testament prophets were when they told people about Jesus' coming. For 1,500 years, those saints longed for and wrote details about the Messiah. Jesus was a hot topic. Even before He came, Christ provided hope for people. Whenever times got dark, the prophets reminded the people that they had Someone to look forward to, Someone who would bring light to their world.

The prophets did such a good job of preparing the people for Jesus' arrival that even slaves, women, and children (sadly, the least valuable people in society during biblical times) recognized Him and were able to accept that Christ was who He claimed to be, the Messiah.

Have you, like the prophets and the woman at the well, let others know about Jesus? Do you, like people in biblical times, take the time to make your heart and your home a place where Jesus would feel welcome?

Do you really believe Christ is who He says He is?

Discussion Starters:

- Why was the Messiah's arrival so exciting to the prophets and biblical people?
  - If you had lived in New Testament times, would you have believed Jesus when He said He was the Christ? Why or why not?

Lifeline:

Get yourself and other people ready for the Messiah. He's the most important Person you'll ever entertain.

"They Just Don't Get It"

the **WORD** | John 4:44

"For Jesus Himself testified that a prophet has no honor in his own country."

the **Message**

Brett came to camp one summer as a confident 14-year-old to become a better soccer player. He left as an improved athlete, but he also left as a different person. One evening, after a lot of thought and discussion, he accepted Jesus into his heart.

Brett was excited about his newfound faith, but he was a little nervous about what his friends would think. He and the guys had hung out together since kindergarten, but they had been into everything *except* church.

After becoming a Christian, Brett prayed that his friends would see a change in him and accept Jesus into their hearts, too. His first day back, hanging out with the guys, Brett nervously told his friends the news.

"Hey, uh, guess what happened to me this summer?" he asked.

"You met some babes!" Mike guessed.

"Nah. Someone better. Jesus," Brett said and held his breath.

Brett didn't get close to the reaction he wanted. His friends laughed. And they laughed at him for three years. The whole time, Brett prayed, tried to love them, and sought support from his Christian friends. Finally, one day Mike, his best friend, approached him. Mike was hurting from a broken relationship and asked Brett how he could get peace. They talked for hours, and at last, Mike gave his life to Christ.

Brett and Mike are still praying for their other friends who haven't stopped laughing at them. But they aren't too discouraged. They know that even Jesus had a hard time sharing God's truth with the people He knew best. Even Jesus was laughed at and misunderstood.

God is powerful, though. And that fact gives Brett and Mike hope that someday, their friends' sarcastic laughter will turn into real God-given joy.

Discussion Starters:

• Why did those who knew Jesus best (the people of Nazareth) misunderstand Him most?

•• Why is it so hard to live out your faith around your closest unbelieving friends?

••• How can you best be a witness to your friends who don't know Christ?

Lifeline:

It's admirable to have friends you want to lead to Christ, but it's essential to also make friends who know Him so they can encourage you and keep you on track. Thank God for your friends who know Him, and pray for the ones who don't.

Do You Will to Get Well?

the WORD | John 5:5-9

"A man was there who had been ill for thirty-eight years. When Jesus saw him lying there...He said to him, 'Do you wish to get well?' The sick man answered Him, 'Sir, I have no man to put me into the pool when the water is stirred up, but while I am coming, another steps down before me.' Jesus said to him, 'Get up, pick up your pallet and walk.' Immediately the man became well, and picked up his pallet and began to walk."

the Message

Beth was a sweet, cute sophomore at Texas Tech University. She came to me confused and in need of counseling as I traveled through Texas to hire summer staff for our sports camps.

"I feel so awful these days," she said as tears threatened to fill her huge brown eyes. "My relationship with God is going nowhere right now."

"What's going on in your life?" I asked, concerned.

"Well, there's this guy..." Beth began, nervously tapping her fingers.

We talked for a while, and she sobbed. She told me her boyfriend was taking advantage of her and drawing her away from God.

"I know I'm not making God happy, but I can't break up with my boyfriend. I've always dated someone. I don't want to be alone," she said.

"Beth," I said, "if you really want to make your heart and your relationship with God better, then you've got to give God your will."

She looked up, astonished. "How'd you know that? How did you know my boyfriend's name is Will?"

A lot of people want to solve their problems—but not enough to give those people and issues over to God. That's why Jesus asked the sick man if he wanted to get well. The man would have to believe that Jesus had the power to heal him. He'd have to surrender his will to God, no longer trying it on his own. The man did, though, so Jesus healed him. Beth, on the other hand, didn't really want God to heal her problem. She didn't want to give God either of her "wills" and tried instead to handle the situation herself.

It's hard to give your will up to God and say, "I want what You want. I believe You can heal me—I can't do it myself."

But if you are *willing*, He is able. He can heal you.

Discussion Starters:

- What's the difference between wanting and deciding to do something?
  - What does it mean to have Jesus own your will?

Lifeline:

Are you willing to let Jesus take control and own your will? Discuss.

Instant Replay

the WORD | John 5:22-24

"For not even the Father judges anyone, but He has given all judgment to the Son, so that all will honor the Son even as they honor the Father. He who does not honor the Son does not honor the Father who sent Him. Truly, truly, I say to you, he who hears My word, and believes Him who sent Me, has eternal life, and does not come into judgment, but has passed out of death into life."

the Message

The game was intense. The crowd was jeering. I was a college football player, facing a tough national championship team. And we were playing on their turf. At least 80,000 biased fans watched from the stands, and millions more were viewing the game on TV.

The pressure got to me, and I made an embarrassing mistake during the game. I was the quarterback and accidentally handed the ball off to an opposing defensive player, giving them possession of the ball. I tried to hide my number under the pile of players. The play went by fast. Since our coach couldn't see clearly from the sidelines, I hoped he hadn't noticed.

No such luck. Later, after we lost the game, the team gathered in the locker room, where our coach saw a film of the game. He zeroed in on my mistake immediately and played the tape over and over again.

"Hey, White," he bellowed, "do you realize what you did here? You didn't think. You're partly responsible for losing this big game!"

I felt as small as a squashed bug, standing in the film room with my teammates as we watched the replay on the screen. *If only I could've erased the film before he saw it!* I thought as my stomach dropped.

I think God is like a coach in some ways, too. He sees it all and knows it all. He has "filmed" every sin, every mistake, every failure. He's no fool. But when you meet Him face-to-face, the judgment scene will be different. If you've accepted Christ into your heart and asked Him to forgive your sins, you'll step over to God's right hand and enjoy eternal life. Your sins will be erased, your heart will be "white as snow," and Jesus will say, "This one is My child. Her sins are forgiven. I died to erase them."

Thank You, God, for deleting our mistakes and loving us in spite of them.

Discussion Starters:

- Why do we sin? How can Jesus erase our sinful pasts?
  - Why is God's forgiveness such a big deal?

Lifeline:

Your family members should be able to learn from their mistakes without being judged and ridiculed for mess-ups.

Bearing Witness

the WORD | John 5:32-34

"There is another who testifies of Me, and I know that the testimony which He gives about Me is true. You have sent to John, and he has testified to the truth. But the testimony which I receive is not from man, but I say these things so that you may be saved."

the Message

Little Emma had been blind since birth. Poverty-stricken and basically abandoned by her parents, Emma had to make a living on her own. Every morning at six, she bundled up and walked 10 blocks to the Chicago train station and sold pencils to buy food and clothing. Most people in the station rushed by her each day, hardly noticing her raggedy clothes and white cane. Occasionally someone would drop a quarter in her moneybox and grab a pencil to do a good deed for the day.

One winter morning, the station was unusually crowded. Emma could hear hundreds of thumping feet rush from train to train. She scooted her chair closer to the wall, trying to keep out of the way. But as the people dashed into the crowded trains, one careless businessman ran into the blind girl and knocked her out of her chair. Emma's coins and pencils flew across the floor. Desperately, she crawled around, feeling for her precious coins and pencils. As she sat on the cold ground, whimpering, an elderly man gently picked her up, gathered her pencils and coins, and helped her get started again. Then the man handed Emma a $20 bill and began to walk away.

Emma, wanting to know who her rescuer was, cried out, "Mister, are you Jesus?"

"No, honey, I'm just one of His followers," the man answered, smiling.

Tears fell from Emma's unseeing eyes as she cried, "I knew you had to at least be related to Him."

Being a witness for Jesus isn't that hard. There are people everywhere who need your help and love. All you have to do is pay attention. Do people know you're a member of His family?

Discussion Starters:

* How do we bear witness for Christ?
** Name one situation you were in yesterday where you had a chance to be a witness. Did you demonstrate Christ's love? Why or why not?
*** How can you be a witness for Jesus in your family?

Lifeline:

Home should be the first place you give witness of Christ's love. Let your family members see Christ in you today!

Whom Do You Please?

the **WORD** | John 5:44

"How can you believe, when you receive glory from one another and you do not seek the glory that is from the one and only God?"

the Message

Leroy is a smart high school junior. Lately, his friends have been mad at him because he won't give them the answers to the history take-home tests. Every time they ask, he says no. Where does he get his courage? Leroy cares only about pleasing God.

Anne is 19 and is still a virgin. Several boys have tried, but no one has been able to so much as kiss her. She's waiting for the right guy, but it's not easy. She's always getting teased about her purity. Where does she get her conviction? Anne cares only about pleasing God.

If it's not an extra-clean flick, Krista doesn't go to the movie. She's left slumber parties when the movie rental was inappropriate. Last week, Krista even pulled her date out of the theater because the movie made fun of her Christian beliefs. Where does she get her confidence? Krista cares only about pleasing God.

Scott is a professional jeweler. Nine out of 10 jewelers he knows lie about diamond purity to make more money. Last week, Scott turned down $20,000 profit on a diamond deal because it was dishonest. Where does he get his integrity? Scott cares only about pleasing God.

Theresa is a successful doctor. Today, while preparing for surgery with seven other doctors, the conversation turned to faithfulness in marriage. All the doctors were cheating on their spouses. Theresa stood alone, the only one who had remained happily committed to her husband. Where does she get her loyalty? Theresa cares only about pleasing God.

Following God is often difficult. But it's a lot easier to walk with Him when you're focused on Who's really important. What your friends, coworkers, and even family members say doesn't matter a hill of beans if their words aren't matching up with God's Word.

Work to gain God's approval. You'll gain an eternal reward that will far outweigh your friends' acceptance.

Discussion Starters:

* What does it mean to work for God's approval and not people's?
  ** In what ways are you living for God's blessings? How are you relying too much on what your friends think?

Lifeline:

It takes a strong person to focus on what God wants. Encourage one another to do that today.

By Himself

the **WORD** | John 6:15

"So Jesus, perceiving that they were intending to come and take Him by force to make Him king, withdrew again to the mountain by Himself alone."

the *Message*

When I first met Sam, I thought his schedule was going to flatten him. Sam was a junior in high school, working to get into a prestigious college. He had a 4.0, ran track, played basketball, was vice president of his junior class, volunteered with his church's junior high group, and had a steady girlfriend. At first, Sam kept up his activities and friendships by living on adrenaline. But as time passed, I could see he was losing gas.

Sam stopped sleeping. *Resting is a waste of time. I have more important things to do and people to be with,* he thought.

Soon, though, Sam's head began to drop in calculus class. He got circles under his eyes and also started getting irritable, snapping at his girlfriend and losing it on the basketball court.

His relationship with God began to slide, too. Quiet times became a thing of the past.

One day, after Sam fell asleep in class for the hundredth time and his girlfriend told him to straighten up, he decided to make some changes.

"I picked up the Bible and asked God to tell me how I should live my life. So He showed me what Jesus did when He was busy. And I couldn't believe it...Jesus slowed down and rested," Sam explained to me.

Jesus knew the value of solitude. He sure needed it after He fed the 5,000. It had been a long, tiring day. He'd spent His time surrounded by people who were clamoring for His attention, hanging on to His every word, and nudging Him for another miracle.

Jesus needed time with the Father after that. He knew He needed to rest and rebuild His strength in the Lord.

Jesus was perfect, but even He still needed to slow down.

Jesus was popular, but even He knew He couldn't find fulfillment from the multitudes of people who always flocked to Him or from the miracles He performed.

Solitude is important. And if God needs it, you do, too.

Discussion Starters:

- Why is it so hard to slow down? To be alone?
  - What are some other instances in which Jesus was alone?

Lifeline:

If you're always running around, you won't be able to hear God's voice. Encourage one another to stop occasionally and listen to Him.

Wake-Up Call

"For I have come down from heaven, not to do My own will, but the will of Him who sent Me. This is the will of Him who sent Me, that of all that He has given Me I lose nothing, but raise it up on the last day. For this is the will of My Father, that everyone who beholds the Son and believes in Him will have eternal life; and I Myself will raise him up on the last day."

the *Message*

A good friend of mine, Kyle Rote, Jr., won the "Rookie of the Year" award several years ago in professional soccer. Shortly thereafter, he received a call from the president of the United States. When Kyle picked up the phone, the president introduced himself. Kyle thought it was a prank call from a buddy who often called, disguising his voice as a famous person's.

Kyle muffled his laughter and said, "Sure—the president of the United States. You're a big fake, a fraud, and you're crazy if you think I'm going to believe something as stupid as this joke, *Donny*."

The president paused, cleared his throat, and said, "Kyle, this is the president of the United States—not Donny—and I want to invite you to the White House to congratulate you on your recent honor."

Kyle was embarrassed beyond words.

Imagine being invited to a famous person's home and, like Kyle, humiliating yourself by not giving that person the respect he or she deserves. Well, Jesus tells us that one day, we're going to live in His home (if we're His child) after we pass away. If you don't know Him during this lifetime, it will be an awkward experience—you'll be sent away to hell. But if you do know Him, if you can recognize His voice, coming to His home will be wonderful—you'll live eternally with the Savior.

You need not fear going home to Christ. It'll be the most welcoming, joyful homecoming you've ever known. But you should ensure that you know His voice so that when He calls, you'll be able to answer.

Discussion Starters:

* Why do most people fear death?
** What do you think it will be like to pass away and wake up in Jesus' home?
*** Where can you improve in recognizing His voice?

Lifeline:

Encourage each other with the hope that life ends with a wake-up call from the greatest man who ever lived—Jesus.

The Battle Belongs to the Lord

the WORD | John 6:65-68

"And He was saying, 'For this reason I have said to you, that no one can come to Me unless it has been granted him from the Father.' As a result of this many of His disciples withdrew and were not walking with Him anymore. So Jesus said to the twelve, 'You do not want to go away also, do you?' Simon Peter answered Him, 'Lord, to whom shall we go? You have words of eternal life.'"

the Message

For decades, countless faithful American young men followed the pointed finger and expectant scowl of the Uncle Sam posters plastered on draft buildings from the Atlantic to the Pacific. "Uncle Sam Wants You!" the posters read, urging young men to join the military and fight for their country.

As a citizen, you have a responsibility to your country. But as a child of God, you have a responsibility to the Lord. God wants you to fight and win a different sort of war. His desire is that you will join His eternal army and fight to win the souls of everyone He puts in your path. That's His will for your life.

God asks us to tell others about Him, but He also wants us to remember that salvation is up to Him. You can witness to a friend, but whether or not she accepts Jesus is in God's hands.

Remember—God has words of eternal life. Your role is to be a tool, someone God can speak through. It's essential to "fight" for your friends and relatives who don't know God. But only God can win the ultimate battle.

Discussion Starters:

• How do we know that true Christians go to heaven?
•• What role does God's army play in bringing people to salvation? How can you, as a member of His army, fight for Him?
••• In order to be part of the battle to win others over for Christ, you'll have to put on God's heavenly armor (see Ephesians 6). In what ways are you donning the armor of God in school? At work? At home?

Lifeline:

Have someone in your family tell about a time he or she led someone to Christ. Answer: What was the experience like? How was God working in that person's life before he actually accepted Christ? What was your role in the experience?

A Never-Ending Class

"But when it was now the midst of the feast Jesus went up into the temple, and began to teach. The Jews then were astonished, saying, 'How has this man become learned, having never been educated?' So Jesus answered them and said, 'My teaching is not Mine, but His who sent Me. If anyone is willing to do His will, he will know of the teaching, whether it is of God or whether I speak from Myself. He who speaks from himself seeks his own glory; but He who is seeking the glory of the One who sent Him, He is true, and there is no unrighteousness in Him.'"

the Message

You're going to be in school for your entire life.

Before you panic, think about it. Everything in your environment teaches you something. You learn from the TV, music, movies, and books. Ten billion cells in your brain take in every sound and sight you hear and see. Those sights and sounds are stored for later.

Jesus knew learning is important—it affects who you become.

The first American teachers taught the Bible. For America's first 100 years, *The New England Primer* showed every American kid how to read with the alphabet taught like this:

A—"A wise son makes his father glad" (Proverbs 10:1).

B—"Better is a little with the fear of the Lord" (Proverbs 16:8).

C—"Come unto Christ all you who labor" (Matthew 11:28).

Kids spent hours reading Bible verses, but now most of our time is in front of the TV. God's prescription for living is not often found there, though. I challenge you to turn off the TV once in a while and involve yourself in activities that would make God smile. Try to relate what you're learning in school to God's Word. Discuss current events and figure out how to take a biblical stand. Critically evaluate media. What is it saying? Do your values agree?

Unscriptural teaching is everywhere. But we don't have to accept it. The Bible is and always will be relevant—and what you learn from it will have eternal significance.

Discussion Starters:

* Who are your main teachers? Whom do you listen to most?
** According to John 7:18, what's the test for a good teacher?

Lifeline:

Help each other identify negative teachers and decide how to respond.

"I Had the World"

the WORD | John 7:31-33

"But many of the crowd believed in Him; and they were saying, 'When the Christ comes, He will not perform more signs than those which this man has, will He?' The Pharisees heard the crowd muttering these things about Him, and the chief priests and the Pharisees sent officers to seize Him. Therefore Jesus said, 'For a little while longer I am with you, then I go to Him who sent Me.'"

the Message

One of the richest and most famous athletes who has ever lived is a world champ, millionaire boxer named Muhammad Ali. No doubt, in his prime, Ali was a boxing phenomenon. He even said it himself: "I am the greatest! I am the greatest!" Just a short 15 years after Ali quit boxing, *Sports Illustrated* did a cover story on him. The writer visited Ali's farm one cold winter day and candidly traced the champ's rise—and fall. Once a legend, Ali had now become a memory. Most of what was left filled the training barn behind Ali's house, which was full of his trophies and life-sized posters—pictures with Ali's arms thrust high overhead in defiant victory. As the writer and the champ toured the old barn, the writer noted that pigeons in the rafters had left droppings streaked across Ali's posters and trophies. One by one, Ali turned them toward the wall in shame and disgust. He walked outside and said softly in self-pity, "I had the world, and it wasn't nothin'."

"I had the world…and it wasn't nothin'."

You can get so much that you don't need God; you can get so famous and successful that you might think you sort of *are* God.

The Pharisees were like that. Those religious bigwigs were so full of pride and arrogance that they didn't recognize the Son of God when He was standing right in front of them. Like Muhammad Ali, they had too much stuff in the way. Their rules and legalism clouded their ability to see Jesus for who He really was.

Don't let other things get in the way of your relationship with the Messiah!

Discussion Starters:

° Jesus said, "For what will it profit a man to gain the whole world if
he forfeits his soul?" (see Matthew 16:26). What does that mean to you?
°° Is there anything in your life that's getting in the way of God? If so, what?
°°° What will you do about it?

Lifeline:

Home is the place to remind one another that there's no way to God but through Jesus.

Man of Prophecy

"Others were saying, 'This is the Christ.' Still others were saying, 'Surely the Christ is not going to come from Galilee, is He? Has not the Scripture said that the Christ comes from the descendents of David, and from Bethlehem, the village where David was?' "

the *Message*

In his book *Evidence That Demands a Verdict,* Josh McDowell showed that during the 1,000 years before Jesus' birth, several hundred specific prophecies were recorded that accurately predicted the birth, life, death, and resurrection of the Messiah[2]:

	Prophesied	Fulfilled
1. Born of a virgin	Isaiah 7:14	Matthew 1:18, 24-25
2. Family line of Jesus	Isaiah 11:1	Luke 3:23-33
3. House of David	Jeremiah 23:5	Luke 3:23-33
4. Born in Bethlehem	Micah 5: 2	Matthew 2:1
5. His pre-existence	Micah 5:2	Colossians 1:17
6. He shall be called Immanuel	Isaiah 7:14	Matthew 1:23
7. Preceded by a messenger	Isaiah 40:3	Matthew 3:1-2
8. Ministry begins in Galilee	Isaiah 9:1	Matthew 4:12-13, 17
9. Sold for 30 pieces of silver	Zechariah 11:12	Matthew 26:15
10. Hands and feet pierced	Isaiah 53 & Psalm 22:16	Luke 23:33

The odds that any man could fulfill all these and the hundreds of other prophetic claims about the Messiah are statistically impossible: about the same as filling the entire solar system with golf balls and asking a blind man to find a specific one.[3]

Discussion Starters:

• What do Jesus' fulfilled prophecies reveal about your faith?
•• How else can we be sure that Jesus is who He claimed to be?

Lifeline:

The Jesus of prophecy lives in His believers and will work through them!

Red-Handed

the **WORD** | John 8:3, 5, 7, 9-11

"The scribes and the Pharisees brought a woman caught in adultery. … 'Now in the Law Moses commanded us to stone such women; what then do You say?' But [Jesus] said to them, 'He who is without sin among you, let him be the first to throw a stone at her.' …When they heard it, they began to go out one by one.… Jesus said to her, '…Did no one condemn you?' She said, 'No one, Lord.' And Jesus said, 'I do not condemn you, either. Go. From now on sin no more.'"

the **Message**

Growing up, pennies were tight. We didn't have money to play video games or buy soda. But God always provided—He was good. As a junior higher, it didn't seem enough, though.

One Friday night, I wanted to see the high school football game, but my pockets were empty. Those games were big in my hometown. I had to get inside. So I schemed, *I'll just crawl over the fence and get in free.*

Up I went, climbing the chain-link fence. I knew it conveniently led to the top of the grandstands. I'd have no problem getting a seat once I arrived there safely. But when I got two-thirds of the way up, I saw Mr. Ozment, the high school principal, peering down at me through his spectacles. I froze. *I'm gonna be an endangered species,* I realized, gulping.

"Mr. White," Mr. Ozment said sternly, "report to my office after school on Monday."

"Yes, sir," I managed to squeak out.

I could already feel the sting of the paddle. It made me miserable the whole weekend.

That Monday Mr. Ozment smiled at me. The paddle was absent. He saw I was sorry. And he forgave me.

Christ forgives us so much more! Like the adulteress, we all get caught. We all mess up. But if we repent, Christ simply says, "It's forgiven. Go and sin no more."

Discussion Starters:

* Why did Jesus tell the woman she was forgiven?
** What does that say about God's love for us?

Lifeline:

Although the Bible commands parents to discipline at times, family members should also give each other the grace Jesus gave the adulteress.

Make Him Smile

the WORD | John 8:28-30

"So Jesus said, 'When you lift up the Son of Man, then you will know that I am He, and I do nothing on My own initiative, but I speak these things as the Father taught Me. And He who sent Me is with Me; He has not left Me alone, for I always do the things that are pleasing to Him.' As He spoke these things, many came to believe in Him."

the Message

I love to please my daddy. He's over 80 years old, and I still get thrilled when he notices something I've done. It makes me feel loved when I get his approval. In fact, when I was in college, playing football was worthwhile because Daddy was watching.

We should try to please our earthly fathers, but even more, we ought to win our heavenly Father's favor. A whole bunch of people in the Bible pleased God—and made history.

God flooded the world but spared Noah's family (Genesis 6:8).

God built the entire Jewish nation on David's strength (see 1 Samuel 16).

God built His kingdom for Jesus because He was happy with His Son (see Matthew 3).

God loves it when we live a life pleasing to Him! Julie went to the sophomore party after the game one Friday night. About 11:30 that evening, things got wild. Two football players brought a fifth of Jack Daniel's and poured it into the punch. "Everybody" started getting crazy. Julie didn't care that it was uncool to leave before midnight. She headed for home.

Andy sat scrunched in the backseat of Mike's Bronco with all five of the starters on the basketball team. A joint was passed from player to player. "Everyone" was getting crazy. Andy felt the heat as his turn came up. "No thanks," he said.

Every day, you make a choice: *Will I make God happy?* Do you want to have Him look at you proudly and say, "That's My child"? Make Him grin: It's the best decision you can make.

Discussion Starters:

• What other people in the Bible were examples of being God-pleasers?
•• Why did God create people with a choice to please or displease Him?
••• How can you make God happy this week? Why is it so important to gain His approval?

Lifeline:

It takes the encouragement of a caring family to be a God-pleaser.

Freed from Slavery

the WORD | John 8:34-36

"Jesus answered them, 'Truly, truly, I say to you, everyone who commits sin is the slave of sin. The slave does not remain in the house forever; the son does remain forever. So if the Son makes you free, you will be free indeed.'"

the Message

Harriet was a dear African-American lady who lived in America's historic Civil War days. Born into slavery, at age seven Harriet Tubman was told by her mom that she might as well face the fact that she was a slave, she'd always be a slave, and she'd die a slave.

Harriet didn't buy it. That day, she determined in her heart that she would either be free or die trying to attain liberty. And she reached her goal. By age 40, not only had she crossed the dangerous pathway to freedom by fleeing north, but she had also helped others find dignity, hope, and freedom. Harriet escorted more than 300 slaves from slavery to freedom—or from death to life on the Underground Railroad.

People called her "Moses."

America is now slave-free, but in some ways we're all enslaved. Sin traps us and restricts us. If we don't have Christ, sin leaves us hopeless. If we do have Christ, it can interfere with our relationship with God.

Be wary of sin. It's sneaky and subtle. No one holds a grudge and intends to end up bitter and hateful at the world. No one "borrows" a few dollars and intends to end up a full-fledged shoplifter. No one starts out with a tiny lie and intends to become outright dishonest. But sin is like that. It starts off seemingly innocent and then leads to a trap of slavery.

Next time you're tempted to cut a few corners, to fudge a bit on the truth, or to indulge in a bad relationship, remember where those things can lead.

Jesus warns, "I love you too much to see you become a slave. Don't give in to the lies. Don't let your foot get caught."

And don't let sin get the better of you.

Discussion Starters:

• What are some other sins that lead to slavery?

•• How does Satan make sin look so appealing?

••• How can you gain freedom when you find yourself in a sin trap?

•••• Why can only Jesus truly set you free?

Lifeline:

Resolve to help one another avoid the trap of sin. Then pray together that God will make you strong enough to resist the sin temptation, and thank Him for ultimately making you free.

Lord, Liar, or Lunatic?

the WORD | John 8:54-56,58

"Jesus answered, 'If I glorify Myself, My glory is nothing; it is My Father who glorifies Me, of whom you say, "He is our God"; and you have not come to know Him, but I know Him; and if I say that I do not know Him, I will be a liar like you, but I do know Him and keep His word. Your father Abraham rejoiced to see My day, and he saw it and was glad.' ...[Then] Jesus said to them, 'Truly, truly, I say to you, before Abraham was born, I am.' "

the Message

What if one of your friends stood up at lunchtime and announced to the rest of the school (or restaurant) that he was the president of the United States? How would people respond?

They would yell, "You're crazy! Sit down."

Or they'd laugh, saying, "You're either kidding or you're lying."

No one would respond, "Well, now that I think about it, you *do* look like the president. Maybe you're right."

Your friend would be a liar or a nutcase if he claimed to be the most powerful political figure in the United States...unless he really was who he claimed to be.

In the same way, Jesus Christ didn't say He was just another prophet. He didn't tell everyone He was simply a good man with some great moral teachings. Jesus claimed to be God in the flesh.

The Jews thought Jesus' claim was blasphemous, so they decided to crucify Him. But I believe Jesus was 100 percent truthful when He told everyone He was God. Jesus knew that statement would lead to His death. Why would He allow Himself to be crucified if He wasn't who He said He was? If He wasn't truly God, Jesus would've confessed at the last minute, "I lied. It's not true! Don't crucify Me!"

But He didn't back down one bit.

As C. S. Lewis pointed out, we all have to decide who Jesus was. Either Jesus was God, He was lying, or He was crazy.

Easter morning and history stand as witnesses that Jesus wasn't a liar or a lunatic. That leaves us with only one choice—He is Lord.

Discussion Starters:

- Why do some people try to make Jesus out to be less than who He is? Why is He different from Muhammad, Buddha, or Confucius?
- What difference does it make in your life that Jesus is Lord?

Lifeline:

How can Jesus be Lord of your household?

Blind Spots

the WORD | John 9:1, 6-7

"As He passed by, He saw a man blind from birth.... [So] He spat on the ground, and made clay of the spittle, and applied the clay to his eyes, and said to him, 'Go, wash in the pool of Siloam' (which is translated, Sent). So he went away and washed, and came back seeing."

the Message

Jerry rips on every kid in school.

Melinda wears clothes that are too tight. Trevor shows off his muscles. Doug, a smart businessman, thinks constantly about his computers and his money. Anna likes her 16-year-old boyfriend more than she loves God. Stephanie won't listen to her friends' problems, but when she's got a crisis, she expects them to be all ears. Marvin will do anything to be popular...even dishonor his parents. Sylvia, a 42-year-old mom, complains constantly about how hard her life is. Byron, an unemployed father, becomes so preoccupied with finding a job that he virtually ignores his kids. Adrienne tunes out her best friend when she tries to point out a major red flag in Adrienne's life.

Sports in college made me increasingly self-centered. I had a blind spot in my ego.

Blind spots—places in our lives where we can't see the truth. God knows that we all, in some ways, are spiritually blind. We often don't perceive ourselves clearly. We can't tell when we're in a rut. We overlook the not-so-good things we say and do.

That's why God created accountability—relationships that are close enough and safe enough that our friends can point out blind spots and bad habits that we've chosen not to see.

Make sure you have someone in your life to whom you're accountable. Someone who will pray with and for you. Someone who will point out the blind spots and, with God's help, help you to avoid crashing.

Discussion Starters:

° How can we get blinded to the truth that's around us?
°° How can Jesus heal our blind spots? How does He use people to help us?

Lifeline:

Jesus can heal physical and spiritual blindness. But He also gives relationships to help us see clearly. Does your family have accountability?

Can You Believe It?

the WORD | John 9:35-38

"Jesus heard that they had put [the blind man] out, and finding him, He said, 'Do you believe in the Son of Man?' He answered, 'Who is He, Lord, that I may believe in Him?' Jesus said to him, 'You have both seen Him, and He is the one who is talking with you.' And he said, 'Lord, I believe.' And he worshiped Him."

the Message

Tim couldn't believe his parents were moving the family to a new town. His anger got him into fights with his friends. He mouthed off to his parents. Most of all, Tim was mad at God.

Seeing that my friend was in trouble, I confronted him. "Tim, why are you striking out at everyone?"

Tim mumbled through hot tears, "My dad's moving us across the country away from my friends. I can't believe God would do this to me. I don't believe in anything anymore. What's the point?"

I took off my watch and handed it to him. Tim looked up.

"Whose watch is this?" I asked.

"Yours," he said gruffly.

"But *you're* holding it."

"It's still yours," Tim said, exasperated.

"Well, I want you to have it. It's a gift." He looked puzzled.

"Whose watch is it now, Tim?" I said with a grin.

"Uh, it's mine, I guess. Yeah, it's mine."

"When did it become yours? When I handed it to you or when you accepted it into your heart?"

Tim gave a weak grin. Like the blind man Jesus healed, he knew he believed.

You can't fight belief or give up the gift—it's yours because God loves you that much.

Discussion Starters:

• Why did the blind man instantly worship Jesus once he believed?
•• What does it mean to believe in Jesus?
••• What happens when a person puts his or her faith in God?

Lifeline:

How can you help one another when struggling with unbelief?

More Than Enough

the **WORD** | John 10:7-10, emphasis added

"So Jesus said to them again, 'Truly, truly, I say to you, I am the door of the sheep. All who came before Me are thieves and robbers, but the sheep did not hear them. I am the door; if anyone enters through Me, he will be saved, and will go in and out and find pasture. The thief comes only to steal and kill and destroy; I came that they might have life, and have it *abundantly.*'"

the *Message*

The original *Webster's Dictionary* was written by a devoted Christian man who, like many of Western society's great early scholars, knew the Bible backward and forward. Webster defined the word *abundant* as "more than enough."

More than enough. Think about it. Jesus came to give abundant life, abundant peace, and abundant joy. Can beer, popularity, sports, money, a car, or a girlfriend do that? How much beauty is more than enough? How much pleasure is more than enough? How much fame and success are more than enough? How much money is more than enough?

When Jesus healed the hemorrhaging woman, she didn't need to go visit more doctors. She was completely well!

When Jesus fed the 5,000, they didn't leave the conference and head for McDonald's. They were full, and there were even baskets of food left over!

When Jesus gave the Samaritan woman His living water, she didn't go buy a Big Gulp at 7-Eleven. She was satisfied.

When will we stop trying to get high on this world's stuff? Ten thousand kids come to our Christian camps every year, and they get high on God! I see kids tapping into Christ's abundance all over this country, attending Bible studies, listening to Christian music on the stereo, enjoying quiet times before bed, participating in youth groups with a purpose, and having parents who encourage their kids to make honest, godly choices. All those things bring fulfillment to their lives because God is in them.

Life with God is abundant. Don't try living any other way.

Discussion Starters:

• What's the difference between living and abundant living?

•• Why do real believers have more fun?

••• Why did God invent fun and happiness and pleasure, and how did He intend for us to have it?

Lifeline:

Ask one another, How abundant is your life today? How can you, as a family, help each other to make it better?

Twice Mine

"Jesus answered them, 'I told you, and you do not believe; the works that I do in My Father's name, these testify of Me. But you do not believe because you are not of My sheep. My sheep hear My voice, and I know them, and they follow Me; and I give eternal life to them, and they will never perish; and no one will snatch them out of My hand. My Father, who has given them to Me, is greater than all; and no one is able to snatch them out of the Father's hand.'"

the Message

Joey was only 12 years old, but he was especially handy with a pocketknife and a block of wood. Because he was quite poor, his few precious toys were all handmade.

For three months, he poured his spare time into carving a beautiful little boat...a miniature replica of the Pinta that brought Columbus across the Atlantic Ocean. Joey took his boat to a nearby creek after a rain shower to test his prize. As the boat took off in the current, Joey's expression of satisfaction and accomplishment quickly turned to panic as the water rushed off with his one-of-a-kind masterpiece. He ran and ran to catch up with it, but the shore was too muddy and the waters were too swift to save the boat. In tears, he wandered back home.

Two months later, Joey was walking by a hobby shop when he saw his boat for sale in the window. Someone had found it! He rubbed his eyes in disbelief. The price tag was $10, but it might as well have been $100. He rushed home, emptied his entire piggy bank, scraped the $10 in change into a paper bag, and hurried back to town.

He bought his boat back and walked proudly out of the store. With tears in his eyes, he looked down at the boat and said, "Little boat, I made you, and you ran away. But I bought you back. So now you're twice mine."

Do you ever wonder if God loves you? Well, He does care for His sheep (that's what the Bible calls God's children). He looks after them, holds them, and, as Joey did, will fight to bring them back if they drift.

Next time you get carried away on the waves of life, remember that your Father in heaven is closer than you realize. He loves you—and He won't let *anything* separate you from Him (see Romans 8:38-39).

Discussion Starters:

- How are we like Joey's little boat?
    - What did God do to buy us back?
        - How does it make you feel to be God's beloved child?

Lifeline:

Let's remember our God who gave us His Son so we could be twice His!

My Father in Me

the WORD | John 10:37-38

"If I do not do the works of My Father, do not believe Me; but if I do them, though you do not believe Me, believe the works, so that you may know and understand that the Father is in Me, and I in the Father."

the Message

Yesterday had to be one of the most "sheer fun" days of my life. I flew across the Tennessee pasture on a red-hot four-wheeler behind Paul Overstreet, one of country music's greatest songwriters and recording artists. Paul loves Jesus Christ. He writes and sings to help families love the Lord and serve each other. One of my favorite songs of Paul's says:

I'm seeing my Father in me, I guess that's how it's meant to be.

And I find I'm more like Him each day.

I notice I walk the way He walks.

I'm seeing I talk the way He talks.

I'm starting to see my Father in me.

Jesus had all of His Father in Him. People could tell that Jesus was completely God because His actions were totally consistent with God's will. Jesus never wavered in producing a godly lifestyle.

Our responsibility as Christians is to follow God at home, work, and church, making sure our lifestyles are in line with the Lord. It's important for two reasons: First, we're supposed to become more like Christ as we grow in relationship with Him. Second, we're called to be witnesses to unbelievers, and they will be watching our words and actions.

If imitation is the sincerest form of flattery, pay Jesus a compliment—mold your life after His.

Discussion Starters:

° How could people tell that Jesus was, indeed, God in the flesh?

°° Parents, how are your kids becoming more like Christ? Kids, in what ways do you see Jesus in your parents?

°°° Practically speaking, in what ways can you more closely model your life after Christ at school? At home? At work?

Lifeline:

People can best see God when they see His love in Christians.

The Human Maze

the **WORD** | John 11:9-10

"Jesus answered, 'Are there not twelve hours in the day? If anyone walks in the day, he does not stumble, because he sees the light of this world. But if anyone walks in the night, he stumbles, because the light is not in him.'"

the **Message**

Last week, my son Brady drew a maze on a sheet of paper for me to try to solve. There were so many detours and dead ends that I never did get to the finish.

In our tourist town, there's a human maze. It's designed for people to race one another to the finish line. You have only five minutes to run through the giant hallways and walls and discover four carefully hidden stations. At those stations, you get the marks "M" "A" "Z" "E" on a card. If you make it in time, you get a free T-shirt.

I went through that maze once. After I lost the race to my son, a curious thing occurred to me. I climbed the stairs to an observation deck where I could see the pathways and walls clearly from above. It was simple to memorize the path to victory. Anyone could win after a careful view from the top.

If we could see the outcome of our actions or what the future holds, we'd be less likely to run into sin. I'm sure Wendy would agree. On a dare, she once stole her biology teacher's master test and passed it out to her friends. She was caught and immediately expelled from school. Now she's in a different school, struggling to make friends and to get rid of her bad reputation.

Wendy couldn't have known what was going to result from her dare. But she could have consulted a Guide—Jesus. He knows the future (see Psalm 139), and He works all things out for our good (see Romans 8:28). If we call on Him, He will help us make godly decisions. His Spirit will direct us through our lives (see Psalm 48:14).

Jesus will be your light and your leader if you call on Him. He knows what's best for you. After all, He's got the view from above.

Discussion Starters:

* What does it mean to walk in the light?
** How is life like a maze?
*** What "walls" and "dead ends" do we often run into as we're growing up?
**** How can we get the view from above—God's perspective?

Lifeline:

Discuss how your family can help each other keep a godly perspective.

Jesus Wept

the **WORD** | John 11:32-36

"Therefore, when Mary came where Jesus was, she saw Him, and fell at His feet, saying to Him, 'Lord, if You had been here, my brother would not have died.' When Jesus therefore saw her weeping, and the Jews who came with her also weeping, He was deeply moved in spirit and was troubled, and said, 'Where have you laid him?' They said to Him, 'Lord, come and see.' Jesus wept. So the Jews were saying, 'See how He loved him!' "

the **Message**

Have you ever wondered where tears come from? Have you cried so long that you wondered if your tear ducts would dry up? Physical hurt from life's bumps and bruises brings a certain kind of tears. But real tears come from heart pain—when you're emotionally upset. That usually happens when friends move, relationships break up, loved ones pass away, and people disappoint you.

In the original Greek language in which the New Testament was written, the apostle John said that Jesus sobbed, boo-hoo'd. He actually groaned with pain when Lazarus died. *Why?* we might wonder. *Didn't He know that He'd bring Lazarus back to life again?*

I think Jesus wept because He loves His people so much that although He knows all our pain will eventually be over forever, He feels every hurt we have. He cares deeply and knows your pain when your boyfriend breaks up with you. He grieves when someone calls you names or spreads rumors about you. He empathizes when you lose your job or when your dog runs away.

Only a deeply caring, loving, sensitive God would weep real tears for His children. What was the source of Jesus' tears? Love.

Discussion Starters:

* What do Jesus' tears say about God's love for you?
  ** When was the last time you cried over someone else's pain? What did those tears mean?
  *** Who needs your empathy right now?

Lifeline:

Empathy means feeling someone else's pain and caring deeply for him or her. Sometimes at home it's easy to overlook your family members' hurt. How can your family become more compassionate?

Security

"Therefore the chief priests and the Pharisees convened a council, and were saying, 'What are we doing? For this man is performing many signs. If we let Him go on like this, all men will believe in Him, and the Romans will come and take away both our place and our nation.'"

the **Message**

Fear of losing our security—wherever we place it—can tempt us to do wrong things. I admire people who face up to that fear and take a stand for what's right.

Yesterday, a grateful mom came and told me about her daughter, Janis, who was running for junior class president. Janis was well liked in her public high school and prepared an excellent campaign. At the completion of her "make it or break it" 20-minute speech, which she gave in front of the entire student body, the panel of judges asked her, "Janis, who is your hero?" Janis responded quickly, "My hero is undoubtedly Jesus Christ, who died for my sins." She didn't care that the truth could make her unpopular.

I know some businessmen who are so secure in their faith that they're able to make choices that cost them, both professionally and financially. My friend Michael Jones recently refused to negotiate a $100,000 real estate deal because it was unethical. And Dr. Cristman passes up thousands of dollars each year because he won't do abortions. His pro-life stance has hurt his reputation, but he doesn't care. He knows his standing with Christ is more important.

Jill also knows about finding security in God. Last week at a youth group party, she told me how tough junior high social life is.

"I couldn't believe it," Jill said. "This guy brought some stuff to this party that went way against my morals. Almost everyone told him he was cool. But I didn't think so. I called my mom, and she came to get me. No one thought I was cool, but I know that Jesus thinks I am."

It's tough to stand up for what you know is right. But if you find your security in Jesus and not in what others think, you'll be standing on eternally solid ground.

Discussion Starters:

* How did Jesus shake the Jewish leaders' security?
  ** How does being a Christian put your temporary security at risk?
  *** Why is it often difficult to find our security in Jesus?

Lifeline:

Encourage each other to build your security in Christ.

Parades

"On the next day the large crowd who had come to the feast, when they heard that Jesus was coming to Jerusalem, took the branches of the palm trees and went out to meet Him, and began to shout, 'Hosanna! Blessed is He who comes in the name of the Lord, even the King of Israel,' Jesus, finding a young donkey, sat on it; as it is written, 'Fear not, daughter of Zion; behold, your King is coming, seated on a donkey's colt.'"

the **Message**

Kids of all ages used to wait in line for days to buy a ticket to an Elvis Presley concert. Tens of thousands would scream 'til they were breathless when the Beatles or the Jackson Five played at a show.

What would we do if Jesus came to town?

Rock stars travel in personal jets. Jesus rode on a donkey.

Rock stars make so much money that they could walk into their concerts on carpets of gold.

Jesus entered on simple palm leaves.

Music stars are raised up on concert stages, which are arrayed with hundreds of lights and lasers.

Jesus was raised up on a Roman cross.

Your favorite rock stars will be forgotten almost before they play their last chorus. Jesus' words will be remembered forever.

Christ's coming changed the world. Do *you* want to make a difference in your lifetime? Well, you sure can't do it through money, popularity, achievement, or power. Those things will mean nothing in God's eternal perspective...unless you use them— your gifts, finances, and talents—to glorify Jesus. Want to make an impact on the people around you? Talk about Christ. He's the Alpha and the Omega, the beginning and the end.

And His name will be life-or-death significant in the long run.

Discussion Starters:

* Why did the crowd say on Palm Sunday, "Blessed is He who comes in the name of the Lord"?
** Why didn't Jesus demand royal treatment?
*** Why do money, talent, and fame mean nothing in God's perspective?

Lifeline:

How can your family make an impact for Jesus?

The Pack

the **WORD** | John 12:27-28

" 'Now My soul has become troubled; and what shall I say, "Father, save Me from this hour"? But for this purpose I came to this hour. Father, glorify Your name.' Then a voice came out of heaven: 'I have both glorified it, and will glorify it again.' "

the *Message*

Jim Ryun has a great talent and an even more terrific heart. When he was in ninth grade, Jim wanted to run track, but he was too slow, so he got cut from the team. The setback didn't make him angry, though. It just made him eager to train even harder. He ran hours and hours every day. When asked if he was in pain, Jim would say, "Yes, but I've learned to run with the pain." Jim was the first high school runner to break the four-minute mile. He held the world record in the mile for 15 years.

But he never won the Olympics.

I watched him run for the U.S. track team at the Munich Olympics in Germany. There, a tragic event occurred. As Jim rounded the curve on the last lap of the race, he got caught—and trapped—in a pack of runners. I could see the pain etched on his face as he tripped and fell. Although he was the best in the world, Jim finished last. But his spirit and smile never dimmed. He continues to be one of the greatest men I've ever known, someone I and thousands of others admire.

Jim demonstrates the grace of Jesus Christ, and it is evident to those around him.

Jesus showed even more dignity on His way to the cross. Like Jim, He had a tough obstacle in His path. He was troubled, too (see verse 27). But Jesus knew that even the hardest things in life can glorify God. He was able to endure His pain on the cross because God had a purpose in it.

God has a purpose for your pain, too. Maybe that seems unthinkable. Maybe you feel hopeless. Maybe you're trapped in the pack of peer pressure, disappointment, or brokenness. But God will help you through it, and He can be glorified through your suffering.

He did it in Jim Ryun's life. But if you really want proof, look at how God's love broke through Jesus' pain.

Discussion Starters:

- How was God glorified through Jesus' suffering?
  - What difficulty are you facing? How can God work in your situation?

Lifeline:

Pray that God would enable your family to see His purpose through hard times.

Are You a Judge of Character?

the **WORD** | John 12:47

"If anyone hears My sayings and does not keep them, I do not judge him; for I did not come to judge the world, but to save the world."

the Message

"Pssst. Hey, did you hear what that Jesus guy said in the synagogue yesterday?" one Pharisee whispered to another.

"I know. What a joke! He didn't come to *judge* the world? That's what religion is all about. We're supposed to watch for all those bad people out there and then tell God about them," the other Pharisee said confidently.

"It's a good thing God has us to keep everyone else in line," the first Pharisee agreed. "What would He do without us to—?"

"Hey," the second Pharisee interrupted, "look at Joseph with that woman over there. Isn't he supposed to be in the synagogue, praying? We'd better go talk to him...."

And they walked off, thankful to be doing "God's work."

The Pharisees' biggest downfall was their judgmental attitude. They were so determined to set other people straight that they couldn't see their own crookedness.

The funny thing is, Jesus said He didn't come to earth (the first time) to judge His people. He came to save the world instead.

So why do we as Christians often feel it's our responsibility to criticize everyone around us? We're not much different from the Pharisees of Jesus' time when we condemn others. But it's easy to think:

Marc goes to those bonfire parties. How can he say he's a Christian?

Or, *I saw Suzie holding a beer. She's really gone downhill.*

Even, *Joanna's never prepared for Bible study. She has a weak faith.*

Maybe those things are true about Marc, Suzie, and Joanna. But our job as believers is to love others, not judge them. Sure, we should be concerned when those we love are sinning, but judging them isn't going to do us—or them—any good. God will deal with those people in His time.

Discussion Starters:

* What did Jesus mean by saying He wasn't going to judge the world?
* What are the dangers of being judgmental?
* How can we love others without condoning their sins?

Lifeline:

Together, thank God for His continual forgiveness. Then ask Him to help you love others and avoid being judgmental.

Washing Feet

"Jesus, knowing that the Father had given all things into His hands, and that He had come forth from God and was going back to God, got up from supper, and laid aside His garments; and taking a towel, He girded Himself. Then He poured water into the basin, and began to wash the disciples' feet and to wipe them with the towel with which He was girded."

the Message

The dishes get dirty three times a day. Who's going to wash them? The front porch is filled with leaves every time the wind blows. Who's going to sweep it? The dog wets the rug. Who will clean it? The baby needs a bottle. Who's gonna feed her? Dad had a hard day at the office. Mom's back is killing her. Larry just lost the student council elections. Angie missed becoming a cheerleader by one vote. Who will encourage them?

Opportunities for foot washing are all around the house. These are great times to show your love for Jesus.

No one should brush off Jesus' commandment to follow His example of service (see John 13:15).

Jesus is Lord, and He still washed His disciples' feet, which was the lowliest chore He could've done back then. He even initiated the whole thing. He *wanted* to do it. Wow!

It's so easy to let your parents serve, or your wife serve, or to make your kid brother serve while you lord your authority (while sitting on a La-Z-Boy) over them. But until you serve others, you'll never know how fulfilling it is to "wash feet" and express your care to those you love. Foot washers hold homes together. They bring love to relationships and meaning to Christianity. Do you really want to imitate Christ and follow His commandment? Wash other people's feet; serve them.

And, for good measure, start with the person who has the dirtiest feet.

Discussion Starters:

- Why did Jesus decide to wash the disciples' feet? Why were they so surprised?
  - Why is it hard to be a "foot washer"?
    - What are some practical ways to "wash feet" in your home? At your school? Your job?

Lifeline:

Have each family member decide to concentrate on serving three people for the next week. Then report back on your results. How did you feel? How did those people respond? Why is it so important to wash feet?

The Broken Finger

the **WORD** | John 13:21, 23-26

"When Jesus had said this, He became troubled in spirit, and testified and said, 'Truly, truly, I say to you, that one of you will betray Me.' ...There was reclining on Jesus' bosom one of His disciples, whom Jesus loved. So Simon Peter gestured to him, and said to him, 'Tell us who it is of whom He is speaking.' He, leaning back thus on Jesus' bosom, said to Him, 'Lord, who is it?' Jesus then answered, 'That is the one for whom I shall dip the morsel and give it to him.' So when He had dipped the morsel, He took and gave it to Judas, the son of Simon Iscariot."

the Message

Have you heard the joke about the man who went to the doctor? Well, the guy was in pain, so the doctor asked him, "Where do you hurt?"

The man, gritting his teeth, replied, "Doc, I hurt everywhere."

"Show me where," the doctor said with concern.

The man placed his right forefinger on his knee and said, "Doc, every time I touch my knee, I hurt bad." Then he touched his forehead. "Every time I touch my head, I hurt bad." Then he pressed his finger to his chest. "Every time I touch my chest, I hurt bad." Then he touched his nose. "Every time I touch my nose, I hurt bad."

The doctor took the man's hand and said, "Buddy, let me examine your finger." One close look was all it took. The doctor exclaimed, "You crazy boy, you've got a broken finger. No wonder it hurts!"

Well, maybe the joke wasn't *that* funny. But it does illustrate a profound truth. Sin is like having a broken finger. When you let sin run your life, everything you touch hurts! If you make money, you become greedy. If you make a friend, the relationship turns sour. If you succeed, you become arrogant. You wonder why you're struggling until someone points out your "broken finger"—the sin in your heart.

Judas was exactly like that. He spent years listening to Jesus talk, watched His miracles, and saw prophecies fulfilled, yet he was willing to betray Jesus for 30 pieces of silver. Judas had a "broken finger," and after he handed his Lord over he died of a broken heart (see Matthew 27).

We all are broken and sinful. But we can decide either to allow sin to taint us or go to the great Physician—Jesus—and let Him heal us.

What will you choose to do?

Discussion Starters:

• What was the root of Judas' sin?

•• What are some ways we betray Jesus? How is betrayal a sin?

Lifeline:

Make a family pact that you will be loyal to Jesus every day, in every way.

Whose Way?

the WORD | John 14:6

"Jesus said to him, 'I am the way, and the truth, and the life; no one comes to the Father but through Me.'"

the Message

America has over 1,800 active religious cults (at the time of this writing), and they all have a lot in common. Each one has a self-righteous leader who claims to be the only way to God. Every cult makes Jesus less than He truly was and elevates its leader until he or she is like a god. They all claim to have a special word from God, and to verify their unique message they add to or replace Scripture with their own personal beliefs, which are supposedly obtained from "divine revelations."

Listed below are some popular cults. Read what the cult leaders have said about faith and how their words conflict with Christianity:

- Joseph Smith (founder of Mormonism) said, "All Christian denominations are wrong, and their creeds are an abomination in God's sight."[4] Mormon church father Joseph Fielding Smith said, "There is no salvation without accepting Joseph Smith."[5]
- Shirley MacLaine (part of the New Age movement) said, "I was one with the water.... I am God, I am God."[6]
- Mary Baker Eddy was the founder of Christian Science. Her "Bible," *Science and Health,* reads, "The material blood of Jesus was no more efficacious to cleanse from sin when it was shed upon 'the accursed tree,' than it was when it was flowing in His veins as He went daily about His Father's business."[7]
- The *Watchtower* (of the Jehovah's Witnesses) teaches that Jesus was not God incarnate and that the doctrine of the Trinity is false.[8]

These cults are all tragically mistaken. Jesus stated simply and firmly, "I am the [only] way, the [only] truth, the [only] life; no one comes to the Father but through Me" (John 14:6).

Jesus is the true God, and you can find salvation only in Him. Don't let any cult tell you otherwise.

Discussion Starters:

- Why do people follow cult leaders?
- What's wrong with cults and other world religions? How are they different from Christianity?

Lifeline:

Some cult members are more devoted to their faith than Christians are to Christ. Is your family following Christ and His Word closely enough?

In God We Trust

the **WORD** | John 14:18,26

"I will not leave you as orphans; I will come to you. But the Helper, the Holy Spirit, whom the Father will send in My name, He will teach you all things, and bring to your remembrance all that I said to you."

the **Message**

I had just spoken to a terrific group of high school athletes in Kansas City when the point guard of the girls' basketball team came up to me, wanting to talk. Melinda, a dynamic athlete, spoke softly as tears pooled in her beautiful brown eyes.

"Last summer," she began, "I was going to come to your camp for the whole month of July. I was so excited, it was practically all I dreamed about for nine months. Then—" her voice broke off "—four days before Kamp started, I got mono. I was so sick, I had to be put in the hospital. I almost died. I felt so alone and betrayed. I kept asking God why He took Kamp away from me."

She stopped and wiped her eyes. "But one day, my friend gave me a cross. Over and over again, I kept looking at that cross and thinking about all Jesus had done for me. I knew He said He'd never leave me, and His promise pulled me through." She continued, saying, "I got better—miraculously—and in a couple of weeks, I left the hospital. I drove to Kamp at the end of the term to see my friends, and the neatest thing happened. A girl I'd never met walked up to me and told me she got to go to Kamp in my place. Just seeing her so happy about it made me feel a lot better."

Melinda grinned and added, "You know what happened? She became a Christian at Kamp! If I hadn't gotten sick, she never would've been able to come. But because I had mono, she came to know God. Now I understand what Jesus meant when He said He'd never leave us. He worked everything out and brought the Holy Spirit to comfort me. God is good!"

Amen.

Discussion Starters:

* Jesus knew we'd be put to the test as Christians, so He gave us the Holy Spirit to live in our hearts. How does the Holy Spirit comfort believers when troubles come?
 ** What is the Holy Spirit's role in your life as a believer?
 *** How did the Holy Spirit help Melinda? How can He encourage you?

Lifeline:

When you accepted Christ, the Holy Spirit came into your heart. Make your heart a good home for the Spirit by getting rid of your worries and doubts. Trust the Lord when He says He won't leave you.

Friends with God

"This is My commandment, that you love one another, just as I have loved you. Greater love has no one than this, that one lay down his life for his friends. You are My friends if you do what I command you. No longer do I call you slaves, for the slave does not know what his master is doing; but I have called you friends, for all things that I have heard from My Father I have made known to you."

the **Message**

Do you have a best friend who will never let you down?

Greg saw the power of friendship as a soldier in Vietnam. During one battle, he and three other guys were in a foxhole, into which the enemy threw a hand grenade. Instantly, one of the other soldiers dove on the grenade and took the explosion so his friends would live. The soldier died instantly, but his commitment will live forever.

God's friendship with us is even more powerful.

It's easy to see God as Lord, as a taskmaster, and as the almighty Ruler. But it's often hard to see Him as your best friend, too. *Why would God want to be friends with little ol' us?*

Because He loves us.

God's the best friend you've got. He knows all your hopes, secrets, and needs. He's a gift giver, a comforter, and a helper. Jesus is completely unselfish. In fact, He literally died for you.

The word *friend* originally comes from the Bible. It's translated as "loving kindness." It means the amount of love you have for someone isn't based on what he has done for you, but on what *you've* done for him!

Have you kept up your end of the friendship with God? Jesus wants you to talk with Him, to spend time with Him, and to share your gifts with Him. You wouldn't expect to stay friends with someone from school if you only talked with the person once a month—and you can't expect to be great friends with God if you only call on Him when you feel guilty or in an emergency. ("Lord, save me from this math test!")

Are you cultivating your friendship with God?

Discussion Starters:

• Is Jesus your best friend? How can you be a better friend to Jesus?
•• What has Jesus done for you? How much does He love you?

Lifeline:

Do you give your friendship with Jesus as much attention as your human friendships? Write Him a letter as you would to a good friend.

The Counselor

the WORD | John 15:26

"When the Helper comes, whom I will send to you from the Father, that is the Spirit of truth who proceeds from the Father, He will testify about Me."

the Message

Clink. Rattle. Clink. The dishes in the Kanakuk kitchen passed from hand to hand as dinner was prepared for the hungry campers. Cassandra, one of the college-aged cooks, sighed as she grabbed her spatula and leaned over to look into the oven. As I chatted with the other kitchen staff, I noticed a tiny tear run down Cassandra's cheek.

"Hey, Cassandra," I called to her, "can we talk for a minute?"

She nodded her head hesitantly, and we sat down at a table in the corner. After we had talked for an hour and she had cried enough to finish a box of tissues, Cassandra told me she'd been abused as a small child.

"I feel hopeless, like I can't escape my problems," she admitted.

"Cassandra," I said gently, "God knows that you have needs and problems. He loves you so much—unconditionally—that He gave you His Word (the Bible) and a counselor (the Holy Spirit) to live in your heart. The Spirit will help you work through these issues."

After our talk, Cassandra realized she had a problem-solver living in her heart. She began to memorize God's Word so she'd feed her mind with her "Counselor's" thoughts. She prayed constantly that God would fill her heart with her Counselor's love. She trusted Him continuously to fill her soul with her Counselor's assurance.

A week went by, and I saw her smile. A month went by, and I saw her happy heart. A year went by, and I saw her dance. The Lord was working in Cassandra.

Cassandra's not the only one with a built-in Counselor. The Holy Spirit comes into your heart the moment you accept Christ as Savior. He comes from the Father to testify about the Son. The Spirit is your Helper and your Teacher, and His purpose is to be with you and enable you to become more like Christ. Give your problems to the Holy Spirit.

There's nothing He can't handle.

Discussion Starters:

• What are some other names for the Holy Spirit?
•• How can His ability as a counselor help you today?
••• Why did God give us His Spirit?

Lifeline:

How can your family recognize the power of the Holy Spirit in your prayers, and especially in your daily lives?

That Voice Inside You

the WORD | John 16:8-11

"And [the Helper], when He comes, will convict the world concerning sin and righteousness and judgment; concerning sin, because they do not believe in Me; and concerning righteousness, because I go to the Father and you no longer see Me; and concerning judgment, because the ruler of this world has been judged."

the Message

Mary is a Christian psychologist who specializes in helping people get rid of their bad habits, relieve their stress, and put their lives back on track. Early last fall, a young lady named Rachel entered her office. Her eyes were dark and disturbed. After just one look, Mary could tell she was dealing with someone deep into a life of misery and sin.

As Rachel sat down, Mary asked what was wrong.

Immediately, Rachel told her that she was involved in an affair with a married man and felt really guilty about it. Rachel threw up her hands, saying, "I'm just completely miserable!"

Mary asked her, "Do you want me to help you change your ways?"

Rachel crossed her arms and quickly replied, "No, I don't want to change—I just want you to weaken my conscience."

Unfortunately, Rachel didn't realize that your conscience is actually helpful. It protects your heart just as the nerves in your hand protect your skin by making you pull away from a hot flame.

Your conscience keeps you from jumping into spiritual bonfires.

Your conscience is actually the Spirit of God. If you're a believer, the Spirit will guide you into the things that are right and will lead you away from sinful mistakes. The Holy Spirit will put the red sirens on when you say or do something displeasing to God. (That's how conviction works.) On the flip side, the Spirit will also let you know if you're becoming a righteous young man or woman of God.

The Holy Spirit is important. Who else could really let us know whether we're pleasing God?

When your conscience speaks, you'd better listen! God's still, small voice knows best.

Discussion Starters:

° How does the Holy Spirit speak to us?   °° How does the Bible speak to our conscience?
°°° What happens when we ignore God's voice inside?
°°°° How does the Holy Spirit glorify Jesus?

Lifeline:

As you keep God's Word alive at home, you'll keep your conscience sharp.

Do You Suffer from Prayer Procrastination?

the **WORD** | John 16:23-24

"In that day you will not question Me about anything. Truly, truly, I say to you, if you ask the Father for anything in My name, He will give it to you. Until now you have asked for nothing in My name; ask and you will receive, so that your joy may be made full."

the *Message*

Some people will try anything to avoid doing their chores. And it seems some Christians will do anything to avoid praying.

Prayer procrastination. Everyone does it. We reason, *I'm too tired to pray right now. I'll do it when I'm fresh, when I have something interesting to say to God.* We put it off, thinking, *I'll pray after I finish this assignment,* or, *I need to run some errands, get advice from my best friend, and clean my room first.*

Why do we put off praying when it's so powerful?

I think it's because we forget how effective prayer really is. We forget that God is listening and that He promised to answer us.

Jesus said that if we pray in His name, He will hear our prayers. Every prayer we send toward heaven is answered—not always in the way we'd like, but always in God's timing (which, as we know, is best). There is no Call Waiting in heaven. God will not "click over" to someone else while we're pouring our hearts out to Him.

Simply worrying about getting a job isn't going to help make you employable, but prayer can. Trying to do too many things will only tire you out unless you enlist God's help. Merely wishing for a new friend won't go as far as praying about finding a Christian buddy.

Why does prayer work? Because God cares about every detail of your life. He wants to provide for all your needs (see Matthew 7). But He desires for you to *rely on Him* for those things. He commands you not to be stressed, fearful, or anxious. God wants you to pray instead.

Jesus said prayers are best when they're honest, from the heart, simple, and not done for show (see Matthew 6). All you've got to do is ask in humility and faith. The rest is up to God.

Discussion Starters:

* Since God can accomplish everything He wants to anyway, why did He give us the gift of prayer?

** Why is prayer such an important part of our lives as Christians?

*** Who or what do you pray for the most? Why?

Lifeline:

Committed prayer will bring your family closer together, allowing you to grow in Christ. Don't put off prayer. Make sure it has top priority.

One Nation Under God

the WORD | John 17:4-6

"I glorified You on the earth, having accomplished the work which You have given Me to do. Now, Father, glorify Me together with Yourself, with the glory which I had with You before the world was. I have manifested Your name to the men whom You gave Me out of the world; they were Yours and You gave them to Me, and they have kept Your word."

the Message

Have we kept our word of commitment to God? If you look at the United States, it sure doesn't appear that those of us who live here have.

Did you know the phrase "One nation under God" is being thrown out of the Pledge of Allegiance in many public places, including schools?

Or that the Boy Scouts are under legal fire for saying "I will do my duty to God and my country"?

Have you heard that it's illegal in some cities to put up a manger scene on government grounds? Courts say it's a violation of the First Amendment. But the politics are pretty twisted. According to the same courts, the First Amendment also makes it illegal to deny government funding to a national art program that paints pornographic pictures of Jesus and mocks His work on the cross.

The laws that govern America are being twisted from their original God-fearing meaning to an anti-God bias that makes it more difficult every day for Christians to live for and worship God.

This shouldn't come as any surprise, though. Jesus told us we would be persecuted by a hostile world because of His name (see Matthew 24).

He also promised to guide us through it.

How can we live in a world that disrespects the One we love and honor? We can persevere, trusting that God is stronger than this world and that He will give us the ability to stand firm. We can give Him the honor and glory He deserves, regardless of what others are doing around us.

When it seems that everything in society is crumbling, your faith should only get stronger. After all, as the prophet Isaiah said, "If you do not stand firm in your faith, you will not stand at all" (Isaiah 7:9, NIV).

Discussion Starters:

- How is your country turning its back on God?
  - What does today's scripture say about reverencing God?

Lifeline:

Focus on keeping your word to God and, as a family, standing up for Him.

Family Ties

the WORD | John 17:19-23

"For their sakes I sanctify Myself, that they themselves also may be sanctified in truth. I do not ask on behalf of these alone, but for those also who believe in Me through their word; that they may all be one; even as You, Father, are in Me and I in You, that they also may be in Us, so that the world may believe that You sent Me. The glory which You have given Me I have given to them, that they may be one, just as We are one; I in them and You in Me, that they may be perfected in unity, so that the world may know that You sent Me, and loved them, even as You have loved Me."

the Message

Unity. What does it mean to your family?

To Grant, family love and unity were of life-or-death importance. During the Vietnam War, Grant and his son, Mickey, both military men, watched battlefield reports carefully from their home base as thousands of American soldiers lost their lives in the fierce battles overseas. Not far into the war, Grant was called to do a 12-month duty on the worst battlefront. Miraculously, he returned home without injury. A few months later, when Mickey was called to Vietnam to fight, Grant asked the commanding officer if he could take his son's place on the battlefield so Mickey could stay home. The substitution was approved, and Grant returned to battle. Grant was so bonded to his son that he risked death so Mickey might be safe.

That's the kind of unity Jesus was talking about—love, devotion, and selfless acts of courage done in His name. Is your family that unified?

Jesus also wants His divine family to be bonded together. If you're a Christian, you have countless brothers and sisters in Christ, and you are all called to be one body. That means you don't laugh when John in the pew next to you raises his hands and sings off-tune on Sunday mornings. You also don't let petty arguments or cliques drive your youth group apart. And you build your brothers and sisters up by praying for them, encouraging them, and sometimes even confronting them in love.

As much as you need unity within your family at home, you also need it in the church around the world. You've got millions of brothers and sisters in Christ. Make your Father proud—be unified.

Discussion Starters:

* How can our family and church body be one as God the Father and Son are one? How does God unify us?
** Why does our love for each other reveal Christ in us?

Lifeline:

They'll know we're His disciples if we love one another.

Holy

"Judas then, having received the Roman cohort and officers from the chief priests and the Pharisees, came there with lanterns and torches and weapons. So Jesus, knowing all the things that were coming upon Him, went forth and said to them, 'Whom do you seek?' They answered Him, 'Jesus the Nazarene.' He said to them, 'I am He.' And Judas also, who was betraying Him, was standing with them. So when He said to them, 'I am He,' they drew back and fell to the ground."

the **Message**

Jesus' bold statement struck those who had come to arrest Him with a sense of awe. It seems as if they got a glimpse of His power as the Son of God—power and glory that ought to get more respect today than they usually do.

Long before copy machines, during a wonderful era of early Jewish tradition, a scribe would make copies of holy Scripture by taking his feather pen (quill) and carefully, accurately, perfectly hand-copying God's Word from one scroll to another. When the scribe would get to the word *God*, he would stop, pray, undress, take a bath, put on clean clothes, get a new quill, and then go back to his work and write "God."

It's quite a bit different today. Now we defy God's fourth commandment—"Don't take the Lord's name in vain"—by trampling God's name as if it's dirt. We degrade Him in our conversations, on TV, in movies, and in books. "Oh, my God!" "My God!" "Jesus Christ!" people exclaim when they're mad, upset, or just want words to fill in the blanks of day-to-day conversation.

It's no longer necessary to bathe and change clothes before we say or write God's name, but Jesus made it clear that God is holy and awesome. He should be revered and respected. Do your language and attitude reveal that you honor the living God?

Discussion Starters:

- What did Jesus mean when He said, "I am He"?
    - What did God mean when He said, "You shall not take My name in vain" (see Exodus 20:7)?
  - In what ways is God holy? Why is His holiness so powerful?

Lifeline:

As we've discussed, each day Christians are surrounded by others who take God's name in vain. How should your family respond to those who don't give God the respect and honor He deserves?

Spread the Good News!

the **WORD** | *John 18:25-27*

"Now Simon Peter was standing and warming himself. So they said to him, 'You are not also one of His disciples, are you?' He denied it, and said, 'I am not.' One of the slaves of the high priest, being a relative of the one whose ear Peter cut off, said, 'Did I not see you in the garden with Him?' Peter then denied it again, and immediately a rooster crowed."

the **Message**

Amanda didn't know *what* to do. After a long, lonely semester, Stacey, a popular girl in the ninth grade, had started talking to her. Stacey sat behind Amanda in fifth-period history and, lately, she'd been passing notes to Amanda during class. Ordinarily, Amanda would've been thrilled with the other girl's attention. She knew that if she became friends with Stacey, she'd be in with the popular group. But strangely, Stacey's notes focused on questions about God and church.

Stacey doesn't seem like the kind of person who'd go to church, Amanda thought. *She must be making fun of me. If she thinks I'm a nerdy Christian, I'll never make friends in this school.*

So after the third note, Amanda stopped beating around the bush and instead lied. "I don't know what you're talking about, Stacey. I don't go to church. Its boring," she wrote back. Amanda took a deep breath, leaned back, and slipped the note under Stacey's elbow.

When the bell rang, Stacey got up, brushed past Amanda's desk, and hurried out the door.

The following Sunday morning, Amanda found out why she'd been snubbed. As she stood talking with her youth pastor, Amanda felt a tap on her shoulder.

"Hi, Amanda," Stacey said. She was clutching a new Bible.

Amanda smiled meekly, feeling about as low as pond scum.

Selfishness and insecurity—that's why Peter denied his Lord. Next time you've got an opportunity to talk about Christ, don't look around to see who's watching. Be bold. Be courageous. Someone else's eternal life could hinge on what you say.

Discussion Starters:

• What keeps you from witnessing to others about Jesus?
•• How can you be bolder in talking about Christ? More prepared?

Lifeline:

Some people are afraid to tell others about Jesus because they don't feel they know enough about Christianity. How can your family learn more?

Take It There, Put It There, and Leave It There

the WORD | John 19:4-6

"Pilate came out again and said to them, 'Behold, I am bringing Him out to you so that you may know that I find no guilt in Him.' Jesus then came out, wearing the crown of thorns and the purple robe. ... So when the chief priests and the officers saw Him, they cried out saying, 'Crucify, crucify!' Pilate said to them, 'Take Him yourselves and crucify Him.'"

the Message

I looked across the sea of multicolored faces and whistled. Our summer camp for forgotten kids had gathered 300 teenagers from projects, gangs, and city streets. As I attempted to explain the miracle of the cross, I could see the question marks in their eyes.

With a large ax and a 15-foot elm tree, I hacked out the form of a huge cross. The kids were silent, watching and thinking.

I finished hacking and said, "You've all heard a lot about how Jesus died to forgive your sins," I said. "Well, take Him up on His offer. Write your sins and come nail them to the cross."

The atmosphere grew somber as each kid made his way and pounded his sins into the cross.

The cross was already filled with paper when Dustin stopped. One of the youth workers noticed. He put his arm around Dustin's shoulder and simply said, "What's wrong?"

Dustin mumbled, "I dunno." He shuffled his feet in the dirt.

The youth worker pointed to Dustin's filled paper, showed him the hammer and nail, then motioned to the cross and said, "Just take it there, put it there, and leave it there."

"That's it?" Dustin asked.

'That's all there is to it.'

Jesus is the only person who never sinned, yet He died to save us. Once you've confessed to Him, your sins are gone. Has He pronounced you not guilty?

Discussion Starters:

• Why is Jesus the only One who is able to forgive our sins?
•• What happens when we repent and ask forgiveness?

Lifeline:

Give your sins to Jesus daily.

Don't Forget the Cross

the **WORD** | John 19:17-18

"They took Jesus, therefore, and He went out, bearing His own cross, to the place called the Place of a Skull, which is called in Hebrew, Golgotha. There they crucified Him, and with Him two other men, one on either side, and Jesus in between."

the Message

Albert, an elderly friend of mine, has worked closely with Billy Graham, helping him and a large team of committed evangelists put on thousands of crusades across America. One summer evening in New York, during one of Dr. Graham's early crusades, the fiery evangelist left the event disheartened, believing the crusade was weak and ineffective. He walked to a bench and slumped, holding his head in his hands.

Dr. Graham tells my friend that in his moment of disappointment, he got a "word" from God. Just as Graham was about to walk back inside the building, an old German man spotted Dr. Graham and, seeing him upset and disillusioned, firmly but lovingly confronted the young evangelist.

"Dr. Graham," the old man said gruffly, "you forgot the cross tonight. Don't forget the cross, Billy! Don't forget the cross."

These words rang in Graham's ears—he knew God had planted that message for him to hear The old man's advice has since guided Billy Graham and his staff through years of crusades. Graham has led more people to faith in Christ than any person alive. What's his secret?

Dr. Graham reaches the lost when he talks about the cross.

Jesus' death on the cross is what makes the Christian faith powerful and meaningful—it saved you (and all believers) from your sins. The cross isn't just another piece of jewelry. It's not simply another symbol. It's the centerpiece of your faith, the hope of your life, and your ticket to heaven. Does your life reflect the significance of what Jesus did for you on the cross?

Discussion Starters:

* Why was Jesus' crucifixion so powerful?
  ** What happens when you forget Jesus' death on the cross?
  *** What does the cross mean to you? Why?

Lifeline:

Christ loved you enough to endure the cross. Make sure you're modeling His sacrificial love in your family!

When All Is Said and Done

"'Therefore when Jesus had received the sour wine, He said, 'It is finished!' And He bowed His head and gave up His spirit.'"

the *Message*

During President Bush senior's term, I toured the White House with his receptionist, Kathy Wills. Kathy took me to the Oval Office where the president did his daily work. In a pencil holder on his desk stood a 2" x 4" American flag—the kind you buy at Wal-Mart for 49 cents.

"Why is that in such a prominent place in his office?" I asked, intrigued about why, out of all the beautiful gifts the president no doubt possessed, he'd decided to go with that.

Kathy explained that as the president was visiting some injured soldiers in a military hospital, a badly wounded paratrooper called him over to his bedside. The president greeted the soldier, and the man gave him the flag. The soldier shook the president's hand, looked him in the eye, and said, "Mr. President, my only regret is that I can't fight again."

Of all the famous and invaluable historical relics in the Oval Office, that tiny flag meant more to the president than anything else. It stood for the perseverance, dedication, and love of Americans.

Jesus finished His fight with the same integrity. He lived an exemplary life. He loved, taught, turned the other cheek, remained devoted to His Father, and died self-lessly. He had no regrets about the things He had done at the end. Jesus didn't say, "Wait, I need to patch things up with Peter," while they dragged Him off to be cruci-fied. He didn't exclaim, "You think *I'm* a sinner? Wait 'til *you* die. Then we'll see who goes where!"

Christ simply looked upward, where His Father was watching from heaven. It gave Him the strength to finish His life honorably and blamelessly. Jesus' death was brutal, but even then, He still glorified God.

You, too, will have obstacles and suffering in life. How will you live? Will you have regrets when all is said and done?

Discussion Starters:

* Why was Jesus able to die without regrets about what He had done?
** How can we be as dedicated to God as the soldier was to his country?
*** What qualities do you want to cultivate so you will live with no regrets?

Lifeline:

What kind of "flag" will your family give God when life is over?

Much Love, Long Walk

the WORD | John 19:32-34

"So the soldiers came, and broke the legs of the first man and of the other who was crucified with Him; but coming to Jesus, when they saw that He was already dead, they did not break His legs. But one of the soldiers pierced His side with a spear, and immediately blood and water came out."

the Message

Abigail was a missionary teaching African kids how to read, write, and understand Jesus. She spent time tutoring a nine-year old orphan boy, Eman. As the boy grew in his skills, he also grew to love his teacher who had given him the gift of knowledge.

One Christmas, Abigail taught the children about Jesus' birth, and Eman worried about what to give his teacher. Without any money, what could he do? Then he remembered reading about a rare seashell that could be found on a secluded beach three walking days from his hut. So a week before Christmas, Eman began his long walk of love.

Early on Christmas morning, the teacher heard a knock on her door. As she opened it, she saw the giant grin lighting up the boy's face. He opened his hand and presented his valuable and unusual gift.

"Oh, this is so beautiful! Where did you get it?" Abigail asked.

"Three days' walk down beach."

"Why? Why did you go get it for me?"

"Much love," Eman said and smiled again.

"I know, but you walked so far!" Abigail exclaimed in amazement.

And Eman humbly replied, "Much love, long walk."

Eman's love for his teacher reminds me of our Lord's love for His children. The day of His crucifixion was excruciating. The humiliation and pain Christ went through are unimaginable. The ordeal seemed to linger forever. Even after Jesus was dead, the soldiers still stabbed Him in the side.

And He endured it all out of love for us.

Discussion Starters:

* What does sacrifice have to do with love?
** What do you think was the longest part of Jesus' day of pain? Why?

Lifeline:

How can we, like Eman, sacrifice to thank Jesus for His incredible love?

He's Not Finished Yet

the WORD | John 20:1-2, 9-11

"Now on the first day of the week Mary Magdalene came early to the tomb, while it was still dark, and saw the stone already taken away from the tomb. So she ran and came to Simon Peter and to the other disciple whom Jesus loved, and said to them, 'They have taken away the Lord out of the tomb, and we do not know where they have laid Him.' ...For as yet they did not understand the Scripture, that He must rise again from the dead. So the disciples went away again to their own homes. But Mary was standing outside the tomb weeping; and so, as she wept, she stooped and looked into the tomb."

the Message

Dashed dreams. Everyone struggles with disappointment, even the most successful people. But losing a battle doesn't have to mean losing the fight. For example, did you know Abraham Lincoln lost at least six elections before he became one of the most famous presidents in U.S. history? Or that Michael Jordan was cut from his ninth-grade basketball team because he wasn't good enough? Even Joe Montana was knocked from the game "permanently" (so they said) before he led the 49ers to four Super Bowl championships.

And Jesus was buried as a dead man before He rose from the grave. No one thought He had a chance of rising on the third day. The stone was too heavy, the entrance too guarded. Jesus was dead, and His disciples all decided they'd just have to deal with it.

They were going to the tomb to mourn.

They got even more discouraged when they arrived. Someone had taken Jesus! It was another slap in the face.

Little did they understand what God was doing. The disciples didn't realize Jesus had risen and that His ascent to heaven had fulfilled the Scriptures. The fact that Jesus wasn't there even further backed up His claim to be the Son of God.

The disciples didn't get it. They thought their beloved Lord was gone forever. But Christ was already working in ways they couldn't see.

God is more powerful than your disappointments. He knows your dreams, and He won't leave you hanging.

I think the disciples would tell you that.

Discussion Starters:

• Why do you think God allowed the disciples to mourn His death?
•• What did Jesus promise the disciples about His death?

Lifeline:

Describe a time when God worked through your disappointments.

Wings

the **WORD** | John 20:27-29

"Then He said to Thomas, 'Reach here with your finger, and see My hands; and reach here your hand and put it into My side; and do not be unbelieving, but believing.' Thomas answered and said to Him, 'My Lord and my God!' Jesus said to him, 'Because you have seen Me, have you believed? Blessed are they who did not see, and yet believed.'"

the **Message**

Have you ever stood at the airport and watched the planes take off? Do you know how those big metal birds lift themselves off the ground? Well, when an airplane shoots down a runway, the wind rushing over the top of the wing creates a vacuum under it. The air that rushes up to fill the vacuum under the wing pushes the wing upward and gives the plane the lift it needs to get off the ground. If you didn't have that rushing air, you couldn't fly the friendly skies.

There's a good parallel here with our faith. Thomas had "wings." He knew Jesus intimately and should have had a faith that soared. He didn't have to run or do a bunch of work to activate his wings, but he needed to trust that Jesus would provide the wind and the lift.

Thomas wanted evidence. Like a baby bird, he stayed perched on the nest of familiarity. He was afraid to take that step of faith into the unknown. He wanted proof from Jesus before he'd exercise his wings.

You've got wings, too. The more you swiftly activate the wings—your faith—the higher you'll go. Jesus promised that. He knows you haven't seen Him, and He'll bless you for stepping out in faith.

How can you make your faith soar? By trusting God with your needs, hopes, and plans. By reading God's Word carefully and doing what it says, believing that God knows better than the world. By praying to God sincerely, with total dependence on Him.

Christians shouldn't be doubters.

Ask yourself some questions. Do you constantly worry about your life? Do you doubt God will come through in a crisis? Are you too self-reliant? Must you always see proof? Is it hard for you to release things?

The Lord knows it's tough to have faith. But you don't have to stay on the spiritual runway. If you'll trust Him, He will enable you to "mount up with wings like eagles" (Isaiah 40:31).

Discussion Starters:

* Why did Thomas need to touch Jesus to believe?
** How can you put faith in Jesus if you've never seen Him?
*** Why do you have to put your wings in motion before you can fly?

Lifeline:

Read Isaiah 40:28-31. How do Isaiah's words encourage your family?

Just Do It—Jesus' Way

the WORD | John 21:1, 3-6

"After these things Jesus manifested Himself again to the disciples at the Sea of Tiberias, and He manifested Himself in this way.... Simon Peter said [to the disciples], 'I am going fishing.' They said to him, 'We will also come with you.' They went out and got into the boat; and that night they caught nothing. But when the day was now breaking, Jesus stood on the beach; yet the disciples did not know that it was Jesus. So Jesus said to them, 'Children, you do not have any fish, do you?' They answered Him, 'No.' And He said to them, 'Cast the net on the right-hand side of the boat and you will find a catch.' So they cast, and then they were not able to haul it in because of the great number of fish."

the Message

There weren't any grocery stores back in biblical times. So when the disciples went fishing, they didn't go for fun—they went out of necessity.

All night they stood in that boat, casting their nets and waiting. Well, Jesus wasn't going to let them starve. Miraculously, He appeared just at the right time to help. The disciples obediently cast their nets on the right side of the boat and caught enough fish to feed the entire community.

Notice that Jesus told them to cast on the *right* side? That's the side He'll call His children to sit on when they enter heaven (see Matthew 25). When Jesus commands us to do things a certain way, there's always a reason. And since the disciples fished in God's way, they were rewarded.

Few of us fish for a living nowadays, but we do decide on which side of the boat to "cast our nets" in life. The left side is the world's way of fishing, or living. Drop your net there and you'll join the crowd in gossiping, cheating, lying, drinking, watching questionable movies, and taking advantage of others. Most people have fished on the left side of the boat. Often it feels good over there, but the net always comes up empty in the long run. You can't be truly successful fishing the way the world does.

Just as Jesus called the disciples to fish in His way, so He commands us to live in His way. We're still to live our lives on the right side of the boat—on His side. It might seem awkward. It might look as if everyone else is fishing on the left. You might feel as though you're not reaping any rewards. But although your catch might not always be in material possessions, it'll be eternally abundant.

Discussion Starters:

* What are the benefits of fishing on God's side of the boat?
** When is it tempting for you to fish on the world's side? Why?

Lifeline:

Together, make a list of what your family has gained from doing things God's way.

Desire

"So when they had finished breakfast, Jesus said to Simon Peter, 'Simon, son of John, do you love Me more than these?' He said to Him, 'Yes, Lord; You know that I love You.' He said to him, 'Tend My lambs.' He said to him again a second time, 'Simon, son of John, do you love Me?' He said to Him, 'Yes, Lord; You know that I love You.' He said to him, 'Shepherd My sheep.' He said to him the third time, 'Simon, son of John, do you love Me?' Peter was grieved because He said to him the third time, 'Do you love Me?' And he said to Him, 'Lord, You know all things; You know that I love You.' Jesus said to him, 'Tend My sheep.'"

the **Message**

A poor, young boy in India sought out a great Indian sage (wise man) to ask him a pressing question. When the boy found the sage, he said to him, "Sir, how might I find the kingdom of God?"

The sage looked carefully into the boy's eyes and said, "You don't want it bad enough."

The boy departed, greatly disappointed. But the next day he returned and asked, "Sir, how might I find the kingdom of God?"

Again the sage said, "Boy, you don't want it bad enough."

The third day, the boy repeated his question persistently.

So the sage replied, "Meet me at the river tomorrow."

The next day, the boy arrived at the river, ready for his answer. The sage walked into the water with the boy until they were waist deep. Then the man abruptly dunked the boy under the water and held him there until he ran out of breath. The boy jerked his head up, gasping for breath.

The old sage said to him, "Boy, when you were under the water, what did you want more than anything?"

"Oxygen, sir, oxygen. I wanted air!"

"Well, boy," the sage said, "when you desire the kingdom of God as much as you desired that breath, you'll find it!"

With his equally challenging words to Peter, Jesus asked His disciple to demonstrate his love for God by caring for His people. It's easy to say "I love God," but to show it to others takes great commitment and desire.

Discussion Starters:

* How can great desire enable you to love God by loving others more?
** What did Jesus mean when He said to Peter, "Tend My lambs"?
*** Why must we love others if we truly love Christ?

Lifeline:

Love begins at home. If it doesn't happen there, it can't truly happen anywhere.

acts

The book of Acts was written by Luke primarily as a historical account of the early church. It begins by documenting the risen Savior and His last discourse with His disciples and continues by focusing on the powerful work of the Holy Spirit. Luke emphasized the work of the early believers and their heroic quest to make Christ known to all the world.

This book is an encouragement for all of Christ's followers to utilize the power of the Holy Spirit who lives within us. If we are sensitive to God's Spirit we will live pure and purposeful lives that seek to bring others into a relationship with Jesus Christ.

Waiting

the WORD | Acts 1:4-8

"Gathering them together, He commanded them not to leave Jerusalem, but to wait for what the Father had promised, 'Which,' He said, 'you heard of from Me; for John baptized with water, but you will be baptized with the Holy Spirit not many days from now.' So when they had come together, they were asking Him, saying, 'Lord, is it at this time You are restoring the kingdom to Israel?' He said to them, 'It is not for you to know times or epochs which the Father has fixed by His own authority; but you will receive power when the Holy Spirit has come upon you; and you shall be My witnesses.'"

the Message

Waiting. I'm the world's worst sport when it comes to being patient! Red lights, grocery store lines, drive-thrus, and—I have to admit—God's promises can all get me frustrated if they don't fit into my schedule.

The disciples were weary and impatient from Israel's long years of political unrest. And since Jesus had been crucified, they were understandably worried about what would happen to them. *Who will be the next to hang on the Roman cross?* they wondered. They wanted an end to it all and knew that if Jesus set up His kingdom, their fears would be gone.

"C'mon, Jesus, set up Your kingdom. Let us rule with You," they said.

"Wait," was His disappointing reply. "God promises He'll be with you. That's all you need to know. I told you I'll be back, and I told you My Spirit would come to live inside you. Now wait. Believe and wait."

Like the disciples, we, too, know a lot about waiting for God. Growing up requires lots of believing and waiting, doesn't it?

"Sex is for marriage only," God says. "Wait. It's best that way."

"I want you to be happy, so leave drugs and alcohol alone. I'll bring all the joy you need. Wait on Me."

"I know you need direction in your life, and you want the answers right now. But I'll guide you. Wait and listen for My voice."

It's tough to be patient. But God will bless us when we wait. The disciples were patient, and God sent His Spirit. Together, they changed the world.

You can, too—if you wait for God's hand on your life.

Discussion Starters:

• How can God enable you to wait on Him?
  •• What other biblical figures had patience and waited on the Lord? How did God reward them?

Lifeline:

Ask the Holy Spirit to help your family *wait* for God's best in your lives.

A Mistaken Case of the Wobbles

the **WORD** | Acts 2:4-6, 12-13

"And they were all filled with the Holy Spirit and began to speak with other tongues, as the Spirit was giving them utterance. Now there were Jews living in Jerusalem, devout men from every nation under heaven. And when this sound occurred, the crowd came together, and were bewildered because each one of them was hearing them speak in his own language.... And they all continued in amazement and great perplexity, saying to one another, 'What does this mean?' But others were mocking and saying, 'They are full of sweet wine.'"

the Message

Phil, a college student, loved Jesus, Carol, and a good laugh. One night in October, Phil took Carol out for a date. They arrived at the Beta Theta Pi house, where the fraternity was putting on its annual skit night. Sitting on the lawn were at least 100 students crammed knee to knee, watching the frat boys ham it up for their peers. Everyone was having a blast.

Except Phil. He'd been squeezed into the center of the crowd, sitting cross-legged for much too long. He and Carol decided to leave early. They stood up, brushed the backside of their jeans, and prepared to go.

Then it happened. Phil fell straight into the lap of a muscle-bound Theta. But even worse, Phil couldn't get up. He rolled off the Theta and ended up whacking a sorority girl in the face as he tried to stand.

"What are you—drunk?" the Theta shouted.

The crowd joined in with the accusations. They didn't know Phil's foot had fallen asleep. And they'd never understood that Phil's joyful attitude came from Christ—not alcohol. So they decided he'd been drinking.

The disciples were also misunderstood. The crowd at the Pentecost couldn't grasp the power of the Holy Spirit. When the disciples were given the gift of speaking in tongues, they, too, were mistaken for being drunk.

If you're a Christian, a lot of people will misunderstand you. Having the gifts of the Spirit or the joy of God won't make sense to others. They won't comprehend that as a child of God, the Lord lives in you.

When that happens, don't worry. As He did with Peter, the Holy Spirit will give you the words to say to those who don't believe.

Discussion Starters:

• How did Peter refute the accusation that the disciples were drunk (see verses 14-22)?

•• Besides speaking in tongues, what are the other gifts of the Spirit (see 1 Corinthians 12)?

Lifeline:

Will you let God's Spirit rule your life, even if it makes you look different?

Taking Notes

the WORD | Acts 3:2-4, 6-7

"And a man who had been lame from his mother's womb was being carried along, whom they used to set down every day at the gate of the temple which is called Beautiful, in order to beg alms of those who were entering the temple. When he saw Peter and John about to go into the temple, he began asking to receive alms. But Peter, along with John, fixed his gaze on him and said, 'Look at us!'… But Peter said, 'I do not possess silver and gold, but what I do have I give to you: In the name of Jesus Christ the Nazarene—walk!' And seizing him by the right hand, he raised him up; and immediately his feet and his ankles were strengthened."

the Message

A root canal. A disloyal friend. Losing a job. Pain is an inevitable part of life. And there are few things more painful than hearing a sermon on charitable giving. We fidget, sweat, and squirm under the pastor's gaze. No matter how much we try to avoid eye contact, the minister still seems to stare straight into our hearts and wallets.

Now, the preacher enjoys the experience even less than we do. Nevertheless, he knows that—like the lame man in Acts 3:5—the needy are looking to the church, expecting help from us. And like Peter and John, we have two options. We can try to meet their needs, or we can keep walking.

If we do pass them by, we're not exactly being obedient to Jesus' command to "feed His sheep." As Christians, we're called to reach out to others less fortunate by giving our time, money, and love. When we help others, we're revealing Jesus and His power.

You may not have gold or silver, but you do have a powerful Savior. And everyone, especially the poor and hungry, deserves to hear about Him and what He's done for us. People need to know the saving grace of Jesus.

As Peter and John did, we're to give of ourselves and allow others the chance to hear the gospel. When we do, the world around us will be taking notes on Christian charity. What notes are they taking on you?

Discussion Starters:

• Peter and John were going to the temple to pray. How can prayer be an act of service? How do we give to others through prayer?

•• How did Peter and John use their charitable act to point to the incredible charity of the Crucifixion?

Lifeline:

Make your monthly financial giving a family experience. Pray together for the ministries you help before you mail the checks. And discuss with your kids the importance of giving from their money, too.

Drivers' Ed

the WORD | Acts 3:17-18

"And now, brethren, I know that you [crucified Jesus] in ignorance, just as your rulers did also. But the things which God announced beforehand by the mouth of all the prophets, that His Christ should suffer, He has thus fulfilled."

the Message

"Ignorance is no excuse." Every day, that statement is proved true all over the highways and streets of this world.

Driver: "Sixty-eight! Gee, officer, I thought I was only doing 55."

Police officer: "Son, this is a 25 mph school zone. Did you miss the sign?"

Driver: "Um...I guess."

Police officer: "Did you miss the swing set?"

Driver: "Er...yes."

Police officer: "The slides? The teeter-totters? The bright yellow buses?"

Driver: "Well..."

Police officer: "What exactly *did* you see?"

Driver: "I saw the building—just before I hit it!"

Ignorance is no excuse for irresponsibility, even more so for Christians. If we don't talk about the Lord, every day people will speed a little closer to the brick-hard realities of hell.

The apostles Peter and John didn't just stand by, watching humanity collide with destiny. They warned the people about the consequences of their wicked ways. They told them how to avoid disaster.

Peter and John made sure everyone knew about Jesus. You have the same responsibility. How are you educating your fellow travelers?

Discussion Starters:

• What's the difference between being ignorant of Christ and outright denying Him? Give some examples.

•• Who do you know that claims to be ignorant of Christ? How can you educate him or her?

Lifeline:

Role-play presenting the gospel to one another. Anticipate questions and objections, and help one another form a clear plan of evangelism. Then pray for the people to whom you'll be witnessing.

The Educated Fool

| Acts 4:8-10, 12-14

"Then Peter, filled with the Holy Spirit, said to them, 'Rulers and elders of the people, if we are on trial today for a benefit done to a sick man, as to how this man has been made well, let it be known...that by the name of Jesus Christ...this man stands here before you in good health.... And there is salvation in no one else; for there is no other name under heaven that has been given among men by which we must be saved.' Now as they observed the confidence of Peter and John and understood that they were uneducated and untrained men, they were amazed and began to recognize them as having been with Jesus. And seeing the man who had been healed standing with them, they had nothing to say in reply."

the **Message**

There are many smart people in this world. Look at John, who lives in my town. This pastor holds theological degrees from prestigious colleges and sits on synod committees that shape the thinking of his entire denomination. In a lot of ways, John is a great guy. But although he's respected by many, John's an educated fool. Every Sunday, he puts on his robe, pounds his pulpit, and demonstrates the little respect he has for God's Word. He twists and alters Scripture to maintain his popularity with his congregation and to fit his own faith. His faith is intellectual—not heartfelt.

Chuck was also an educated fool. He was president of his fraternity in the late '70s and even a member of the student council and the Blue Key organization. Chuck was handsome, athletic, popular, and smart. He almost had a double major in German and marketing. But he wasn't smart about everything. In the spring of '79, he drank himself to death at a rush party.

Peter and John, on the other hand, never had a lick of schooling. In fact, their educational shortcomings were glaring. They were simple men with simple solutions. No degrees. No robes. No impressive titles. But the Pharisees and learned scholars looked at them and marveled. Why? Because Peter and John were so confident and eloquent, and there was no mistaking that they had been Jesus' disciples.

You don't need to be a scholar to talk confidently and accurately—as the disciples did—about Jesus. Christ will give you all the knowledge you need to witness. You'll never be a fool if you hang with Him!

Discussion Starters:

- How could the Pharisees tell that Peter and John had been "with Jesus"?
  - Peter's sermon was short. Why was it so powerful?
    - Which Christians do you admire for their deep knowledge of God? Why?

Lifeline:

Does your family know Christ as Peter and John did?

All Lies Are Big

the WORD | Acts 5:1-5

"But a man named Ananias, with his wife Sapphira, sold a piece of property, and kept back some of the price for himself, with his wife's full knowledge, and bringing a portion of it, he laid it at the apostles' feet. But Peter said, 'Ananias, why has Satan filled your heart to lie to the Holy Spirit and to keep back some of the price of the land?... You have not lied to men but to God.' And as he heard these words, Ananias fell down and breathed his last; and great fear came over all who heard of it...[and the same happened to Sapphira, his wife]."

the Message

Have you ever wondered why we use the words "falling in love" to describe such a blissful state? "Falling in love" sounds so painful.

Kent fell hard when he was 14. Like all the boys in his eighth-grade class, Kent thought Sharon was a goddess. Unfortunately, Sharon had her eye on Andy, which made Kent wonder what Andy had that he *didn't*.

Soon Kent figured it out. Andy had a broken leg!

Girls must fall for guys who are injured! Kent deduced. So he quickly settled on the least painful way to injure himself.

"I'm getting my tonsils out this weekend," he told Sharon on Friday.

"Oh! That sounds awful!" Sharon said with more sympathy than she'd ever shown him. "I hope it doesn't hurt too bad."

Of course, Kent soon realized that his lie had put him in a terrible mess. So that December night, Kent stripped down to his T-shirt, went out into the backyard, and screamed until he was hoarse. At any rate, by Monday, Kent definitely sounded as if he'd had his tonsils removed.

Now, I'd love to tell you Kent got the girl. But he didn't. Andy won Sharon's affection. Kent got a wonderful case of pneumonia.

As Kent discovered, lying will always backfire on you. If the person you lied to doesn't discover your fib, God always will. You can't pull *any* wool over God's eyes; even a half-lie will be found out. And if Ananias and Sapphira were still alive, they'd tell you the same thing.

Discussion Starters:

* How was Ananias and Sapphira's lie only a "half-lie"?
** What were the consequences of their lie? How did others respond?
*** When is it tempting for you to lie? Why? How can you avoid lying?

Lifeline:

Promise one another to be honest at all times in your household. Then decide together what the consequences will be for dishonesty. (Parents should ensure those consequences are administered immediately and effectively.)

Suffering Shame for His Name

the **WORD** | Acts 5:17-18, 29, 33, 40-41

"But the high priest rose up, along with all his associates (that is the sect of the Sadducees), and they were filled with jealousy. They laid hands on the apostles and put them in a public jail.... [And after they'd escaped,] Peter and the apostles answered [the priest and Council], 'We must obey God rather than men.' ...But when they heard this, they were cut to the quick and intended to kill them.... [Instead] they took [Gamaliel's] advice; and after calling the apostles in, they flogged them and ordered them not to speak in the name of Jesus, and then released them. So they went on their way from the presence of the Council, rejoicing that they had been considered worthy to suffer shame for His name."

the Message

Persecution didn't just take place in biblical times. In fact, today 2.5 billion people are denied freedom of religion, and 1 million are imprisoned because of their faith. More Christians have been persecuted for their beliefs in the twentieth century than in any other century.[1]

Ha Sieng, of Vietnam, is an evangelical Christian preacher who endured a life-threatening beating when police arrested him for preaching the gospel in 1996. Sieng had been repeatedly warned by the police to stop evangelizing the Koho people, a poor tribe that lives in the central highlands of Vietnam. But Sieng adamantly refused to quit preaching and wouldn't hand over any Bibles or spiritual books to the authorities. For that, he was whacked with a heavy iron rod for seven straight days. On the last day, his body couldn't bear the pain any longer, and he passed out.

The police sent him home, and soon after, he fell into a coma. Sieng became delirious, and hospital authorities told his wife that Sieng might never regain consciousness or be his normal self again.

Miraculously, he left the hospital a few weeks later, completely well. Despite the terrible suffering Sieng endured, he still continues his work undaunted. He claims that neither laws nor persecution will stop him from telling people about Jesus Christ. And to date, about one-third of the 150,000 Koho people have become Christians as a result of Sieng's work.

Many of them believed because of Sieng's strength in suffering.[2]

Discussion Starters:

* Why is it important to rejoice when we suffer for God?
* * Have you ever suffered for your beliefs? If so, when?

Lifeline:

People are often persecuted today for speaking the truth. Make a pact that your family will always follow God's Word, no matter what.

Every Busboy Has His Day

the **WORD** | Acts 6:8, 10, 12, 15

"And Stephen [one of the deacons], full of grace and power, was performing great wonders and signs among the people.... But they were unable to cope with the wisdom and the Spirit with which he was speaking.... And they stirred up the people, the elders and the scribes, and they came up to him and dragged him away and brought him before the Council.... And fixing their gaze on him, all who were sitting in the Council saw his face like the face of an angel."

the **Message**

One summer, I ate in the same restaurant, at the same table, by the same window, every day. I always ordered chocolate pie for dessert. I always read the paper with my pie. And I always said hello to Frank, the redheaded busboy who cleared my table.

Frank and I got to be friends. So of course I missed him when one day I noticed he was no longer working at the restaurant.

"Oh, Frank's still here," my waitress said when I asked about him. "That's him back there in the kitchen. He's a prep cook now. The hours are a little earlier. The pay's a little better. You understand."

I understood perfectly. The boy was moving up in the world.

Ten years have passed, and Frank has long since left his cook position. After three other kitchen jobs, a stint behind the cash register, and a year and a half of management, the boy has become a man—and part owner of one of America's fastest-growing restaurant chains.

At one point, Stephen was also a strong, silent, behind-the-scenes server. As one of the support deacons, his main responsibilities were far from the limelight. But when God planted him in the Council to testify about Jesus, he amazed and angered people with his grace, knowledge, and eloquence. The crowd was shocked to see that Stephen, the "blue-collar deacon," had the face of an angel.

Work hard where God has placed you, and do your best to follow His will. In the meantime, remember this: Every busboy—every silent server—has his or her day. Serve well, and God will bless you.

By His Spirit, He will make you great.

Discussion Starters:

* Quiet servants still have an obligation to speak up for Christ. When it was Stephen's turn to speak, what inner qualities aided him?

** Where do you think Stephen acquired his incredible wisdom?

*** What is your definition of godly "greatness"? How can you attain it?

Lifeline:

Pray for grace and power as you serve in God's world today.

"Hey! Taxi!"

the WORD | Acts 7:51-53

"You men who are stiff-necked and uncircumcised in heart and ears are always resisting the Holy Spirit; you are doing just as your fathers did. Which one of the prophets did your fathers not persecute? They killed those who had previously announced the coming of the Righteous One, whose betrayers and murderers you have now become; you who received the law as ordained by angels, and yet did not keep it."

the Message

I was standing outside the airport recently and heard a man calling a cab. "Hey! Taxi!" he shouted as the yellow car pulled forward. The taxi stopped, the man got in, and quickly he drove off in the rain.

But his two words, *Hey! Taxi!* remained with me. They reminded me of a painful time in my childhood. See, I was born with ears the size of Africa, just like my dad, who took after *his* dad, who took after *his* dad. Our ears go back centuries, to the time when real men carried clubs.

It's hard for me to hear the word *taxi* without cringing. When I was in sixth grade, Tommy Kite said my ears made me look like a taxi going down the street with its doors open. Tommy was twice my size, so I never said anything back, and eventually, most of the sting went away. But since that day, I've always grown my hair fairly long—especially on the sides. My ears are still a big part of my inheritance I'd love to hide.

In some ways, we're all an extension of our families. I inherited my dad's big ears. My son got my skill in football. And the religious people Stephen spoke to had inherited their parents' rebellious, godless, hypocritical natures. Unfortunately, they were still so blind that they couldn't accept the truth of who they'd become. So they stoned Stephen for being honest (see Acts 7:54-60).

The reality is, we've all inherited a little doubt, deceitfulness, and dishonor. But we have a choice. We can break from the problems of the past and follow God as others before us should have done, or we can continue old patterns and walk in the footsteps of our not-so-good Israelite ancestors. What heritage will your family leave behind?

Discussion Starters:

* We inherit both good and bad attributes from our parents. In what ways are you like your stiff-necked, hard-hearted Israelite ancestors?
  ** As Stephen pointed out earlier in his speech, the Israelites built golden calves. What "idols" do you focus on in your life?

Lifeline:

Ask God to help you break from the negative parts of your past.

Passing Down the Tie

"Now in Joppa there was a disciple named Tabitha (which translated in Greek is called Dorcas); this woman was abounding with deeds of kindness and charity which she continually did. And it happened at that time that she fell sick and died; and when they had washed her body, they laid it in an upper room. So Peter arose and went with them. When he arrived, they brought him into the upper room; and all the widows stood beside him weeping and showing all the tunics and garments that Dorcas used to make while she was with them. But Peter sent them all out and knelt down and prayed, and turning to the body, he said, 'Tabitha, arise.' And she opened her eyes, and when she saw Peter, she sat up."

the *Message*

Our actions should always point back to God's glory and goodness. Peter's did. When he raised Tabitha from the dead through the power of God, Peter was imitating the ministry of his Lord, Jesus Christ. Peter's decision to model Jesus reminds me of an incident that took place not so long ago.

In the back of the van, Grayson was in tears.

"What's wrong?" my son Cooper asked as we sped toward the kids' Christian school, 20 miles away.

"I forgot my tie! I f-f-forgot my tie!" blubbered Grayson.

Cooper immediately knew why the boy was so upset. You see, at Riverview Baptist School, Tuesdays are chapel days. And forgetting to wear a tie spells "D-E-M-E-R-I-T." To a boy as sensitive as Grayson, getting a demerit is as bad as getting the death penalty. Cooper considered the consequences, then slowly removed his own tie.

"Here, Grayson," said Cooper. "You can wear mine."

Grayson's face lit up.

It was moving to witness Cooper's act of compassion. But the best part about the incident was that four years earlier, my elder son, Brady White, had done the same thing for Cooper. (Way to go, guys!)

There are countless opportunities to imitate Christ's ministry of compassion. How can you model God's love to those around you?

Discussion Starters:

- Why did Peter send the crowds outside before he raised Tabitha?
- How well are you imitating Christ these days? Explain.

Lifeline:

Think of a Christian brother or sister who has been kind to you in the past. Imitate that kindness as soon as you have the opportunity.

Just a Man!

the **WORD** | Acts 10:25-26

"When Peter entered, Cornelius met him, and fell at his feet and worshiped him. But Peter raised him up, saying, 'Stand up; I too am just a man.' "

the **Message**

I'm always impressed with humility—especially when I see it in people who have reason to brag.

The late U.S. Senator Stuart Symington used to breeze through Kamp—and I do mean *breeze*. He brought a freshness and love of life. He never put on any stuffy airs or acted important. Stuart just blended in to the point that when you went looking for him, he was difficult to locate.

You'd never find him signing autographs for the campers. He'd never be seen giving impressive speeches. Not Stuart. We usually found him in the kitchen, with his sleeves rolled up and his forearms plunged into a sink full of suds. This politician, who could probably afford 10 maids, would be cleaning pots and pans!

He wasn't campaigning for votes because he wasn't running for anything. Stuart was simply a man who loved God and people, plain and simple. Senator Stuart Symington modeled the humility and grace of Jesus, his Lord and Savior.

Maybe in the world's eyes, you have a reason to flaunt your feathers. Maybe you're the most popular kid in school, a talented musician, or a young Einstein. If you've been given gifts or popularity, thank God for those blessings, and be humble. You can't manufacture your gifts. The Lord is responsible for every one of them (see James 1:17).

That's why when Cornelius fell to the floor, Peter said, "Get up!" Peter knew he was just a man. Any strength or power he had was from God.

All glory should go to God. He's the only One who deserves to be exalted. Next time you're complimented, don't pat yourself on the back. Humbly give God the praise.

Discussion Starters:

• How do you think Peter felt when Cornelius began to worship him?
•• What does Cornelius's reaction reveal about the culture in which he lived?
••• What's the difference between having low self-esteem and being humble?

Lifeline:

Have each family member name someone they know who is humble and Christlike. What qualities does he or she have that make him or her that way? How can you learn to be more humble, too?

It's Big News

"But Peter began speaking and proceeded to explain to them in orderly sequence, saying, 'I was in the city of Joppa praying; and in a trance I saw a vision, an object coming down like a great sheet lowered by four corners from the sky; and it came right down to me, and when I had fixed my gaze on it and was observing it I saw the four-footed animals of the earth and the wild beasts and the crawling creatures and the birds of the air. I also heard a voice saying to me, "Get up, Peter; kill and eat."'"

the *Message*

God is imaginative. He finds all sorts of ways to speak to us—through friends, books, sermons, the Bible, and even, as Peter found, in dreams. My friend Whit would tell you that, too. This author spent two years writing a novel, and a week before its publication date, he had a dream.

"I've got big news!" his editor said over the phone in Whit's dream.

Whit smiled and rolled over in bed. *I must be a Pulitzer Prize candidate. Why else would he call?* Whit thought.

"We're not going to publish your novel," came the voice.

At that, Whit woke up and told his wife the story. They both laughed, reassuring themselves it was only a dream.

But the next day, Whit's editor did call. "I've got big news for you," he said. "Your book is canned."

Whit could've been mad. But he trusted God. Just six months after his novel was canceled, the largest Christian publisher in the nation printed it.

Sometimes dreams are big news, indeed! Peter's dream/vision sure was. God intentionally spoke to him in that vision and, as we discussed before, He changed society through it. What if Peter hadn't listened to God's voice? What if he'd just decided his mind was playing tricks on him? Fortunately, Peter knew God well enough to recognize that it was the Lord talking—he wasn't just going crazy.

God will often communicate to us in creative ways. Be prepared. Study Him and His methods. Otherwise, you'll never know when He's sending you a message. And when God talks, it's *always* big news.

Discussion Starters:

* How did the people respond to Peter's dream (see Acts 11:18)?
    ** How can we tell if God is speaking to us through our dreams?
   *** In what ways does God speak to you about important things?

Lifeline:

Describe another time in Scripture where God spoke to someone through a dream. What was He trying to say? How did the person respond?

What Were You Thinking?

| Acts 12:13-16, 18-19

"When [Peter] knocked at the door of the gate, a servant girl named Rhoda came to answer. When she recognized Peter's voice, because of her joy she did not open the gate, but ran in and announced that Peter was standing in front of the gate. They said to her, 'You are out of your mind!' But she kept insisting that it was so. They kept saying, 'It is his angel.' But Peter continued knocking; and when they had opened the door, they saw him and were amazed.... Now when day came, there was no small disturbance among the soldiers as to what could have become of Peter. When Herod had searched for him and had not found him, he examined the guards and ordered that they be led away to execution."

the Message

One winter, Seth was skiing in Colorado, tackling an expert slope. When he was just 30 yards from the end of the run, Seth saw a familiar brunette standing in the lift line. Actually, he saw only a tuft of brown hair sticking out from under a ski cap. But Seth was so overjoyed that he overlooked the fact that the skier was hidden beneath layers of thermal clothing. He was sure it was Valerie, the prettiest girl at his university.

"Valerie!" Seth shouted, elated to bump into her so far from home. Unfortunately, he didn't check his speed, and he *did* bump into her—or rather, *him*. When Seth looked up, he realized he'd mistaken a 40-year-old man for the cutest girl on campus. Seth's ego was shattered.

As Seth found, joy can make you impulsive. The servant girl who heard Peter at the door got so excited that she forgot about Peter, leaving him out in the cold—right where Herod's men could have found him. She wasn't thinking clearly, and her jubilation actually endangered Peter's life.

Emotions are great! God created them. But they need to be tempered with sound judgment. When you let your feelings run wild, it becomes easier to say yes to sex and no to God, to be self-absorbed and forget your friends' needs, and to dismiss your promises to the Lord.

In the heat of the moment, call on God. Ask Him to help you make a sound decision. It's important. Your feelings will come and go, but what comes from them—the results of your decisions—will stay with you forever.

Discussion Starters:

* Why are impulsive acts (like the servant girl's) sometimes dangerous?
** How can you let God take control of your feelings?

Lifeline:

Does anyone in your family have an important decision to make? If so, pray together that God would enable him or her to use godly discretion.

Pray Fast!

the WORD | Acts 13:1-3

"Now there were at Antioch, in the church that was there, prophets and teachers: Barnabas, and Simeon who was called Niger, and Lucius of Cyrene, and Manaen who had been brought up with Herod the tetrarch, and Saul. While they were ministering to the Lord and fasting, the Holy Spirit said, 'Set apart for Me Barnabas and Saul for the work to which I have called them.' Then, when they had fasted and prayed and laid their hands on them, they sent them away."

the Message

Wouldn't it be great if our relationship with the Lord was so intimate that we always heard His instructions clearly and obeyed Him? We'd know exactly where to go to college, what job to take, which friends to hang with, what things we should be doing.

Of course, no Christian has a perfect pipeline to God. But the Bible does prescribe some things for us to do that will open the channels of communication with Him—in particular, prayer and fasting.

Now, most of us confuse prayer and fasting with praying fast so we can get on with the meal. We say, "God is great, God is good. Lord, we thank You for this food. Let's eat!"

But that's not how the Bible portrays the disciplines of prayer and fasting at all. There are times when we must empty our stomachs in order to receive spiritual food from heaven.

Paul and Barnabas knew that. They'd been fasting and praying with the prophets and teachers in Antioch when the Holy Spirit spoke to them.

"I've prepared Paul and Barnabas to do My work. I want them to go preach the gospel," the Spirit said.

It was clear God had spoken, and the church leaders understood what He wanted. So right away, they sent Paul and Barnabas on a worldwide (well, almost) missionary journey.

Those first-century Christians didn't have a perfect relationship with God—but they knew that when they prayed and fasted, the Holy Spirit would give them direction.

Discussion Starters:

• Paul and Barnabas were sent out after they'd spent a lot of time praying and fasting. How did doing this help the disciples to discern the Holy Spirit's guidance?

•• How does praying and fasting enable us to make better decisions?

Lifeline:

Next time your family is facing a big decision, choose a day to fast and pray. Then use the time you'd normally eat to consult God about the matter. The following day, break the fast and share your insights with each other.

Whom Do You Fear?

the W**O**RD | Acts 13:26, emphasis added

"[Paul said to the people,] 'Brethren, sons of Abraham's family, and *those among you who fear God,* to us the message of this salvation has been sent.' "

the Message

Parachuting, bungee jumping, cliff diving, and hang gliding may sound really exciting to you. I'm so afraid of heights, though, that I'd rather fight a rattlesnake than do any of those things.

What scares you? Spiders? Car accidents? Earthquakes? Big dogs? What about God?

I'm not afraid of God any more than I'm afraid of the picturesque Table Rock Lake that we play on at our sports camps. We jet ski, sail, kayak, wind surf, and do a zillion other fun sports on that lake. But let me tell you, we deeply respect Table Rock. Why? A few years ago, Ricky, a 19-year-old dear friend of mine, drowned in that lake. One minute he was playing sports, and the next minute he was gone. Ricky didn't respect that the lake had the potential to take his life. He went out by himself at night—when he shouldn't have—and was caught in some of the lake's thick reeds.

It's a poor comparison, but I respect God in the same way I respect that lake. God is my Father, my almighty Lord and Savior. There's no comparison to what I can do and what God can accomplish through His enormous power. But His power and holiness don't make me afraid of Him—those qualities cause me to respect Him immensely.

God doesn't want you to tremble when you pray or be afraid to spend time with Him. But He does want you to honor Him and His ways. One way to do that is to turn your back on evil (see Proverbs 8:13). Evil is anything that defies God and His Word. So because I love and fear God, I choose—every day—to walk away from evil of any kind: evil movies, TV, music, and magazines; evil thoughts, motives, and lies.

God will bless your socks off when you fear Him. When you respect the living God, He'll give you abundant life (see Proverbs 14:27).

Discussion Starters:

* Why must we respect God if we claim to fear Him? How do respect for and fear of God go hand in hand?
  ** Why do only those who fear God understand the gospel message?
  *** Why does Proverbs say that when you fear the Lord, you'll hate evil?

Lifeline:

Discuss God's different characteristics. What makes you respect, honor, and fear Him? How can your family encourage a healthy fear of the Lord?

Home Base

the WORD | Acts 14:21, 25-28

"After they had preached the gospel to that city and had made many disciples, they returned to Lystra and to Iconium and to Antioch.... When they had spoken the word in Perga, they went down to Attalia. From there they sailed to Antioch, from which they had been commended to the grace of God for the work that they had accomplished. When they had arrived and gathered the church together, they began to report all things that God had done with them and how He had opened a door of faith to the Gentiles. And they spent a long time with the disciples."

the Message

Dorothy was right about one thing—there's no place like home!

About 25 years ago, I left my boyhood home in Texas. But last week, I did something I've wanted to do for a long time. I went to Texas and took a nostalgic four-mile run up and down the streets where I grew up.

I jogged by my elementary school and reminisced about Mrs. Manning, my dear first-grade teacher, who once cracked my knuckles with a yardstick. (I deserved it.) I passed my junior high girlfriend's house, remembering when she dropped me for my best friend. (So much for that!) As I got closer to home, my heart quickened. In my mind, I could see the yard I mowed, the pond where I caught crawdads, and the dog pen I built.

When I reached my boyhood home, I became overwhelmed with memories. I could picture Mom in the kitchen, loving us with her good Texas hospitality. I saw Dad out on the old baseball field behind the house, teaching me to play catch. At least a dozen memories flooded me.

That jog back home was one of the greatest adventures of my life. Our house wasn't perfect. But it was and always will be home base to me.

Paul and Barnabas also knew the value of home. After their journeys, they returned to Antioch. For them, it was a place where they could rest, catch up with the disciples they loved, and report to the church on their ministry. Their travels were grueling. They needed the support of home.

Be sure your family makes its home an encouraging environment. The world can be tough. Allow God to turn your home into a retreat.

Discussion Starters:

• Why was it so important for Paul and Barnabas to return to Antioch?
   •• What did they do when they arrived back home?

Lifeline:

Paul and Barnabas spent a lot of time with the disciples at their home base in Antioch. Make one night this week a family night at home. Play a game. Talk. Pray. Tell jokes. Discuss a video. Enjoy some quality time together.

A Weighty Matter

the WORD | Acts 15:1, 7, 10-11, 19-20

"Some men came down from Judea and began teaching the brethren, 'Unless you are circumcised according to the custom of Moses, you cannot be saved.' ...After there had been much debate, Peter stood up and said to them,... 'Why do you put God to the test by placing upon the neck of the disciples a yoke which neither our fathers nor we have been able to bear? But we believe that we are saved through the grace of the Lord Jesus, in the same way as they also are.... Therefore it is my judgment that we do not trouble those who are turning to God from among the Gentiles, but that we write to them that they abstain from things contaminated by idols and from fornication and from what is strangled and from blood.' "

the Message

Brad's mom often warned him not to lift weights alone. But Brad always said, "Aw, Mom, I can take care of myself." Then he'd smile and point to his biceps. "Look at these guns! I'm invincible!"

One day, when Brad was home alone, he went for a personal weightlifting record. He didn't have the proper equipment, so he balanced the weights on two stacks of encyclopedias. Lying on the floor between A and Z, Brad bench-pressed 250 pounds *10 times*! But when he lowered the weights, the books fell over, and the bar pinned his throat to the floor.

Brad was too tired to move it off, so he inched along the floor, rolling the bar as he moved toward a phone on a corner table. He reached the table, yanked the phone's cord, and the phone crashed down on his head. He groaned, then dialed his neighbor. But Brad's mother got home first. She lugged the weights off her son, wrapped his head in a towel, and drove to the hospital, chuckling inside at her "invincible" son with the weird turban.

Strapped and weighted down. For years, the Pharisees made religion out to be a burden. The apostles didn't want Christianity to be a weighty matter, though. They knew Jesus had saved people by grace, not by burdensome works. So they made careful decisions about what Christians should be required to do, and they focused on the core issues of the faith.

Next time you feel trapped by rule-based religion, remember that Jesus' message was plain and simple What you do for God is important, but what He did for you on the cross matters more. Following burdensome rules won't help you get to heaven—but having a deep faith in Jesus will.

Discussion Starters:

* How do you think the disciples decided what was important?
  ** How are we saved by grace? How should works fit in with our faith?

Lifeline:

Read 1 John 5:3. Why isn't it a burden to keep God's commandments?

Bad Things and Good People

"When [the chief magistrates] had struck [Paul and Silas] with many blows, they threw them into prison, commanding the jailer to guard them securely.... But about midnight Paul and Silas were praying and singing hymns of praise to God, and the prisoners were listening to them; and suddenly there came a great earthquake...and immediately all the doors were opened and everyone's chains were unfastened. When the jailer... saw the prison doors opened, he drew his sword and was about to kill himself, supposing that the prisoners had escaped. But Paul cried out with a loud voice, saying, 'Do not harm yourself, for we are all here!' ...And after he brought [Paul and Silas] out, he said, 'Sirs, what must I do to be saved?' They said, 'Believe in the Lord Jesus, and you shall be saved, you and your household.'"

the Message

I was married my junior year in college and faithfully loved my wife for 14 months. I was a college football player, and the life was fun and glamorous. But when I graduated and began working, my wife fell in love with my best friend and left me. After a few months, they were married.

I cried for months—I was heartbroken, without hope. But by God's grace, I never got bitter or blamed either of them. I still respect them both and realize now that I could have been a much better husband and friend.

You know what? I survived! And after I'd healed, God led me to Debbie Jo, my life-time bride and the mother of our four kids, whom I *adore*. Every year I love Debbie Jo more than I first did 25 years ago.

God hates divorce. It's totally wrong. God wants men and women to marry for life. But God is merciful and gracious, able to work through any circumstance and bring good from it (see Romans 8:28). He did in my case.

Bad things *do* happen to good people. Paul and Silas didn't have it easy. They were beaten, mocked, and jailed for preaching the gospel. But although Satan might have worked to get them behind bars, God had the last word. That night in prison, the jailer and his household accepted Christ.

God doesn't cause the messes in our lives, but He uses them to draw us closer to Him. He worked through my difficulty and Paul and Silas's crisis, and He'll bring good from your problems, too. Do you believe that?

Discussion Starters:

- Name three good things that came from Paul and Silas's imprisonment.
- What do you think was the purpose of the earthquake?
- How do we grow closer to God through tough times?

Lifeline:

Describe a time when God used a crisis to bless you and others as well.

When Reason Fails

the WORD | Acts 17:1-3

"Now when they had traveled through Amphipolis and Apollonia, they came to Thessalonica, where there was a synagogue of the Jews. And according to Paul's custom, he went to them, and for three Sabbaths reasoned with them from the Scriptures, explaining and giving evidence that the Christ had to suffer and rise again from the dead, and saying, 'This Jesus whom I am proclaiming to you is the Christ.'"

the Message

I like to debate with evolutionists. I try to reason with them about the pitfalls and problems the evolutionary theory poses. To the scientist who believes Piltdown Man was the bridge between ape and Adam, I'll say, "That's impossible. Fifty years after its discovery, Piltdown Man was proved to be the clever combination of an ape jawbone and a modern human skull, planted as a fossil to fool the experts." To the scientist who believes Nebraska Man was the missing link, I'll remark, "Hold your horses. We can't base our beliefs about the existence of humanity on a single pig's tooth found in a Nebraska cornfield."

Unfortunately, my reasoning with the scientific elite usually has little effect on them. They go on believing in pig teeth and monkey mandibles because that's what they want to believe.

I could talk to these staunch evolutionists until I was blue in the face, but I've realized that even reason has its limits. Paul discovered this when he tried to reason with the Jews at Thessalonica. Sure, he may have persuaded some of them to join the faith. But the rest of the Jews mobbed Paul and even tried to hurt his friends. Nevertheless (as the book of Acts reveals), Paul continued his custom of reasoning with the Jews and kept trying to convince them to follow Christ. And as his letters to various churches reveal, Paul never ceased to pray for them.

You, too, might have friends who don't support your faith. What should you do when they won't listen to you or they mock your beliefs? As Paul did, keep preaching the gospel and praying for your friends.

Don't give up. You never know what God can do in a person's life!

Discussion Starters:

* Note that in Thessalonica, Berea, and Athens, Paul always preached to the Jews first. Why do you think he did that?
** As Paul experienced rejection, what did he do in the next town? When has reasoning with someone for Christ failed for you?

Lifeline:

Do you know any unbelieving people—Jews or Gentiles? If so, pray consistently that the Father would direct them to the Son.

Holy Dirt

the WORD | Acts 18:2-5

"And [Paul] found [in Corinth] a Jew named Aquila, a native of Pontus, having recently come from Italy with his wife Priscilla, because Claudius had commanded all the Jews to leave Rome. He came to them, and because he was of the same trade, he stayed with them and they were working, for by trade they were tent-makers. And he was reasoning in the synagogue every Sabbath and trying to persuade Jews and Greeks. But when Silas and Timothy came down from Macedonia, Paul began devoting himself completely to the word, solemnly testifying to the Jews that Jesus was the Christ."

the Message

Over the years, there has been such a separation of the spiritual and secular that it would take a rocket to launch a Bible across the chasm—especially when it comes to what we do, our occupations.

Maybe you're a student, a business professional, or a parent. Maybe you spend your days going to class, or you're top dog in the office, or you home school your kids.

But whatever our jobs, shouldn't we all be pastors first? In other words, shouldn't we be messengers of Christ who also happen to work for a living?

Isn't the Christian who hauls trash a minister of sorts? Or how about the truck driver, attorney, or homemaker who loves Jesus? Isn't it his or her business to work heartily for the Lord as well? My favorite pastors are those who wear their jeans to the office occasionally and spend their lunch hours at the playground with their kids. I also like those ministers who pour concrete with the construction guys in the church parking lot, pray for their fellow students, or cook meals for families who need help.

Paul was a tent maker when he first arrived in Corinth. He stayed with Priscilla and Aquila because they made tents, too. But Paul's *lifestyle* showed that he was an apostle. His true job was ministry.

All Christians are, in some ways, ministers. The world is our church—humanity, our congregation. Whatever your occupation, make sure you live as Christ's evangelist. There are a million ways to touch the people around you. Don't just leave it up to your pastor to fulfill the Great Commission.

Discussion Starters:

* How do you think Paul ministered to people while making tents?
  ** When Silas and Timothy arrived, Paul was free to devote himself to preaching. How do you think he was supported?

Lifeline:

How can you be a pastor in your neighborhood, school, or workplace?

Hankies and Hoodwinkers

"God was performing extraordinary miracles by the hands of Paul.... But also some of the Jewish exorcists, who went from place to place, attempted to name over those who had the evil spirits the name of the Lord Jesus, saying, 'I adjure you by Jesus whom Paul preaches.' ...And the evil spirit answered and said to them, 'I recognize Jesus, and I know about Paul, but who are you?' And the man, in whom was the evil spirit, leaped on them and subdued all of them and overpowered them, so that they fled out of that house naked and wounded. This became known to all, both Jews and Greeks who lived in Ephesus; and fear fell upon them all and the name of the Lord Jesus was being magnified."

the Message

I was in the lobby of a college dorm one Sunday morning and overheard some students talking as they watched a religious show on TV.

"Here's another one of those hokey handkerchief guys. Could someone please change the channel!" a young man said as the televangelist prayed over a piece of cloth, promising to send it to some viewer for a donation of $100 or more.

I shook my head and walked away. But I couldn't blame the young man. He was right. Too many people in this world have tried to reproduce the work of the Spirit without first letting the Spirit work in *them*.

Satan laughs at such vain attempts. In fact (as you probably noticed in verse 16), he waits for just the right moment—then he pounces on the unsuspecting hoodwinker, and the gig is finished. No more fame, money, or reputation. Without the work of the Holy Spirit, many ministries—like the Jewish exorcists—are stripped naked and made into a joke.

You should respond to supernatural power as the Ephesian Christians did in verse 17. They realized that only the power of the Holy Spirit can subdue evil, and it made them honor God even more.

God's miracles are a far cry from the world of fluffy preaching. He sovereignly chooses to perform miracles in His timing, with His discretion, and solely for the purpose of glorifying His name and deepening His relationship with us. There's nothing hocus-pocus about His power.

Discussion Starters:

- What was the purpose of such miracles in Paul's day?
  - What was the difference in motive between Paul and the exorcists?
    - What miracles have you seen God work in your own life?

Lifeline:

Pray for Christians involved in healing ministries. A lot of good can result from the ministries, but the people involved need guidance and protection.

God Bless Tears

"And when they had come to him, he said to them, 'You yourselves know, from the first day that I set foot in Asia, how I was with you the whole time, serving the Lord with all humility and with tears and with trials which came upon me through the plots of the Jews.' ...And they began to weep aloud and embraced Paul, and repeatedly kissed him, grieving especially over the word which he had spoken, that they would not see his face again. And they were accompanying him to the ship."

the *Message*

Whenever I see an unusual word more than once in a passage, I take note of it. This passage describes grown people crying. And Paul stated that he served "with tears," indicating that he probably cried many more times as well.

Apparently Paul cried freely. And because he did, his audience heard the Word of God seasoned with emotion. They were able to see God's hand on Paul's heart, and it inspired his Ephesus congregation to be more open with their feelings as well.

Our faith should touch our emotions. We should cry tears of joy when our friends meet Jesus and weep with sorrow when people reject Him. I don't know where society got the idea that people—especially men—who show emotion are weak. Our Lord was emotional, and He modeled the perfect life. Jesus sobbed in the Garden of Gethsemane. He wept over His dear friend Lazarus's death. And He cried out to God twice when He was being crucified on the cross.

Most men (and some women) struggle with being open about their feelings. If you're a stoic, I challenge you to learn from Christ's (and Paul's) example. It is possible to be both strong and emotional. Expressing your feelings at the appropriate times will strengthen your relationships—with people and with God.

Let the One who's Lord over your life be Lord over your heart.

Discussion Starters:

* How do you think Paul's tears strengthened the Ephesians?
** How can revealing your emotions strengthen your relationships?
*** Does your family encourage everyone to be open with his or her feelings? Explain.
**** When are tears inappropriate?

Lifeline:

Read Ecclesiastes 3:1-8. As Solomon noted, there's a time for everything. How do you know when it's appropriate to talk about your feelings?

Hold the Line

the **WORD** | Acts 21:11-14

"And coming to us [the disciples], [Agabus] took Paul's belt and bound his own feet and hands, and said, 'This is what the Holy Spirit says: "In this way the Jews at Jerusalem will bind the man who owns this belt and deliver him into the hands of the Gentiles."' ...[So] we as well as the local residents began begging him not to go up to Jerusalem. Then Paul answered, 'What are you doing, weeping and breaking my heart? For I am ready not only to be bound, but even to die at Jerusalem for the name of the Lord Jesus.' And since he would not be persuaded, we fell silent, remarking, 'The will of the Lord be done!'"

the Message

In my opinion, God gets blamed too often for our dumb moves. We pray, and we think we heard Him correctly. So we rush into action, never once imagining that our ears were full of wax and we hadn't heard Him at all. Oh, the things we do in the name of God's will!

Intelligent men propose marriage to women, claiming that God has told them she's "the one." They're astounded when the women say, "Well, He hasn't told me that yet."

Pro-lifers murder abortionists because they think it's God's will.

Cult leaders everywhere lead their members to steal, lie, and sometimes even commit suicide—based on a "word" they've gotten from God. I'm certain those cult leaders need to swab their ears with Q-tips.

With all the confusion over God's voice, how do you and I know if we've really heard Him? Well, we do what Paul did (see Acts 21).

We pray (verse 5).

We listen (verses 4, 12).

We consider the advice of other Christians (verses 4, 11-12).

We study Scripture.

But most importantly, we *wait* (verses 4, 10). When all else fails, and we can't figure out God's will when we need to make tough decisions, we should "hold the line" until we can hear His voice clearly.

Then, like Paul, we must go forth boldly to do God's will—regardless of what He has in store for us.

Discussion Starters:

* Why do you think Paul's friends urged him not to go to Jerusalem?
  ** Was Paul being stubborn not to heed their advice? Why or why not?
  *** Is it possible that Paul's friends advised him according to their own emotions rather than God's will? Have you ever done that? If so, when?

Lifeline:

Describe a time you were certain of God's will for you in a particular area.

romans

"The just shall live by faith" (Romans 1:17, KJV).

The entire Protestant Reformation took place largely because Martin Luther spent a lot of time thinking about this single verse. John Wesley pioneered the Methodist movement in England (which led to much of the evangelism of America) because of his understanding of that same verse.

And that's just one verse from a magnificent book of the Bible. The book of Romans is a masterpiece in the way it helps us understand the concept of grace. As a new Christian at age 17, I read it like there was no tomorrow. It laid the foundation for my faith. This is a book that stands staunchly and sternly, directing us away from the gates of hell. The book of Romans is where millions and millions of people have discovered the love and the salvation of God. As you read it, may you do the same.

Not Ashamed

the WORD | Romans 1:16-17

"For I am not ashamed of the gospel, for it is the power of God for salvation to everyone who believes, to the Jew first and also to the Greek. For in it the righteousness of God is revealed from faith to faith; as it is written, 'But the righteous man shall live by faith.'"

the Message

Karen McGregor had wanted a horse since she was three years old. She had spent so many nights falling asleep thinking about horses that she began to dream about them. Alas, to a rural girl in Calgary, Alberta, money didn't come easy. The $1,500 price might as well have been a million dollars. She had never seen that kind of money. But her desire grew even stronger as she worked and saved every penny she could.

Just as Karen finally scraped together enough money to buy her dream horse, she happened to hear about a mission trip to San José, Bolivia. The only thing stronger than the desire to own her first horse was her desire to tell others about her tremendous love for Jesus, who had died to set her free from the penalty of her sins. But the mission trip had a hefty price tag.

Karen's dilemma became painfully apparent. She couldn't have both of the things she wanted; one of the two had to go. After some time devoted to intense prayer, she made her decision. The horse had to wait (maybe forever). The needs of the mission kids in Bolivia outweighed Karen's personal dreams. And as a result, Bolivia will never be the same. Neither will Karen. She will have all the days of eternity to claim her highest prize.

Discussion Starters:

* Because Karen was not ashamed of the gospel, other people's lives were changed for the better. Can you envision potential life changes if you were to take a bolder stand for what you believe? Explain.
** Have you ever felt ashamed or embarrassed to share your faith? Why? How did you deal with your feelings?
*** What personal desire would be hardest for you to sacrifice in order to share your love for Jesus? (Your boyfriend or girlfriend? Your group of friends? Your car?)

Lifeline:

Shame results in timidity. Love produces bold sacrifice.

Michelangelo of the Sky

the **WORD** | Romans 1:20

"For since the creation of the world [God's] invisible attributes, His eternal power and divine nature, have been clearly seen, being understood through what has been made, so that [unrighteous people] are without excuse."

the **Message**

"Been there, done that." That was Rob's motto.

Drugs? He'd done them all. Assault? He had beaten numerous of his fellow teens in fits of rage. Lockup? Though only 17, he had heard many jail gates and doors close in cold finality behind him. Gang life? He was one of his neighborhood's most notorious members.

Rob's parents were 15 and 16 at the time of his out-of-wedlock birth. Eight years later, a disastrous car accident left Rob an orphan with more psychological baggage to haul than a cargo jet could carry. To put it mildly, Rob was mad. The chip on his shoulder left no room for trusting relationships. And God was definitely at the bottom of his list of priorities.

Rob attended our summer camp in Missouri, where he and I became close friends. We spent hours talking about God…about forgiveness…about a person's ability to receive supernatural help to dispel guilt, anger, and rage. Rob asked a lot of questions, but his heart remained cold and hard toward God.

Mysteriously, he sought me out one night just after sunset. He wrapped his arms around my neck and hugged me for 10 long minutes as he sobbed a river of tears onto my shoulder. He was finally able to explain that he had been watching the majestic sunset. It was as if he had seen a painting, a masterpiece like he'd never seen before. He told me, "I knew a painting that spectacular *had* to have a painter, so I asked that 'Master painter' to reside in my heart and to forgive me for all the wrongs that I had done."

When God makes Himself evident to us, even the most resistant among us will eventually sit up and take notice.

Discussion Starters:

* What are some ways that God reveals Himself to you through the wonders of His creation?
** Why do you think some people choose to reject God even after they witness His many wondrous expressions in nature?
*** What are the short-term results of a person's refusal to acknowledge God's existence? What are the long-term results?

Lifeline:

Take note of God's many "paintings" today. Stand in awe of them and watch your affection for Him grow.

The Balance Beam

the WORD | Romans 2:1

"Therefore you have no excuse, everyone of you who passes judgment, for in that which you judge another, you condemn yourself; for you who judge practice the same things."

the Message

My palms still threaten to break out in a nervous sweat when my mind recalls watching my girls in gymnastics. No event was as grueling for the young athletes, nor as gut-wrenching for their dads, as the balance beam. The beam requires a series of feats on a surface no more than four inches wide, spanning a length of 16 feet, and perched more than four feet off the floor.

The plank between tolerance and judgment is the balance beam of the Christian life. Perhaps you've heard condemning statements where the gavel falls with resounding finality as the speaker piously declares:
- "You're going to hell for that."
- "Do that one more time and God will get His due revenge."
- "That politician is a pervert."

Yet just as we can be too judgmental, we can also be too tolerant:
- "Your rules are fine for you, but they don't apply to me."
- "If it feels good, do it."
- "Truth is relative."

A careless gymnast is penalized for falling off either side of the balance beam. Similarly, a careless Christian can experience distress from harsh judgment as well as excessive tolerance. It isn't easy, but we strive to remain upright on the beam. Whenever we feel ourselves beginning to tumble off, we can always count on God being there to help us keep our balance.

Discussion Starters:

In what ways have you seen tolerance for the behavior of others taken too far?

What judgmental statements have you heard directed at others lately?

Do you tend to be judgmental or tolerant? How can you find balance between the two?

Lifeline:

Referring to a down-and-out person, Albert Camus said, "There, but by the grace of God, go I." What do you think he meant?

The Walking Sermon

the WORD | Romans 2:21-23

"You, therefore, who teach another, do you not teach yourself? You who preach that one shall not steal, do you steal? You who say that one should not commit adultery, do you commit adultery? You who abhor idols, do you rob temples? You who boast in the Law, through your breaking the Law, do you dishonor God?"

the Message

Rather than reading something from me today, here are some words of wisdom by an unknown author from a poem called "I'd Rather See a Sermon."

I'd rather see a sermon than hear one any day;
I'd rather one should walk with me than merely show the way.
The eye's a better pupil and more willing than the ear;
Fine counsel is confusing, but example's always clear.
And the best of all the preachers are the ones who live their creed;
For to see good put in action is what everybody needs.
I soon can learn to do it if you let me see it done;
I can watch your hands in action, but your tongue too fast may run.
And the sermon you deliver may be very wise and true;
But I'd rather get my lesson by observing what to do.
For I might misunderstand you and the high advice you give;
But there's no misunderstanding in how you act and how you live.

Discussion Starters:

* Describe a family member who has "walked his talk," or point out a "walking sermon" quality in each family member.
  * Why do you think it is so difficult for nonbelievers to believe in Jesus when they observe a Christian who doesn't practice on Saturday night what he or she sings about in church on Sunday morning?
  * What is an area you've identified lately where you could stand to do a better job of "walking" more like you "talk"?

Lifeline:

The next time you take a walk, look for some "sermons" of your own.

Pop Quiz

the WORD | Romans 3:10-12

"There is none righteous, not even one; there is none who understands, there is none who seeks for God; all have turned aside, together they have become useless; there is none who does good, there is not even one."

the Message

The students have just zipped up their backpacks to dash home from school after a hard day of classes. But the principal's bizarre announcement over the P.A. system stops them in their tracks: "Students, we have an unexpected guest visiting us today, and I want everyone to immediately proceed to the auditorium for an assembly."

Some people grumble as they head for the auditorium. Others are curious and wonder, *Who is this guy who thinks he's important enough to extend an already long day? He'd better be good.*

The auditorium fills with whispers of complaint and speculation. Soon the guest walks onto the stage. He has a wise face with a long white beard. He wears a flowing white robe. His voice resonates throughout the assembly as the crowd becomes silent.

"Hello, students. I am God. Some of you don't recognize Me, and I'm concerned that many of you are going to flunk My final exam. Therefore, I've come to give you a little pop quiz." He begins to pass out copies of the Ten Commandments. His voice is deep and solemn as He continues. "You may score yourselves. If you have kept a commandment perfectly, give yourself a 10 for that one. Otherwise, give yourself a zero. Do that for each of the commandments. A perfect score is 100. That's the only passing grade. Any score less than 100 means complete failure."

Everyone is finished in 15 minutes. No one passes.

Attempting to achieve righteousness on our own would require that we score 100 on the Ten Commandments as well as the hundreds of other laws in the Bible. Only one person has ever achieved that feat—Jesus. He doesn't expect the same of us. That's why He provided a better way to "pass the test." All we have to do is put our faith in Him, and He covers our sins, shortcomings, and failures with His love, mercy, and forgiveness. If you believe in Him, congratulations! You've passed!

Discussion Starters:

* If you would like to see how well you would have done on the pop quiz, turn to Exodus 20:1-17. (But also read Matthew 5:21-30 to see that murder = name-calling, and adultery = lust.) What's your score?
  ** Why does everyone fail the test?
    *** How can a holy God allow unholy people into heaven? What is His remedy for this eternal dilemma?

Lifeline:

Without the cross, heaven would be an empty dream.

The Gift

the **WORD** | Romans 3:23-25

"For all have sinned and fall short of the glory of God, being justified as a gift by His grace through the redemption which is in Christ Jesus; whom God displayed publicly as a propitiation in His blood through faith."

the **Message**

How would you like a brand-new Porsche or Lexus—for free? How about a MasterCard with unlimited spending and no bills to pay…ever?

God has an even better offer. Today's passage gets to the very heart of Scripture. It tells us that we all have sinned. The wages of sin is death. The horror of death is separation from God in hell. That's where we're headed and what we deserve. But wait! God is offering us a gift—an amazing, overwhelming, unparalleled, unmatchable gift.

Step forward and receive your gift of being justified. (Say what?)

Justification is a big word that means your glob of accumulated sins has been totally forgiven and you have been declared righteous. How do you become justified? It's a gift from God—no charge. What did you do to deserve this life-saving gift? Not a thing! That's the definition of *grace*, bestowing something that is completely undeserved. *Redemption* is the process by which all this happens—Jesus' blood being shed for you on the cross. And the last big word in today's passage is *propitiation*, which is a sacrifice that appeases the wrath of God toward our sin and prevents us from receiving the brunt of His judgment.

Recently a college athlete came to my office to talk about God. He had caused two abortions. His wife had left him. His drinking was out of control. In his search for meaning in life, he scoffed at the idea of a personal, loving God.

At the very moment I began to explain the Bible's description of the love of a heavenly Father for His Son, my daughter brought my 12-day-old grandson to see me. He was dressed in a tiny hat and pajamas. As she placed the precious package in my arms, my daughter spoke for him: "Granddad, I want to go hunting with you."

I was overcome with a dad's love too powerful for words. The athlete saw the picture of God's redemption unfold before his eyes. That night he gave his life to Christ and has since dedicated his life to purity so others might see the truth as well.

Discussion Starters:

* How can you explain God's amazing grace?
** How should His grace motivate you?
*** Why is grace so hard to comprehend?

Lifeline:

Grace is getting good things we don't deserve. Mercy is not getting bad things we do deserve.

Meet the Twins

the **WORD** | Romans 4:3-5

"For what does the Scripture say? 'Abraham believed God, and it was credited to him as righteousness.' Now to the one who works, his wage is not credited as a favor, but as what is due. But to the one who does not work, but believes in Him who justifies the ungodly, his faith is credited as righteousness."

the Message

In Genesis 25 we read about a pair of remarkable twins born to the Jewish patriarch Isaac and his wife, Rebekah. The amazing account includes a play-by-play description of the birth of Jacob and Esau. Esau actually was born first, with Jacob close behind, grasping Esau's heel. In their culture, the firstborn son—even the firstborn of a set of twins—was traditionally given a special blessing. But through a long and complicated chain of events, Jacob was the one who ended up with the majority of the birthright, blessings, and rewards. Romans 9 refers to this pair of twins to illustrate how the Gentiles came to receive God's blessings even though they weren't "firstborn."

But today I'm more interested in another set of twins whose importance is emphasized in Romans. As significant as birth order was in the Old Testament, it was no more important than understanding the birth order of the twins we're going to call "Faith" and "Works." Many Christians get confused about the birth order of this pair. But today's passage is clear: As it was with Abraham, so it is with us.

Faith is the firstborn and therefore should come first in our lives. We are saved by faith. Through faith we are able to trust Christ and give our lives to Him (Ephesians 2:8-9). Faith is necessary for joining God's family (John 1:12) and being declared righteous before God (James 2:23). Nothing else can get you to heaven—no good deed, church ritual, sacrifice for another, or life of absolute piety.

If the second twin, Works, tries to come before Faith or stand apart from him, there will always be problems. But when he comes second in the birth order, things go as God planned. In fact, if Faith is genuine, he will always have Works along with him (James 2:17-18). And they make a dynamic duo you don't want to miss out on.

Discussion Starters:

* Why don't works play any part in saving you?
  ** Why can't faith be genuine if not accompanied by good works?
  *** Can you think of any church rituals that may be good but can never take the place of faith? What are they?

Lifeline:

Are the Faith and Works twins alive and well in your life today?

What a Team!

the **WORD** | Romans 4:16

"For this reason it is by faith, in order that it may be in accordance with grace, so that the promise will be guaranteed to all the descendants, not only to those who are of the Law, but also to those who are of the faith of Abraham, who is the father of us all."

the **Message**

When I first walked onto the field as a member of the Southern Methodist University football team, I found myself surrounded by large, fast, confident athletes who towered over my six-foot, 195-pound frame. They had the moves, the biceps, and the scholarships!

Hayden Fry was the head coach of the Mustangs in those days. Although I was a seventh-team defensive noseguard as a freshman, he took a special liking to me. (Who knows why?) He "adopted" me during my sophomore year, maybe because I was too stupid to give up. The first game of my junior year, he started me—and he never put me on the bench again. He played me at Ohio State, Michigan State, Tennessee, Texas, and Arkansas. He even tried to send me to the Hula Bowl, but the regulating committee found out I wasn't the superstar he had made me out to be.

He took me off the bench and put me in the game, and for that I'll be forever grateful. As a result, I played my guts out for him. I'll love him until I die.

It wasn't too hard to figure out that playing on Astroturf in Dallas on Saturday afternoons with a free college education was better than paying hundreds of thousands of dollars to get educated and then sitting on the sidelines.

Paul makes a similar point in Romans. Instead of attempting to pay for my own sins and ending up in hell for all eternity, my faith in Jesus is like a "scholarship" that entitles me to full tuition in heaven forever and allows me to see some terrific action in the game of life in the meantime. The deal gets even better when I realize that God becomes not only my Coach, but also my Father.

And as good as that sounds, the final bonus is that this "team" has no cutoff. I hope you've already joined. If so, there's still room for all your friends. Why not let them know about it?

Discussion Starters:

* What does it mean that Abraham is "the father of us all"?
* * Becoming a Christian is like being adopted by God (Romans 8:23). How can an adopted orphan show gratitude to his or her new family?
* * * How can you do more for our "team"? Who else can you recruit?

Lifeline:

Gratitude builds commitment. Commitment builds obedience. Obedience builds countless blessings.

Pain and Promise

"We also exult in our tribulations, knowing that tribulation brings about perseverance; and perseverance, proven character; and proven character, hope; and hope does not disappoint, because the love of God has been poured out within our hearts through the Holy Spirit who was given to us."

the **Message**

My first girlfriend left me for my best friend in junior high. That was puppy love, but it still left a pain in my gut.

My first wife left me for my best friend in college. That was true love which left a pain in my heart that lasted for many months. It almost killed me.

Both my first wife and my college friend are wonderful people. Although there's little doubt that initiating divorce is wrong in most circumstances, I've never blamed them, nor have I ever been bitter. I cried my eyes out for a few months. Yet during that horrible time I fell completely in love with God for the first time. I learned to give Him my todays as well as my tomorrows.

God not only healed my broken heart, but He also brought Debbie-Jo to me. (In case I haven't told you, she is the greatest woman alive and the mom of my four kids.) God also gave me a passion for people who, like myself, find themselves in the bottom of an emotional canyon with no apparent way out.

I learned a lot in my brokenness before God. I can see Him at His best when I am at my worst. He is never closer than the day I fall on my face. Pain gives me a choice. When I choose to run to God, I get *better*. If I choose to rely on my own answers, I get *bitter*.

I discovered that my pain is like a golf tee. I can use it to be "teed off" or "teed up." Pain either makes me mad and useless or else it helps me go a lot farther than I might have otherwise.

God is never more ready to fill our hearts than when we're deep in the canyon of despair. As we learn to rely on His Holy Spirit, our tribulations turn to perseverance, then to proven character, and finally to hope. Our painful times will come and go, but God's promises remain available to us all the time.

Discussion Starters:

* How do trials build character when God is in charge?
  ** What has been the greatest time of brokenness you've ever faced? Did it eventually result in stronger character and/or hope? Explain.
  *** How can you prepare yourself to endure painful trials that lie ahead?

Lifeline:

Bitter or better? It's your choice when the painful ball of failure lands in your court.

Dying for an Enemy

"For while we were still helpless, at the right time Christ died for the ungodly. For one will hardly die for a righteous man; though perhaps for the good man someone would dare even to die. But God demonstrates His own love toward us, in that while we were yet sinners, Christ died for us."

the Message

It was Christmas Day in the cold, damp foxholes on a European battlefield during World War I. The details of the story remain foggy, but I remember reading long ago of an unprecedented event that took place on this particular day set aside to honor the Christ Child's birth.

A platoon of Germans had made a run across the coiled barbed wire barrier to ambush their American enemies, but the raid was called off when heavy gunfire stopped them in their tracks. Several Germans died on the spot. But one German soldier took a hit in the shoulder, became tangled in the barbed wire, and lay there helpless and screaming.

His painful wails persisted until one brave young American soldier stood and ran to the German's rescue. As he removed his enemy from the entanglement, all gunfire stopped in grateful astonishment. The heroic American freed the wounded warrior and carried him to his friends. Without fear, he then turned and walked gallantly back to his foxhole. Eventually the battle resumed. But on one Christmas Day, for a brief shining moment, two groups of soldiers saw what it meant to be willing to die for one's enemy.

What the American soldier did for his German foe is a picture of what Jesus has done for each of us. We're tangled in sin, writhing in emotional and spiritual pain, and vulnerable to attack. Nobody said Jesus had to come and die for us. It was His idea. He volunteered for the mission and carried it out to the end. In doing so, we all learn that "the end" is not death but resurrection and eternal life.

In response, perhaps more of us can begin to bravely reach across barriers to show love and compassion to others we usually don't care much about. It's a risky mission that will require faith and courage. Are you up to it?

Discussion Starters:

* How does this story remind you of Jesus and His heroic death on the cross?
** Why were we considered enemies of God before we surrendered our lives to His leadership?
*** Who are a few "enemies" whom you would eventually like to see put their faith in Jesus?

Lifeline:

Since Jesus was willing to die for us as His enemies, think how much He will love us as His friends!

A Grace Trip

the WORD | Romans 6:1-4

"What shall we say then? Are we to continue in sin so that grace may increase? May it never be! How shall we who died to sin still live in it? Or do you not know that all of us who have been baptized into Christ Jesus have been baptized into His death? Therefore we have been buried with Him through baptism into death, so that as Christ was raised from the dead through the glory of the Father, so we too might walk in newness of life."

the Message

"What's the big deal? Jesus will forgive me anyway!"

Married businesspeople sometimes use this phrase when they're traveling alone and have the opportunity to spend the night with a lovely young stranger. College students sometimes say it when they're at a party where everyone else is getting drunk. High school kids may think it when a joint is passed around or when a make-out session starts to get out of control.

We read that twice as many "Christian" kids watch MTV as non-Christian kids. We read that "Christian" teens have sex almost as often as non-Christian kids. "Christian" adults in Hollywood, in the NBA and NFL, in the White House, in Congress, on Wall Street, and elsewhere in the country rationalize alcohol abuse, cheating in business, pornography, and sexual promiscuity. "It's okay. Jesus will forgive me."

Paul states in no uncertain terms how God feels about our naïve rationalizations. "May it never be!" In the original Greek language, he uses the most forceful negative statement available.

If you truly become a follower of Christ, your old "self" who tends to commit such acts of lawlessness *dies*. That's not you anymore; that's the *old* you. That person is dead. Gone. Kaput. The *new* you exists only because Christ brought you to life. You should, therefore, be attuned to His desires rather than your old, sinful ones. The new and improved you says, "If it pleases God, I do it. If it doesn't please God and conform to His Word, I say no."

God's grace doesn't cost you a cent, but it cost Jesus His life. Overlooking it or trying to abuse it is just about the worst insult we can direct at God.

Discussion Starters:

* What does living on a "grace trip" mean to you?
** Why do some people treat grace like a disposable toy?
*** After studying today's passage, what do you plan to do in response?

Lifeline:

True grace produces true obedience.

Dead to Sin

the **WORD** | *Romans 6:8-11*

"Now if we have died with Christ, we believe that we shall also live with Him, knowing that Christ, having been raised from the dead, is never to die again; death no longer is master over Him. For the death that He died, He died to sin once for all; but the life that He lives, He lives to God. Even so consider yourselves to be dead to sin, but alive to God in Christ Jesus."

the Message

My son Cooper played football like there was no tomorrow. Some of the fans called him "Missile Man." At age 17, though only 5'10" tall and 160 pounds, the way he ran down the field on a kickoff, blasting defenders off their feet, reminded me of a bowling ball rocketing down the alley, spreading pins everywhere.

But there was a time when the Missile Man was temporarily knocked out of commission. A series of concussions put Cooper on the sidelines.

After a hard game, Cooper had been warned by his doctor how concussions have a "mounting effect" as each one makes the brain more susceptible to the next, opening the door to brain damage and severe post-concussion syndrome. But Cooper had begged to play in one more game, and the doctor reluctantly granted his wish.

Early in the second half Cooper tackled a runner with a hard hit. The ball carrier was knocked to the ground and jumped back up; Cooper's body went completely limp. For many weeks after that game, Cooper experienced painful headaches, insomnia, and dizziness.

Sin works much the same way as a series of concussions. The first blow doesn't seem so bad, maybe even harmless. We can't detect any damage. We don't change our behavior even when the second sin adds to the effects of the first, as do the third, fourth, and fifth. By then a caring "doctor" has issued the warning, "You're going to hurt yourself." If we don't heed His wise advice, we may experience a knockout blow that sidelines us longer than we might wish.

Is it time for a spiritual CAT scan to ensure that sin is not accumulating in your life and threatening serious damage? Listen to the Great Physician. Take care of yourself. We need you in this game!

Discussion Starters:

* What does it mean to consider yourself "dead to sin"?
* * How does a healthy relationship with Jesus enable you to stop sinning willfully?
* * * What can you do if you discover apparent sin in your life today?

Lifeline:

To be alive to God is to be dead to sin.

"I Can't Stop Sinning!"

the WORD | Romans 7:15-17

"For what I am doing, I do not understand; for I am not practicing what I would like to do, but I am doing the very thing I hate. But if I do the very thing I do not want to do, I agree with the Law, confessing that the Law is good. So now, no longer am I the one doing it, but sin which dwells in me."

the Message

When I used to cohost Focus on the Family's *Life on the Edge Live!* teen call-in radio show, I'd talk to a lot of teens. I talked to a girl in New York who got a thousand friends in her public high school to wear Christian T-shirts. I talked to a guy in Las Vegas who witnessed to his unsaved friends daily. I talked to a Christian in Florida who told his girlfriend that all forms of sex are for marriage only. And I talked to a Dallas girl who set some strong standards that excluded drinking, tobacco, drugs, and petting.

Some calls, however, were painful to hear. Once, a 15-year-old girl from California pleaded for help. Her involvement in drinking, drugs, and sex was out of control and affecting her physically and emotionally. She told me, "I want to stop but I just can't." I encouraged her to put an end to her sexual involvements and save herself for her true love who would someday seal his commitment to her with a wedding ring. She wasn't convinced: "I can't quit. I just can't do it."

So many of us understand her desperation. Guilt and failure are two of Satan's favorite tools to eliminate any motivation to repent and turn to God in obedience. They speak to our inner spirit and incapacitate us.

You've blown it in the past? Join the club! Jesus knows you're not perfect. That's why He came to earth in the first place. But He wants us to trust Him and keep trying. Every day is a brand-new opportunity to say, "I might have failed yesterday, but today is the first day of the rest of my life. Christ can give me the grace to never sin like that again!"

Discussion Starters:

* Why is it impossible to do all the right things in our own power?
  ** How do guilt and failure work together to defeat us? Do you have any personal examples?
 *** How does Christ help us break free from the cycles of guilt and failure that try to keep us down?

Lifeline:

Pointing out someone's failures spells failure. Pointing out someone's successes spells success.

Free at Last

"But if I am doing the very thing I do not want, I am no longer the one doing it, but sin which dwells in me.... Wretched man that I am! Who will set me free from the body of this death? Thanks be to God through Jesus Christ our Lord! So then, on the one hand I myself with my mind am serving the law of God, but on the other, with my flesh the law of sin."

the *Message*

I saw a television interview with a 65-year-old man who spent four years in a Nazi slave camp. He was part of a group forced to burrow a huge tunnel through a mountain of rock to conceal German covert bombing and missile operations. Many of his friends died in that tunnel. They all were starved beyond belief and beaten unmercifully.

When the Allied soldiers defeated Germany and arrived at the tunnel to free the slaves, the men literally clasped their hands together in prayerful celebration. They were finally free to eat, free to laugh, free to cry, free to go home to their families. They probably had a better understanding of freedom than most people ever will because they were deprived of it for so long.

It's a terrible thing when we *choose* slavery. Yet all of us occasionally choose to be slaves to sin—alcohol, tobacco, drugs, pornography, sex, or any number of other "masters." In most cases, we start out with willful participation but find ourselves enslaved and miserable before we know it. And we discover we aren't able to break free on our own power.

But when we turn to Jesus, He forgives us and frees us. He lifts us from our sin and severs our chains with His chisel of grace. I know this is true because people tell me.

That's how Diane stopped smoking.

That's how Wes stopped having sex with his girlfriend.

That's how Lori stopped using drugs.

That's how Bill stopped cheating his customers.

That's how Bryce stopped looking at nude pictures in magazines.

No chain around your heart is too powerful for Jesus to break. He can free you whenever you are ready.

Discussion Starters:

* Why do so many people allow sin to enslave them?
** What kinds of "slavery" do you see among other people your age?
*** If someone asked you how to break free from some sin that was enslaving him or her, what would you say?

Lifeline:

When we agree to let God be our Master, nothing else has the power to make us slaves.

The Law of the Spirit

the WORD | Romans 8:1-3

"Therefore there is now no condemnation for those who are in Christ Jesus. For the law of the Spirit of life in Christ Jesus has set you free from the law of sin and of death. For what the Law could not do, weak as it was through the flesh, God did: sending His own Son in the likeness of sinful flesh and as an offering for sin."

the Message

The following declaration of freedom is true and was candidly expressed by a 16-year-old friend of mine.

Joe,

Thanks for your letter and the book. It is very good and has helped me greatly with some problems I have been facing lately. I can feel myself changing greatly every day since I decided to let God run my life. It is truly amazing. I get so excited about life now, it is just unbelievable. Before I accepted Jesus Christ into my heart, I had a problem with drinking.

At first, I thought drinking was all right since I grew up around it. How terribly wrong I was! I tried to stop drinking after realizing I was putting myself in bodily harm. The first night of that month was one of the toughest struggles I've been through. I felt that I needed to drink more than anything else. But I didn't. The second night of that month, I gave in. My strength was not strong enough to overcome my dependency. I felt like a failure. I knew I could not do it alone.

Now, as a true Christian, I've tried to stop again. This time it was different! I asked Jesus to help me with my problem and to show me the way to a happy life, and that is exactly what He did. When I tried to stop drinking for the second time, it was one of the easiest things I have ever done. I felt no need whatsoever to have alcohol in my system. It was amazing how much easier it was that second time. But we both know why it was so easy. It was because Jesus was in the driver's seat.

I have never been so happy, and this happiness will be growing more and more every day! I know there will be trials, but I also know that whatever comes my way, with the Lord's help, I will be able to handle anything!

Discussion Starters:

* What was the secret of the 16-year-old's success?
** Why did he fail the first time he tried to stop drinking?
*** How can the Romans 8:1-3 passage help you with your own struggles to overcome a problem you are facing?

Lifeline:

When I try, I fail. When I trust, Jesus succeeds.

A Winner Every Time

"Who will separate us from the love of Christ? Will tribulation, or distress, or persecution, or famine, or nakedness, or peril, or sword? ...But in all these things we overwhelmingly conquer through Him who loved us. For I am convinced that neither death, nor life, nor angels, nor principalities, nor things present, nor things to come, nor powers, nor height, nor depth, nor any other created thing, will be able to separate us from the love of God, which is in Christ Jesus our Lord."

the *Message*

Every day countless millions of dollars are literally thrown away. They are thrown into slot machines, onto blackjack tables, beneath rolling dice, and in various other games of chance in the alluring casinos that sparkle like diamond-studded earrings across our country.

When you walk in the door of a casino, your odds of walking out a winner are usually less than 40 percent. In addition, income from many such establishments supports organized crime. Still, there is no shortage of people who continue to dream big and "lose their shirts" night after disappointing night.

Even worse than losing money is losing someone close to you, especially if you have invested your heart in the other person. It may be that *you* do everything possible to salvage the relationship, but the other person simply decides to walk away. My mom lost her father that way. I lost a girl that way—one I loved very much. Your heart breaks in two as the door slams shut. The pain is indescribable.

Losing makes you cautious. It makes you wonder about commitments. It makes you doubt the sincerity of others.

Well, there's one person on whom I would bet my entire savings—and even my life. I know for a fact that Jesus already laid His life on the line for me. He has promised never to leave me, and I believe Him. Why? Because "while we were yet sinners, Christ died for us" (Romans 5:8).

Christian faith rarely involves bright neon lights, clanging slot machine bells, or glitzy entertainers. But it's a sure thing that never stops paying off. You'll be counting your winnings for eternity. You can bet on it.

Discussion Starters:

* Why might you be cautious about believing someone will never leave you?
** Why is God's Word believable? What portion of it do you really need to believe right now?
*** How does it make you feel knowing for sure that God will love you forever?

Lifeline:

Memorizing today's passage is like having a priceless gold coin in your pocket.

Oh, Those Names!

the WORD | Romans 9:25-26

"As He says also in Hosea, 'I will call those who were not My people, "My people," and her who was not beloved, "beloved." And it shall be that in the place where it was said to them, "You are not My people," there they shall be called sons of the living God.' "

the Message

As I think back over my growing-up days in grade school, junior high, and high school, I still grieve a little over the names that people called me: Wimp! Loser! Quitter! Jerk! Two-faced! Punk! Shorty! Fatty! Chicken!

Ouch! Those names (and you may have been called worse ones) cut like a knife, don't they! But I've also found that other names have just the opposite effect: Teammate! Coach! Leader! Friend! Lover! Sweetheart! Honey!

It doesn't take long to forget petty, negative names slipping off someone's loose tongue when I dwell on the names used by people I truly care about (who also care about me). Of all the names I've ever been called, two will be my favorites for all time. I never cease to appreciate when my mom and dad smile and call me "son." And I don't think any name will ever compare to the title my kids give me: "Daddy."

God could have called you and me "slaves." He could have called us "losers." He could have called us "unlovable." He could have called us "strangers."

But the moment we put our faith in Jesus, He calls us "sons" and "daughters." God has big plans for us as His children—plans more grandiose than the very creation of the universe. His plans unfold continually as He looks into our hearts, where His Holy Spirit is at work. With God as our Father, every day is a new adventure.

Discussion Starters:

* What are the most positive associations you have with being called "son" or "daughter"?
** God could have kept us at arm's length. Why do you think He chooses such endearing names for us and invites us to get closer to Him?
*** What are some of the names for God that mean the most to you? (Father? Shepherd? Counselor? King? Others?)

Lifeline:

Prayer is participation in a Father/son or Father/daughter banquet.

Young Heroes

the WORD | Romans 10:9-10

"If you confess with your mouth Jesus as Lord, and believe in your heart that God raised Him from the dead, you will be saved; for with the heart a person believes, resulting in righteousness, and with the mouth he confesses, resulting in salvation."

the Message

Kathy D.'s father was an alcoholic who darkened his daughter's junior year in high school by committing suicide and leaving his family in utter dismay. Kathy soon turned to drugs in her desperate attempt to numb the pain and escape a cruel reality that left her hopeless.

Then, like a laser light from heaven, a bright-eyed, 17-year-old named Kathy Adams showed up and invited her to the Young Life club my wife and I led in our small Ozark mountain community. Kathy A. took Kathy D. under her wing like a mother eagle covering her nesting chicks, providing warmth and protection. Kathy D. soon allowed Christ to fill the void in her heart left by her disturbed father. The two Kathys lit up the local high school with their warmth, and soon they had many of their friends coming to Young Life club. One night 30 students gave their hearts to Christ. Over the years, more than 500 others have asked Jesus into their hearts in that little three-room house.

If you look for them, I think you'll find modern-day heroes in every high school in America. They are the valiant teenagers who not only believe that Jesus died and rose from the grave, but also are eager to tell their friends about Him. They guide a searching generation of their peers to Bible studies, prayer groups, and youth meetings so as many as possible will find purpose, meaning, and eternal life in heaven.

Discussion Starters:

• Do you know any modern-day heroes in your school? How can you be supportive of the stand they are taking for Jesus?

•• What does it mean to "confess with your mouth that Jesus is Lord" in practical ways? Is it enough to "believe in your heart" if you never get around to telling people about it? Explain.

••• Who are three people you can invite to a church activity before the week is over?

Lifeline:

Believing in your heart and confessing with your mouth are the "heads" and "tails" of the same coin.

Amazing Faith

"So faith comes from hearing, and hearing by the word of Christ."

the **Message**

It's not hard to be amazed at God's design for the world when we take a close look at nature. Who would ever believe that a tiny little acorn could get covered with a little dirt and, in time, become a mammoth tree capable of providing shade to a country home, supporting a swing from an upper limb, and cradling a tree house for dozens of neighborhood kids? Yet we've all seen enormous oak trees, so we can marvel at God's design.

Who would ever believe that a Canada goose would sense a change in the weather, lift off from the shores of Alaska, and migrate all the way to the Gulf of Mexico? Yet we know that's what happens, and we see God's plan for the goose quite clearly.

The great thing about faith is that people, too, can tap into God's plan for them and find inner peace and satisfaction in an otherwise hectic world. The Word of God says to guard your heart (Proverbs 4:23), and my beautiful 19-year-old friend Kalene has the faith to hear and respond. She "saves her kisses" for her future husband, and him alone. She passes up other would-be suitors most Saturday nights, believing that some day she will find "Mr. Right" and will be able to offer him the virgin soil of her heart that has never been tampered with.

The Word of Christ says that no one can serve two masters (Matthew 6:24). So with great faith, Jason, Jarred, Jill, Erin, and others avoid the potential masters of drugs, alcohol, sex, pornography, blasphemous music, and wild weekend parties. They remain faithful to their pure Christian convictions.

Faith is belief accompanied by commitment. The words of Christ through Scripture fill our minds with His precious promises, and our hearts turn those words into a lifestyle that sets us free. Faith comes from hearing, and hearing by the Word of Christ. Most of us have heard. But do we have the faith to act?

Discussion Starters:

 • How does the Word of Christ eventually become a living and active faith?
 •• What portion of Scripture did you hear recently that you responded to in faith? What was your response?
 ••• How does someone's inner faith manifest itself for others to see?

Lifeline:

Hearing with your ears produces interest. Hearing with your heart produces faith.

A Second-Round Graft Pick

the **WORD** | Romans 11:17-19

"But if some of the branches were broken off, and you, being a wild olive, were grafted in among them and became partaker with them of the rich root of the olive tree, do not be arrogant toward the branches; but if you are arrogant, remember that it is not you who supports the root, but the root supports you. You will say then, 'Branches were broken off so that I might be grafted in.'"

the **Message**

A recent season of professional football featured a Cinderella story that surprised the critics and amazed the analysts. The Randy Moss story was everywhere. Though his speed, size, and vertical jump had tantalized every scout in the NFL, he was also well known for his explosive behavior on and off the field. He was considered an undisciplined street fighter and therefore not much of a draft choice. Sixteen teams passed over him in the draft.

Then came the Minnesota Vikings and a veteran all-pro receiver named Cris Carter, who is a Christian. Cris Carter agreed to "adopt" Randy Moss and pour his life into the young rookie. The covers of *ESPN Magazine, Sports Illustrated,* and *USA Today* told us the rest of the story. The young rookie was nothing less than sensational. The throwaway became a star. The long shot became a sure shot. The team who adopted him became division champions! A "wild branch" was grafted in and became a part of a team—a team that went to the Super Bowl.

Likewise, the Jews were (and always will be) God's chosen people. For years the Gentiles were "out of the loop" when it came to getting to God. But Jesus' death changed all that. God "so loved the *world,*" not just the Jewish people. With incredible genius and love beyond belief, God reached down to a wild and unattached branch and grafted us into a nurturing and growing tree. We didn't really belong there, but God made it happen.

Randy Moss joined Cris Carter and the Vikings in the streets of Minneapolis for a night of celebration. The believing Gentiles will someday join the Hebrew children of God in the golden streets of heaven for a celebration that will never end!

Discussion Starters:

* Has anyone ever stood up for you, allowing you to be accepted by a group who might have otherwise rejected you? Give some specific examples.

** How does it feel to realize that God personally reaches out to include you in His great love?

*** Since God has grafted you into His family, what are some victories you hope to achieve for Him someday?

Lifeline:

Amazing demonstrations of love deserve equally amazing responses of obedience.

Fascination

"Oh, the depth of the riches both of the wisdom and knowledge of God! How unsearchable are His judgments and unfathomable His ways!"

the *Message*

Are you ready to be fascinated? Consider with me for a moment some awesome facts that reflect the wisdom of our Creator expressed through His creation.

The human body has 100 trillion cells. A single cell contains enough information to fill 10 million volumes of literature.

The human eye can handle 1.5 million simultaneous messages. One hundred thirty-seven million nerve endings pick up every message that the eye sends to the brain. Even Darwin wrote in his book *The Origin of Species*, "To suppose that the eye with all of its inimitable contrivances for adjusting focus to different distances, for emitting different amounts of light, and for the correction of spherical and chromatic aberration could have been formed by natural selection seems, I freely confess, absurd in the highest degree."

The inner ear contains as many circuits as the telephone system of most cities. The information in the brain could fill approximately 20 million books. The brain has 10 billion circuits, each five to 10 times more complex than any computer ever built.

The universe has millions of galaxies. The Milky Way galaxy alone has over 100 billion stars. If our universe were on a scale where the earth and moon were only one inch apart, you would still have to travel 10 million miles just to reach the center of our galaxy. (And after 4,000 years of scientific effort, our greatest space accomplishment has been to successfully transport a person to and from the moon.)

Some people say all these amazingly intricate designs and massively expansive spaces happened by chance. They theorize that the creation of the universe and of human beings is nothing more than a lucky accident. But it doesn't require much of an IQ to see the wishful thinking in modern science. Likewise, it doesn't take much faith to believe in an intentional and loving Creator, and to stand in awe of His work all around us.

Discussion Starters:

- Do you believe you were designed by a divine Creator, or are you the result of a lucky accident? Why?
- How does the awesome complexity of God's world affect your faith?
- Why do so many men and women try to refute God and His majestic power?

Lifeline:

George Beverly Shea says it best when he sings, "My God, how great Thou art."

Conformed or Transformed?

the WORD | Romans 12:1-2

"Therefore I urge you, brethren, by the mercies of God, to present your bodies a living and holy sacrifice, acceptable to God, which is your spiritual service of worship. And do not be conformed to this world, but be transformed by the renewing of your mind, so that you may prove what the will of God is, that which is good and acceptable and perfect."

the Message

The Japanese kamikaze pilots of World War II flew their fighter bombers directly into the decks of American aircraft carriers, giving their lives for the country they loved. An American soldier dives on a live hand grenade in a German foxhole to shield four buddies from the explosion. Sacrificial deaths. We are amazed by them. They inspire us with undaunted courage and valor. My 17-year-old friend George lunged in front of his girlfriend during a drive-by shooting in Boston. The shooter unloaded his pistol into George's neck and back. His girlfriend was unharmed. George also miraculously survived, but his act was no less a sacrifice.

Living sacrifices don't get as much press coverage, but they can be equally courageous. Some kids abstain from drinking at parties, for which they are ridiculed and never asked to return. Some teenage guys protect their dates' purity at all costs, fighting off peer pressure, raging hormones, and cultural acceptance of "safe sex." Some Christian teens go to Bible studies and youth groups, and then live out their faith the other six days of the week.

These people all make sacrifices for God. They are on the altar, offering their very bodies and souls to Him and showing others what Christian faith is all about. I admire girls like Jill and Johnia, who date the two best football players in our school. The guys didn't have a lot of Christian background when they met Jill and Johnia, but they're catching up quickly. Not only do both of them now know Christ as their Lord and Savior, so do many other guys on the team who have seen a difference in them—all a result of what God did in response to Jill's and Johnia's unwavering stand for Christ.

When God is at work you can "get a life" *and* be a holy sacrifice. Being a living sacrifice is the best of both worlds!

Discussion Starters:

* What happens to someone who becomes conformed to this world? Why do so many people tend to conform?
** How does a person become *transformed* rather than *conformed* to the world around him or her?
*** What makes a living sacrifice "holy and acceptable to God"?

Lifeline:

Conforming or transforming? You're always doing one or the other.

Overcoming Bitterness

the WORD | Romans 12:17-21

"Never pay back evil for evil to anyone. Respect what is right in the sight of all men. If possible, so far as it depends on you, be at peace with all men. Never take your own revenge, beloved, but leave room for the wrath of God, for it is written, 'Vengeance is Mine, I will repay,' says the Lord. 'But if your enemy is hungry, feed him, and if he is thirsty, give him a drink; for in so doing you will heap burning coals on his head.' Do not be overcome by evil, but overcome evil with good."

the Message

"I pledge allegiance to the flag of the United States of America and to the republic for which it stands, one nation, under God, indivisible, with liberty and justice for all."

The Pledge of Allegiance was written by Francis Bellamy in 1892. I like to connect the concepts of "freedom" and "under God." We may tend to think of freedom in terms of winning wars. Our soldiers from the Revolutionary War to Desert Storm have fought for freedom. Yet "freedom under God" is even more significant. God frees us from inner voices that threaten to enslave us in sin or trap us in mental instability, envy, anger, jealousy, or hatred.

The Civil War divided our nation, yet it brought to an end the insidious practice of slavery in America. Freedom under God promotes liberty and justice *for all*. Yet slavery in another form continues to rage in America. I see it in teenagers who want to kill themselves and couples who want to divorce. It's a slavery that cannot be ended with weapons or eloquently phrased proclamations. This freedom *does* require bloodshed— the blood of Christ applied for our sins.

Otherwise we all remain slaves to bitterness, which makes us hold grudges like a three-year-old holds a Butterfinger bar. Maybe your boyfriend was cruel to you. Your dad called you names. Your sister wore your favorite shirt and tore it. Your football coach kept you on the bench. The bitterness we harbor from such offenses burns like a hot coal inside of us.

We need freedom…under God. And we can receive it the moment we pledge Him our allegiance.

Discussion Starters:

• Why is bitterness such a powerful slave master?

•• How does today's passage relate to the "freedom under God" concept?

••• Whom do you need to forgive today? How can Jesus' death on the cross help you?

Lifeline:

"Father, forgive them; for they do not know what they are doing" (Luke 23:34).

A Higher Law

the WORD | Romans 13:1-2

"Every person is to be in subjection to the governing authorities. For there is no authority except from God, and those which exist are established by God. Therefore whoever resists authority has opposed the ordinance of God."

the Message

As a high school student, Brandon had the good looks that could have taken him to Hollywood. His speed and strength could have taken him to all-star status in Division I football. His personality could have taken him on a date with almost any girl in Houston. But at 16 Brandon began to drink beer on Saturday nights, and within two years he was an alcoholic. His alcohol and drug habits led to failure in his high school football career, many broken relationships, two car wrecks, and even some prison time.

Alcohol is responsible for more automobile deaths, fire deaths, broken homes, wife abuse, child abuse, murders, and burglaries than any other single factor. Our government says it's illegal to drink alcohol if you're under 21. While that should be enough of a deterrent for Christian teenagers, God's law also says "strong drink" is wrong at *any* age.

The Bible refers to two kinds of alcoholic beverages. The first is *oinos,* a fermented grape juice purified by a small alcohol content. Historical research suggests that *oinos* had a maximum content of 2 percent alcohol. Jesus turned water into this kind of wine (John 2:1-11). The other biblical word is *shekar*, which refers to strong drink and is condemned many times in Scripture (Proverbs 23:29-35, for example).

Alcoholic consumption by teenagers is a case where our national laws confirm what the Bible teaches. But what if the law of the land contradicts God's law? For example, our government allows abortion, pornography, adultery, and homosexual sex, yet such practices remain in direct opposition to God's law. Even though they are legal, our Christian convictions should prevent our involvement in such things.

God has established governments, and we are to support them as much as we can with a clear conscience. But governments won't be standing before Him on judgment day. We remain responsible for our actions *as individuals.* And there's no better time to begin than during your teenage years.

Discussion Starters:

* When civil law and God's law don't agree, which should you obey? Why?
    ** Scripture doesn't address certain governmental laws (such as speed limits). How should we respond to such laws? Why?
    *** Which current laws do you most tend to resist? Why?

Lifeline:

God's law always has a purpose: to protect us and provide for our well-being, happiness, and peace.

Lust Kills

the **WORD** | Romans 13:13

"Let us behave properly as in the day, not in carousing and drunkenness, not in sexual promiscuity and sensuality, not in strife and jealousy."

the **Message**

Recently I received yet another letter that tells the tragic story of what happens when someone mistakes lust for love.

> I just want to tell you I've made a terrible mistake. I had been dating a Christian guy for 11 months, [and] we both told each other our physical limit was kissing. A few months ago we began to go further than that. We never went all the way, though. I felt terrible every time we went further. My relationship with God was almost nonexistent. I still feel guilty. Please tell other teens how they should totally wait for their future spouse. I wish more than anything that I would've completely waited. Tell them to make a physical limit and stay behind that line. Tell them that no matter how much the temptation is to go further, don't give in. It will be worth the wait. Just to top things off, we broke up yesterday.

There's a huge difference between love and lust, but lust is such a chameleon that it's often hard to tell the two apart. I do know that most of the "I love you's" exchanged between guys and girls in high school and college are actually "I want you's." Otherwise, why do so many people break up when things don't go exactly as they had hoped?

If you're ever confused between love and lust, turn to the reassuring words of 1 Corinthians 13. Here are just a few verses: "Love is patient, love is kind and is not jealous; love does not brag and is not arrogant, does not act unbecomingly; it does not seek its own, is not provoked, does not take into account a wrong suffered, does not rejoice in unrighteousness, but rejoices with the truth" (verses 4-6).

If this isn't your working definition, you don't yet know genuine love. And in this case, what you don't know *can* hurt you.

Discussion Starters:

* How would you explain the difference between love and lust in your own words?
** Do you know anyone who's struggling with lust? How can you help?
*** How can you keep your core values strong throughout your teenage years?

Lifeline:

"Lust can't wait to get. Love can't wait to give" (Josh McDowell).

Put on Jesus

the **WORD** | Romans 13:14

"But put on the Lord Jesus Christ, and make no provision for the flesh in regard to its lusts."

the *Message*

My Labrador retriever seldom leaves my side. His shiny black coat glistens in the sunlight as he gallantly retrieves the doves, ducks, pheasants, and quail we hunt together each winter. He will chew on a sorry little gnawed-up chicken bone for hours, and you might lose a hand if you try to take it away from him. But if you lay a piece of freshly cooked sirloin steak on the sidewalk beside him, he'll drop that old bone in a split second!

Sin is *so* much like Ol' Brave's chewed-up chicken bone. It may satisfy your craving for a while, but only because you don't realize you could have something much better.

Take a look at these quotes from letters I received from high school friends:
- "I knew it was wrong, but I did it anyway."
- "I felt like I had 600 knives go through me. I was crushed."
- "I feel so used and ashamed."

Drinking *looks* fun. Sex *looks* fun. Sin *looks* cool. But when we get drawn into sinful activities, they all seem so meaningless, don't they?

God, as usual, is way ahead of us. He doesn't only tell us not to sin, but He also provides us with a much better option. Paul says to "put on the Lord Jesus Christ." In other words, we can access Jesus' continual companionship, friendship, and unconditional love. Anything else we pursue to fulfill our needs is a lame substitute.

Now take a look at these quotes from some of my other high school friends:
- "I have fallen in love with Jesus this year. God has blessed me with the strength to stay free from drugs, alcohol, and sex."
- "I have acquired this sense of peace that only He could bring."
- "While doing my Bible study this year my relationship with the Lord has grown greatly.... I used to rely on drugs and sex for fun, but now I know that God has forgiven me and loves me like none of that ever happened."

Discussion Starters:

- What are some enticing sins you've encountered lately?
  - How can "putting on the Lord Jesus Christ" actually replace our desire to sin?
    - How can Jesus truly become a friend and source of fulfillment?

Lifeline:

When something you love is removed and you feel a void in your life, you can successfully replace it with something you love more.

Judge Not

the **WORD** | Romans 14:10, 12-13

"But you, why do you judge your brother? Or you again, why do you regard your brother with contempt? For we will all stand before the judgment seat of God…. So then each one of us will give an account of himself to God. Therefore let us not judge one another anymore, but rather determine this—not to put an obstacle or a stumbling block in a brother's way."

the **Message**

No one knew why the beautiful blonde drove her baby blue BMW convertible to the school principal's house each evening at 6:30 and stayed until 10:00. The principal was 35; the blonde was barely 22, fresh out of college and a new resident in the small community.

The community *did* know that the principal had lost his wife to cancer only a year before. Now rumors of his new "affair" spread across town like wildfire. What must the principal's 12-year-old daughter be witnessing? How could the principal appear so pious each Sunday morning in his Baptist church, nodding his head in response to the preacher's comments?

To add fuel to the fire, the blonde became obviously pregnant after a few months. She looked like she had swallowed a basketball. It was clear to everyone at school that she had also swallowed "a line" from the suave principal.

Tempers raged at the next school board meeting. A unanimous vote of the board expressed the town's judgment in a firm and final manner. The principal was asked to resign.

Forced to look for work in another town, the principal sorrowfully began to pack his 12-year-old daughter's clothes, dolls, and priceless books—books which happened to be in Braille. His daughter would have to look for another teacher who was specially trained to teach blind kids to read—just as she was finally finding hope after living in darkness since birth.

The blonde woman's grief at losing a client was minor compared to the pain she felt over the recent loss of her husband—the father of her new baby—a casualty of the war in the Persian Gulf. The sorrow of three people was intensified by the harsh judgment of a town that all too quickly formed erroneous opinions and spread false rumors.

Discussion Starters:

* Why does today's passage come down so strongly against judging others?
** Have you struggled with this problem in your own life? In what ways?
*** What steps can you begin to take in order to leave all matters of judgment in God's hands?

Lifeline:

It has been said that God hates the sin but loves the sinner. We should learn to do the same.

Stumbling Blocks

the WORD | Romans 14:19-21

"So then let us pursue the things which make for peace and the building up of one another. Do not tear down the work of God for the sake of food. All things indeed are clean, but they are evil for the man who eats and gives offense. It is good not to eat meat or to drink wine, or to do anything by which your brother stumbles."

the Message

Is it wrong to wear a low-cut dress?

Is it wrong to wear tight pants?

Is it wrong to French-kiss passionately and then make the other person stop before petting begins?

Is it wrong to drink a beer at a party?

Is it wrong to say you love someone so he or she will go further with you on a date?

Is it wrong to let a seductive undergarment show through a light-colored blouse or pants?

Is it wrong to wear powerful perfumes, hoping to arouse men's sexual fantasies?

To answer these all-important questions, define the word *enticement* in your mind. Then look closely at how the models are dressed in car ads and beer commercials. Ask a boy what he was thinking about when you wore those tight shorts to the Fourth of July picnic. Ask a younger friend what that can of beer in your hand does to your Christian witness.

Not everyone is necessarily pulled into sin by each of these things, but some people *are*. It's not enough to simply think about ourselves; it's just as important to consider our weaker Christian brothers and sisters, as well as those who haven't yet become Christians. Satan is a master at causing people to stumble. He knows our weaknesses like he knew Eve's craving for the forbidden fruit in the Garden of Eden. And if we're not careful, he uses us to initiate sin in other people's lives.

Some of our choices are obviously right or wrong. Others are less clear. But anything that threatens to trip up a fellow follower of Jesus should be avoided—because we *want* to, not because we *have* to. Our call is simple. Let's leave the blocks in the toy box and stop using them to make our brothers and sisters fall.

Discussion Starters:

- What are some stumbling blocks that have been placed in your path? Did you get tripped up?
  - Can you recall causing anyone to "stumble" in the past?
  - Even if you're convinced that you're doing nothing wrong, is it possible that any of your behaviors might cause problems for someone else? If so, what do you think you should do?

Lifeline:

When we're free to do something, we're usually just as free not to.

Three Little Words

the WORD | Romans 15:1-3, 7

"Now we who are strong ought to bear the weaknesses of those without strength and not just please ourselves. Each of us is to please his neighbor for his good, to his edification. For even Christ did not please Himself.... Therefore, accept one another, just as Christ also accepted us to the glory of God."

the Message

One of my sons gets his feelings hurt far too easily. The other one shoots his mouth off too much. One of my daughters has a hard time saying she's sorry. The other one demands too much attention. My wife can't remember my favorite recipe and keeps adding onions to the meatloaf.

I used to fuss about their inconsistencies. Now, by God's grace, I hardly notice. In return they don't seem to mind my oversized feet and nose—not to mention my thousands of other faults too numerous to list in this book.

"Accept one another" is a simple three-word phrase that is the best possible prescription for holding a family together. Acceptance is the strongest glue for relationships. No earthquake or tornado can compare to its power.

My wife had a rocky childhood from contending with generations of family idiosyncrasies. At first her emotional wounds didn't fit into my pious formula for "the perfect wife." Yet we have a blast together these days because I've learned to accept her just as she is and thank God for giving me far more than I deserve!

My good buddy Lee Eaton raises horses in the bluegrass hills of Kentucky. A few years ago he bought a young colt that turned out to be crippled. The previous owner offered to refund Lee's money, but Lee had grown to love the young horse and accepted her as if she were perfect. A couple of years passed and the filly gave birth to a beautiful little foal...that grew up and won the Kentucky Derby! Lee has given away a good share of the $35 million that little crippled horse made for him. More important to him is his priceless family, who have learned from Lee that good things happen when we "accept one another."

Discussion Starters:

* What does it mean to "accept one another"? Think of some specific examples.
  ** What "faults" have you noticed in those you love? How can acceptance help you downplay those faults and see more clearly the worth of each person?
  *** What changes would you expect to see if everyone in your family began to accept one another completely?

Lifeline:

Acceptance prevents any shortcoming from diminishing a person's sense of worth.

Speak Up!

"For I will not presume to speak of anything except what Christ has accomplished through me, resulting in the obedience of the Gentiles by word and deed, in the power of signs and wonders, in the power of the Spirit; so that...I have fully preached the gospel of Christ."

the **Message**

Jill Brawner was recently crowned homecoming queen at my son's public high school. Early in the football season, Jill began to date the all-state running back on the team, a handsome senior named Matt Fisher. They've dated for a whole year, and everyone thinks Matt is the luckiest guy alive.

You say you've heard this story? Small town. Homecoming queen dates the football star. Nothing to do on Saturday night but drink _____ and have _____. But before you fill in the blanks too hastily, let me set you straight about Jill. She's a virgin who has never tasted alcohol or been touched sexually by a guy. Her consistent Christian witness has led Matt to a closer walk with Christ. Within the last two years, many other guys on the football team have chosen to become Christians as well.

No one in the locker room dares to ask Matt, "How far did you get on your last date with Jill?" It's not that they fear his crushing right fist. Instead, their respect for his southern Missouri girlfriend won't even allow them to think such things.

Jill's best friend is Erin Teeter. Hardly a day goes by that Erin doesn't have her arm and her huge heart around some new girl in town or a freshman searching for God's answers to a lifetime of hurt. While small-minded gossipmongers gather in cliques and spread rumors about girls with problems, Erin is busy getting those girls to church, to small-group Bible studies, or to hook up with Christian teens who can give them a "light" to find their way out of the darkness.

The apostle Paul enjoyed any opportunity to preach, but he especially liked to talk about Jesus to people who had never heard before (Romans 15:20-21). Jill and Erin are fellow apostles on the mission field of their campus. Can you identify anyone in that role at your school? If not, that means the job is still open...maybe for you.

Discussion Starters:

* What can we learn from Paul about speaking up for Jesus?
** What are some ways to "preach the gospel" without using words?
*** Where is a mission field you can get involved with today?

Lifeline:

"Witness always. Use words when necessary" (St. Francis of Assisi).

Honest to God?

"I urge you, brethren, keep your eye on those who cause dissensions and hindrances contrary to the teaching which you learned, and turn away from them.... By their smooth and flattering speech they deceive the hearts of the unsuspecting."

the *Message*

It seems I have a problem with integrity. A close look at my heart reveals I have erred in this area of life.

Take a look at these potential verbal problems, nicely summarized by Nancy Leigh DeMoss.[1] Look up the verse(s) provided and read the short explanation of each. Which ones are true of you?

Exaggeration (Proverbs 8:8; 30:5-6)
- Overstating the truth by using words like "always" or "never."
- Making sweeping generalizations about people or situations.

Flattery (Psalm 12:2)
- Giving insincere praise.

Misleading Others (2 Corinthians 8:21)
- Leaving a false impression (though my own spoken words may be true).

Inaccuracy (Hebrews 13:18)
- Carelessness with regard to factual details of stories.

Deception (Psalm 120:2)
- Attempting to create a better impression of myself than is honestly true.

Hypocrisy (Psalm 62:4b; Proverbs 26:23)
- Speaking kindly to another while harboring bitterness in my heart.

Inconsistency (Malachi 3:6; James 1:17)
- Flip-flopping on issues as my "audience" changes.

Guile (Psalm 32:2)
- Maintaining hidden agendas and ulterior motives when dealing with people.

Broken Promises (Psalm 15:1, 4)
- Agreeing then failing to be somewhere at a certain time or to meet a need.

Discussion Starters:

- In what areas do you want to improve your integrity before God?
  - What is the difference between honesty before men and honesty before God?
    - How do you evaluate your personal integrity?

Lifeline:

Integrity means "knit together," and integrates your walk and your talk.

1 corinthians

An hour's drive from Athens, Greece, lays the rediscovered ruins of ancient Corinth. Of all the places in the world I've ever visited, Corinth is the most impressive. Here, early Christians stood against an oppressive, sinful culture. Corinth was a crossroads for Christianity. Towering over the city like a huge, golden idol was a mountain where thousands of prostitutes practiced illicit sex as a heathen religious practice. Each day a Corinthian Christian awoke, he stood in the shadow of sin.

Ancient Corinth was much like our society today. The TV set in my house, like the mountain above their city, is a daily reminder of the sin around me. Believers in Corinth made the difficult choice to walk away from sin and trust God. We have much to learn from them in 1 and 2 Corinthians.

My friend and fellow counselor, Will Cunningham, joins me to write the following devotionals. He has much experience as a professional counselor and an abiding love for God and His people.

Divided We Fall

"Now I exhort you, brethren, by the name of our Lord Jesus Christ, that you all agree and that there be no divisions among you, but that you be made complete in the same mind and in the same judgment. For I have been informed…that there are quarrels among you. Now I mean this, that each one of you is saying, 'I am of Paul,' and 'I of Apollos,' and 'I of Cephas,' and 'I of Christ.' Has Christ been divided? Paul was not crucified for you, was he? Or were you baptized in the name of Paul?"

the *Message*

Coaches get excited when their players are working together. Dads get even more excited when their kids work together. To the church at Corinth, Paul was both father and coach. Before his arrival, these unbelievers on the Aegean Sea had never had anyone explain the gospel to them, much less show them how to live by it. Paul's preaching had made him their spiritual father, and he was just as interested in coaching them to maturity. Unfortunately, the Corinthians were anything but unified. As other church leaders became popular, the church members began to argue like a football team squabbling in the huddle.

"I was discipled by Apollos," someone would say, "so I'm the quarterback!"

Another disagrees: "Paul was my mentor, so I get to call the plays!"

"Big deal! Peter's the main man, and that's who I follow, so both of you stand aside."

Not surprisingly, the church at Corinth was not having much success on the field, which made Coach Paul both angry and sad. His appeal to unity flows through his entire letter to them.

Teams go nowhere when they quarrel and fight. They succeed only if they work as a unit. This is what Paul wanted the Corinthian Christians to know more than anything else. And it is what God wants today's Christians to know, too.

Discussion Starters:

* Football teams get penalized if they spend too much time quarreling in the huddle. What are some consequences the church faces when Christians don't work together?

 ** What was the source of the Corinthians' squabbling? Do you ever see a similar problem in your own church?

 *** What is one way you can become more unified with your fellow Christians?

Lifeline:

Just as a sports team must unite, so we as Christians must lay aside our petty differences and unify in the work Jesus has called us. What inhibits your family unity?

Fools and Fighters

"For the word of the cross is foolishness to those who are perishing, but to us who are being saved it is the power of God."

the Message

Muhammad Ali was unsurpassed. Of all his fights, most memorable are his bouts with Smokin' Joe Frazier. Joe was half a foot shorter than Ali, but built like a block of granite and noted for his hard, straightforward punches. Frazier was known to pursue his opponents relentlessly, moving in tight, taking blow after blow, until he finally wore them down enough to move in for the knockdown. Ali was the champ, but many sports analysts were picking Frazier to win.

For weeks prior to the match Ali did nothing but abdominal work—sit-ups and more sit-ups—even to the neglect of his other skills. It was baffling to the media, and Ali's explanation wasn't much clearer: "If you're coming to see me float like a butterfly and sting like a bee, you're in for a surprise! I'm going to use the rope-a-dope on Mr. Frazier, and he'll never know what hit him."

The *rope-a-dope?* No one had ever heard of it. It seemed foolish for Ali to alter from his proven style. When the fight began, Ali backed into the ropes. Frazier followed and pummeled Ali's midsection for round after round, with little retaliation from Ali. Eventually it became evident that Frazier was the "dope." Worn out by his unsuccessful attack on Ali's muscled torso, Frazier found little strength left in his arms. Soon the victory was Ali's. For weeks afterward, the media praised Ali's "rope-a-dope" tactic. What had once been considered foolish had become a thing of wisdom.

Paul knew that human wisdom could be a treacherous opponent. At its core is the proud belief that we are clever enough to earn God's favor on our own. The thought of Christ dying on the cross for us seems like foolishness. But in the end it will be the power of the cross that delivers the final knockout blow to Satan.

Discussion Starters:

• When has your human wisdom (pride) hindered you from following Christ?
•• When was a time you felt foolish for following Christ but followed Him anyway?
••• Why does Paul call the cross "the power of God"?

Lifeline:

Spiritual fitness is our "rope-a-dope" strategy that eventually defeats Satan.

Simple Talk

the **WORD** | *1 Corinthians 2:4-5*

"My message and my preaching were not in persuasive words of wisdom, but in demonstration of the Spirit and of power, so that your faith would not rest on the wisdom of men, but on the power of God."

the *Message*

During the past year, I had dinner in the homes of two different ex-NFL linebackers. Both were godly men with good wives who treated me with such hospitality that you would have thought I was an ambassador. Their children were conversational. Their homes were in order. Even their pets were polite. From what I could tell as a guest, they seemed to live a perfect life.

Of course, I know things are not perfect for them all the time. But they learned to experience a lasting peace—not from knowing they had earned Super Bowl rings, but because of their relationships with an awesome God. In both homes I noticed that their trophies were nowhere in sight. When I pressed them, one led me to the basement and the other to an obscure closet. The evidence of their careers was collecting dust.

In one home, a Super Bowl game jersey, long forgotten by the public, was tucked in a corner. Underneath a stack of boxes was the pair of shoes the owner had worn to run the 40-yard dash in 4.3 seconds. One day even Darryl Green, the fastest man in the NFL, will fade from people's memory. Somehow, my two linebacker friends had kept all the fame of their lives in proper perspective. Instead of talking about their accomplishments both nights, we spent our time together talking about the Lord.

These were two noted football players, yet they were not in the least flashy or ostentatious. Similarly, Paul was perhaps the best-known preacher of his time, yet he took great care to avoid sounding stuffy or talking over people's heads. He knew if he could just stand back and let God act, everyone would be a lot better off. My two NFL friends seem to have learned that lesson. I hope it sinks in for me and for you as well.

Discussion Starters:

* If you won an honor, where would you display your trophy?
  ** Have you ever felt let down when you relied on someone (or God)?
  *** When you experienced that disappointment, how did you handle it?

Lifeline:

Take inventory of the things you rely upon. Are they anything less than God's power?

Mind Reader

the WORD | 1 Corinthians 2:16

"For who has known the mind of the Lord, that he will instruct Him? But we have the mind of Christ."

the Message

I once read that every successful father knows one good magic trick. So I dutifully learned my trick and repeated it hundreds of times to the delight of squealing kids. Then came Henry. After I did the trick for him, he ran and told his mother I was a mind reader. Henry's mom came to see if her son's head was being filled with mumbo-jumbo.

I explained that my trick was only about 1 percent "magic" and mostly required distracting the kids while I prepared the deck. She still looked skeptical, and Henry didn't help things. "That's not true, Mom. He closed his eyes and told me to pick a card. Then he put his hand on my forehead, rubbed a little bit, and told me the exact card I picked. He's a mind reader!"

By now Mom was really frowning, so I held out the deck and said, "Henry, pick a card." I knew that without stacking the deck, there was no chance I would guess which card he chose. Henry picked a card. And I'll be the Queen of Artichokes if my wild guess wasn't right. He picked again. I guessed again, *correctly!* By this time, I was too baffled to reply. A third time Henry chose, and *again* I guessed his card. To this day, I have no idea how.

At that point the mother hastened Henry away from what she must have considered my hypnotic, evil gaze. And as I watched them drive away, I promised never again to amuse a child with "magic"—a promise I have kept.

Yet when I read 1 Corinthians 2:16, I discover I *can* be a mind reader. It's as if Paul is saying, "I know it seems a little hard to believe, but we can know Christ's thoughts because we have the mind of Christ."

If you're a Christian, you too have the mind of Christ. His thoughts are available to you in Scripture, and the Holy Spirit helps you remember and understand what you read. So why not open your Bible today and start practicing a little "mind reading"?

Discussion Starters:

• Have you ever had the mind of Christ—a time when His thoughts helped you make a decision, withstand a temptation, etc.?

•• Have you ever ignored good directions to follow your own mind? What happened?

••• What does it say *about God that He is willing to share* His thoughts with you?

Lifeline:

As important as asking "What would Jesus do?" is knowing what He would think.

Foundations for Living

the **WORD** | 1 Corinthians 3:10-11

"According to the grace of God which was given to me, like a wise master builder I laid a foundation, and another is building on it. But each man must be careful how he builds on it. For no man can lay a foundation other than the one which is laid, which is Jesus Christ."

the Message

In my neighborhood we have what I would guess to be, oh, about 5,000 little boys, each with a bike and a dog. If eight of them come to your house for cookies, you can be sure there will be eight bicycles in your driveway and eight lazy dogs lying in your front yard.

The other day I was walking through our woods and noticed some of their handiwork. Every other tree had the beginnings of a tree house in it. Over here was a chunk of two-by-four nailed to the trunk of an oak. Farther off, an irregular piece of plywood formed a seat in the crook of an ash tree. But in the center of the woods was the grandfather of all tree houses—a finished product nestled high in the arms of an alder tree.

I use the word *finished* loosely, but to a 10-year-old boy it must have seemed so. More accurately, it was a ton of lumber teetering on a toothpick. It was a deathtrap! How could any child play there without plunging to his demise? I had the urge to call the Department of Urban Renewal, but then I remembered my own childhood, smiled to myself, and went on my way.

Unfortunately, a lot of people's lives are on foundations just as shaky as that tree house. Everything seems okay at first glance, but a closer look reveals that things aren't quite right. Paul wanted the Christians at Corinth to know that only one foundation is stable enough to build a life upon. If we try to build on anything else—money, accomplishments, physique, possessions—the foundations will crumble, and the fall will be tragic.

At all costs, build on the foundation of Jesus—and nothing else.

Discussion Starters:

* Are you building on some "foundations" other than Christ? If so, what are they?
  ** When people have built on other foundations, is it better for them to "do the remodeling" themselves or wait until those foundations crumble? Explain.
* *** What is the best symbol for your current relationship with Jesus: A shaky tree house? A log cabin? A brick home? A stone fortress? Other? Explain your answer.

Lifeline:

Discuss ways you can build your life on the foundation of Jesus Christ.

The Real Thing

"Now if any man builds on the foundation with gold, silver, precious stones, wood, hay, straw, each man's work will become evident; for the day will show it because it is to be revealed with fire, and the fire itself will test the quality of each man's work. If any man's work which he has built on it remains, he will receive a reward."

the **Message**

My friend Andy went to marvelous measures to ask his girlfriend to marry him. Being an actor, he invited her to a play in which the character he played (a very stuffy aristocrat) was in a marriage proposal scene but could not bring himself to pop the question. After the play, the curtain came down and the lights went on. But before people could exit, Andy stepped to center stage and, in front of his college peers, delivered two dozen roses to his girlfriend in the audience.

He announced: "My character in the play was unable to receive and give love. But I'm not him and he's not me, and I can think of nothing more wonderful than to share our love together for the rest of our lives. Will you marry me?" Then he pulled a box from his pocket and opened it to reveal a shining diamond ring.

The girl said yes. I think I was happier than most of the others in attendance, because she happened to be my daughter. Andy, who is now my son-in-law, won my admiration for a lifetime.

Now imagine if, after all the creative energy Andy poured into his proposal, he had offered Jamie Jo a cheap, little, plastic ring he tried to pass off as the real thing. Trust me, the evening would have turned ugly.

Paul told the Christians at Corinth that it was their choice to build upon the foundation of Christ with either precious jewels or materials that were worthless. We have the same choice today. Of course, it is by God's grace that any of us will get to heaven in the first place. But our works determine the quality of the gift we present to Jesus when we get there. I'd much rather hand Him a diamond than a piece of plastic. How about you?

Discussion Starters:

* What are some "works" that are jewels?
** What are some "works" that are worthless?
*** Do you need to improve the quality of your "works"? If so, how?

Lifeline:

Jewels and precious metals survive the test of fire. Will the value of your work for Jesus endure, or will you stand before Him empty-handed?

Dead Man Writing

the **WORD** | *1 Corinthians 4:9*

"For, I think, God has exhibited us apostles last of all, as men condemned to death; because we have become a spectacle to the world, both to angels and to men."

the **Message**

Twice I have written to a dead man. On both occasions, his response showed me I was less alive than he was.

When I sent my first letter to Darrell in the fall of 1998, I half expected to get back the ramblings of a stir-crazy inmate. After all, he had been on death row for over 10 years. How fluent can a man be in his situation? Yet his reply was immediate and filled with wit, country humor, and spiritual wisdom. It turns out that Darrell's only conversation partner is God—24 hours a day—so his letters are filled with scriptural references.

After entering Potosi Correctional Center, he gave his life to Christ. At that moment, his old self died—the old, awful self who had shot his former drug dealer and two other human beings with a 12-gauge shotgun. Since then, Darrell has become the self-appointed chaplain of death row.

Not long ago, I saw that Pope John Paul II had taken up Darrell's case and had asked the governor of Missouri to pardon him after 10 long years. Darrell's letters reveal that he believes he will one day be released.

In today's verse, Paul compares Christianity to a death sentence. Without crucifying our old, evil natures, we could never enter the perfection of heaven. But Christianity is also a full pardon that flings our cell doors open wide and frees us to walk with God.

Have you died to sin? Like Paul and Darrell, are you a dead-to-self person who now lives in the abundant life of Christ? If not, consider the cold, hard walls of your existence and the bleakness of your future. Then come to Jesus, the doorway to life, and leave your cell behind forever.

Discussion Starters:

* Do you have the hope of eternal life with Jesus Christ? If so, who are some "imprisoned" people you could free with the good news of the gospel?
** As believers in Jesus Christ, we are spectacles to the world (1 Corinthians 4:9). What does the world see in you: a dead person or a live one? A death sentence or a pardoned sinner?
*** What old behaviors do you need to "crucify" to strengthen your relationship with Jesus Christ?

Lifeline:

The more dead you are to self, the more alive you will become in Christ.

Climbing Toward Servanthood

the WORD | 1 Corinthians 4:11-13

"To this present hour we are both hungry and thirsty, and are poorly clothed, and are roughly treated, and are homeless; and we toil, working with our own hands; when we are reviled, we bless; when we are persecuted, we endure; when we are slandered, we try to conciliate; we have become as the scum of the world, the dregs of all things, even until now."

the Message

In the world of technical climbing, one person leads the group and another follows behind. The leader has the job of getting the team of climbers safely up the cliff by "setting protection" along the way. Into one crevice he places a cam; into another, a chalk or a wedge. And into each of these devices he fastens the climbing rope. The safety of his comrades depends on how well he does his job. If the climb is successful, the lead climber gets the glory.

On the other hand, the climber who follows—known as "the cleaner"—has the unheralded job of unfastening ("cleaning") the protective devices set by the lead climber as the team advances up the cliff. There is nothing flashy about the role he plays. Consequently, he rarely gets acknowledged.

The role of the Christian servant is like that of "the cleaner" on a treacherous mountain climb. If he does his job well, the whole team advances. But his negligence can result in disaster. I knew a man who broke his leg on an ice climb—snapped the bone in two—because the cleaner had not paid attention to his job.

Paul wanted the Corinthians to take servanthood seriously. He didn't try to hide the challenges and "down" sides of service because he knew the rewards were even greater. And he made it clear that he was right there with them, even admonishing his readers to imitate his example (1 Corinthians 4:16).

Whether God calls you to be a "lead climber" or a "cleaner," there is no place for arrogance in the Body of Christ. We are all servants, just as our Lord Jesus was a servant. When we get this point straight, our journey upward will be a thrilling one. And the view from the top, when we finally get there, will be glorious.

Discussion Starters:

Do you see yourself more as a "lead climber" or a "cleaner"?

Are you aware of any disasters that have happened because Christian leaders were either arrogant or negligent?

Think of one servant-leader you know.

What characteristics distinguish his or her servanthood?

Lifeline:

How can your family be servants to each other, the church, and your neighborhood?

Weeds and Worse Problems

"It is actually reported that there is immorality among you, and immorality of such a kind as does not exist even among the Gentiles, that someone has his father's wife. You have become arrogant and have not mourned instead, so that the one who had done this deed would be removed from your midst."

the Message

A high cholesterol count.

A rumor.

A child near a socket with a paper clip.

A fever.

A disagreement with the wife or kids.

A bag of weed in Johnny's bedroom.

A spot on an X ray.

The letter "E" on the gas gauge.

Some problems in life are trivial. Others, such as the ones listed here, demand immediate attention. If we don't take action, they will only get worse.

The church in Corinth had a serious problem. One of the church members had an ongoing sexual relationship with his mother (or maybe stepmother, but still…!). And he kept coming to Sunday services as if nothing were wrong. Amazingly, no one in the church was doing anything about it. In fact, it had become a point of arrogance for them. They thought it made them cool and free-thinking—sort of like a guy who brags about how many beers he drank at a party. But such an attitude eventually brings you down.

Paul's advice was twofold: (1) they should change their attitude about the sin before it infected the entire body; and (2) they should remove the man until he repented.

Maybe it isn't something as drastic as this, but are any problem areas being left unattended in your own life that could do you harm?

Discussion Starters:

* Do you think it's right for churches to kick people out who don't conform to biblical teaching?
  ** Is there anything you need to repent of? If you are willing, share it with someone.
    *** What do you think could happen if you don't repent?

Lifeline:

Confessing sins ensures there will be no rift in our relationships with God.

Crate Expectations

"I wrote to you not to associate with any so-called brother if he is an immoral person, or covetous, or an idolater, or a reviler, or a drunkard, or a swindler—not even to eat with such a one."

the *Message*

I have helped train several Labrador retrievers, so I can chuckle to watch my son-in-law going through the same painful process. Andy doesn't have a single mean bone in his body. His pupil, Ty, on the other hand, is a tail-wagging terror. It is high comedy watching the gentle master with his not-so-eager pupil.

Yet I get more than grins from observing Andy and Ty. Their back-and-forth struggle reminds me that love is not always comfortable. At times one must direct a dog with painful consequences for him to become more teachable, useful, and, in the long run, happier. The same is true of people. In spite of what we hear in this age of tolerance, our failure to apply discipline in our deepest relationships has led to the breakdown of families, businesses, governments, and even churches.

One of the hardest things for a dog trainer to do is put his animal in a crate. It separates the dog from the company of all living creatures by confining him to a box barely bigger than a suitcase. But the procedure is necessary when the trainee habitually rebels against the trainer's voice. After the confinement, when the doors to the crate are flung wide again, it is often a much more submissive dog that emerges.

Paul faced a similar problem in the Corinthian church when he learned a man was sleeping with his own mother (or stepmother). The church leaders had given their stamp of approval.

"Crate the man!" Paul says in essence.

Tough love. Sometimes that's what it takes. Complete obedience is something dogs and people must have for their Master.

Discussion Starters:

* What is a situation where you have seen "tough love" applied? What were the results?

** What might have happened if a softer approach had been taken?

*** How can people avoid finding themselves in a spiritual "crate" to be disciplined?

Lifeline:

Loving parents will express tough love to their children when necessary. And loving parents will also accept tough love *from* their children.

Court Adjourned!

the WORD | *1 Corinthians 6:5-7*

"I say this to your shame. Is it so, that there is not among you one wise man who will be able to decide between his brethren, but brother goes to law with brother, and that before unbelievers? Actually, then, it is already a defeat for you, that you have lawsuits with one another. Why not rather be wronged? Why not rather be defrauded?"

the Message

Several years ago, a woman sued a major fast-food chain after receiving a serious burn from spilling a cup of coffee in her lap. Never mind that in her haste to pull away from the drive-through, she had placed the cup between her legs instead of in a cup holder. Rather than assuming responsibility for her haste and acknowledging that "accidents happen," she hired a lawyer and charged the restaurant with serving coffee that was too hot. The amazing thing is, she won.

In an age when people would rather sue than accept the consequences of their actions, Paul's words in 1 Corinthians 6:1-11 are a breath of fresh air. The passage exposes what is at the heart of so many of our lawsuits: greed, a desire for vengeance, and a disregard for the forgiveness we have received.

Paul explained that the whole church suffers whenever Christians "air their dirty laundry" in public. Lawsuits in a secular court of law may be unavoidable at times. But more often than not, we Christians should be able to settle our differences without the aid of attorneys—even if we receive less than we hope for. Paul points out that one day we are to "judge angels" (verse 3), so we should be eager to concern ourselves more with God's style of justice (which is heavy with mercy and forgiveness) rather than demand a precise eye-for-an-eye compensation.

Do you have a grievance with a friend? A teacher? An employer? Rest assured that for each of your gripes there is a lawyer who would like to turn it into money for you (and him). With Paul, I urge you to resist the temptation to pursue quick financial gain, striving always to settle your disagreements in a godly manner.

Discussion Starters:

* What is the silliest lawsuit you've heard about lately?
  ** How do you think so many people's haste to sue one another has affected our country? How might it affect the church?
  *** Have you ever willingly let someone else take advantage of a situation in order to put a quicker end to a conflict? How did you feel?

Lifeline:

Whenever you have a dispute you'd like to settle, ask Jesus to help.

How's Your Appetite?

the WORD | 1 Corinthians 6:19-20

"Or do you not know that your body is a temple of the Holy Spirit who is in you, whom you have from God, and that you are not your own? For you have been bought with a price: therefore glorify God in your body."

the Message

If you hang around kids for a weekend, you'll hear them say some pretty funny things. One of my camp directors coaches a second-grade boys' basketball team in his spare time, and one of his players told him, "My sister can't eat much 'cause she has a little stomach. But I can eat 17 pieces of pizza. Deep dish."

That guy sounds like a classic overachiever. Don't you get a sick feeling picturing 17 wedges of meat sauce, cheese, and bread dough all mashed together inside a single second-grader? Such a binge may be legal, but it can't be natural.

The people of ancient Corinth had some pretty heavy appetites as well—but not for food. Their city was known for fertility cult temples. It was not only lawful, it was fashionable to have sex with prostitutes who lived in them! It was part of their religion. Supposedly, the sex helped gain favor from the gods to bring blessings on crops (lame excuse).

Paul wanted the Corinthians to acquire a righteous repulsion to their city's sanctioned immorality. He used the examples of both food and sex to make the point that our bodies are not our own. We belong to the One who bought us with everything He had. How dare we allow ourselves to become mastered by our inner appetites!

Whether it's a little boy packing pizza in or a teen allowing his hormones to run wild, we grieve any appetites that are out of control. Paul concludes with the best reason in the world to submit our desires: "You have been bought with a price: therefore glorify God in your body."

Discussion Starters:

• Besides food, what are some human appetites people tend to run away with?
•• Why are our appetites so difficult to master?
••• What appetites do you struggle with? What is the secret to mastering them?

Lifeline:

If an appetite is too strong, perhaps something else is causing the imbalance.

The Wedding Singer

the WORD | *1 Corinthians 7:3-4, 32-34*

"The husband must fulfill his duty to his wife, and likewise also the wife to her husband. The wife does not have authority over her own body, but the husband does; and likewise also the husband does not have authority over his own body, but the wife does.... One who is unmarried is concerned about the things of the Lord, how he may please the Lord; but one who is married is concerned about the things of this world, how he may please his wife, and his interests are divided."

the Message

A friend of mine used to sing in a lot of weddings…until one particular ceremony cured him. He was early, his guitar was in tune, and he had the song down perfectly.

Then in the middle of the song, all recollection of the English language fled from his memory. He stood there gaping like a codfish for a split second and then immediately plunged into wedding singer suicide: he improvised. He made up words. He even attempted to hideously wedge both the bride's and groom's names into the lyrics. The result was a cross between a bad singing telegram and a clichéd fortune cookie to music.

Now, whenever my friend is asked to sing in someone's wedding, he has an answer: "The marriage of two people is such a beautiful thing. Why would you want me to mess it up?"

Paul, too, believed that marriage is a beautiful thing. Yet he also knew about some potential problems that are unforeseen by many single people. As soon as you say "I do," two things change: (1) your body is no longer yours (verse 4); and (2) your interests will forever be divided (verses 32-34).

During our single years, we have only ourselves to think of. Marriage quickly changes that, and Paul wants us to be prepared rather than surprised. Are you selfless enough to sacrifice your body for another? Your quiet times? Your needs, interests, hobbies, and more? If so, you are a candidate for marriage. Just remember—there's no need to rush it.

Discussion Starters:

* What does Paul mean when he says that husbands and wives no longer have authority over their own bodies? Is this only in a sexual sense, or might it be interpreted more broadly?
* Why did Paul feel compelled to warn prospects for marriage about their interests becoming divided?
* What are the advantages of postponing marriage until after your teenage years, or even longer?

Lifeline:

Over every couple entering into marriage hangs a big sign: "All you who enter here, prepare to give yourself away!"

Fiery Love

"It is better to marry than to burn with passion."

the Message

Most of us are drawn to a fire in the dead of winter. When all is bleak and white out-side, nothing beats sitting around a crackling campfire with close friends, sharing stories and a bag of marshmallows. But we grow somber when witnessing the terrible devasta-tion of a fire out of control. Fires remind us that every good gift of God can go awry if not managed properly.

Sex is a gift from God, intended to be the fulfillment of marriage. I am intrigued by the analogy of fire and human sexuality. Every good fire requires three elements: fuel, oxygen, and spark. Remove any of these elements and you decrease the possibility of combustion. Let's think of the "spark" as our hormones, the "oxygen" as our environ-ment, and the "fuel" as our emotions. We can't do much about our hormones or envi-ronment, so let's focus on the fuel of sexual involvement: emotions.

We have a choice of fuels. One common one, though not a particularly good choice, is fear. Have you ever been so afraid to try something that you actually got a "rush" when you finally did it? That's why snowboarding, whitewater rafting, roller coasters, and similar things are so popular.

Lots of dating couples start having sex and experience the "fire" fueled by fear. Will they get caught, will they cheat the rules and come out clean? But using fear as a fuel for sex is like replacing your dinner candles with a big bowl of gasoline. By the time you get married (if you ever do), little fuel remains. The flames of passion burn less brightly, and many quickly decide they are "no longer in love."

The fuel of genuine love, on the other hand, will never ignite the sexual fire prema-turely because love is patient. But on your wedding night, love will produce fireworks galore—and the fire will never go out. Indeed, genuine love just burns warmer the longer you stay together.

You're going to have a fire one way or the other. Just choose your fuel wisely.

Discussion Starters:

• What are some ways people can get "burned" by experimenting with premarital sex?

•• Besides fear, what are some other emotions that can ignite a sexual relationship?

••• With hormones and environment creating sexual drive, what steps can you take to remain faithful to God and your future spouse by saving sex for marriage?

Lifeline:

Sex outside of marriage is unbelievably damaging. If you have experienced such damage, God forgives you and honors your commitment to make a fresh start.

What Do You Know?

the **WORD** | 1 Corinthians 8:1-3

"Knowledge makes arrogant, but love edifies. If anyone supposes that he knows anything, he has not yet known as he ought to know; but if anyone loves God, he is known by Him."

the **Message**

Just when I think I know everything, someone asks me a question I can't answer. Here's one that humbled me recently: "What is uglier than the devil, more beautiful than God, possessed by the poor, and desired by the rich?"

If you said "nothing," you are smarter than I.

Sometimes on the ladder of knowledge, a person must be knocked down a step or two in order to realize how little he or she truly knows. The universe is a vast vault of secrets still undiscovered by even the world's greatest thinkers.

Know-it-alls are like party balloons, all puffed up and full of themselves. Yet it only takes one simple question they can't answer, one tiny pinprick of doubt or ignorance, for their pride to be popped. Then everyone can see them as they truly are—empty windbags.

Paul tells us that loving God is more important than accumulating an ever bigger database of facts and figures. Knowledge can make you look good to others, and you may feel good that others look up to you, but it's a false sense of security. As we begin to believe we know it all (or at least most of "it"), we develop an arrogant attitude. Frequently people with strong personalities and opinions have a hard time learning from others and listening to God.

We must come to realize that if we have developed that kind of sinful mind-set, we *don't* know it all. We still have a lot to learn about love. "Love edifies," says Paul, meaning that it builds other people up. Love is more important than worldly knowledge because it is the key to tapping into God's knowledge. A genuine love for God soon blossoms into an active love toward others by becoming compassionate and attentive to their needs. If you learn to do that, you won't need to know it all. You'll already have more friends than you know what to do with.

Discussion Starters:

* Knowledge can be both a blessing and a curse. Give examples of each.
** What do you know a lot about? Have you ever become proud or arrogant because of it?
*** How can God help you avoid becoming a know-it-all?

Lifeline:

All that you learn may be great and vast, but it only comprises a grain of the past. The future is held by God.

In a Corner

the **WORD** | 1 Corinthians 8:9

"But take care that this liberty of yours does not somehow become a stumbling block to the weak."

the *Message*

Many times I have "painted myself into a corner" in a symbolic sense. But never have I seen this saying fulfilled quite as literally as when I worked with Tom Boggins.

It was a hot day in June. We were hard-pressed to paint six tennis courts before foul weather arrived, as the weatherman had predicted. "Slop it on good and fast," I ordered the crew as I eyed the sky.

Tom took his paint tray and long-handled roller and headed for the spot where we had stopped the day before. I left to go make my rounds and check on several other projects. When I got back, Tom Boggins stood on a tiny island. All around him was an ocean of wet blue paint—and no way out.

I told him to stand still until the paint dried, and he did just that—all the way through lunch and supper. Then, when the paint was finally dry enough, Tom tiptoed back to freedom. To my knowledge, he has not picked up a paint roller since.

Later I found out that Tom hadn't painted himself into that predicament. His fellow workers had been so free with their brushes that they'd isolated him and forced him to forfeit his freedom. They just weren't thinking.

In the same way, it's possible to behave so freely that we don't even notice how we're stealing other people's freedom and forcing them to struggle. If our Christian liberties cause anyone annoyance or discomfort, it damages our testimony. Paul had no problem eating meat offered to idols because he knew idols were nothing more than sticks and stones. But if others took offense, Paul wouldn't do that anymore. We might substitute drinking or wearing tattoos or even dating—things that are lawful for Christians but may cause others to stumble in their faith.

As you paint the canvas of your life, do you notice all the others around you? Or do you slop paint so freely that they will eventually find themselves isolated?

Discussion Starters:

- How has some other Christian's behavior caused you to stumble?
  - What are some other practices Christians could feel free doing but might voluntarily avoid in order to not cause others to take offense or stumble?
- Have you ever been a stumbling block for others? How? What did you do about it?

Lifeline:

There are situations where forfeiting your freedom can cause another to stumble as much as exercising your freedom. Let your desire to show others Christ's love be your guide.

Right of Way

the WORD | 1 Corinthians 9:11-12

"If we sowed spiritual things in you, is it too much if we reap material things from you? If others share the right over you, do we not more? Nevertheless, we did not use this right, but we endure all things so that we will cause no hindrance to the gospel of Christ."

the Message

I once saw a man's car get smashed on his left while he was exercising his rights. "But I had the right of way," he told the officer who surveyed the scene. "The other guy didn't stop at the intersection." The officer replied, "Sometimes our rights don't keep us from getting wronged."

I am astounded by the rights we have in America. If I choose to do so, I can own a gun to protect my family against evil intruders. I can get legal representation in a court of law even if I can't afford it. I can disagree openly with our government. These rights and dozens like them are unheard of in many countries. In fact, we have so many rights that we have begun to expect everything we want. Some of us have even begun to identify wrong as "right" and the pursuit of wrong as a right endeavor.

A popular TV network tells its viewers that "kids rule." Way back in the eighties, the Beastie Boys declared, "You've got to fight for the right to party." Wouldn't it be scary if kids did rule? And I think we all agree life, liberty, and the pursuit of happiness are nobler goals than partying.

The next time you feel like demanding for your "rights," stop and recall the words of today's passage. Paul knew he had rights. When the situation was appropriate, he applied them with great skill (see Acts 16:35-39). Yet if more people could be won to Christ, Paul was willing to give up all entitlements, even his meager preaching income. In short, Paul exercised his rights with wisdom. It is always more important to do right than to demand rights.

Discussion Starters:

* People who don't always stand up for their rights are often seen as spineless or weak. What do you think?
** What rights did Jesus Christ give up?
*** Have you ever willingly yielded your rights? Explain.

Lifeline:

Jesus Christ and the apostle Paul gave up their rights, and great numbers of people received the love and forgiveness of God as a result. What rights could you give up that might help someone know Christ as Savior?

Decks

"For though I am free from all men, I have made myself a slave to all, so that I may win more. To the Jews I became as a Jew, so that I might win Jews; to those who are under the Law, as under the Law though not being myself under the Law, so that I might win those who are under the Law; to those who are without law, as without law, though not being without the law of God but under the law of Christ, so that I might win those who are without law. To the weak I became weak, that I might win the weak; I have become all things to all men, so that I may by all means save some."

the *Message*

It was brought to my attention this summer that some of my staff members had gotten creative in their quest to keep in shape. "They're doing decks," my source told me. Two (or more) guys, eager to pump up their pectorals, would take turns drawing a card and doing that number of push-ups until they had gone through the entire deck. Depending on the luck of the draw, one participant could end up doing a lot more push-ups than the other guy. You ought to see some of my counselors go at it. Talk about a passion for winning!

Paul expressed the same kind of tenacity when he used the phrase "I might win" five times in four verses. He was trying to win souls—any souls. Paul prioritized evangelism over every other aspect of his life.

Paul even had a "workout regimen" to help him achieve his spiritual goals (verses 26-27). Because he could not bear the thought of anyone missing out on the salvation of God, he was always willing to go the extra mile, do the "extra push-up" for the sake of those who were lost. He worked hard, prayed hard, preached hard, traveled hard, loved hard, and trained hard.

And he wanted to know, 2,000 years before Nike asked the question, "What are *you* training for?"

Discussion Starters:

* What word would you use to describe your "walk" with Christ: a stroll or a marathon?
** What are you training for spiritually? Do you have a workout schedule?
*** When you're passionate about something, you work harder. How passionate are you about the gospel? How can you become more?

Lifeline:

If spiritual performance were an Olympic event, what score do you think you would receive from the judges?

Rattler

the WORD | 1 Corinthians 10:12

"Let him who thinks he stands take heed that he does not fall."

the Message

Bill was a rancher, which meant he spent a lot of time alone. He quickly developed a habit of taking action at the first sign of trouble. One night he went to bed and felt something move against his leg beneath the sheets, so up he sprang, grabbing a broom to defend himself. *Whack! Whack! Whack!* With no electricity in the bunkhouse where he slept, Bill beat the bed blindly until he broke a sweat. He stopped to catch his breath and listen. Silence. Bill turned back the covers and swept vigorously until he was sure the mysterious bedfellow was gone. Then he lay back down and went to sleep.

Just before dawn, Bill was awakened by a noise—a sound every rancher has learned not to ignore: a *rattle*. As the sound grew louder, an object fell onto the bed from the bookshelf above. Up Bill sprang again with his trusty broom. *Whack! Whack! Whack!* He pounded until the broomstick snapped and flew across the room. This time he dared not go back to bed but decided to take his chances under the stars.

The next morning, when Bill returned to the bunkhouse, he found a six-and-a-half-foot rattlesnake, dead, stretched out in a patch of sunlight. From that point on, whenever Bill hears the sound of a rattlesnake's rattle, he associates it with the goodness of God's protection.

First Corinthians 10:1-12 is a passage filled with warnings telling us to walk carefully, keep a sharp eye out, and avoid the mistakes of the Israelites (idolatry, immorality, discontent, grumbling, etc.). Just when we think we're immune to these things, they strike. So as today's verse says, we need to "take heed." If we keep our ears open to God's voice, we'll always hear the "rattle" before such dangers can get close enough to hurt us.

Discussion Starters:

* What are the warning signs that someone's life is being threatened by idolatry? Immorality? Grumbling?
** In each of these areas, how can the person heed the warning signs?
*** What are the things that regularly threaten to trip you up and make you fall?

Lifeline:

Identify any "idols" in your life. What steps must you take to diminish each idol's power?

Escape Route

"No temptation has overtaken you but such as is common to man; and God is faithful, who will not allow you to be tempted beyond what you are able, but with the temptation will provide the way of escape also, so that you will be able to endure it."

the **Message**

I heard about some snowmobilers in Lake City, Colorado, who ignored a winter storm alert they heard during a lunch break. An hour later they were high atop Bristol Head, groping along in a whiteout, when suddenly the ground dropped from under them. Days later a rescue team found their shattered bodies at the base of an enormous cliff. Because they ignored a storm warning, they found themselves in a whiteout. Because of the blinding snow, they missed the sign that warned of the dangerous cliff. And because they missed the sign, their lives were tragically cut short. It is now impossible for me to pass that landmark without thinking of the terror that must have been theirs during that unexpected plummet.

When I read 1 Corinthians 10:13, I find both comfort and caution. It's a relief to know that I'm not the only person experiencing the strong temptations I face. But in spite of this comfort, I realize that even a "common" temptation can lead to a disastrous fall if I yield to it. So I must look for God's "way of escape" before I end up endangering myself.

Many are the imprisoned guys and pregnant girls who say, "When I was tempted, God didn't provide *me* with a way of escape. Now look at the mess I'm in!" Yet if you press them, they know that what they did was wrong and that God had provided a clear sign that read: "DO NOT PROCEED BEYOND THIS POINT."

Oh, how I wish teenagers would look ahead far enough to see the tragedies that might result from giving in to common temptations! The longer we ignore God's initial "way of escape," the more impaired our vision becomes and the more difficult it is to find our way back to safety.

Watch for God's signs today. And when you see one, don't just read it and roar past it. Heed it and soar successfully through life.

Discussion Starters:

* What are some "common" temptations you regularly face?
** Is it comforting to know that lots of other people face those same temptations? Why?
*** Have you ever suffered after recognizing, yet refusing to heed, God's "way of escape"? What were the results? What potential problems have you avoided by heeding God's signs for righteous living?

Lifeline:

God's ways of escape will always be on His paths, not ours.

Order and Teamwork

the **WORD** | 1 Corinthians 11:3

"But I want you to understand that Christ is the head of every man, and the man is the head of a woman, and God is the head of Christ."

the *Message*

"Who wants to play quarterback?" the coach asked at the first football practice of eight-year-old gridiron warriors. He then had to explain why 15 quarterbacks might be a few too many. So most were doomed to become linemen. A few were chosen as running backs or for other positions of honor. And finally Zach became the object of envy when he was named quarterback. As the coach told him, "You da man."

Zach beamed. He had never felt so elated in his life. He was "da man." And he lived in that blessed state until Saturday, a minute and 20 seconds into the first quarter of game one. As he looked up from the indentation he had just made in the ground after being sacked by the other team's linemen, he suggested: "Maybe someone else would like a chance to play quarterback."

Those eight-year-olds learned a lesson that day: Without organization, every team fails. Players must accept their positions and play heartily for the good of the team. The people scoring touchdowns and kicking field goals usually get more recognition than others, because points win games. But without those mud-encrusted linemen doing their jobs equally well, no one's going to score many points.

In a society that values political correctness, a lot of people like to skip 1 Corinthians 11. But the Bible indicates there is order in marriage relationships, just as in peewee football and in heaven between Jesus and His Father. What Paul is saying is that, yes, a husband is the "head" of a woman in the same way that God is the head of Christ. Can you imagine Jesus and God getting into a screaming contest over who's number one? No way! They have an order in their relationship that has nothing to do with personal value and everything to do with function.

When men and women get this straight, their mutual interdependence brings glory to God. Failure to accept it brings chaos—and lots of fumbles.

Discussion Starters:

• Why are many people offended by the phrase "the man is the head of a woman"?

•• Paul also says, "Christ is the head of every man." How would you describe this?

••• Is it possible for people to practice the same kind of headship as Christ? If so, how?

Lifeline:

Identify what you think your "position" is on Jesus' team at this point in your life.

The Heart of the Matter

the **WORD** | *1 Corinthians 11:27*

"Therefore whoever eats the bread or drinks the cup of the Lord in an unworthy manner, shall be guilty of the body and the blood of the Lord."

the **Message**

I'll never forget one lineman from Texas Tech—I'll call him Alex—who had the biggest biceps I've ever seen and could eat more food than any two other men. Because he was a gentle giant, Alex was assigned to counsel our smallest campers. One day I noticed Alex engaged in a classic contest with a boy the size of his thigh. They were spinning a spoon to determine who got the last pancake on the plate.

Alex won. Just as he was about to take his first bite, he saw the boy was crying. With little ado, Alex simply slid the pancake over to the boy's plate. Later I discovered Alex had been tending to one of his sick campers in the infirmary that morning and was late to breakfast. That last pancake was going to be his only one to prepare him for a long day of hard work.

After Alex left camp, I never heard of him again. But that day in the Kanakuk dining hall, he became an all-American in my book.

The mark of an all-star Christian is love. Paul's big complaint with the Corinthians was that they were treating Communion (the "Lord's Supper") as if it were a buffet table rather than a holy sacrament. They were beginning to fight over it as if it were the last pancake.

The early church combined its communal "agape" meal with the Lord's Supper to commemorate the most selfless act of all times, the Crucifixion. Yet, sadly, it had become a "me first" grabfest. Some church members were eating their fill while others went hungry.

Do you get satisfaction beating everyone to the last pancake, or passing it up for someone else?

Discussion Starters:

* Besides food, what other appetites reveal a person's heart?
    ** What are some of your appetites? How do you handle them?
    *** What are some ways people can still abuse the Lord's Supper?

Lifeline:

Jesus is the bread of life (John 6:48). Are you sharing that "bread" with others?

The Five-Legged Steer

the **WORD** | 1 Corinthians 12:7

"To each one is given the manifestation of the Spirit for the common good."

the *Message*

In the grammar school I attended, the boys couldn't wait until sixth grade and Mr. Cottle's field trip to see the five-legged steer. We endured the first five years of school primarily for the opportunity to board the bus for the field trip we knew would be the zenith of our lives. (The girls were somewhat less enthusiastic.) After a 65-mile trip discussing where the fifth leg would be on this steer and how much faster it should be able to run, we finally arrived at "Lester's Little Sahara—Home of Exotic Delights."

Before seeing the star attraction, we looked at newborn baby pigs, a bunch of tarantulas, some ostrich eggs, live rattlesnakes, and a three-ton prairie dog made of crumbling plaster. But our eyes didn't light up until we reached a door on which was scrawled, "Behold the Five-Legged Steer."

It is with the deepest regret that I must tell you it was one of the biggest disappointments in my life, over in a matter of seconds. We were hurried past a dismal-looking bovine with what looked like a woman's stocking filled with sawdust strapped to its back. Then we went through another door and found ourselves back in the parking lot, blinking at one another in the bright sunlight. Sadly, the highlight of our trip was the stop at Dairy Delite on the way home. But you can bet that when we got back we bragged about the five-legged steer as if we had seen the Taj Mahal.

If Paul had been in Mr. Cottle's class, he might have subtitled 1 Corinthians 12: "Beware the five-legged steer!" Church members were envying one another's God-given gifts and were trying to be things they weren't. Subsequently, the "body of Christ" was taking on the phoniness of a five-legged steer. (Paul used equally ludicrous examples of feet trying to be hands and "bodies" consisting of a single large eye or ear [verses 15-17].)

God knows what He's doing. Don't let envy turn you into a useless appendage.

Discussion Starters:

* What are a few things *all* Christians should be involved with in the church?
  ** Who are some people you know who have unique and specific spiritual gifts?
  *** Have you ever experienced problems trying to be like someone else?

Lifeline:

If you don't want to feel like a useless fifth leg, you need to identify what special gifts God has entrusted to you. How can you begin to discover your individual gift(s)?

Marching Orders

the **WORD** | *1 Corinthians 12:27*

"Now you are Christ's body, and individually members of it."

the **Message**

When my friend Bill was in the military, he was assigned to a platoon of illiterate men, so he went to his superiors to request a transfer.

"Request denied," they told him.

"But I have an education," said Bill. "I can read."

"Sorry, there's too much red tape involved. Besides, we need a leader in this group of ragtags. I guess you're it."

At first Bill was angry, but soon he began to feel honored. After all, he had two years of college and was planning to go to medical school. He could lead these men. He could teach them to read. Why, he might even get a medal for it!

Because of Bill's height, he was given the lead position in the marching formation, which meant he was in front of everyone. The first day of drills, a sergeant was barking out commands, but not very clearly. Bill guessed right on the first two turns, but the third time he went right when everyone else went left. He didn't notice for several paces. After the other men had a good laugh, the sergeant gave Bill a brick to carry in his right hand for the rest of boot camp (to help him learn right from left). In the end, Bill made a fine soldier, spending months in the Philippine Islands as a radio operator. On breezy days, he kept his door propped open with a brick—the same brick that would keep him humble until he died at the age of 69.

It's easy for Christians to get a "big head." We love to be perceived as spiritual giants, but we need to be reminded daily that there is only one head of this platoon of Christian soldiers—Christ Himself.

Paul makes it clear that love must prevail in the church so we as individuals can achieve unity. We're all marching in the same direction. The better we keep in step, the more pleasant and efficient will be the journey to our final destination.

Discussion Starters:

• How is it possible for people in positions of Christian service to become arrogant?
•• What does it mean to submit to Christ? Give some examples.
••• When have you been humbled in front of a crowd? What is a "brick" you could carry with you or post in a prominent place to remind you to be humble?

Lifeline:

It's a lot less embarrassing to humble ourselves than to have others do it for us.

"XXX"

the WORD | 1 Corinthians 13:8, 13

"Love never fails.... But now faith, hope, love, abide these three; but the greatest of these is love."

the Message

I opened a valentine the other day and saw a string of X's at the bottom of the card, accompanied by the words "I love you, Dad." After being touched by the sentiment, I began to ask myself one of the age-old questions: What is love? Psychologists tell us that without love we shrivel up and die, yet hardly one in a hundred people could come close to defining it.

Many people who sign an X to a card or letter simply intend it to represent a kiss. Actually, however, the sign goes back to the days of the early Christians. "X" was the first letter in the Greek word for Christ as well as a symbol for the cross. As a symbol it conveyed the power of an oath, and because it was associated with goodness and honor, it became an acceptable substitute whenever a signature was needed from an illiterate person. So, in an age when few people could write, the "X" began to appear on many documents. To prove the sincerity of a transaction, a person would kiss the "X". It was this practice that led to its becoming a symbol of a kiss.

So much for our fascinating history lesson, but we still haven't defined love. It seems easier to nail Jell-O to a tree than to arrive at a good definition. It's more than an emotion, more than a decision. The best definition I can offer is found in 1 John 4:8: "God is love." Love must ultimately be defined as a person, and must include all the traits that person possesses.

God's loving characteristics are found in 1 Corinthians 13. Read the entire chapter and substitute the word *God* wherever the word *love* appears. Your daily need for more of God in your life will quickly come into focus.

Love is not a string of X's. It is not merely an emotion, a decision, or even an action. True love is a Person—God Himself. Be filled with God, and you can't help but be filled with love.

Discussion Starters:

* Read through 1 Corinthians 13 and write down all the qualities of love.
  ** How many of these descriptions are true of you? Which ones are most lacking?
*** How can you "fill in the gaps" so your love toward others is more complete?

Lifeline:

You can't have love without sharing it.

Droopy Drawers

"When I was a child, I used to speak like a child, think like a child, reason like a child; when I became a man, I did away with childish things."

the Message

I have a friend—I'll call him Reggie to spare him some embarrassment—who has a great underwear story. Every guy knows that when you keep a pair of boxers for too long, the waistband gives out. What starts as a size 32, over time, becomes a 58. Reggie had one such pair that he had failed to retire to the rag box. Once, in a hurry to get to a game, he put on that last pair in the drawer and rushed out the door.

He had no problems during the pre-game warm-up. But when the game began and the sweat started to roll, his undies started a migration south. At first only a hint of white cotton appeared below the hem of Reggie's blue basketball shorts. But after a few more trips down the court, they became a white flag, flapping at his knees.

Every time there was a break in the action, Reggie would try to tuck everything back into place, but nothing worked for long. He says, "My face was red, my boxers were white, and my uniform was blue—I must have looked like Old Glory with high-tops on."

Reggie went on to play for the Arkansas Razorbacks, and then for the Spirit Express, a Christian team that travels around playing exhibition games and sharing the gospel. But he never again left for the gym without checking the waistband of his underwear.

Sometimes neglecting a childish habit is a bit like those droopy drawers. Paul's comments to the Corinthian church were about the childish ways in which they were using their spiritual gifts. In essence, he was telling them to grow up, throw out those old, ratty undies, and change their unloving, childish ways.

Everyone knows some difficult-to-tolerate person who flaunts his or her gifts. But God has gifted *all* Christians. When we apply them properly, the church grows stronger. But if we use them to show off, we are like a pair of old droopy drawers: an embarrassment to the body of Christ.

Discussion Starters:

• Have you ever seen people abuse or misapply their spiritual gifts?
•• How can *you* prevent becoming a source of embarrassment to the body of Christ?

Lifeline:

The gifts God gives us are of little benefit unless we "open" them and put them to use.

Paul's Top Five

the WORD | 1 Corinthians 14:19

"In the church I desire to speak five words with my mind so that I may instruct others also, rather than ten thousand words in a tongue."

the Message

Just over a year ago, Julia went in for routine thyroid surgery. But while she was on the operating table, the surgeon severed one of her vocal cords with the scalpel. Immediately, her voice was reduced to a painful whisper. Attempts at rehabilitation weren't working well. But exactly a year after the surgery that rendered her mute, Julia again found herself on an operating table—with a different doctor. This time the surgery was successful and Julia had her voice back.

Her new doctor advised her to take it easy for 10 days until he was sure her voice would still work. But Julia decided that if there was any possibility her voice might disappear again, she was going to make the most of the time she had. She used her new-found voice like there was no tomorrow.

She told her husband, "I love you," 50 times a day. She told her kids how proud she was of them. She told knock-knock jokes, read bedtime stories, sang in the shower, and laughed at every opportunity. And she made sure every night to say "thank You" to God for returning her voice—even if it was just temporary. I'm glad to report that after two months, her voice is still going strong.

As I read today's passage, I think of Julia and wonder why Paul chose "five words" instead of two, or 12, or 25. Something tells me Paul was a lot like Julia in that both had learned the value of speech and were eager to use their voices as a blessing for others.

I don't think Paul had five specific words in mind, but if he did, I suspect they might have been "Jesus Christ, God's Son crucified." That phrase was the basis of everything Paul stood for, a common theme in his writings, and a bond that united a thriving church. Uninterpreted tongues could never have the same effect as those five words.

Spend some time thinking about your own words. Do you use your tongue to edify others? Or would the world be a better place if you were mute?

Discussion Starters:

* What does your speech tell others about your heart?
** Who has the most edifying speech that you know? What makes that person stand out?
*** What can you do to build up others with your words?

Lifeline:

What five words best describe your feelings about God? How can you influence others with those words?

Tongues of Fire

the **WORD** | *1 Corinthians 14:22-23*

"So then tongues are for a sign, not to those who believe but to unbelievers....Therefore if the whole church assembles together and all speak in tongues, and ungifted men or unbelievers enter, will they not say that you are mad?"

the *Message*

A friend of mine shared a story I would like to pass along as he told it to me:

"A boy named Larry lived on my street, and he was a bona fide pyromaniac. One Christmas his parents gave him a magnifying glass. When he got tired of using it to melt tar and herd bugs, he gave me a call. I think he was looking for an accomplice.

"I met Larry beside a Dumpster at the Piggly Wiggly supermarket. Next to the Dumpster was an old mattress, its cottony guts protruding from a gash down the middle. Larry had found (or maybe stolen) a gross of bottle rockets and had dumped their gunpowder into a substantial pile in the center of the mattress.

"'This is going to be cool,' he bragged. 'Since we're not using any matches, there'll be no evidence to prove who did it.'

"Larry carefully focused the sun's rays through the glass until a tiny, orange tongue of fire sprang up. Larry leaned closer to study his project just as a gust of Oklahoma wind reached the flame, igniting the gunpowder. A flash blew Larry's eyebrows from his forehead, and he stumbled back into the Dumpster. In a matter of seconds, the flames had reached the Piggly Wiggly.

"We ran away as fast as we could and then watched the arrival of the fire department from a nearby tree house while eating Oreos. The blaze was out in less than 10 minutes, but the lesson has lasted a lifetime—at least for me. It wouldn't surprise me if Larry is still somewhere playing with matches in a prison cell."

Christians disagree on the significance of tongues in today's church. But Paul makes it clear: Misusing the gift of tongues can be as dangerous as a fire out of control. Used inappropriately, speaking in tongues can create confusion, disunity, and even ill feelings toward the church. A fire under control can be a blessing, but fire in the hands of folks like my friend's friend Larry is always destructive.

Discussion Starters:

* What's your opinion about the gift of tongues?
** How might this gift be threatening to others?
*** How can it be a blessing when used appropriately?

Lifeline:

When kids abuse new toys, they break. Similarly, the misuse of *spiritual* gifts is always disappointing and unrewarding.

The Spotlight of Truth

the WORD | 1 Corinthians 15:3-5

"For I delivered to you as of first importance what I also received, that Christ died for our sins according to the Scriptures, and that He was buried, and that He was raised on the third day according to the Scriptures, and that He appeared to Cephas, then to the twelve."

the Message

We've all seen a police helicopter whirring across a city sky, its spotlight probing the ground for some fleeing villain. But one of my friends actually witnessed one that had the hunted person pinned down in a circle of light.

"I was coming home from church with my family one night," he told me. "We had just entered an overpass, and below us the highway was dotted with traffic. Suddenly, my son shouted, 'Hey, Dad, look at that car down there. It looks like it's on stage.' Sure enough, ahead of the other cars sped an old, black van—smack-dab in the middle of a fluorescent halo. Above it, flying as low as possible, a police helicopter kept its search beam trained on the suspect. The light was so bright that every detail of the van stood out—license number, missing taillight, rust on the back. Nothing was hidden from view. No doubt, the police had their man."

In 1 Corinthians 15, Paul has his spotlight trained on the resurrection of Jesus. His light shines so brightly that nobody can be mistaken about the identity of the man "on stage." The man had a name: Christ Jesus. The man had a purpose: to die for our sins. The man was buried and stayed in the grave for three days. The man was raised from the dead. Finally, the man appeared to many people after His resurrection, and in a specific order: first to Peter (Cephas), then to His disciples, then to a group of 500, then to James, then to the apostles, and finally to Paul (verses 5-8).

In short, the Resurrection is illuminated by facts and eyewitnesses. When we study it in light of Paul's evidence, we can arrive at only one conclusion: Jesus Christ most certainly rose from the dead.

Discussion Starters:

• What are four pieces of evidence that verify Christ's resurrection?
•• How does the Resurrection give you hope?
••• If it were your job to try to disprove the Resurrection, what questions would you ask?

Lifeline:

Take the spotlight off the resurrection of Jesus, and you'll be left in the dark.

The Last Trumpet

"Behold, I tell you a mystery; we will not all sleep, but we will all be changed, in a moment, in the twinkling of an eye, at the last trumpet; for the trumpet will sound, and the dead will be raised imperishable, and we will be changed."

the Message

For years at Kanakuk, we began each morning with reveille. How would you like to be responsible for waking up 220 sleepy, grumpy boys and men every morning? No, you didn't get to quietly sing them awake or entice their eyes open with a terrific-smelling breakfast.

Here's how reveille works. A young boy is enlisted for his musical talents (primarily being that he owns a trumpet). It becomes his job to rise early, pull a T-shirt over his nappy head, grab his instrument, and shuffle to the bluff that overlooks beautiful Taneycomo Lake. There he starts blaring on his trumpet as loudly as he can—occasionally hitting the correct notes. To his sleeping peers he is, in every sense of the word, "unpopular."

Once an anonymous hero arose in our midst. In the quiet hours of the night he sneaked into the reviled bugler's cabin and plugged his horn with a big, wet wad of toilet paper. When the boy tried to bugle, nothing came out. We had 15 minutes of extra sleep that day, and the anonymous vandal gained the admiration of the masses.

The apostle Paul tells of another "bugle"—a trumpet that will one day sound so loudly that no plug can mute it. No one will sleep through it because even the dead will be awakened. In fact, it will be those of us who are awake and ready who will respond positively to this heavenly trumpet call. In an instant we will be changed, given immortal bodies that are fit for heaven in every way.

How can someone prepare for this day? He or she must be a Christian, rescued from the clutches of death by Christ Himself. Those who are not ready will never hear the bugle again. For them, there will be no more mornings to wake up to. Are *you* ready?

Discussion Starters:

* Christ's return to earth seems too fantastic for some people to believe. Why do you think this is so?

** Would you like to be living when Christ returns? What do you think it would be like to go straight from algebra class to heaven?

*** How does someone know if he or she is ready to meet Christ?

Lifeline:

Spend an hour or so determining how to be ready to hear that final trumpet.

The Stickies

"On the first day of every week each one of you is to put aside and save, as he may prosper, so that no collections be made when I come. When I arrive, whomever you may approve, I will send them with letters to carry your gift to Jerusalem; and if it is fitting for me to go also, they will go with me."

the Message

At least twice a year, "the stickies" would arrive. You could always recognize them by the fingerprints on the packaging and the card that read: "I lov yew, Dady." They came at Christmas, on my birthday, and sometimes for no special occasion at all. The stickies were always the same—a scrap of cloth, a tattered item from the garbage can, or perhaps a little wad of yarn with feathers glued randomly to it.

One time I ran my fingers across the colorful plumage and remarked, "Gee, Cooper, this is the most beautiful bird I've ever received."

Silence intruded—followed by correction.

"It's a hand gwenade."

His hand grenade is only one of the many tokens of love I've received from *my kids* over the years. They were always so touching, so personal...so sticky. But it didn't matter that they were coated in the goo that covers every child's hands. They were *sincere*, and I would never dream of throwing them away. I keep them in a special drawer, where my now-grown children can one day bring their children to rummage through the stickies.

Paul's closing instructions to the Corinthians begin with an appeal to practice *sincere* giving. Perhaps no mark of Christianity is more significant than one's willingness to give to others. And Paul didn't just instruct the Corinthians to give; he told them to give *habitually*—once a week, as soon as the paycheck comes in.

The Corinthians' gift was headed to the church in Jerusalem from where Christianity had spread. When we remember people or ministries that have been instrumental in our spiritual lives, we should ask God to bless them. Then *we* should bless them with a gift they'll never forget.

Discussion Starters:

* Who would be the top three people or ministries you might want to give to?
   ** Other than shelling out money, in what ways do you give?
   *** In what ways would you like to become more giving?

Lifeline:

We don't actually give to God. The best we can do is return some of the abundant gifts with which He has blessed us.

2 corinthians

Second Corinthians is Paul's second biblical letter to the church at Corinth. This fantastic letter is one of my personal favorites because it is packed full of godly wisdom. It relates to teenagers with amazing clarity and gives us a chance to see a spiritual X-ray view of the apostle Paul's heart. You see his highest highs and lowest lows. His openness and his honesty will help you see God and yourself in a way that will probably influence you for a lifetime. I pray that through our time together in this tremendous book, it will touch your heart and your character the way it has mine.

Bravery

the **WORD** | 2 Corinthians 1:3-4

"Blessed be the God and Father of our Lord Jesus Christ, the Father of mercies and God of all comfort, who comforts us in all our affliction so that we will be able to comfort those who are in any affliction with the comfort with which we ourselves are comforted by God."

the *Message*

War Memorial Stadium in Little Rock, Arkansas, is not the place to be when the Razorbacks boast the number-two team in the nation and you're dressed in the red, white, and blue uniform of Southern Methodist University. My 20-year-old rookie legs shook as I staggered onto the field for the opening kickoff. My dismay intensified as the Razorbacks scored 35 unanswered points.

With 10 minutes, 53 seconds left in the game, we were still behind 35 to zero. That's when a fiery-eyed linebacker named Bruce Potillo pulled our battle-weary defense together and screamed to us above the Arkansas roar, "Men, these guys aren't that good. We're better than they are. They're not going to make one more first down for the rest of this game. Let's go out there and play like we are capable of playing."

Our offense scored on the next series. Our defense stopped them like a concrete wall. Three more times our offense scored. Three more times our defense held. As the clock ticked down to 28 seconds remaining, the stadium had become deathly quiet. We had held the powerful Razorback offense yet again.

Our offense had one more shot at the ball—or so we thought. Somehow the refs let the clock tick down to zero. Game over. We were certain that if we had touched the ball just once more, the upset of the year would have taken place. Although our 28-point scoring spree left us one touchdown short of catching up, I would never again experience a "victory" so sweet, because a word spoken by a friend gave our entire team the "bravery" (which is exactly what the biblical word *comfort* means) to pick ourselves up, return to the battlefield, and play like we had never played before. Whether you need comfort or courage, you'll find both in Paul's words as we begin this series in 2 Corinthians.

Discussion Starters:

• How does the Holy Spirit give you "bravery" (comfort) when you need it most?
•• How do you transfer the comfort you receive from God to others who need it?
••• What trials have you faced (and endured) that allowed you to later minister to someone going through the same thing?

Lifeline:

Comfort is never found in attempting to sidestep difficult circumstances, but in bravely facing them with the strength God provides.

The Pledge

the WORD | 2 Corinthians 1:21-22

"Now He who establishes us with you in Christ and anointed us is God, who also sealed us and gave us the Spirit in our hearts as a pledge."

the Message

The air seeped out of the front right tire of our van with a steady swoosh. It was just after midnight and definitely no time for a flat tire, especially for a group of weary travelers with no spare who were planning a nine-hour, all-night drive to Kansas City. To my amazement, we found an open tire store with one tire on the shelf exactly the right size. As I reached for my billfold, I realized I had left it—with all my travel money—at a McDonalds across town. With frantic determination, I pleaded with the mechanic to trust me and put the tire on our van while I hitched a ride to retrieve my billfold.

"How do I know you'll return to pay me?" he asked with a shout.

"I'll leave Brad Friess with you. He's my close friend," I said clumsily.

It was enough to seal the deal. Brad was my friend, and no fool would abandon a friend for the price of one measly tire! Besides, he was a handsome, intelligent, talented, 6'5" basketball standout for the University of Arkansas cagers.

When I returned with billfold in hand, I received Brad back along with the new tire. During our starlit trip to Kansas City, my friends laughed at me all night long for exchanging Brad for, of all things, a steel-belted radial worth no more than $99. But I didn't trade Brad. He was my *pledge* to the mechanic. It's how he knew I would return.

When Jesus had to go away, He knew some of His followers might be afraid He would never return. So, as Paul tells us, He left the Holy Spirit as His pledge. When Jesus returns, we'll all be together again. Until then I can take Him at His word because I am holding His pledge—one I trust even more than my friend Brad.

Discussion Starters:

• When a person receives Christ as personal Savior, what is the significance of the Holy Spirit entering his or her heart to stay?

•• Sometimes Christians talk about "the security of the believer." In light of today's passage, what does the phrase mean to you?

••• What does it mean that God "sealed us"?

Lifeline:

The most hope-inspiring words in Scripture may be "I will never leave you or forsake you" (Deuteronomy 31:6; Hebrews 13:5).

Forgiven

the **WORD** | 2 Corinthians 2:10-11

"But one whom you forgive anything, I forgive also; for indeed what I have forgiven, if I have forgiven anything, I did it for your sakes in the presence of Christ, so that no advantage would be taken of us by Satan, for we are not ignorant of his schemes."

the *Message*

The chair lift in Park City is the longest one in Utah. I was riding with my 22-year-old friend Emily, an energetic snowboarder who can run circles around this "gray-haired knuckle dragger" (as the young snowboarder crowd terms old guys like me). It took the entire trip for Emily to tell me her emotional life story. At age 15 she thought she had a model family until her mother announced she was in love with the school music director and would be leaving home with all the furniture and as much of the family's savings as she could get her hands on. Emily's world immediately shattered into small fragments.

In contrast to her gentle-spirited, forgiving father, Emily's rage toward her mom boiled inside. Her anger seemed unquenchable. The inner fire of hatred blazed hotter with each passing year as her mom demanded more and more from the family and updated them on her continuing extramarital affair.

Five years later, Emily showed up at our sports camp to counsel teenagers. From all appearances, she was a talented athlete with a smile as beautiful as a Rocky Mountain sunrise. Yet in addition to all her talents and Christ-filled beauty, Emily also brought a loaded suitcase of bitterness that was crippling her like a case of spiritual arthritis.

During staff training week, I spoke frequently of God's amazing love for us and of my boundless love for my wife and kids. During the week, the Holy Spirit purposely and mysteriously melted Emily's hard heart toward her mom, allowing her to completely forgive her mother for five long years of hurt. Like a mighty wall of water caged behind a huge concrete dam, the healing power of forgiveness was released to flow into Emily's life and enable her to be truly well, truly whole, and truly free.

Discussion Starters:

- Why does God expect us to forgive others as He forgives us?
- What specks of bitterness might be hidden in your heart that you need to get rid of today?
- Review today's passage. How does Satan take advantage of us when we refuse to forgive one another?

Lifeline:

The healing power of forgiveness is God's greatest medicine for you and your family.

Boy, Do We Smell!

"But thanks be to God, who always leads us in triumph in Christ, and manifests through us the sweet aroma of the knowledge of Him in every place. For we are a fragrance of Christ to God among those who are being saved and among those who are perishing; to the one an aroma from death to death, to the other an aroma from life to life."

the Message

My walk along the 2,000-year-old original stone Appian Way into the ancient walled city of Rome is without a doubt the most memorable of my life. Peter and Paul walked on those very stones as they went about their historic, gospel-spreading ministry. On those stones, too, marched Roman soldiers attempting to silence the testimony of early Christians, bringing capital punishment as a final judgment to many who faithfully gave testimony of their risen Savior.

The Appian Way into Rome was also "Main Street" on which the Roman armies would return in their famous "parade of triumph." Proud generals would display their troops, as well as throngs of captured slaves and condemned prisoners, while wildly cheering crowds lined the thoroughfare into the heart of the city.

According to tradition, burning aromatic incense would accompany the chariots and officers in the parade. To the Roman conquerors, it was an aroma of life. To the prisoners, it was an aroma of death because this would very likely be their final walk. A cruel death awaited, perhaps the same fate that was given to Jesus, or something almost as cruel.

Paul passes along the good news that those who are led by God *always* march in triumph. For us, the stench of death is left behind and replaced by salvation and victory in Christ. As Christians, we are a "fragrance of Christ to God." As far as God is concerned, we really smell! And we can be happy we do.

Discussion Starters:

* As you speak up for Jesus, Christians may support you while others give you a hard time. Why is your witness an "aroma of life" to one group and an "aroma of death" to the other?
** What's the worst you've ever suffered because you were a Christian? How does that compare to the treatment received by Peter, Paul, and other early Christians at the hands of the Romans?
*** How noticeable is your "aroma of triumph"? How can you make it stronger?

Lifeline:

Commit each day to be an "aroma of life" to your family.

A Strange-Looking Letter

the WORD | 2 Corinthians 3:2-3

"You are our letter, written in our hearts, known and read by all men; being manifested that you are a letter of Christ, cared for by us, written not with ink but with the Spirit of the living God, not on tablets of stone but on tablets of human hearts."

the Message

The highways that lead into our highly traveled tourist town of Branson, Missouri, are lined with huge, illuminated billboards that literally number in the thousands. Numerous country music stars have elegant theaters here, each seating from 2,000 to 4,000 people. Music fans travel here by the millions. The billboards are part of a strategy that marketing experts call "intercept marketing," and are intended to influence the plans of tourists who don't have their vacation schedules finalized.

I'm not sure how the tourists feel about the billboards. But to many of us who live here, the signs are flashy…glitzy…gaudy…and nauseating.

Believe it or not, you and I have billboards around our necks, on our cars, in our homes, in our classrooms, and where we work. As true believers, our billboards all display the same message: "JESUS LIVES HERE!" It's a simple but profound statement. *Jesus* lives here. Jesus *lives* here. Jesus lives *here*.

It's true. We are part of God's intercept marketing. Many people sense they are headed for death and hell, but they haven't finalized their decisions yet. Any one of the Christian "billboards" God puts in front of them might sway their decision so that their destination becomes eternal life in heaven.

Sometimes I realize my billboard needs a bit of repair. Perhaps the light is beginning to burn dimly or I need a fresh coat of paint to make the message easier for others to see. How about you? You will reach dozens (or hundreds, or thousands) of people I'll never see. The way you talk, act, and treat others will make your billboard either a repulsive sign that causes them to reject the message or perhaps the most attractive piece of artwork they will ever see. Shine on!

Discussion Starters:

* A popular chorus says, "They'll know we are Christians by our love." What kind of love will attract your friends to Jesus?
* Do you know someone who consistently displays a "Jesus Lives Here" billboard?
* What can you do this week to make your message clearer to others?

Lifeline:

Someone may be looking for a "sign" from God, and you just might be it!

Let Freedom Ring

the WORD | 2 Corinthians 3:17

"Now the Lord is the Spirit, and where the Spirit of the Lord is, there is liberty."

the Message

The liberated woman…"feminist," "tramp."

The liberated man…"chauvinist," "pig."

The liberated teen…"druggie," "rebel," "alcoholic."

The liberated Christian…"guiltless," "sin-free," "forgiven and free to forgive," "pure," "godly," "knower of grace," and "heaven-bound."

Sometimes we tend to translate "liberated" as "liberal." The press often refers to active Christians as "fundamentalists," "extremists," "narrow-minded," "judgmental," "zealots."

Amy and Marcus had been dating for over a year. Marcus convinced Amy that if she would be more open to sex, she could be free from her parents' grip on her life and could experience "free love" in their relationship. Three months later Amy stares into the impersonal eyes of an abortion clinic doctor, trapped in a web of guilt that only Christ can unlock. Marcus is nowhere to be found.

Steve, Jason, and Jared hounded their friend Sam for four months to party with them. "C'mon, Sam. Have some fun, man. Loosen up a bit." Sam started going to their parties and developed a serious alcohol problem. Jason is in drug rehab.

Melissa used to party. She thought she had to be high for people to like her, but she didn't even like herself for what she had become. Then at a Young Life club she met Jesus and she was released from guilt and found freedoms she never knew—including the freedom to stay home on Saturday nights, or go to church with her family.

Paul says, "Where the Spirit of the Lord is, there is liberty." And he should know: he learned it from a master—*the* Master—who promises, "If the Son makes you free, you will be free indeed" (John 8:36).

Discussion Starters:

• How is the word *freedom* abused in today's society?
•• What are other biblical words that have become twisted?
••• What does being "free indeed" mean to you?

Lifeline:

Every day we choose to be either freer or less free.

Peanut Butter Jars

the **WORD** | 2 Corinthians 4:7-10

"But we have this treasure in earthen vessels, so that the surpassing greatness of the power will be of God and not from ourselves; we are afflicted in every way, but not crushed; perplexed, but not despairing; persecuted, but not forsaken; struck down, but not destroyed; always carrying about in the body the dying of Jesus, so that the life of Jesus also may be manifested in our body."

the **Message**

When I was a kid, my dad worked hard to provide for us. We didn't go hungry, but we ate a lot of beans, burgers, and peanut butter and jelly. And our dog, Pixie, never got fat on leftovers because we hardly ever had any.

My mom was a champion at stretching a dollar, and she would save everything that had potential value. Nothing went into the trash. Her mom had taught her to save buttons, rare coins, toy marbles, trading stamps, and other things that could be put to use at some time in the future. She accumulated these things in peanut butter jars. I remember one Friday night we even put a bunch of fireflies in a peanut butter jar to create a natural flashlight for a game we played in our dark room!

Treasures in peanut butter jars: It sounds contradictory, but it's a biblical image that's important to understand. The basic concept: God is great and powerful, and we're pretty insignificant in comparison. Yet God Himself chooses to live within us when we turn to Him for salvation. Paul refers to this as "treasure in earthen vessels" (or some versions say "jars of clay"). In other words, the jar is only valuable because of what it contains.

I thought my family kept some pretty good treasures in our peanut butter jars. But when I think of God putting His greatest treasure into someone like me with all my failures and weaknesses, I am humbled and ecstatic. It's the least I can do to share my "hidden treasure" with those who come my way.

Discussion Starters:

• How valuable is an empty peanut butter jar, i.e., how valuable are you without Jesus?
•• What are some benefits of having the treasure of God within us?
••• How might today's passage motivate you to be more humble?

Lifeline:

When empty, the jar that I am is meaningless. When filled with the treasure of God, it is the strongest treasure chest on earth.

Skin Deep

the **WORD** | 2 Corinthians 4:16-18

"Therefore we do not lose heart, but though our outer man is decaying, yet our inner man is being renewed day by day. For momentary, light affliction is producing for us an eternal weight of glory far beyond all comparison, while we look not at the things which are seen, but at the things which are not seen; for the things which are seen are temporal, but the things which are not seen are eternal."

the Message

"Man, she's hot!"

Sex-saturated sitcoms, thousand-dollar exercise machines, fitness centers, celebrity diets, fat-free potato chips: We are driving ourselves crazy with an obsession for "perfect" bodies. As the values of our country continue to slide, we continue to concern ourselves with shallow, surface images.

We need a reminder about stark reality from the commonsense writing of David: "As for man, his days are like grass; as a flower of the field, so he flourishes. When the wind has passed over it, it is no more, and its place acknowledges it no longer" (Psalm 103:15-16).

Imagine the freedom we would find if, instead of a size two dress, we concentrated on having a Jesus-sized heart!

Think how enormous our love for God could become if we encouraged spiritual growth in each other as much as we stress low-carb diets.

If we started "working out" to purify our hearts and build others up instead of building up our own image, think how our homes, schools, and workplaces would be.

No doubt, beauty is only skin deep. But that skin we strive to keep so perfect is destined to decay one day. The sooner we abandon our fixation with the outer shell and concentrate on what's beneath, the happier and *truly* healthier we will be.

Discussion Starters:

What are some influences that focus primarily on external beauty?

What happens if we're deceived into fixating on the external rather than the eternal?

How can you minimize the impact of potentially destructive influences in your home?

Lifeline:

How beautiful are you on the inside?

Earth Suits

the **WORD** | *2 Corinthians 5:1-3*

"For we know that if the earthly tent which is our house is torn down, we have a building from God, a house not made with hands, eternal in the heavens. For indeed in this house we groan, longing to be clothed with our dwelling from heaven, inasmuch as we, having put it on, will not be found naked."

the Message

Randy Odom is a counselor at Kids Across America, our summer sports camp reserved for some of America's most deserving kids who come from the financially challenged concrete world of urban inner cities. Not only does Randy love God, but he also loves urban kids with a passion.

One stormy spring day, Randy pulled up in front of his trailer home at the exact moment a tornado hit. He jumped out of his car as the door was ripped from its hinges and dove into his "home on wheels," just as he was met by another door flying down the hallway. The door pinned him to the floor as his whole house was literally demolished above him. Although his home and possessions were scattered for city blocks, miraculously, Randy was protected by the door and escaped uninjured.

The bodies we inhabit are about as reliable as Randy's mobile home in a tornado. They are "earth suits" we wear while we're here. But like NASA astronauts', they will eventually wear out and need to be replaced. We can exercise them, feed them, and doctor them all we want, but the tornado of time will eventually reduce them to dust. When Christians die, our bodies are traded in for eternal ones (1 Corinthians 15:40-44). Our eternal spirits, protected from destruction by the Spirit of Christ, are sealed by grace, destined to live with God forever—unchanging, unharmed, and free to live with the King forever.

Discussion Starters:

* What do you like best about your appearance? How will you feel when those features are gone?
** What blinds us and causes us to focus on our "earth suits" rather than our hearts?
*** Can you rearrange your priorities to focus on the part of you that will live forever?

Lifeline:

When you realize you'll live forever, you're more likely to focus on the parts that will last.

Metamorphosis

the WORD | 2 Corinthians 5:17

"Therefore if anyone is in Christ, he is a new creature; the old things passed away; behold, new things have come."

the Message

After elementary school we often take "metamorphosis" for granted, but think about it for a moment. The entire biological makeup of a creeping caterpillar somehow transfers into a majestic butterfly. And that butterfly can travel from deep in the heart of Mexico to the exact tree in the northernmost part of the United States where its ancestors lived! God is supernatural. He is unexplainable. He is unprovable.

To God, the caterpillar-to-butterfly and tadpole-to-frog transformations are a breeze. Even more amazing is the metamorphosis of a vicious murderer into a tender-hearted minister...a "hopeless" alcoholic into a trustworthy husband and father...lost and depressed teenagers into dynamic teachers, sports figures, counselors, musicians, and all sorts of other successful adults.

Recently a 17-year-old boy told me at a youth rally, "Last year when you spoke here, I was a heroin addict. But I became a Christian a month later, my drug habit has ended, and now I've been called to be a pastor someday."

I have failed in this life way too many times to count. So I can tell you from experience that when you feel like a caterpillar, the best thing to do is crawl into the "cocoon" of God's grace. Before long, like a butterfly, you'll be lighter than air and flying high.

Discussion Starters:

What does it mean to be a "new creature"?

Have you been through a spiritual metamorphosis? Is the transformation complete, or is it an ongoing process? Explain.

What other "new things" (2 Corinthians 5:17) do you have to look forward to?

Lifeline:

Try to always forgive the "caterpillar" state of others, and look for the "butterfly" in everyone around you.

Bound Together

the **WORD** | 2 Corinthians 6:14

"Do not be bound together with unbelievers; for what partnership have righteousness and lawlessness, or what fellowship has light with darkness?"

the **Message**

Imagine you're an ox named Bill. Your job is to pull the king of Turkey in a cart. You love the king and serve him willingly. After all, it's a pretty good gig for an ox. But one day someone places you in a yoke with Sam. Although Sam is a big, strong ox, he also turns out to be lazy, rebellious, and stubborn. Although you work hard, you can't compensate for Sam's hoof-dragging. The king becomes frustrated with both of you and sells you to a much less compassionate owner.

Okay, I know oxen don't have hearts that can be broken or a strong love for their owners. But the story is similar to what Paul is warning about in today's passage. Many teen letters I've received tell the same story. A few examples:

"My friends told me that getting high would make my problems go away. That wasn't true at all. First we tried speed, then pot, angel dust, and LSD. Although I only tried LSD once, it was an experience I'll never forget."

"He told me he loved me and that we'd get married someday. He talked me into sex and then we broke up. I was crushed."

"I began to hang out with the wrong friends. They were always partying and drinking. Before long, they took me down with them."

And here's one from an adult Christian businessman:

"The worst mistake I ever made was building a business partnership with [an unbeliever]. I'll be paying for it (literally) for years to come."

Christians are not to ignore unbelievers—by no means. We need to share the gospel with them and show them the love of God. But we must beware of becoming "bound together" with people who don't have our same moral base or faith in God. The pairing might be in a business partnership, marriage, dating relationship, etc. It may start out well, but it can easily become the "yoke" that drags you down.

Discussion Starters:

* Can you relate to being "bound together" with a nonbeliever? In what ways?
** If you find yourself "unequally yoked" with someone, what do you need to do?
*** If you feel an attraction to a nonbeliever, what can you do before problems arise?

Lifeline:

Pull your own weight in helping your family continue growing strong.

An Inside Wedding

the **WORD** | 2 Corinthians 6:16, 18

"For we are the temple of the living God…. 'I will be a father to you, and you shall be sons and daughters to Me,' says the Lord Almighty."

the **Message**

Candy Irwin was stunning on her wedding day as she walked down the colorful, laced pathway into the picture-perfect chapel. It was without a doubt the most beautiful wedding I have ever seen and her wedding budget was only $100! Candy was a country girl and money was scarce. She had spent all summer hand-sewing beads and sequins to a simple white dress until she produced a wedding gown far superior to anything Saks Fifth Avenue ever dreamed of. Candy had no money for flowers, but God took care of that with majestic splendor. The silver leaf maple trees surrounding the outdoor chapel had turned a myriad of fall colors. The gentle Ozark breeze blew brilliant leaves across the ground, decorating her footsteps.

By the time Candy arrived at the altar, I was speechless and her groom was in tears. The anticipation of this moment was overwhelming. He had patiently waited for three years while Candy attended to an ailing grandmother every day until her hero went to her heavenly rest. The thought of Candy's pure and loving heart intensified her beauty as she stood at the altar.

Yet as breathtaking as Candy's wedding scene was, it pales in comparison to a ceremony that takes place within each Christian. In the chapel of your heart, your soul becomes wedded to the Holy Spirit of God. No planner could design a more beautiful wedding.

Paul says that each Christian is "the temple of the living God." That's why Scripture calls us to a high standard of living. That's why we're selective with our music, movies, television, and conversation. That's why we don't abuse alcohol, drugs, or tobacco. That's why we don't have indiscriminate sex.

When we're married to Christ, we don't mind a bit.

Discussion Starters:

• How do you feel about your body being God's "temple"?
•• How do your eyes and ears allow things into the temple that ought not be there?
••• If your temple needs a good "housecleaning," how can you go about it?

Lifeline:

The joy of a wedding ceremony with Jesus Himself should quickly flow into your home.

Perfecting Holiness

the **WORD** | 2 Corinthians 7:1

"Therefore, having these promises, beloved, let us cleanse ourselves from all defilement of flesh and spirit, perfecting holiness in the fear of God."

the **Message**

Erin now laughs at her earliest athletic setback—getting kicked off the gymnastics team at eight for being "too fat." She also laughs off the title of "Best Body" her high school peers recently voted to bestow on her. The honor was far from a joke, yet Erin doesn't let such ideas affect how she feels about herself. She's dedicated her mind and body to Christ. To put it simply, Erin is "pure" and has dedicated herself to staying that way.

My son Cooper is one of Erin's close friends, and they frequently go out on weekends. She recently asked him to the prom and wrote him a "love letter," which he shared with me. It had a hand-drawn picture of a flower and looked something like this:

God's
Riches
At
Christ's
Expense

Dear Cooper,
Did you know the Bible mentions grace 131
times? Isn't that cool! See you Saturday. Erin

Seventeen magazine has said that prom is like a miniature honeymoon for many couples. Supposedly more virginity is lost on prom night than any other night of the year. Not so for Erin. The grace she knows as a true believer has given her the determination to save her "best body" (every inch of it!) for her husband.

My oldest son, Brady, recently asked Erin what she liked best about Cooper. She was quick to respond, "His Christian character." When the question was reversed, Cooper replied with eloquent candor: "Same for her."

Most of us are willing to "dabble" in holiness, but Paul reminds us that our ultimate quest should be "perfecting" holiness. May we all come a little closer to perfection week by week.

Discussion Starters:

* What does the term "purity" mean to you?
** Why is purity such an attractive quality?
*** How do you interpret "perfecting holiness" when it comes to how you live your life?

Lifeline:

A pure heart permeates all the senses: what you see, what you say, what you hear, what you touch, and what you feel.

Without Regret

the WORD | 2 Corinthians 7:10

"For the sorrow that is according to the will of God produces a repentance without regret, leading to salvation, but the sorrow of the world produces death."

the Message

M. Scott Peck's insightful best-selling book *The Road Less Traveled* begins with a profound insight: "Life is difficult."

The French say *la vi est dure* ("the road is difficult"). But this popular phrase is immediately followed by *mon dieu est bon* ("my God is good").

In case you haven't noticed, this planet we live on is not heaven. Satan wreaks havoc on us in the form of crime, disease, heartaches, and heartbreaks—all of which we must contend with throughout our lives.

Josh McDowell says that trials will either make us bitter or better. If we trust God in all circumstances and hold Him sovereign in our lives, difficulties bring out the best in us. If the pleasures of the world become our ultimate aim, letdowns and disappointments make us bitter.

Some people are "groaners" while others are "praisers." The difference is not the size of the trial but the size of their hearts. If my ultimate goal is to get to heaven and take a lot of people with me, I can appreciate trials because they tend to humble people and make them receptive to the help, forgiveness, and power God offers.

The day my young friend Ricky died in a drowning accident, seven people who knew him accepted Christ as their personal Savior. Martin has had 14 major surgeries on his face to correct a birth defect, yet he called from his hospital bed to praise God for his medical care. Lauren lost a leg to cancer yet continues to excel at our sports camp, blessing and amazing everyone with her fantastic attitude and Christ-given smile.

I'm not trying to tell you that sufferings don't hurt. They do! It usually takes a significant period of time and personal struggle—and perhaps even fear, anger, or doubt—before you get over them. God understands because He has been there! Even Jesus expressed a desire to avoid a painful trial (Mark 14:34-36). But He submitted to God's will and eventually was rewarded with a magnificent triumph. The same future lies ahead for those of us whose sorrows produce "a repentance without regret."

Discussion Starters:

* How do trials separate genuine Christian faith from counterfeit faith?
  ** Think of a trial you are now facing. How might it help make you better rather than bitter and turn you into a "praiser"?
*** How can trials help us appreciate Jesus and identify with Him? (See Hebrews 5:8-9.)

Lifeline:

Home should be a "comforting place" when the trials of life wound a family member.

Recapturing the Joy of Giving

"They gave of their own accord, begging us with much urging for the favor of participation in the support of the saints, and this, not as we had expected, but they first gave themselves to the Lord and to us by the will of God."

the Message

Nothing this side of heaven is as fun, as rewarding, or as fulfilling as giving. Just watch children pick out that very special gift for Mom or Dad at Christmas. They almost burst with excitement until the parent opens the gift and says, "Wow! Just what I've always wanted!"

But many of us seem to lose the joy of giving somewhere along the line. One day as 200 hungry teenage boys entered our dining hall for lunch, they found one table set with an abundance of food. Fourteen lucky guys were randomly chosen to sit at that "America" table. The rest of the famished young athletes sat at "Third World" tables—a few of which had beans, rice, and water, and others of which had nothing at all.

The "America" table was lavished with steaks, fried chicken, vegetables, and all sorts of desserts. The "Americans" were free to roam, and I watched with amazement. Four boys filled their plates to overflowing and ate like pigs without regard for their friends. Nine boys ate their fill but were willing to share leftovers. But one fantastic kid spent the entire meal giving away everything he had—and he had a blast! He had more fun than anyone. And when supper rolled around, you can believe he enjoyed his meal to the max.

Today's passage is Paul's praise for the Christians in Macedonia, who were struggling to get by and yet were willing and able to collect an offering to share with others who might need it more. Just off the coast of Florida 2 million children are starving on the tiny island of Haiti—and that's just one small area of poverty. If more American churches discovered the joy of giving known by those wonderful people in Macedonia, the kids of Haiti, as well as many others around the world, would have no want for food. We might not be able to feed the whole world, but we can do more than we're doing now. This week—today—let's try to do *something*.

Discussion Starters:

• How can you and your family clean out a closet, a cupboard, or even a savings account to help the poor of this world?
  •• How would you expect the recipients (and God) to respond to an act of joyful giving on your part?
  ••• How can your giving become more satisfying and joyful?

Lifeline:

Cast out a few crumbs and you get back a whole loaf.

For a While

"For you know the grace of our Lord Jesus Christ, that though He was rich, yet for your sake He became poor, so that you through His poverty might become rich."

the Message

Not much space remained in my assigned seat because the huge fellow in the next seat overflowed into mine. But it turned out to be one of the most interesting flights of my life. Not only was he rich in size, but he was rich in finances as well...very rich. The purpose of his trip was to meet 10 close friends and give each of them a very expensive gift. But after I complimented his generosity, he gave me a piece of wisdom I have found far more valuable than what his friends were to receive the next day. He said, "Aw, it's nothin'. I never saw a hearse followed by a U-Haul trailer."

My new friend was right. You can't take it with you. He reminded me of a favorite saying of my dad: "You can only sleep in one bed at a time. Why build an empire to yourself when it's so much more fun to give it away?"

Paul reminds us of the overwhelming example Jesus provided for us. He was God. He was in heaven with His Father. Yet He gave it all up—for a while—to come to earth and be a human being. Not only that, but He also willingly died a horrible death as a condemned criminal. He challenged us in His Sermon on the Mount, "Do not store up for yourselves treasures on earth, where moth and rust destroy, and where thieves break in and steal. But store up for yourselves treasures in heaven" (Matthew 6:19-20).

Jesus willingly became poor for us. We can choose to do the same for others. Just remember that whatever you give in God's name is never lost. It is "stored up." It's out of your possession—but only for a while. Keep in mind that Jesus certainly didn't *stay* poor. Similarly, at the end of this earthly life we can expect to get back more than we can even imagine. And that time it won't be for a while. It will be forever.

Discussion Starters:

* Why is it so hard to follow Christ's example of giving?
** Would you consider yourself more of a giver or a taker? Why?
*** How can you improve your giving skills? Be specific, and consider time, talents, and possessions as well as money.

Lifeline:

Your family members have given a lot for you. What can you give back this week?

Give Until You Giggle

the WORD | 2 Corinthians 9:6-7

"He who sows sparingly will also reap sparingly, and he who sows bountifully will also reap bountifully. Each one must do just as he has purposed in his heart, not grudgingly or under compulsion, for God loves a cheerful giver."

the Message

Fifteen thousand of God's most beautiful kids go to school in and around Port-au-Prince, Haiti, in the 22 schools built by my dear friend Pastor Jean Edmond. The children get a good Christian education, one shirt per year, and a meager meal that they get to eat after they finish their math assignment. Yet this is the happiest bunch of kids you've ever laid your eyes on!

Recently some friends and I decided to take Christmas to Haiti, so we prepared 15,000 gift bags packed with Frisbees, stuffed animals, Bibles, and a few other treats. The bags were filled with things the kids had never even dreamed of. Santa Claus ("Papa Noël" to them) went along for the festive presentation to each school. The kids went nuts!

Something happened that Christmas, however, that will forever redefine my concept of "the fun of giving." In each gift bag was a tiny roll of Lifesavers. Try to imagine how much the children loved their very first taste of a Lifesaver. They smiled from ear to ear!

One little boy stole my heart and changed my life as he took the first Lifesaver out of the pack and ate it. He found it so tasty that he immediately wanted to share the experience. In fact, he tried to give the whole pack back to me. That's right—the whole pack! One for him, the rest for me. And he couldn't have been happier!

It's a great principle, whether you're talking about Lifesavers or anything else we tend to accumulate. One of these days, try the "one for me, the rest for others" principle and see how happy it makes your heart.

Discussion Starters:

* What does today's passage mean when it says (in my own translation), "Give until you giggle"?
** Why does it sometimes become harder to give after we've accumulated a lot?
*** What needs do you see around you today? How might you give "the whole pack of Lifesavers," so to speak, to help one or more of the people in need?

Lifeline:

What special giving project are you willing to commit yourself to this year?

Captive Thoughts

the **WORD** | 2 Corinthians 10:3-5

"For though we walk in the flesh, we do not war according to the flesh, for the weapons of our warfare are not of the flesh, but divinely powerful for the destruction of fortresses. We are destroying speculations and every lofty thing raised up against the knowledge of God, and we are taking every thought captive to the obedience of Christ."

the Message

A review of almost any year's top 10 movies, CDs, and TV shows will yield a parade of pornographic scenes, raw lyrics, and profanities woven into addictive soundtracks and seductive stage productions. According to *Preview*, a family movie and television review magazine, one recent top-10 list contained a total of 436 crude, obscene, and/or profane references. Media moguls walk away with hundreds of millions of teenage dollars. In return, they leave an entire generation of kids spiritually and morally confused.

Is it right or wrong to listen to a CD that promotes premarital sex?

Is it right or wrong to go to a movie that takes God's name in vain?

Is it right or wrong to watch a TV show filled with sexual innuendoes, crude humor, and sexual jesting?

Should I continue to berate myself for the mistake I made last year?

Should I continue to harbor bitter thoughts against my dad?

Today's scripture is probably the clearest answer to these and many other questions. It tells us that Satan wages war for the control of our thoughts. Not content to stop with unholy thoughts, Satan also builds mental fortresses to encompass those thoughts so that our entire thinking process is corrupted.

Paul provides the military strategy to defeat Satan's schemes: Take every thought captive to the obedience of Christ. In other words, every thought that crosses our minds should be subject to Him. Certainly profanity, pornography, guilt, bitterness, and similar thoughts are not appropriate. Submit your thought life to the lordship of Jesus. Once your thoughts are "captive to the obedience of Christ," you will experience unprecedented freedom.

Discussion Starters:

How do Satan's fortresses become entrenched in our minds?

What are some practical ways you can take every thought captive to the obedience of Christ?

What divine weapons do you have in your arsenal? Are you using them all?

Lifeline:

Your mind is either your biggest friend or your biggest foe.

God's Stamp of Approval

"But he who boasts is to boast in the Lord. For it is not he who commends himself that is approved, but he whom the Lord commends."

the **Message**

When *Newsweek* asked thousands of Americans who would be most likely to get to heaven, Mother Teresa came in second. Billy Graham was third. Michael Jordan was high on the list, as were the president and first lady. But the winner, by a whopping majority, was "me." More people thought themselves more likely to be approved and get to heaven than any other person they could think of.

This may not seem surprising at first. After all, those of us who are Christians can be certain of our salvation. And it makes sense that we should be surer about ourselves than other people.

But on the other hand, the *Newsweek* poll was a national, random survey. It was conducted among the same group of people as other polls that tell us two-thirds of the male population will have sex before age 18, and more than half will have sex with other people after marriage. Many people don't think there's anything wrong with a president who cheats on his wife. Most don't think twice about attending movies where God's name is repeatedly profaned. And still, a vast majority of them can think of no person of faith more likely to get into heaven than "me."

Let's make one thing clear. Your behavior has nothing to do with whether or not you go to heaven. First comes a commitment to Christ. His salvation is the only key that fits heaven's door. Yet as we show Him our love, our behavior should improve. Sometimes people who receive Christ's offer of salvation go on to live lives that don't honor Him. But they shouldn't.

Paul wanted us to be sure that if we're boasting about going to heaven, it's because we've made a conscious decision to do so and are living as Jesus has taught us to—*not* because we think we've been good enough to get there. Those in the first group will one day hear the voice of God saying, "Well done, good and faithful servant" (Matthew 25:21). Those in the second are in for a big surprise.

Discussion Starters:

- What makes some people so proud of themselves and arrogant toward God?
  - Why does God humble the proud and give grace to the humble (James 4:6)?
  - What does it mean to be "approved" by God?

Lifeline:

We who have received God's stamp of approval should live like it.

Angel of Light

"Even Satan disguises himself as an angel of light."

the **Message**

A letter I just received, like so many others from teens I have befriended through the years, bleeds with rationalization. The person writes, "I know the Bible says sex before marriage is wrong, but my boyfriend and I love each other and it seems so right. Something this beautiful just can't be wrong, can it?"

The beer commercials on TV really do look like fun! Those parties on sandy, tropical beaches with hot cars, hot girls, and fun and laughter really make drinking look great. And "TV love" is just as promising, the way those gorgeous couples fall in love and head off to their steamy bedrooms. Anything that's that simple and that rewarding really makes you want to try it yourself.

If you think heavy drinking or premarital sex is either simple or rewarding in the long run, you're fooling yourself. Or more accurately, you're being fooled.

Believe me, we all think sin looks like fun in its earliest stages. But no one ever set out to become an alcoholic with their first drink. No one ever planned to become a heroin addict when they took a hit off of their first marijuana joint. During the passion of their first heavy kiss, no couple ever expects to deal with pregnancy or sexual disease. Satan is a master at getting you started down a path of sin by making it appear to be all fun. But after you're hooked, you *always* discover that there are consequences—many which are worse than you ever could have expected.

"Hey, smoke this great joint." "Take this cool pill." "Drink from this shiny bottle." "Live it up." "Go for it."

Take Satan up on his offer, and you may have fun tonight. But later you will pay. That's why he is the master of deception and your number-one enemy. But all you have to do is stand in the true Light that gives life (John 1:4-9), and the phony "angel of light" will be revealed for what he is—the devil himself.

Discussion Starters:

• Why does the title "angel of light" fit Satan so perfectly?
•• Can you think of a sin you've faced lately that looked really fun at first, but the more you evaluated it, the more you saw its danger?
••• How can you tell for sure whether something is a sin?

Lifeline:

"How can a young man keep his way pure? By keeping it according to Your word" (Psalm 119:9).

Mount Perspective

"Five times I received from the Jews thirty-nine lashes. Three times I was beaten with rods, once I was stoned, three times I was shipwrecked, a night and a day I have spent in the deep. I have been on frequent journeys, in dangers from rivers, dangers from robbers, dangers from my countrymen, dangers from the Gentiles, dangers in the city, dangers in the wilderness, dangers on the sea, dangers among false brethren; I have been in labor and hardship, through many sleepless nights, in hunger and thirst, often without food, in cold and exposure."

the Message

If you want to climb "Mount Perspective" to get a better view of just how fortunate you are, read today's passage several times. Then ask yourself: *What have I suffered for God lately? What have I sacrificed for Jesus that really cost me something?*

Jennifer told her boyfriend that their relationship would have to be pure or not at all. She was willing to sacrifice it, if necessary, knowing that God would have something better for her later on.

Robert gave his entire savings account to the starving kids in another country as an offering to God. He didn't think twice when he sensed God telling him it was the thing to do.

Lola got 1,000 of her friends to wear "Pray to Jesus" T-shirts to school. I'm guessing some of those kids got laughed at and ridiculed. But they probably won't lose any sleep over it. Compared to Paul's suffering, a few snide remarks don't really amount to much, do they?

A lot of people in this world are doing some *serious* suffering for Jesus. Many die for what they believe. Others relate to Paul's experience of beatings, imprisonment, and perpetual danger. But they continue to believe, and their bold faith continues to demonstrate to others the reality of God. Those dear saints will receive a crown of life the instant they arrive in heaven as they immediately forget the sorrows and pains they faced on earth. It will all be worth it to them. And if we are willing to be a bit bolder for what we believe, it will surely be worth it to us as well.

Discussion Starters:

• How do Paul's sufferings encourage you in yours?
   •• How do our difficulties make us more like Christ? (See 1 Peter 1:6-7.)
      ••• To what extent are you willing to suffer for Jesus?
         Are you truly convinced it will be worth it some day? Why?

Lifeline:

"Consider it all joy…when you encounter various trials, knowing that the testing of your faith produces endurance" (James 1:2-3).

Thorns

the **WORD** | *2 Corinthians 12:7-9*

"Because of the surpassing greatness of the revelations, for this reason, to keep me from exalting myself, there was given me a thorn in the flesh, a messenger of Satan to torment me—to keep me from exalting myself! Concerning this I implored the Lord three times that it might leave me. And He has said to me, 'My grace is sufficient for you, for power is perfected in weakness.' Most gladly, therefore, I will rather boast about my weaknesses, so that the power of Christ may dwell in me."

the *Message*

My daughter Courtney was taking 22 hours one semester in college while working an additional 15 hours a week to pay her way. But 37 hours of work and school (plus homework) is a hefty load.

She was hoping for all A's and B's, but right at the end she was surprised to receive a C in math. She seemed disappointed. I told her, "Courtney, I'd be just as pleased with you if you made *all* C's, because I know you've put your whole heart into this semester." I went on to explain that I don't think God would give me straight A's, even though I work hard to do my best. In fact, I think He sometimes hands out a C here and there so I won't become too proud of myself. None of us is good at *everything*. God has designed us to depend on one another, capitalizing on one another's strengths while minimizing our weaknesses.

If anyone deserved straight A's from God, it was Paul. But God was allowing him to endure some kind of recurring problem that Paul called a "thorn." (People have speculated that it could have been epilepsy, poor vision, or any number of other things.) The point of the thorn, he figured out, was so he would never forget what was allowing him to make all those A's the rest of the time—the grace of God.

I, too, am thankful that God cares enough to see me through my infirmities, failures, and imperfections. In doing so, He gives me a great gift—humility. In response, I can only say, *To God be the glory. Anything good that I've done is because of You.*

Discussion Starters:

• How is God's power made perfect in our weaknesses?

•• How do the C's (or D's or even F's) in our life "torment" us?

••• Why does God show greater love by allowing us to endure difficulties than if He allowed everything to be perfect?

Lifeline:

Identify your ongoing problems and imperfections. Then, if you can be honest about it, thank God for the humility you are learning.

The Strength of Weakness

the **WORD** | 2 Corinthians 12:10

"Therefore I am well content with weaknesses, with insults, with distresses, with persecutions, with difficulties, for Christ's sake; for when I am weak, then I am strong."

the **Message**

I was with Congressman Jim Ryun in Washington, D.C., where I was speaking on behalf of America's teenagers at the National Day of Prayer. I told him how heartbroken I had been watching him get tripped and then fall to the track in the Munich Olympics, dashing his hopes for the gold medal. He had been the best miler in the world for 15 years, but he lay sprawled on the ground as a pack of less talented runners passed him by and captured the gold, silver, and bronze medals.

Jim only smiled until he finally said, "You know? That was the greatest moment of my life because it was on that day, as I lay on the track and lost the race, that I truly gave my heart to Christ and began to live the life God wanted me to."

Jim now has a family of solid Christian kids and a wonderful wife, Anne, who loves him for his Christian character as much as any woman alive loves a man. Do you think he would trade that away for a gold medal? Do you think he would choose that medal over the seat in Congress that he earned because of his godly heart? I don't think so.

If we're expecting a smooth track ahead of us, free from any stumbles or trip-ups, we're in for sure disappointment. Look at the words Paul used to describe his Christian life: weaknesses, insults, distresses, persecutions, difficulties. And he could have gone on. But his point was that even though he faced such things, he was still content because God remained his source of strength.

We generally choose our heroes because of their strengths. Yet we have much to learn from the heroic examples of people like Paul and Jim Ryun. It was in his falling that Jim Ryun became a success. It was in his weakness that he became so strong. It was in dying to himself that he was born into eternal life.

Discussion Starters:

* Why are we actually weak when we think we're really strong?
  (The answer has something to do with pride and humility.)
** When has a problem weakened you and allowed God to use it to make you stronger?
*** On a scale from 1 to 10, how content are you when you're going through difficult circumstances beyond your control?

Lifeline:

When we are strong, we tend to lean on ourselves. When we are weak, we tend to lean on God.

Preparing for the Final

the **WORD** | 2 Corinthians 13:5-6

"Test yourselves to see if you are in the faith; examine yourselves! Or do you not recognize this about yourselves, that Jesus Christ is in you—unless indeed you fail the test? But I trust that you will realize that we ourselves do not fail the test."

the **Message**

Studying medicine with average brainpower and playing football with average talent was brutal when I was in college. The only thing worse than getting battered by a national championship team on Saturday was getting battered by my organic chemistry professor on Monday morning. On any test day, Dr. Jeskey was a master at exposing my lack of discipline for studying. But he was especially good (and I was at my worst) when he would unexpectedly deliver an 8 1/2-by-11-inch missile right to the middle of my desk— a dreaded pop quiz! Oh, I bottomed out on many of them.

Today's scripture is a clear warning that we should prepare for the ultimate "final exam," even though we don't know when it is coming. It will count for 100 percent of our grade, so it's very important we pass. In order to get ready, we should give ourselves a "pop quiz" from time to time. As Paul wrote, "Test yourselves to see if you are in the faith." We must be sure we are ready anytime. (Surprise accidents kill people of all ages every day.)

Below are some basic questions you'll need to be sure about. Look up the Scripture references, give them some thought, and then answer honestly.

1. Have you been born again? (John 3:3) Does Jesus live in your heart? (Revelation 3:20) Do you have a personal relationship with Him? (John 1:12)

2. Is your faith a real, *living* faith? (James 2:14-26) Does your faith produce spiritual fruit? (Galatians 5:22-23)

3. Does your love for Jesus make you *want* to obey Him? (John 14:15)

4. When you commit a sin (which we all do), do you confess it to Jesus, sincerely turn from that sin, and walk in the opposite direction? (1 John 1:9)

You don't have to grade this quiz, but give it some serious thought. You won't ever have to answer questions that are any more important than these.

Discussion Starters:

• What is one question you think God will ask on your final exam?

•• How can we know for sure whether or not we will pass that last test?

Lifeline:

If all your "pop quiz" answers are affirmative, you'll do well on the "final exam."

galatians

The area of Galatia included the cities of Antioch, Iconium, Lystra, and Derbe, where Paul established churches on his famous missionary journeys. Paul's letter to the Galatians shines like a welcome lighthouse to all Christians everywhere. Unlike the myriad other world religions that attempt to please God and gain holiness by good works, Paul makes it clear that the only way to God is by grace, through faith in God's Son, Jesus, our gift of righteousness.

As an acorn must be present before an oak tree can spring up, so must grace first be present before our good works mean anything. Although we want to please God because of the tremendous gratitude that flows from our hearts, the Galatian letter forever frees us from the worry and frustration of attempting to gain God's love by striving to be perfect.

Radically Saved

the WORD | Galatians 1:13-16

"For you have heard of my former manner of life in Judaism, how I used to persecute the church of God beyond measure and tried to destroy it; and I was advancing in Judaism beyond many of my contemporaries among my countrymen, being more extremely zealous for my ancestral traditions. But…God…was pleased to reveal His Son in me so that I might preach Him among the Gentiles."

the Message

The amazing beauty of Disney World in Orlando, Florida, is a tribute to how Walt Disney converted swampland filled with snakes and alligators into an architectural paradise of theme parks, golf courses, and real estate opportunities. It is hard to believe that a CEO of the Disney empire has built upon that wonderful man's dream a film conglomerate that makes more R-rated movies than any other on earth.

Whether you're 16 or 60, a preacher or a prostitute, your life changes when you give your heart to Jesus. His Holy Spirit enters your heart like springtime rain upon dry, parched soil. If your commitment to Him is genuine, positive changes will take place throughout your lifetime. A person "truly saved" becomes more and more like Jesus, more and more loving, joyful, peaceful, patient, kind, and self-controlled. Like a masterpiece of art, your life grows more valuable with each year passed as you celebrate the "spiritual birthday" that turned wasteland into a majestic work of God.

Radically saved Christians treasure their "Jesus-sized hearts" and never again return to the lifestyle of a nonbeliever.

Radically saved Christians don't delight themselves in gossip, coarse language, pornography, or sexual sin.

Radically saved Christians don't profane God or enjoy films that do.

As Paul opens his epic epistle to the Galatians, he bears witness to God's ability to radically change his heart. Today your life is bearing witness to others who will look at you and see the heart of Jesus.

Discussion Starters:

* How does God's willingness to change Paul's life (Galatians 1:11-24) reflect the magnitude of His love?
** In what ways is becoming a Christian a lifetime commitment? Why is it important to follow Christ forever, in all that you do?
*** What can you do if you discover you are falling back into your old ways of living?

Lifeline:

"You will know them by their fruits.… A good tree cannot produce bad fruit, nor can a bad tree produce good fruit" (Matthew 7:16, 18).

Crucified with Christ

"I have been crucified with Christ; and it is no longer I who live, but Christ lives in me; and the life which I now live in the flesh I live by faith in the Son of God, who loved me and gave Himself up for me."

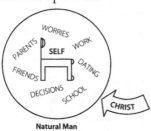

Natural Man

Spiritual Man

the Message

My dear friend Bill Bright and his organization, Campus Crusade for Christ, have shown these two pictures to literally hundreds of millions of people around the world. Bill estimates that over 500 million people have been saved as they have come to understand these concepts.

"Natural" man lives for self. The circle represents the man's life; the throne represents the control center (will) of that life. Without the saving power of Christ, all decisions revolve around self, and the person's life ends up a big, confusing mess.

In contrast, "spiritual" man has given his will (heart) to Christ. Jesus is in control. He's not only Savior, but He's Lord as well. He's not just a compartment in your life; He's the center around which everything else revolves. Where there was confusion, there is harmony; where there was bitterness, there is compassion; where there was immorality, there is purity; where there was guilt, there is forgiveness.

The decision to turn everything over to Jesus is not always easy. Paul compared it to being "crucified with Christ." But the new life that Jesus offers is not possible until the "old life" is dead and gone.

A true Christian is not just a better person; he or she is a *new* person.

A true Christian is not just going to heaven; we're living like we're already there!

Discussion Starters:

• What does it mean to crucify the "old self" with Christ?

•• What does it mean to have Christ "living" in you? How can you allow Him to guide all you do?

••• Is Jesus on the throne in your heart today? How can you tell? If not, what do you need to do to give up your seat?

Lifeline:

If you memorize today's verse, you'll be amazed at how often it comes to mind in the future.

Cursed

the WORD | Galatians 3:13

"Christ redeemed us from the curse of the Law, having become a curse for us—for it is written, 'Cursed is everyone who hangs on a tree.'"

the Message

Eight hundred years before Jesus stepped onto earth in human form, and before His sacrificial death on the cross became an eternal invitation, the prophet Isaiah described in intricate detail what God intended to do and how He would do it.

> But He was pierced through for our transgressions, He was crushed for our iniquities; the chastening for our well-being fell upon Him, and by His scourging we are healed. All of us like sheep have gone astray, each of us has turned to his own way; but the Lord has caused the iniquity of us all to fall on Him. (Isaiah 53:5-6)

I played college football, and as a defensive lineman I endured many crushing Saturday afternoons in stadiums around America. But when I first came to grips with today's passage in Galatians and comprehended that Jesus "became a curse for us," I literally sobbed for an hour like a little boy who'd lost his first girlfriend. I simply couldn't squelch the sadness that welled up in my heart for the injustices inflicted on this dear man.

Paul further explained the "curse" of Jesus in Philippians: "Although He existed in the form of God, [Jesus] did not regard equality with God a thing to be grasped, but emptied Himself, taking the form of a bond-servant, and being made in the likeness of men. Being found in appearance as a man, He humbled Himself by becoming obedient to the point of death, even death on a cross" (Philippians 2:6-8).

Jesus became a curse and died on a cross, all because He loved me and wanted to have a close, personal, intimate relationship with me—just like a father who adopts a beloved child!

His curse became my salvation.

My guilt became His burden.

His purity became my perfection.

Discussion Starters:

* How do you respond when you consider that God made His Son a curse for you?
  ** How would your life be different if Jesus hadn't had the humility and love required to "hang on a tree"?
    *** What are some specific things you can you do to thank Him for such an overwhelming act of love?

Lifeline:

From now on, when you hear a curse of any sort, let it remind you that Jesus was a curse on your behalf.

Daddy

"But when the fullness of the time came, God sent forth His Son, born of a woman, born under the Law, so that He might redeem those who were under the Law, that we might receive the adoption as sons. Because you are sons, God has sent forth the Spirit of His Son into our hearts, crying, 'Abba! Father!' Therefore you are no longer a slave, but a son; and if a son, then an heir through God."

the **Message**

The day was dark and gloomy as I trudged reluctantly to the local high school football field to see David, a 13-year-old football player who had been to our sports camp just a couple of months before. David's eyes were filled with tears of sorrow over the drowning death of his father, reported only a few hours previously. Behind those eyes I could see he was struggling with questions of doubt and sheer disbelief.

I told David I loved him deeply. As I hugged his sweaty frame, I told him that if he ever needed me, I'd be there for him, like a dad—his second dad. All he had to do was call.

Four years went by, and David's life went slowly downhill. I'd see him occasionally, and our chats were always meaningful, but his world without his dad was empty and he wasn't ready to take me up on my offer. Eventually everything fell apart for him; his life became chaos.

But to my sheer delight, he recently came to my house and began to talk to me like I was his daddy. And he gave his heart to Christ! We spent most of three days together, and my feelings for him were much like those toward my own sons. I was thrilled when he prayed an earnest prayer of repentance, turned from his past, and opened up his heart to let the Savior in to reign.

Like Paul, I know what it's like to be "adopted" and to have my status changed from one of "outsider" to that of "son." I can never repay what God has done for me. But as long as there are good kids like David around, I want to keep trying.

Discussion Starters:

• "Abba" is a tender expression, sort of like calling God "Daddy." How do you feel about having that privilege?

•• What does it mean to become not only God's child, but also an heir?

••• Who else this week might like to hear about this opportunity?

Lifeline:

From a slave of sin to freedom…from an orphan lost in the world to an adopted child in heaven…Jesus makes all the difference.

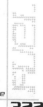

Fruit

"But the fruit of the Spirit is love, joy, peace, patience, kindness, goodness, faithfulness, gentleness, self-control; against such things there is no law."

the **Message**

The black-tie banquet is an incredible event. We sit in formal attire and glittering jewelry beneath vintage crystal chandeliers. The table is spread with the juiciest filet mignon, lobster, fresh mahi-mahi flown in from the Caribbean, and more. Assorted tropical fruits provide color and wonderful aroma—Hawaiian pineapple, papaya, plump strawberries, mangoes, and...

What's this? As a guest reaches for a fresh orange wedge, she is speared by a spiny, prickly pear cactus. Then we begin to notice the slimy, drippy, horse apples...too-hot-to-eat Mexican peppers...bitter, green persimmons...and other inedible, not-yet-ripe fruits.

I'm not describing a literal dinner, but it's a valid illustration of the life of a Christian who first displays "the fruit of the Spirit" and then reverts to "the deeds of the flesh" (Galatians 5:19-21). The old "fruit" is out of place and no longer appealing.

Take a look at the nine qualities listed as "fruit of the Spirit." Once you start to display those things in your life, people take notice. Ask Hally, who was elected homecoming queen of Oklahoma State University after the students were impressed by her godly qualities. Ask Mark Brunnell, who led the Jacksonville Jaguars to the division championship during their first season as an expansion team. His precision passes helped, but they weren't as influential as his Christ-centered, "fruitful" lifestyle that drew the Jaguars together. Ask Michael W. Smith. He's been singing for God so long that he's now more than twice as old as the average age of those who attend his concerts. Yet the fruit of the Spirit continues to exude from his smile, his eyes, and his voice—both on and off the stage.

Without God's Spirit, we're about as appetizing to others as hedge apples, sour grapes, or green persimmons. But when His Spirit controls us, others witness a rich and "fruitful" life devoted to Jesus.

Discussion Starters:

- Read the list of the "deeds of the flesh" (Galatians 5:19-21).
  Which of these has God removed from your life?
  - Have you witnessed the "fruit of the Spirit" in another
    family member? Have you told him or her lately?
- Which quality from today's passage do you most need
  the Holy Spirit's help to cultivate in your life?

Lifeline:

Water and fertilizer enable the growth of rich fruit on orchard trees. Prayer, obedience, and God's Word help the fruit of the Spirit grow ripe in the life a believer.

ephesians

During a three-year stay in the magnificent Macedonian city of Ephesus, the apostle Paul established a church that would become an anchor to the Christian faith. Ephesus was influential as a religious, political, and commercial center, and Paul had quite an impact on the Christians at Ephesus.

Paul's epistle to this church takes on special meaning if we remember it was written while Paul was imprisoned in Rome, possibly chained to Caesar's Praetorian guard. This awareness makes the theme of freedom even more clear and significant.

This letter was so cherished by the early church that it was copied countless times and circulated throughout the many churches in Asia Minor. Thousands of new believers found encouragement and instruction from these words of Paul. I think you will, too.

Who Chose Whom?

the WORD | Ephesians 1:3-5

"Blessed be the God and Father of our Lord Jesus Christ, who has blessed us with every spiritual blessing in the heavenly places in Christ, just as He chose us in Him before the foundation of the world, that we would be holy and blameless before Him. In love He predestined us to adoption as sons through Jesus Christ to Himself, according to the kind intention of His will."

the Message

Did God choose us, or do we choose Him? It's a question that has been debated in the church for centuries. Sadly, it has divided congregations by the thousands. It has started 10,000 arguments. It has created dissension, factions, pride, and insecurity.

God never intended this kind of response! Today's passage *should* be the most wonderful of all the news in the good news of the gospel, and it *will* be if we comprehend two important scriptural truths. First, God chose you! Second, by the grace of God, you choose Him.

God's message to the believer is repeatedly emphasized in Scripture. He chose you. You were handpicked. You were known before you were born. You are His by choice. He created you and was willing to die for you. He couldn't bear the thought of spending eternity without you!

But Scripture is equally clear in stating God's message to the unbeliever: "Whosoever will may come." In other words, if you want to follow God, nothing is stopping you! The heart of the gospel is John 3:16: "For God so loved the world, that He gave His only begotten Son, that whoever believes in Him shall not perish, but have eternal life." (The key word that keeps popping up is *whoever*.)

John tells us, "But *as many as received Him*, to them He gave the right to become children of God" (John 1:12, emphasis added). Peter agrees: "The Lord is not slow about His promise, as some count slowness, but is patient toward you, not wishing for any to perish but for all to come to repentance" (2 Peter 3:9).

How can both be true? Only God knows. But as believers we should be grateful God has chosen us—and motivated us to encourage others to choose Him.

Discussion Starters:

* How does it feel, knowing that you were chosen by God?
** How does such knowledge motivate you to tell others about God?
*** Do you tend to get confused trying to understand God's mysterious truths? If so, how do you handle your confusion?

Lifeline:

By grace we have been chosen by God. By faith we are able to choose Him.

Last One Chosen

the **WORD** | Ephesians 2:12-13

"Remember that you were at that time separate from Christ, excluded from the commonwealth of Israel, and strangers to the covenants of promise, having no hope and without God in the world. But now in Christ Jesus you who formerly were far off have been brought near by the blood of Christ."

the *Message*

The following is a make-believe story, but see what you think about it.

Mike was a running back on a small college football team. He was very good, but his school never got the exposure needed to get him noticed so he could be drafted into the NFL. He felt great disappointment because he truly believed he had the talent to go professional. No matter. He had to watch the pros on television, just like everyone else.

But with only a couple of weeks left in the season, injuries had left the Denver Broncos short of running backs. To Mike's amazement, he was invited to try out. He made the squad and was even able to play a few downs in the season's final games. And as it so happened, the Broncos went to the Super Bowl—and won.

Later, as the players were being called forward one by one to receive their Super Bowl rings, Mike thought to himself, *I'll never get a ring. I just came on at the end of the season and didn't even play that much.* Yet not only did he get the ring (inscribed with his name), he was also prominent in the team picture. He received full rights as a Super Bowl champion even though he joined the team later than all the other members.

Mike's story is a parable for how God has favored those of us who are not Jewish. Before Christ came, we were not among His chosen people. Yet we are now part of His plan because of the work Jesus did on the cross. He died to give salvation to everyone who believes in Him—Jew or Gentile. We may have been the last ones chosen, but thank God, we're now on the winning team!

Discussion Starters:

* What did Jesus do to "bring us near" to God? (See Ephesians 2:13.)
  ** The passage goes on to describe the importance of unity (2:14-16). Who, within the church, are the people you find hardest to get along with? Why?
  *** How can you emulate Jesus in how you include and treat people around you?

Lifeline:

The Lord doesn't care how late in the season you were added. Each and every team member receives full rights and privileges.

Immeasurable Love

the **WORD** | Ephesians 3:17-19

"And that you, being rooted and grounded in love, may be able to comprehend with all the saints what is the breadth and length and height and depth, and to know the love of Christ which surpasses knowledge, that you may be filled up to all the fullness of God."

the **Message**

My longtime friend Dr. Horace Wood was 93 years old when he closed his eyes for a nap and woke up in the arms of the Savior whom he had cherished for over 80 years. I never saw a man so much in love with anything or anyone! Every time Dr. Wood began to talk about Jesus, big tears of affection would stream from his eyes. Every night he went to bed listening to some great preacher teaching him more about his first love.

The breadth and length and height and depth of Christ.

I've been a follower of Christ for 25 years, and every year my love for Him and His Word grows sweeter, deeper, and more intimately fulfilling than ever before. In a similar way, my love continues to grow for my wife of 25 years. I liked her the first time I met her. I loved her the first time we kissed. I loved her more when I hid her engagement ring in a box of Cracker Jack…and more when she walked the aisle in gorgeous white wedding lace…and more when she delivered our first child. The more I know about her, the more I love her. You can't get to the bottom of love. You can't get to the top of it or reach around it.

God is love. The longer you love Him or love someone through Him, the more you realize how little you've seen so far.

In the city on a clear night, you can see about 3,000 stars. In the Ozark Mountains, you can see maybe twice as many. But once I saw the sky from atop a 10,000-foot volcano in Maui, and I could have gazed for a week and never seen all the stars. They go on and on. But even after you get past all the stars in all the galaxies, you'll still find the love of God. And the more of it you comprehend, the more you'll want to know.

Discussion Starters:

* Why should our love for God grow deeper as the years go by?
  ** To what extent have you comprehended the fullness of God's love?
    *** How has your ever-deepening love for a person
        taught you about the ever-deepening love of God?

Lifeline:

Search for deeper love in the people you encounter today.

Precious Treasures

"Do not grieve the Holy Spirit of God, by whom you were sealed for the day of redemption. Let all bitterness and wrath and anger and clamor and slander be put away from you, along with all malice. Be kind to one another, tender-hearted, forgiving each other, just as God in Christ also has forgiven you."

the **Message**

The bottom drawer of my dresser contains the most precious treasures I've accumulated in my lifetime. You'll find no gold, precious gems, or rare coins—I'm talking about *priceless* treasures! That's where I keep Jamie's first pair of size one moccasins her grandma made for her, two plaster casts Cooper had to wear as a toddler to correct a slight birth defect, handmade presents I've received from my children, and, best of all, the love letters my wife and my kids have written me through the years.

"Hey, Dad, I love you. You're the best dad in the world."

"Hey, Dad, thanks for always being there for me."

"Daddy, you're my hero."

"Dad, when I grow up, I want to love my kids the way you love us."

The words, though completely undeserved, place diamonds in my hands and gold in my heart. Showing kindness to those you love is not something you should ever overlook. It will put smiles on their faces and songs in their hearts.

If anything on earth can surpass the value of an act of kindness, perhaps it's the gift of forgiveness. Forgiveness is overlooking someone's mistake, saying, "That's okay. I know you didn't mean it." Forgiveness is choosing to not harbor feelings of resentment against someone who may have wronged us. As we come to realize how much God has forgiven us, it becomes easier to shrug off our hurt feelings when someone else offends us.

Besides, look at what Paul says we can expect if we don't choose kindness and forgiveness: bitterness, wrath, anger, clamor, slander, and malice. What kind of life is that?

So as you go through this week, try to remember: Forgiveness opens the treasure drawer; kindness fills it.

Discussion Starters:

• When those you love check their "treasure drawers," what will they find that you've put there? What else might they like to receive from you?

•• How does forgiveness pave the way for kindness?

••• How does Christ's example make it easier for a believer to be kind and forgiving?

Lifeline:

With the love of Jesus, I can't remember your mistakes...and I can't forget your kindness.

Fill It Up!

the **WORD** | Ephesians 5:18-21

"And do not get drunk with wine…but be filled with the Spirit…singing and making melody with your heart to the Lord; always giving thanks for all things in the name of our Lord Jesus Christ to God, even the Father; and be subject to one another in the fear of Christ."

the *Message*

Pop a balloon and it collapses in an instant. Put an empty glass under a gushing faucet and the air dissipates just as quickly.

The moment you become a Christian, Jesus comes into your heart and His Spirit remains in you forever (2 Corinthians 1:22). That "moment of salvation" is when you become God's child and He becomes your Dad. You are baptized (placed) into the body (family) of Christ, and the Holy Spirit makes His home in your heart.

Then why do Christians sin? Why do Christians hate? Why do Christians fight? Why are Christians unhappy?

Just as a balloon with only a tiny puff of air in it will never fly, so a heart filled mostly with self will never be happy. That's why it's so important to be Spirit-filled.

Being filled with the Holy Spirit automatically makes you smile. Spirit-filled Christians smile a lot and forgive others quickly. Spirit-filled Christians have nice things to say about others, and rid their minds of negative words and harsh thoughts.

Though you receive the Spirit of Christ only once, the filling of the Holy Spirit is a recurring need. Just as you can blow up a deflated balloon, so you can ask God to fill you again with His Spirit as you confess your sins and give yourself to Him wholly.

Alcohol fills a drunk man and controls him. But if you're a Christian, the Holy Spirit will fill you with positive experiences you'll never forget.

Discussion Starters:

* How do you describe a heart filled with the Spirit?
   ** What's the difference between Jesus as *resident* and Jesus as *President* of your life?
*** Would you say you are "filled with the Spirit" today? Explain.

Lifeline:

Just as a car is filled with gas, so a Christian must be filled with the Spirit to accelerate.

God's Family Portrait

"Children, obey your parents in the Lord, for this is right.... Fathers, do not provoke your children to anger, but bring them up in the discipline and instruction of the Lord."

the **Message**

Just as the best and most valuable paintings were rendered at the hands of masters such as Michelangelo, Picasso, and Rembrandt, so a family is at its best when it is painted by the brush of God. Onto a canvas of affection He adds love in various colors, in perfect proportions and intensities. The result, if no one interferes with His original work of art, is a masterpiece with each relationship interacting perfectly with all the others. Today's Scripture passage tells us how God intends for families to operate.

Dads have the greatest jobs on earth! Our calling is to treat our wives like queens by listening to them, caring for them, serving them, and becoming expert in meeting their needs. Similarly, we are to bring up our children with love and devotion, without creating resentment in their hearts by ignoring them or being cruel in what we say or do.

The happiest wives I know are the ones who trust their husbands to captain the marriage ship. They don't mind asking, "Honey, what do you think?" or "What do you think we should do about this situation?" It is their trust and teamwork within the relationship that helps them become secure on their own and confident in the roles they play.

Children who want to live long and live happily obey their parents. Happiest of all are those who honor their moms and dads by maintaining a positive attitude rather than obeying grudgingly.

The Mona Lisa is enshrined in a gallery of the finest works of art where it can be admired. But even more impressive to many people today is seeing a family that operates the way God intends it to. Ephesians 6:1-4 describes God's "family portrait." If your family lives according to these instructions, others will notice. And more importantly, someday you will all be featured in heaven's gallery.

Discussion Starters:

• According to today's passage, what should be your role in your family?
•• How can you become more "picture perfect" in that role?
••• Since God's roles for the family are so clear, why do you think so many families experience serious problems?

Lifeline:

An original Picasso on a piece of canvas can be worth tens of millions of dollars. Imagine the value of a vintage family portrait that is hand-painted by the brush of God.

philippians

The book of Philippians is a letter filled with joy. In this epistle, the love, appreciation, warmth, and affection that flood the apostle Paul's heart shine through as clearly as lighted ornaments on a dazzling Christmas tree. How encouraging it must have been for the Philippian Christians to read, "I thank my God in all of my remembrance of you" (1:3). Yet woven throughout this letter of appreciation, Paul includes a number of strong instructions for harmonious virtuous living:

- "Conduct yourselves in a manner worthy of the gospel of Christ" (1:27a).
- "Have this attitude in yourselves which was also in Christ Jesus" (2:5).
- "I have learned to be content in whatever circumstances I am" (4:11).

It is in Philippians that Paul reveals the source of his seemingly endless energy and devotion: "I can do all things through [Christ] who strengthens me" (4:13). And here Paul exposes the roots of his sacrificial lifestyle and his unquenchable hope: "For to me, to live is Christ and to die is gain" (1:21).

I know committed Christians who have memorized this entire book. It would be well worth your while to do so as well. Whether or not you memorize it, be sure to meditate on it the rest of your life. You'll discover that not only is *joy* the theme of this book, but it will also be the by-product of your study. My son Cooper helped write these devotionals.

To Die Is Gain

the WORD | Philippians 1:19-21

"For I know that this will turn out for my deliverance through your prayers and the provision of the Spirit of Jesus Christ, according to my earnest expectation and hope, that I will not be put to shame in anything, but that with all boldness, Christ will even now, as always, be exalted in my body, whether by life or by death. For to me, to live is Christ and to die is gain."

the Message

When we read about the Christian martyrs of the "Bible days," they seem so far from us. Two thousand years ago and halfway around the world are a lot of time and space that diminish the reality of "dying for Jesus." But Peter did it, Paul did it, James did it, and hundreds of thousands have done it since. In fact, more Christians were martyred for their faith in the twentieth century than in any previous century. They died because they truly believed that "to live is Christ and to die is gain."

Do you agree? If you were presented with the choice to either deny Christ or die for your faith, what would you do?

The reality of this verse came shockingly close to home on April 20, 1999, when 17-year-old Cassie Bernall found herself staring down the barrel of a loaded gun. A classmate on a killing rampage at Columbine High School in Littleton, Colorado, asked Cassie if she believed in God. Cassie declared, "Yes, I believe in God." The next thing Cassie saw was the face of Jesus as He welcomed her home to spend eternity in paradise. Two days before Cassie died, almost as if she somehow sensed the impending disaster, she wrote the following words that clearly expressed her living faith in God, who just two years before had come into her heart and saved her soul.

Now I have given up on everything else.
I have found it to be the only way to really know Christ and to experience
The mighty power that brought Him back to life again,
And to find out what it means to suffer and to die with Him.
So, whatever it takes I will be one who lives in the fresh newness of life
Of those who are alive from the dead.

Discussion Starters:

* What does Cassie's death mean to you?
  ** If faced with the same challenge, what do you think you would have done?
*** What are some practical ways you can "die to yourself" and live for Christ today?

Lifeline:

A martyred Christian is a hero, but it is just as heroic to live for Jesus.

Rewards of Love

the **WORD** | *Philippians 2:1-4*

"Therefore if there is any encouragement in Christ, if there is any consolation of love, if there is any fellowship of the Spirit, if any affection and compassion, make my joy complete by being of the same mind, maintaining the same love, united in spirit, intent on one purpose. Do nothing from selfishness or empty conceit, but with humility of mind regard one another as more important than yourselves; do not merely look out for your own personal interests, but also for the interests of others."

the *Message*

For more than 20 years, I've had the indescribable privilege to have been assigned a 50-yard-line seat in a most amazing "arena" where talent, charm, and character have been displayed like no other place on earth.

The players are male and female. The male team dresses in well-tailored tuxedo uniforms; the female team is in exquisite evening gowns. The star of the show wears a pure, dazzling white gown. Her beauty is beyond my ability to describe.

By now, I'm sure you've guessed that the event is a wedding. My "50-yard-line seat" is the spot between the bride and groom where I can place their hands together and invite them to say "I do."

Almost all the weddings at which I've officiated feature a bride and a groom from the staff of our Christian sports camp who met and fell in love there. The number of couples over the past two decades has become too large to keep up with. Even more amazing is that every one of those couples is not only still married, but also very happily married.

Nationally, about half of all marriages end in divorce, and a large percentage of those who stay married aren't truly happy. The difference between those I've closely witnessed and the rest is the daily reality of the few simple verses of Scripture at the top of this page. If you'll study them and apply them diligently in your life between now and your wedding day, you too can expect rewards of love beyond your wildest dreams.

Discussion Starters:

• Why is putting others' needs before your own so difficult to accomplish?

•• Why does unselfishness bring so much joy to a relationship?

••• What are three specific things you can do, beginning today, to prepare for the selflessness required in a marriage relationship?

Lifeline:

It is in giving that we receive. It is in dying to self that love can truly live.

Just Plain Rubbish

the **WORD** | Philippians 3:8-9a

"I count all things to be loss in view of the surpassing value of knowing Christ Jesus my Lord, for whom I have suffered the loss of all things, and count them but rubbish so that I may gain Christ, and may be found in Him."

the **Message**

What is your favorite title or possession? Is it a tangible item like a car, a girlfriend, a diamond necklace, a letter jacket, a savings account, or your own room? Or is it an elected position like cheerleader, football captain, all-district in basketball, or all-state band? Whatever it is, would you give it up for Jesus? If someone needed it more than you, would you give it to him or her for the sake of Christ?

While you ponder that thought for a minute, let me pose a more practical question. Would you give up your favorite CD if you heard or saw a lyric that was not respectful toward God? How about your favorite TV show? How about a hit new movie at the local theater? What about a relationship that doesn't honor Him? Or a habit? Or a moral value?

Paul has a word for anything that interferes with a truly pure relationship with Christ: *rubbish*. Just as we take out trash before it begins to accumulate and stink, so we need to eliminate anything in our lives that threatens our love and commitment to God—and we need to do so on a regular basis. To be honest, some of us become quite attached to certain pieces of rubbish. But in order to stay focused on the things that are really important, we need to "take out the trash"—all of it.

Jesus made the trip from heaven to earth—and to the cross—to show His love for us. The least we can do is make a trip to the dump and get rid of the rubbish in our lives to show our love for Him.

Discussion Starters:

• What, if anything, have you given up for Jesus lately?
•• What would you be most reluctant to give up for Jesus? Why?
••• What are some things that aren't necessarily bad on their own yet might be classified as "rubbish" because they interfere with a closer relationship with Jesus?

Lifeline:

Are any of your possessions, positions, or relationships beginning to cause a stink in regard to your spiritual growth? If so, are you willing to "take out the trash"?

Contentment

the **WORD** | Philippians 4:11-13

"I have learned to be content in whatever circumstances I am.… I have learned the secret of being filled and going hungry, both of having abundance and suffering need. I can do all things through Him who strengthens me."

the *Message*

An old tale is told of a Texas rancher who said, "I don't want much land. I just want everything that joins mine."

During a professional basketball strike, an athlete who had signed a contract for over $106 million was heard to say, "The problem with the NBA is the owners are just too greedy."

I know a beautiful young lady who won a huge national beauty pageant. Yet her boyfriend would complain that her features just "weren't perfect enough."

Every year thousands of thin girls starve themselves because they "can't get skinny." Contentment is a state of mind that can only be found in God. He makes us happy with what we are given. We find peace with the body He gave us. We discover joy in our circumstances. We are satisfied with our looks and don't worry about money.

Without contentment, you can't get "rich" because there is never enough. You can't become beautiful enough because you're always comparing yourself to others. Someone else always has a hotter car, a faster horse, bigger biceps, more popularity, and so forth.

How can you replace your competitive tendencies with contentment? Get an attitude of gratitude! Start being thankful for what you have. When you're thankful, you see people who have less and who would consider you blessed.

What can you be content about today? Start there, and each day keep developing that attitude until you can say, "I will be content in whatever circumstances I face." Your anxiety will diminish and your smile will increase as quickly as you can change your mind.

Discussion Starters:

• In what area of life do you find it hardest to find contentment?
•• Why is discontentment such a joy stealer?
••• How does drawing closer to the heart of God make contentment more real?

Lifeline:

An old saying goes, "I complained because I had no shoes until I met a man who had no feet."

colossians

Bob Waliszewski is a youth-culture expert from Focus on the Family. He knows movies, music, and other media like no man on earth. Bob applies his accumulated wisdom to the excellent book of Colossians to help you and me in an area that is very difficult for most Christians—how to live in righteousness.

In Colossians, Paul gives the most descriptive picture of Christ found in any of his letters. Colossians 1:15-20 is a "must" for Scripture memory. It can sweeten your walk with Christ and strengthen your understanding of His purpose like no other place in Scripture.

As we understand Jesus' holiness and "fix our eyes on Him," it is easy to apply Bob Waliszewski's insights. May we learn to eagerly respond to God's greatest compliment to us: "Your body is a temple of the Holy Spirit,…therefore glorify God in your body" (1 Corinthians 6:19-20).

Who's Your Hero?

the WORD | Colossians 1:15-17

"[Christ] is the image of the invisible God, the firstborn of all creation. For by Him all things were created, both in the heavens and on earth, visible and invisible, whether thrones or dominions or rulers or authorities—all things have been created through Him and for Him. He is before all things, and in Him all things hold together."

the Message

It never ceases to amaze me to see who some people idolize…and why. In one Letters to the Editor section of the rock music magazine *Rip*, I ran across the following statements from young music fans:

- "Metallica is my number-one sellout and always will be."
- "I have been a die-hard, obsessed fan of Marilyn Manson for four years now…. To show my dedication to [Manson], I just got my seventh tattoo last week…. I'd get a hundred more tattoos for my loving Marilyn if I had to."
- "I'm an enormous fan of Garbage. I've seen them in concert twice and, aside from the first time I had sex, those are the best two nights of my life…. Shirley Manson is the ultimate rock goddess."

Some sad comments indeed, especially when we realize these statements represent the views of millions of other like-minded young people. Yet with the media defining society's heroes, it's often difficult to break away from the pack and choose worthy ones. We're told whom we should esteem by MTV, on magazine covers, and on the big screen. Never mind that these individuals may be bisexual, alcoholics, drug addicts, witches, or on their fifth marriage.

So how do we know when someone measures up? Paul reminds us that Jesus should be our ultimate hero. Why? To begin with, He's God. He created everything. He has "made peace through the blood of His cross" (Colossians 1:20). And the list could go on and on. His nature, His sacrifice, and His love qualify Him to be mankind's most deserving role model!

Discussion Starters:

List your favorite heroes. Why did you include each person? Where would you place Christ on that list?

In your opinion, what constitutes a true hero? Besides the reasons listed by Paul in Colossians 1:15-20, what others can you give for why Christ Jesus is the ultimate hero?

Name 10 individuals who are frequently idolized in the media. Which, if any, do you feel are worthy of admiration?

Lifeline:

Identify an acquaintance who idolizes someone (a rock star, actor, or sports figure) who openly displays hostility toward God and His kingdom. Write down three things you can do to point your friend to the hero from Nazareth.

No Place Too Dark

the **WORD** | Colossians 1:28-29

"We proclaim [Christ], admonishing every man and teaching every man with all wisdom, so that we may present every man complete in Christ. For this purpose also I labor, striving according to His power, which mightily works within me."

the *Message*

Toward the end of the book of Colossians, Paul informs his readers that he is currently serving prison time (4:10). Picture yourself in his first-century living conditions. No electric lights. No flush toilets. No gas furnace. No queen-size mattress. It's dingy. Dreary. Smelly. Bug-infested. Cold. To pass the time, there's no telephone, no radio, no prison library, and no TV (which was perhaps a blessing). Sounds miserable, doesn't it? And certainly, in this situation, ministry to others would seem impossible.

Well, not for Paul. His love for Christ and desire to spread the gospel didn't stop at the jailhouse door. Even while in prison, he could write and challenge others to grow in their faith.

Paul desired to present everyone complete in Christ (Colossians 1:28). What a fantastic goal! Yet he went on to say that his work for God wasn't a casual pursuit. It was a struggle. It was labor. But the key was that Paul's source of strength was Christ's energy, "which mightily works within me" (verse 29). As a result, God's energy gave Paul ideas. It opened doors—even in a dingy jail cell.

Have you ever been in a place that seemed too dark to witness for Jesus? Perhaps at your school? In a certain class? Around your family? On a sports team? Looking at Paul's situation reminds us that regardless of what we're going through, regardless of where we find ourselves, Christ can demonstrate His love through us. The call is universal. The rewards are truly great. All it takes is His energy…and a willingness to let His love compel us.

Discussion Starters:

* If Paul had waited for his circumstances to improve, he would have missed some major ministry opportunities. What situations in your life do you consider obstacles to fruitful ministry? Are they really obstacles, or might they be opportunities to adjust your perceptions and increase your faith?
    ** Can you think of some new and more fruitful ways to share your faith?
    *** What situations has God placed you in that may seem too dark for sharing Christ yet could have great potential if you use Christ's energy?

Lifeline:

Identify a situation you're involved in that has seemed "ministry impossible." Pray to be shown how to present Christ effectively in that situation.

Persuasive Arguments

"I say this so that no one will delude you with persuasive argument. For even though I am absent in body, nevertheless I am with you in spirit, rejoicing to see your good discipline and the stability of your faith in Christ."

the Message

I love this quote from comedian Bill Cosby: "The [TV] networks say they don't influence anybody. If that's true, why do they have commercials?"

The apostle Paul realized people—even Christians—could be easily swayed to believe all kinds of strange ideas if they failed to aggressively keep their minds from being polluted. The entertainment industry is notorious for offering a number of "persuasive arguments" that are deceptive, dishonest, and destructive. Here are just a few (either stated directly or implied) from TV programs I've reviewed recently:

- Sex outside of marriage is acceptable.
- Christians are wimps, hypocrites, or dangerous to others.
- On-screen violence and nudity have no negative effect on anyone.
- Homosexuality is a perfectly legitimate lifestyle.

When our media role models laugh at moral standards, they don't just reflect society; they affect the values and integrity of its people. That's why Bill Cosby's quote has a prominent place in my office. Isn't it bizarre that the same television executives who charge $1.3 million for a 30-second Super Bowl spot to influence purchasing can then adamantly deny that their programming sways others' behavior?

Deceptive messages packaged in "persuasive arguments" are easily rejected when we refuse to allow our minds to be bombarded in the first place. The best approach when considering a certain entertainment option is to ask the question "What would Jesus do?" and then take the appropriate action.

Discussion Starters:

- If Jesus were walking this planet today instead of 2,000 years ago, list three TV shows you think He and His disciples might watch.
  - What are some "persuasive arguments" being promoted on TV and in other media that are actually deceptive and destructive?
  - What do you think are the best ways to guard your heart and mind against alluring, but empty, philosophies?

Lifeline:

Make a card with Psalm 101:3 written on it to place over each family television set as a reminder to think about what you're watching.

Captive or Free?

"See to it that no one takes you captive through philosophy and empty deception,... according to the elementary principles of the world, rather than according to Christ."

the Message

To justify her allegiance to a controversial rock band, "Heather" wrote a letter to Focus on the Family. She said: "You should realize that the world is not fun and full of life—that the world is full of hate, love, suicide, and murder, and we as Christians—I and millions of depressed teens—turn to music that understands that."

Note the "we as Christians" part. Heather is not some out-of-control Satanist. She's a sophomore in high school who claims to love Jesus. Here's my interpretation of what Heather is really saying: "I'm a Christian and I've been hurt. As a result, I'm often down and in despair. To find some relief, I turn to music that wallows in pain, wallows in messages that promote suicide and angst—messages that I know are far from whole-some. But when I'm depressed, this music seems to offer some consolation."

Can you relate? Have you ever justified a questionable entertainment choice for similar reasons? Have you ever found yourself more interested in pop culture than Christian culture?

Paul was aware of the type of temptation Heather faces. He warned, "See to it that no one takes you captive through philosophy and empty deception."

Unfortunately, Heather shows signs of being a captive. Hollow and deceptive philosophies flow through her headphones and threaten to lead her astray. So far they haven't totally shipwrecked her faith, but they have weakened her witness, lessened her joy, and dampened her love and commitment to her Savior. Rather than finding com-fort in the One who truly knows about pain, she has chosen to find "comfort" in the hollow philosophy of musicians who profit from producing troublesome CDs.

Still, it's not too late for Heather to change. It's never too late for anyone. How about you?

Discussion Starters:

* What philosophies being promoted in pop culture would you classify as "empty" or "deceptive"?

** How do you prevent potentially destructive entertainment messages from affecting your faith?

*** What are some possible consequences of indulging in entertainment that applauds behaviors, language, and attitudes that are not Christ-honoring?

Lifeline:

Do any of your favorite music groups, TV shows, or movies contain "empty deception"? If so, what should be your response?

Setting Our Minds

the **WORD** | Colossians 3:1-2

"Therefore if you have been raised up with Christ, keep seeking the things above, where Christ is, seated at the right hand of God. Set your mind on the things above, not on the things that are on earth."

the Message

Have you ever found yourself thinking about something twisted or off-color and wished you could turn your brain off? Impossible, isn't it? Even when we're sleeping, the wheels of our minds are turning. Although there is no off button inside your head, it is possible to redirect your thought life. Paul was so convinced of this that in the first two verses of Colossians 3 he tells us what things should take center stage in the theater of our minds.

Unfortunately, it's easy to get sidetracked and set our minds on worldly—even sinful—things. This is especially true when what enters our ears and eyes is contrary to Scripture. So the key to setting our minds on things above is twofold. First, we must be "transformed by the renewing of our minds" (Romans 12:2). This occurs when we diligently meditate upon God's Word. But equally important, we must avoid things that war against our faith. Reading the Bible and watching *Dawson's Creek* or *South Park* just don't mix.

Christians often fail miserably at avoiding harmful entertainment. For instance, church statistician George Barna found that on a percentage basis, more Christians watch MTV than non-Christians. No wonder many teens continue to struggle with thoughts of lust, rebellion, anger, etc.

Philippians 4:8 goes into more detail about improving our thought life. Paul explains that our minds should focus on those things that are pure, lovely, honorable, excellent, and so forth. Today's media sometimes meet these standards, but more often they don't. When you catch yourself "setting your mind" on things that are less than pure, remember that your brain doesn't have an off switch—but your CD player does!

Discussion Starters:

* Have you had any disturbing thoughts lately? If so, are any related to or reinforced by your media diet?
** What practical steps can you take to renew your mind and set your affections on things above rather than on earthly things?
*** What arguments are you likely to hear from your peers in regard to their choice of movies, music, and TV shows? If they ask why you're concerned about today's media, how would you respond?

Lifeline:

Discuss with a trusted Christian mentor the struggles you face regarding your thought life. Create a plan that will help you more consistently think about things above.

Heartsongs

the WORD | Colossians 3:16

"Let the word of Christ richly dwell within you, with all wisdom teaching and admonishing one another with psalms and hymns and spiritual songs, singing with thankfulness in your hearts to God."

the Message

Something about melody helps us remember things. My son memorized all 50 states alphabetically using a tune his second-grade teacher taught him. The other night my daughter "performed" a rap song she had learned that contained a number of phonics rules. Her teacher did her quite a favor when she set the language basics to music rather than just listing them on paper and commanding, "Memorize!"

But long before my children's teachers discovered how music helps us retain information, Paul asked us to consider getting God's Word in our hearts by this method. Although many of us would never consider singing publicly, all of us can sing as Paul suggests: with thankfulness in our hearts to God. We can sing "in our hearts" while walking down the hall at school, on a crowded bus, or in the numerous lines we find ourselves waiting in. The opportunities are endless.

But what kind of songs qualify? Paul says we should sing psalms, hymns, and spiritual songs. Perhaps you already know a number of choruses that feature verses from the Psalms. But have you tried writing some of your own? Remember that no one has to hear them. You're singing them "in your heart." When it comes to "spiritual songs," there are umpteen thousand to choose from—no matter what style of music you enjoy most. Choose from ska, country, rap, alternative, R&B, swing, and everything in between. The key is to ask, "As I listen to and re-sing this song in my heart, does it edify my spirit?" If so, the Bible says the Word of God will dwell in you more deeply—a promise that's music to my ears.

Discussion Starters:

* Write down as many Bible verses as you can think of that you learned because of a scriptural song. Do you think you would know these scriptures if you hadn't learned them through song?
** When does singing "spiritual songs" mean the most to you?
*** If you were sad right now, what would be a good "spiritual song" to sing? What if you were elated? Lonely? Hurt? Confused?

Lifeline:

Identify a Bible verse that you've always wanted to commit to memory. Use the verse as "lyrics" and set it to a tune you already know (or make one up). Sing through the song a few times until it sticks in your mind. If this exercise goes well, try doing this every day for the next 30 days.

Devoted to Prayer

the **WORD** | Colossians 4:2

"Devote yourselves to prayer, keeping alert in it with an attitude of thanksgiving."

the Message

Did you know that falling TV sets kill about four children every year? That sad and obscure fact was cited in the September 1998 issue of the *Journal of Pediatrics*. The observation got me wondering how many other people are "dead" today because of TV—not because of falling television sets but because of faulty media messages. Consider this statement:

"I personally worry more about television than other forms of media, because it's so pervasive, and it's a primary baby-sitter and value-transmitter for many children.... The constant barrage of violence and explicit sexuality reinforces the loosening of human bonds, undermining the evolution of a mature person. For many people, it is affecting not just what they think about but also how they think."

This concern was expressed by Hillary Rodham Clinton and serves to underscore a widespread concern about TV—not just among evangelicals. Even television mogul Ted Turner echoed similar thoughts regarding the tube:

"As a parent with five children, I don't need experts to tell me that the amount of violence on television today can be harmful to children.... Television violence is *the single most significant factor* contributing to violence in America" (emphasis added).

Besides guarding our own hearts, we need to influence the entire media culture. There are a number of ways, but none is more important than prayer. The apostle Paul says, "Devote yourselves to prayer, keeping alert in it with an attitude of thanksgiving." Later in the chapter, he compliments a fellow believer by saying he is "laboring earnestly for you in his prayers" (4:12). Do you ever "labor earnestly in prayer" for our nation? For Hollywood? For individual actors, actresses, musicians, and industry insiders? God assures us that we can make a difference. But not until we first hit our knees.

Discussion Starters:

• How often do you "labor earnestly in prayer" for influential media personalities? Why do you think many Christians never pray for these individuals?

•• What are the keys to seeing our prayers create change in the culture?

••• What scriptural promises assure us that God not only hears us when we pray but also that He will answer?

Lifeline:

Make a list of 31 popular media personalities, and begin to pray for one person each day for the next month. Be specific. Ask the Lord to bring the person to His Son and give him or her a burden for purity, wisdom, and wholesomeness.

A Little Salty Conversation

the **WORD** | Colossians 4:5-6

"Conduct yourselves with wisdom toward outsiders, making the most of the opportunity. Let your speech always be with grace, as though seasoned with salt, so that you will know how you should respond to each person."

the *Message*

Have you ever wondered what you should do in a situation where someone is talking about a certain movie, TV show, or popular CD that you personally find offensive? Most of us can relate to the uncomfortable feeling of wanting to express our views, but knowing that they could come across as judgmental.

But have you ever considered that these conversations—if done right—could lead to an opportunity to share your faith? The apostle Paul saw the need to encourage the church at Colosse to make the most of *every* opportunity.

Most people love to talk about entertainment: "Did you see *Death Factor IV* yet?" Or "Have you heard Blood Kill's new CD?" Some people respond to such questions by getting preachy—which turns people off. Paul suggests another option: "Let your speech always be with grace."

I suggest we fire up a quick prayer for guidance and wisdom during such times as we look for ways to "salt" the conversation rather than squelch it. I might say something like "I used to love movies like that, but I find I'm having a lot more fun these days since I've quit going. Although entertaining to some degree, they just didn't set well with me in the long run."

This type of response concentrates on what has happened to *me*. It's part of a testimony and is something people just can't argue with. This approach allows you to talk to people without blasting them for making poor entertainment choices. You haven't dumped out the whole saltshaker, but you've salted the conversation.

If they want to hear more, they might ask, "What do you mean you're having more fun? What are you up to?" And their questions may just lead them to the ultimate answer—Jesus Christ. During the next week, let's all look for openings where we can "make the most of every opportunity." May I pass you the salt?

Discussion Starters:

* Why do many Christians dread witnessing? Could it be possible they go about it all wrong?
  ** What are some ways you can "salt" a conversation spiritually?
*** In addition to using the subject of entertainment as an opportunity to witness, what other commonly held conversations can become witnessing opportunities? (Sports talk? Politics? Homework? Hobbies?)

Lifeline:

Write out a paragraph you might use to respond to a friend asking you to go to an R-rated slasher film.

1 & 2 thessalonians

Paul established a church in the European (Macedonian) port city of Thessalonica on his second missionary journey. The gospel was received there with joy and tremendous appreciation. Paul's encouragement echoes throughout these two Thessalonian epistles as he surrounds his message of instruction with words of affirmation and empowerment.

"You show great love for people."

"You're pursuing purity with all your heart."

"Overall, you're doing great! Keep it up!"

Another feature of the Thessalonian epistles is Paul's focus on eschatology (teachings about the second coming of Jesus). Apparently there was a lot of sorrow in this church over fellow believers who had died, so Paul went to great effort to reassure those grieving saints of the return of Christ, the rapture of the Church, and our eternal home with Him after we die.

Finally, it's almost humorous to read Paul's rapid-fire spray of one-line instructions as he closes his first letter. He had so much wisdom and encouragement to pass along that he just couldn't quit writing until he had expressed everything that was on his heart.

I am pleased to be joined in the writing of these devotions by son Cooper, who contributed the poems.

Imitators of God

the WORD | 1 Thessalonians 1:5-6

"Our gospel did not come to you in word only, but also in power and in the Holy Spirit and with full conviction; just as you know what kind of men we proved to be among you for your sake. You also became imitators of us and of the Lord, having received the word in much tribulation with the joy of the Holy Spirit."

the Message

Josh had been in trouble ever since he was kicked out of elementary school for carrying a concealed weapon in fifth grade. In high school, recurring fights and extensive drug use had left his heart cold and hard. Although he had a religious background, he had ceased to believe in God. He preferred his biology teacher's Darwinian explanation that people somehow evolved by chance over a long period of time.

Josh had a friend named Brett who for three years had been a fellow drug user and dealer. Brett stopped at my house one day after a friend had almost died in a heroin overdose. That day Brett gave his heart to Christ with sincerity. I challenged him to give up drugs for 21 days, because psychologists tell us it takes 21 to establish a habit. Brett accepted the challenge, and he said no during those 21 days more times than he could count. He also decided to break up with his "drop-dead gorgeous" blonde girlfriend because their relationship had been sexual. Brett was truly a new person, and Josh saw a complete change in his friend.

Josh asked Brett to take him to my house. We talked about evolution for a while, and I cleared up some misconceptions he had been taught. Then Josh said he wanted to give his heart to Christ. I asked him why he wanted to make such a life-changing decision, and he answered with one word: "Brett."

Paul reminds us that what we believe isn't just a bunch of words. The gospel of Jesus Christ has *power*. If you don't believe me, just ask Josh and Brett.

Discussion Starters:

* Why is a lifestyle dedicated to Christ the most powerful witnessing tool that we have?
   ** How consistently do your friends see you living out your faith in Jesus?
      *** Does your lifestyle lead your unsaved friends to Christ? What changes could you make that might cause your Christian witness to be more effective?

Lifeline:

Other people see you (and your witness for God), whether you notice them or not! Without saying a word, your actions speak volumes.

Our Glory and Joy

"For who is our hope or joy or crown of exultation? Is it not even you, in the presence of our Lord Jesus at His coming? For you are our glory and joy."

the *Message*

Every great company has a vision statement—a lofty, long-range goal that the company is constantly working toward. Everything the company sets out to do is driven by that statement. Lots of good ideas come along, but only those that fit the company's vision statement are pursued.

Individuals can also have clearly defined vision statements. Many of the world's great inventors, ministers, writers, executives, and leaders have carefully thought through what they want to achieve, and they work toward that vision each day with care, passion, and purpose. Such men and women usually get more accomplished in this life, by far, than people who give little consideration to where they are headed.

Paul's vision statement is identified clearly in today's passage. This amazingly selfless, passionate, gospel-spreading apostle was motivated daily to excel at his work by his expectation that someday he would meet Christ face-to-face. In addition, on that day Paul wanted to see men and women from all over the world whom he had led to Christ and nurtured in their faith. Those people, standing by his side in the presence of the Lord and receiving their reward of eternal life in the kingdom of heaven, were Paul's constant source of "glory and joy."

As we read and respond to Paul's writings in 1 Thessalonians (and his other epistles), it's exciting to think that even *we* can benefit from his steadfast vision. Even more exciting is to consider who might benefit from *ours*.

Discussion Starters:

* Do you have a vision statement? If not, what would you want to include in it?
  ** What people would you consider your "glory and joy"?
    *** Who are some of the people you want to see standing before Jesus when you meet Him for your eternal reward?

Lifeline:

If perishable things are your glory and joy, you'll be disappointed. If people's souls are your glory and joy, you'll be motivated.

Growing Hostility

"For indeed when we were with you, we kept telling you in advance that we were going to suffer affliction; and so it came to pass, as you know."

the *Message*

For those of us who live in the United States, active persecution of our Christian beliefs has never been much of a problem. But the times are changing; it seems our nation is turning against Christians! Here are some recent actions taken against Christians, as presented in Allan Bloom's book *The Closing of the American Mind* (New York: Simon & Schuster, 1987; pp. 52-54):

• A federal court, referring to a local school district, said that "nothing can be more dangerous…than an adolescent seeing the football captain, the student body president or the leading actress in a dramatic production participating in communal prayer meetings in the captive audience setting of a school."

• A child in Kentucky was told she could not submit her chosen drawing for an independent school project. She had drawn a cross.

• An Arizona teacher disciplined a second-grader in class for typing the word *Jesus* on her school computer during a computer lab.

• In Virginia, the Department of Motor Vehicles refused a pastor's request to display "4GOD-SO" on his license plate.

• Six students in Illinois were detained in squad cars and threatened with mace because they prayed around their school's flagpole.

I believe we are only beginning to see the tip of the iceberg. If Jesus doesn't return first, you and I will see increased hostility toward Christians and our beliefs.

If you take a pro-life stance, you are labeled "a narrow-minded anti-abortionist." If you believe in marriages only between a male and a female, you are scorned as "a homophobic bigot."

If you believe devoutly in Jesus, you're called "an uneducated freak."

Media mogul Ted Turner has stated that "Christianity is for losers."

Paul warned the Thessalonians that afflictions were coming for devoted Christians. I believe that Christians in America can expect the same.

Discussion Starters:

• In Paul's day, what effect did persecution have on the cause of Christ?
•• Why does suffering tend to strengthen the convictions of Christians?
••• If faced with persecution for your beliefs, how do you think you would respond? How can you be better prepared to respond with boldness?

Lifeline:

Hot fire tempers a band of steel, strengthens it, and allows it to hold a sharp edge. The hot fire of persecution puts the edge on a Christian's lifestyle.

Beyond Morality

the **WORD** | 1 Thessalonians 4:3-5, 7

"For this is the will of God, your sanctification; that is, that you abstain from sexual immorality; that each of you know how to possess his own vessel in sanctification and honor, not in lustful passion…. For God has not called us for the purpose of impurity, but in sanctification."

the **Message**

I received three letters from Jana that arrived in approximate one-year intervals. The first arrived during the spring of her ninth-grade year.

> Dear Joe,
> I'm so afraid of losing my boyfriend. Even though we're having sex and I know it's wrong, I can't stop for fear that I'll lose him.

Seven months later, during her sophomore year, I received Jana's second letter.

> Dear Joe,
> My boyfriend and I broke up, but now I have another problem. I went to spend the night at my girlfriend's house and we started drinking. A boy I'd never met before was there who had been drinking, too. He started messing around with me and before I realized what I was doing, we had sex. The next day when I came to my senses, I confronted him on what he'd done. He called me awful names and said he never wanted to see me again.

A year later, Jana wrote me another letter:

> Dear Joe,
> I've finally realized what I've been doing the past two years was so wrong. Please tell other kids how badly I've hurt my family and myself. Why do I have to learn things the hard way? Why did I have to go through all of this to learn what God had been telling me all along?

Paul uses the word *sanctification* in reference to Christians. *Sanctified* simply means we are "set apart"—*from* sin, and *to* God. So when it comes to things like sex, our standards must be set higher than others'. It's the only way to avoid personal pain and potential danger.

If you don't believe Paul, just ask Jana.

Discussion Starters:

* Read 1 Thessalonians 4:6. What does it mean to "defraud" someone of the opposite sex?
  ** First Thessalonians 4:8 says, "He who rejects this is not rejecting man but the God who gives His Holy Spirit to you." What does that mean?

Lifeline:

Beyond virginity is *purity*. It heals broken hearts. It establishes shame-free boundaries. It builds incredible marriages.

Sons of the Day

the WORD | 1 Thessalonians 5:2, 4-5

"For you yourselves know full well that the day of the Lord will come just like a thief in the night.... But you, brethren, are not in darkness, that the day would overtake you like a thief; for you are all sons of light and sons of day."

the Message

Paul promised the Thessalonians that someday Jesus would return to earth (1 Thessalonians 5:1-11). His followers should be looking forward to the day when He will escort them to an eternal home of joy and safety. Others will be caught completely off guard. For those who don't believe or who aren't prepared, the return of Jesus will be like "a thief in the night."

The book of Revelation confirms what Paul says. Below are a couple of samples: "No one will be able to buy or to sell, except the one who has the mark, either the name of the beast or the number of his name" (Revelation 13:17). With current computer chip technology, one person (the Antichrist, a.k.a. "the beast") could "mark" every human on earth with laser tattoos and control all economic transactions.

"The number of the armies of the horsemen was two hundred million.... [The Euphrates] was dried up, so that the way would be prepared for the kings from the east" (Revelation 9:16; 16:12). Red China has been heavily involved in the military affairs of Iraq and Iran, and it is thirsty for the vast Middle East oil reserves. Israel and the United States stand squarely in the way of a military takeover. China now boasts an army of 200 million.

Dozens of other prophecies about the return of Christ and the rapture of the church are being fulfilled before our eyes. Many are quite alarming. But let's not overlook one final word from Paul to the Thessalonians: "Since we are of the day, let us be sober.... For God has not destined us for wrath, but for obtaining salvation through our Lord Jesus Christ" (1 Thessalonians 5:8-9).

Jesus could return *today*—a scary thought for some people. But for us who are "sons of day," no news could be better.

Discussion Starters:

* How does a "child of the day" behave differently than a "child of the night"?
    ** If you knew Jesus were coming back tomorrow, would you do anything differently? If so, what?
  *** How can you encourage your friends or family members to be ready for Jesus' return?

Lifeline:

Make plans as if Jesus won't return for 100 years, but live as if He's coming back today.

Give Thanks

the **WORD** | 2 Thessalonians 1:3

"We ought always to give thanks to God for you, brethren, as is only fitting, because your faith is greatly enlarged, and the love of each one of you toward one another grows ever greater."

the Message

Today I was broken
and I was made new
in Your image
and by your power
I am redeemed.

Yesterday is but a memory
and seems as though a dream
for I lived not until this day...

As the east is to the west
so are all my sins.
They're gone and out of my life;
it is not a fad or a change of style
but a change of heart and my soul.

As many times as I fall
you will always be there,
and each tear that is shed of mine
is as if it were one of your own,
for you loved me even when I was lost...

Each time I go astray
I pray that you will lead me home,
for it is with you that my soul belongs
and in your presence is where I strive to be;
in your favor is where I desire to live.

Love me today, Lord;
that is my prayer,
for I am so empty without you,
and in your presence
my joy overflows.

Discussion Starters:

* What are a dozen things or people for which you can "give thanks to God" today?
** How does it make you feel to respond to God's good gifts by giving Him the glory?
*** How do you think God reacts when we offer thanksgiving?

Lifeline:

God has been so good that our joy should overflow in thanksgiving.

Deluding Influences

"Then that lawless one will be revealed whom the Lord will slay with the breath of His mouth and bring to an end by the appearance of His coming.... For this reason God will send upon them a deluding influence so that they will believe what is false, in order that they all may be judged who did not believe the truth, but took pleasure in wickedness."

the Message

A trucking company placed the following ad in a local newspaper:

> "Wanted: Conscientious and experienced truck driver to transport dynamite across narrow mountain roads. Pay is very good."

Three brave drivers interviewed for the job. The foreman asked each of them, "When you turn a tight corner on a mountain road, how close to the edge can you drive without slipping off?" The first driver responded, "No problem! I can get within a foot of the drop-off." The second applicant said, "I've had years of experience, so I can hang the outside edge of my tire over the ledge and still keep her on the road." The third man said, "I'm sorry, sir. You're asking the wrong person. I respect the load and the danger and would never get close enough to the edge to find out."

Guess who got the job?

A committed Christian stays far from the edge too. The lukewarm Christian "dances with the devil," dabbling with sin here and there, not respecting the danger:

Just a couple of beers.

Just a little petting.

Just a PG-13 movie—not too much sex or profanity.

Just that new CD and then back to giving offerings to God.

Just one drag.

Just a couple of pictures on the Web.

The trouble is, "just a little" of Satan's deluding influence goes a long way. I think that's why the Antichrist ("the lawless one") will rise to power so easily—many "Christian wannabes" won't even recognize him because our tolerance of sin is deadening our spiritual awareness.

When the Lord returns, truth will once more prevail. All delusions will be shattered. And the groans of disappointment will be everywhere.

Discussion Starters:

• What can you learn about the Antichrist from 2 Thessalonians 2?

•• What are some of Satan's "deluding influences" you are aware of?

••• How can you prevent being deluded—both now and in the future?

Lifeline:

The "angel of light" camouflages sin. Walking in the Light reveals sin.

Steadfast

"But the Lord is faithful, and He will strengthen and protect you from the evil one. We have confidence in the Lord concerning you, that you are doing and will continue to do what we command. May the Lord direct your hearts into the love of God and into the steadfastness of Christ."

the **Message**

Solid.

    Immovable.

        Dependable.

            Loyal.

                Steadfast.

If you were to outline your hand on a piece of paper (like we did in kindergarten) and write one adjective on each digit to describe your feelings about the nature of God and His Word, what would the adjectives be? If the tables were turned, how do you think God would describe *your* commitment to Him?

Last week a sharp 17-year-old friend of mine made the extremely difficult decision to break up with his girlfriend. He knew she wasn't where she needed to be spiritually, and their relationship wasn't leading toward a godly future. My friend is *steadfast*. He has also walked away from countless parties where alcohol and drugs were present, and he has led some of his friends to Christ by his solid example.

In the rural country around where I live, words are few and character is measured by the work you do and the way you walk your talk. One of the biggest compliments you can receive is when an old cowboy tells someone, "I could turn my back on him and never give it a second thought." The comment reflects a trust in the person's steadfastness.

Jesus handpicked a group of disciples He knew He could entrust to tell the world about Him. Although they had failed in the past, as far as the 11 that were left after the Resurrection, He knew He "could turn His back on them" and they wouldn't let Him down. What great selection skills He had!

Jesus is still calling disciples. Why has He chosen *you*?

Discussion Starters:

• What two or three adjectives do you think God would use to evaluate you today?

•• How can a young Christian become steadfast and dependable?

••• Why are steadfast people so respected?

Lifeline:

As you reflect on each of your hard decisions and choices this week, evaluate yourself with an adjective that depicts your character.

1 & 2 timothy

My favorite human relationship in all of Scripture is between Paul and his "true child," young Timothy. Though they weren't related by flesh and blood, they shared a marvelous father-son friendship in their faith. Because of Timothy's undaunted faith in Jesus and his loyalty and love for Paul, he was chosen to carry the baton of leadership to many newly established churches while Paul was imprisoned and awaiting death.

Paul saw much potential in Timothy and wanted his young disciple to be knowledgeable and prepared for the challenge of faithfully upholding the gospel during a time when others were beginning to dilute and distort it. It would be Timothy's assignment (and privilege) to carry the faith onward.

Paul's encouragement and exhortation to Timothy are scattered throughout his two letters:

"My beloved son."

"I thank God for you and pray for you night and day."

What a "father" Paul was to Timothy! He desired to give Timothy protection, passion, and instruction so Timothy would succeed on his own after Paul's death. Next to Jesus, it was Timothy on Paul's heart most as he breathed his last breath before being martyred for his faith.

These highly personal letters are filled with strong, clear instructions to be diligent, not be ashamed, retain the standard, be strong, suffer hardship, remember Jesus, avoid gossip, flee youthful lusts, cling to Scripture, be sober, and preach the Word. Once again, I'm pleased to have the help of my son Cooper in preparing these devotionals.

Fight the Good Fight

"This command I entrust to you, Timothy, my son, in accordance with the prophecies previously made concerning you, that by them you fight the good fight, keeping faith and a good conscience, which some have rejected and suffered shipwreck in regard to their faith."

the *Message*

Each of my last two years in college, our undersized Southern Methodist University team played the number-one and number-two teams in the nation, the University of Texas and the University of Arkansas. Texas had a 38-game winning streak; we didn't beat Arkansas for 13 straight years.

We never won the championship, but we did receive a much bigger prize—we learned to train hard and fight as a team, even in the face of insurmountable odds. Each of those Saturday afternoon games was 60 minutes of all-out war. We fought for every yard of Astroturf and Bermuda grass. My body still aches (literally) from the punishing hits I took from our NFL-bound opponents.

Following Christ is precisely that kind of challenge. In a spiritual sense, it is World War III. When a great movie comes out that is sexually explicit, or you're in love with a promiscuous partner, or you get "caught up in the moment," it is a *fight* to stay pure. You're battling not only your natural desires to sin, but also a personal and evil enemy behind those tendencies. So fight the good fight! Acknowledge that your body is a temple of the Holy Spirit and "go to war" to keep out all substances that would deface or weaken that temple. Fight the good fight!

Few challenges on earth are more difficult than establishing and maintaining Christian character and a godly lifestyle in the wake of our nation's amoral plunge into the jaws of hell. Fight the good fight!

Is the cause worth the sacrificial effort and battle scars? You bet it is! I've read about the victory party, and it will be abundantly more rewarding than any price you paid to be there.

Discussion Starters:

• Do you feel that it's fair to have to "fight" for what you believe? Is it is worth it? Why?

•• Describe a spiritual battle you are in right now.
How are doing? Are you determined to win?

••• Who are some people who might encourage you,
as Paul did Timothy, to "fight the good fight"?

Lifeline:

The goal of your life should be love from a pure heart and a good conscience and a sincere faith (1 Timothy 1:5).

Big Families

the WORD | 1 Timothy 2:3-6

"This is good and acceptable in the sight of God our Savior, who desires all men to be saved and to come to the knowledge of the truth. For there is one God, and one mediator also between God and men, the man Christ Jesus, who gave Himself as a ransom for all, the testimony given at the proper time."

the Message

"Tomahawk" Tom Hund was 6'11" when he played basketball for Kansas State University. Tom was a counselor at our sports camp and had a tremendous love for kids. His huge Kansas smile and his warm, gentle ways gave him a personality more contagious than the chicken pox! Everybody at camp loved him.

As crazy as it sounds, his 6'11" frame wasn't the most remarkable thing about Tom. We all knew that Tomahawk Tom Hund was one of 23 brothers and sisters. That's right, 23. In sports camp talk, that was a complete offense and a complete defense in football (plus a sub), or four basketball teams plus three managers!

As many as 20 of Tom's siblings lived in his home at one time. Four to a bed was the standard in their small Kansas farmhouse. They would all get up early, do the farm chores, and then pile on their own school bus and whisk off to school.

I love big families! So does God! God wants a big family so much that He sent His Son to earth to pass out invitations and adoption papers.

God wants you in His family. He wants the girl who sits next to you in geometry class. He wants the kid who plays third clarinet in your band. He wants the big defensive end on your football team. In fact, he wants your entire school.

God's desire is that *all* men and women be in His family. It's not hard to join. All they have to do is hear the call, lay down their pride, and receive Jesus Christ as their personal Savior and Lord. Nothing to sign.

God is the most loving Father imaginable. He already has a lot of kids. But He won't be satisfied until He gets us all!

Discussion Starters:

* In what ways does today's Bible passage motivate you to tell your friends about Jesus?
** How does this teaching affect your perspective about God's nature?
*** What if God weren't so generous? What could you expect?

Lifeline:

"[God] is patient toward you, not wishing for any to perish but for all to come to repentance" (2 Peter 3:9).

Go Forth

the **WORD** | *1 Timothy 3:16*

"By common confession, great is the mystery of godliness: He who was revealed in the flesh, was vindicated in the Spirit, seen by angels, proclaimed among the nations, believed on in the world, taken up in glory."

the **Message**

It was the greatest
of commands ever given
for we who were left,
the ones that witnessed
the ascension.

To live each day for Him
as if it were to be our last;
none will know the day or hour
when the Lamb becomes the Lion
and takes us away.

We cry out
and in our arrogance
await His return,
wanting to be on His right hand,
yet we aren't worthy
to be in His presence.

The Lamb was slain
and we must preach
no matter violent nor hostile crowds;
we strive on
in the name of Him.

A moment that is without
an utterance of Him
is one that has been wasted,
a chance past
and an opportunity lost.

So we must take
the cup that has been passed
from the Creator to us,
acting on His last words
and GO FORTH!

Discussion Starters:

* What do you find "mysterious" about the godliness Paul refers to in today's passage?
** Read the third chapter of 1 Timothy which describes guidelines for Christian leadership. Is there anything you need to work on to follow God more faithfully?
*** Where can you "go forth" this week to make a difference for God?

Lifeline:

The risk we take for Christ is small compared to the price He paid for us.

Faith Training

"For bodily discipline is only of little profit, but godliness is profitable for all things, since it holds promise for the present life and also for the life to come."

the *Message*

Olympic weights, health clubs, tae bo, step-aerobics, crunches, "Abs of Steel," Jazzercise, Gold's Gym, diet plans, swimming workouts, jogging workouts, biking workouts… America is in a health and fitness craze. Each year tens of billions of dollars and tens of billions of hours are spent on health, training, and diet regimens. But the results aren't all positive. Most boys grow up thinking their biceps are too small, and one in four girls suffers from some kind of eating disorder.

Fitness and healthy diets are certainly good things. But what would happen to America—to your home—to yourself—if you started training your soul as devotedly as you train your body? Can you envision Bible-cise, Souls of Steel, Bible Club, God's Gym, memory workouts, and spiritual growth plans?

Pardon the tongue-in-cheek images, but the concept is straight from Scripture, as Paul points out to Timothy in today's verse. Psalm 1 also says it well: "How blessed is the man who[se]…delight is in the law of the Lord, and in His law he meditates day and night" (verses 1-2).

To meditate on God's Word, you have to memorize the Word.

To memorize the Word, you have to study it.

To study the Word, you have to read it.

To read the Word, you have to open your Bible…often.

To open your Bible, you have to have a heart that is excited about loving God, knowing God, and living a life with Him at its center.

So start with a few stretching exercises. Stand up and stretch your legs. Jog over to where you keep your Bible. Do a deep knee bend until you're within reach. Stretch your arm out and lift the "weight" of God's Word. Do a few repetitions of page turning until you find a section that appeals to you. Then you're ready for the *real* workout: stretching your heart, soul, and mind as you read and apply God's Word in your quest for spiritual fitness. The more often you do these exercises, the stronger you'll become.

Discussion Starters:

* Why is spiritual discipline more profitable than bodily discipline?
** How would you evaluate your current level of spiritual fitness?
*** What kind of a "faith workout" would you like to maintain in the immediate future?

Lifeline:

Lord, give me a heart that wants to know You more.

Respect

the WORD | 1 Timothy 5:1-2

"Do not sharply rebuke an older man, but rather appeal to him as a father, to the younger men as brothers, the older women as mothers, and the younger women as sisters, in all purity."

the Message

It is a virtue
and a blessing
to all who are around;
it spurs on wisdom
and is its friend.

Without it
we are but sinners
and are not in God's will,
for He writes
so it shall be done.

In our ignorance
we fear not
and in our hatred
we receive not,
for we are without respect.

All who surround
are in awe of those
who have this gift,
and throughout the world
they have no enemies.

Once it is given
it is returned in full,
and with its benefits
it carries
a lifelong friendship.

As a smile warms the room,
so does respect
in a hostile environment
and will heap coals on the head
of the aggressor.

As He did
the one who was raised,
so should we,
for we should strive to be
in His shadow of mercy.

Love one another
and respect each other,
for it is pleasing
in His eyes
as we are in His image.

Discussion Starters:

* How can you better respect the older people you know?
** How does respect for other people show respect for God?
*** How would your life and behavior be affected if you treated every stranger
as if he or she were as close to you as your closest family members?
How would it change any tendencies toward name-calling? Swearing? Lust? Etc.

Lifeline:

Respect: The more you give to others, the more you receive in return.

The Root of All Sorts of Evil

the **WORD** | 1 Timothy 6:6-10

"But godliness actually is a means of great gain when accompanied by contentment. For we have brought nothing into the world, so we cannot take anything out of it either. If we have food and covering, with these we shall be content. But those who want to get rich fall into temptation and a snare and many foolish and harmful desires which plunge men into ruin and destruction. For the love of money is a root of all sorts of evil, and some by longing for it have wandered away from the faith and pierced themselves with many griefs."

the *Message*

A better stereo system.

Bigger allowance. Bigger paychecks.

A newer car. A faster car.

The United States is a financial black hole that has enough resources to feed much of the starving world. Yet how many of us are content with what we have? Perhaps we should revise our national motto to "More. Gimme more. I want mo-o-o-ore."

What happened to "Enough already"?

We've told you about the 15,000 kids in Haiti that our camps support. They each have one shirt and one pair of shoes. They live on one bowl of beans and rice per day. That's all they've ever known, and they are thrilled to get it.

Yet in some ways the Haitian children are much more content and happier than the youth of America. I've never seen the Haitian kids shoot each other, threaten a teacher, or call their parents degrading names. In the same way, the American kids I know who are most content are those who really love God and would give the shirt off their back to someone in need. In fact, I believe many of today's teens are less materialistic than preceding generations!

At the bottom line is a continual struggle between contentment and greed. Love of money creates a love of things, which is basically idolatry. Anything you own that you wouldn't immediately give to someone who needs it is probably an idol. And the more you accumulate, the more you want until eventually, you can never have enough.

That's why Scripture puts such a high value on contentment. It is the one commodity you can't get enough of.

Discussion Starters:

* How do material things become idols?
  ** How susceptible are you to the love of money?
  Can you see how it might lead to evils?
*** How do we get out of the cycle of desiring, accumulating, and desiring still more?

Lifeline:

Material things always leave you wanting more, but contentment satisfies.

Bold

the WORD | 2 Timothy 1:7-8

"God has not given us a spirit of timidity, but of power and love and discipline. Therefore do not be ashamed of the testimony of our Lord or of me His prisoner, but join with me in suffering for the gospel according to the power of God."

the Message

Be bold in His name
for He commands us so,
and it is for Him
that we live and strive.
There are none who may stand in His way;
in this we can have all confidence.

Our Savior is above all
and calls us to do His will;
it is for this reason
that we can let none stand
in the way of His teaching
for whatever the cause.

There is not any who can oppose
or successfully question His power;
it is as He says without flaws,
and for us it is all we need
to back us in our struggle.

He is in our corner
and with Him we are assured
nothing less than a victory,
for He will vanquish our foes
for all eternity.

The job we have is simple:
It is to do what we are told
and to back it
with all that we are worth
no matter the odds we face.

Our timidity is a weakness
and is a cop-out
for what we know we must do.
We mustn't hide behind
our fear or any other emotion.

Strength is not possessed
in numbers of people
or numbers of followers
but in our Lord
and our Redeemer, Jesus Christ.

Discussion Starters:

* If you're shy by nature, how can you be bolder when God gives you opportunities to speak up or take a stand for Him?
** When you're at school or work, are you ever "ashamed of the testimony of our Lord"—even a little bit? If so, how do you deal with your feelings?
*** How do you feel after you gather your courage and take a bold stand for God?

Lifeline:

Bold actions are most effective when they spring from a humble heart.

Pleasing the Coach

the WORD | 2 Timothy 2:3-5

"Suffer hardship with me, as a good soldier of Christ Jesus. No soldier in active service entangles himself in the affairs of everyday life, so that he may please the one who enlisted him as a soldier. Also if anyone competes as an athlete, he does not win the prize unless he competes according to the rules."

the Message

The high school football team I coached was, to be kind, mediocre. We trained hard, we played hard, and we had fun. In fact, we did most everything a team is supposed to do…except win.

We had a sophomore named Robert who didn't know squat about the game of football. He was slow and inexperienced, but he had a huge heart for the team and a desire to play. One Friday night, the opposing team's running back was streaking down the sideline right in front of our bench, ball in hand and 10 yards ahead of our pursuing defense.

Suddenly a flash of red shot past me, completely leveling the kid with the ball! And just as quickly, it disappeared. It all happened so fast, the referees didn't even see it.

The opposing coach was livid, as well he should have been. But Robert, who was sick of sitting on the sidelines watching his teammates play and lose, had taken matters into his own hands. He had jumped off the bench, wiped out the guy carrying the ball, and quickly resumed his place on the sidelines. It was over 20 years ago and I'm still laughing.

Everybody wants to play. Nobody wants to sit on the bench!

You can learn a lot about God on a football field. When a coach asks you to play for him, you'd run through a brick wall to please the guy. It sure beats sitting around watching other people who are active in the game.

God wants players, too. Those willing to purify their hearts and live clean lives for Jesus get to play in the greatest, most competitive, most exciting game ever—the struggle for men's and women's souls. The greatest Coach ever has invited you to be on His starting team. But learn from Paul's instructions—and Robert's mistake—play by the rules!

Discussion Starters:

* Can you recall a time when a coach or teacher pointed out how valuable or gifted you were? How did it feel?
** How does it feel to "please the one who enlisted you" as a Christian?
*** Read 2 Timothy 2. What specific things can you do to be useful to your heavenly Coach?

Lifeline:

If you ever feel useless, make yourself useful to the Master.

God-Breathed

the WORD | 2 Timothy 3:16-17

"All Scripture is inspired by God and profitable for teaching, for reproof, for correction, for training in righteousness; so that the man of God may be adequate, equipped for every good work."

the Message

Have you ever wondered what it would be like to hear God talk? Imagine it for a moment. What would He say? How would His voice sound?

Let's say there were some things He really wants you to know. Maybe He wants to give you some clear instructions about a problem you're facing, assurance of His love, or a warning that you're about to get hurt. Would you listen, or would you blow it off? Would you hurry or take your time? Would you want Him to write His message in the sky like a vapor trail, or would you be willing to go out of your way to hear Him?

I suspect that if God literally spoke to you, you would cup your hands to your ears and try to hear every word. If He wrote you a personal letter, you'd rip it open and absorb every page.

Well, guess what? That's exactly what He did. Every page of the Bible is part of God's message to be ripped into and absorbed.

All Scripture is God's voice to you, from "In the beginning..."—the first phrase of Genesis—to "Amen," the last word of Revelation. When Paul tells Timothy that Scripture is "inspired by God," the literal translation means "God-breathed." The Bible contains the thoughts, breath, and voice of God.

Does that sound exciting, or what? I carry God's voice with me everywhere I go. When I have a spare moment, I yank it out of my back pocket to see what He has to say. I stand in awe that God would write a love letter to us, and that I can read it any time I want.

Discussion Starters:

* How is the Bible God's love letter to you, personally?
** What was the last thing you read from God that affected your life?
*** What benefits of Bible reading might you be missing out on? (Review today's passage.)

Lifeline:

"Either this book [the Bible] will keep you from sin, or sin will keep you from this book."

Finish Strong

the **WORD** | 2 Timothy 4:7-8

"I have fought the good fight, I have finished the course, I have kept the faith; in the future there is laid up for me the crown of righteousness, which the Lord, the righteous Judge, will award to me on that day; and not only to me, but also to all who have loved His appearing."

the **Message**

Richard was a talented young man at Kanakuk Kamp, and the fastest kid there. I had never seen anybody faster. Nobody could beat him…that is, until the summer Sam came to camp. Sam was one step faster out of the blocks. He covered the first 10 yards of a race like a bolt of lightning.

We would race in three-person teams, with a total of six runners as teams competed against one another. Whenever Richard and Sam were in the same race, Sam would always come in first, and Richard, of course, would be…*sixth!* Not second. Not third. Every single time, Richard got sixth place.

Why? Whenever Sam took the lead, Richard would quit running. He couldn't stand the idea of second place, so he never crossed the finish line.

My first year in coaching, I was fortunate to coach at Texas A&M University. Our slogan during spring training was "Finish strong." Every race, every drill, every play, you could hear Coach Stallings or one of the other coaches shouting, "Finish strong!" There was no place for any "Richards" at Texas A&M.

Life is so much like a sports competition. Like a football player, we sometimes get knocked flat. Like a basketball player, we may hear a lot of trash talk and get belittled. Like a track event, other people get ahead of us no matter how hard we try to stay out front. We get discouraged. We want to quit running.

But the runner who keeps his eyes on the prize and his legs pumping to the finish line wins every time. All we have to do is finish strong. God guarantees the victory.

Discussion Starters:

- How was Paul able to finish strong? How do his words encourage you today?
  - Why do we tend to quit sometimes when we see others outdoing us? How do you keep the "Sams" in your life from making you feel discouraged?
    - How do you think it would feel to be able to say, at the end of your life, "I have finished the course, I have kept the faith"?

Lifeline:

Determine today to finish the race strong.

titus

I have a friend who refuses to believe in Jesus because of the hypocrisy he sees in Christians. We both know he's not the only one. The non-Christians we encounter want to know if our faith is genuine. They want to know if we have integrity and conviction that influence our day-to-day activities.

Charles Swindoll has said that the letter to Titus teaches us to pay as much attention to our behavior as we do to our beliefs. In this short book (which many seem to skip over), Paul encourages Titus to support his words with actions as he models the gospel. Paul's challenge to Titus serves as a reminder for us to "walk the talk" as we interact with others.

Brett Causey is a friend from Clinton, Mississippi, who says that following Christ is the most incredible challenge he's ever undertaken. Brett and his big heart for God come through in the following section.

Are You Empty?

the **WORD** | Titus 1:10-11

"For there are many rebellious men, empty talkers and deceivers…who must be silenced because they are upsetting whole families, teaching things they should not teach for the sake of sordid gain."

the *Message*

Mike stood on the top rung of a ladder with a paintbrush in his hand, where he had been since 6:00 A.M. He could hear the laughter and shouts of the other kids as they swam and played basketball, and he was mad because he had to paint all day. He had arrived the previous week at the Baptist Children's Village, a residential home for children and teens, because his parents didn't want him. Sure, he had messed up and at 14 had already been expelled from school. But it hurt to be rejected by everyone.

As he painted, his frustration and anger became more intense. He didn't know where to turn for help. In his pain, Mike wrote with his finger the letters "E-M-P-T-Y" in paint on the wall. That one word described his entire life. No one loved him. No one cared. He had been told repeatedly that he would never amount to anything. Everyone expected him to be just like his alcoholic father, who had abandoned him when he was two years old.

There are a lot of "Mikes" in our neighborhoods and cities who have no hope because they have heard only lies about themselves. They think they are worthless because they have never been told differently.

Mike may attempt to fill the emptiness with alcohol or some other substance to distract him from the pain. But maybe—just maybe—someone will love him for who he is and help him discover the truth about his worth as a child of God. It is time we silence the lies by allowing God to love the "Mikes" of this world…through us.

Discussion Starters:

* If you had to describe your life in one or two words, what would you choose?
  ** Have you ever felt separated from God? How did it feel? What did you do to fill that void?
  *** Discouragement and lack of love are two ways the Evil One fills our hearts with lies. What are some others? How can those lies be replaced with truth?

Lifeline:

Make a list of five positive qualities that describe you.

No Compromise

the WORD | Titus 2:11-13

"For the grace of God has appeared, bringing salvation to all men, instructing us to deny ungodliness and worldly desires and to live sensibly, righteously and godly in the present age, looking for the blessed hope and the appearing of the glory of our great God and Savior, Christ Jesus."

the Message

Reggie White is a former defensive end for the Philadelphia Eagles and Green Bay Packers. For 14 seasons, he played in the National Football League, where he terrorized opposing teams' offenses and dominated as one of the best pass rushers of all time. Reggie is a man after God's own heart. He has had the opportunity to stand fearlessly for Christ on the playing field, in the locker room, and before the media. His courage and boldness are rooted in a deep and passionate love for Christ that affects everything he does.

In an interview, Reggie was asked about his views on homosexuality. He responded with the truth of the Bible, proclaiming his belief that homosexual behavior is a sin. His comments brought a tidal wave of insults from homosexual activists, certain media personalities, and even a White House spokesperson. As a result, he lost a pending contract with CBS worth millions, as well as every endorsement he had. All he did was share boldly something from God's Word that he believed to be absolute truth.

Reggie could have prevented a lot of heartache, avoided the insults, and gained millions of dollars if he had been willing to compromise. But instead, he stared the enemy in the face and bore the consequences of the controversy. Praise God he didn't remain silent. He spoke the truth.

Discussion Starters:

• Do you ever feel that you compromise your Christian beliefs? If so, in what ways?
•• Have you ever been silent when you knew you should have spoken? Why were you silent?
••• Do you believe the Bible is absolute truth? What are some of the things you find hardest to believe? What things do you find hardest to defend to others?

Lifeline:

As a family, you must say no to ungodliness and worldly passions. How can you honor God in your home? (Consider the TV programs you watch, music you listen to, etc.)

I Grant You Grace

"But when the kindness of God our Savior and His love for mankind appeared, He saved us, not on the basis of deeds which we have done in righteousness, but according to His mercy, by the washing of regeneration and renewing by the Holy Spirit, whom He poured out upon us richly through Jesus Christ our Savior, so that being justified by His grace we would be made heirs according to the hope of eternal life."

the **Message**

As a young child, Katherine was always the biggest troublemaker in her family. Not many opportunities passed without her managing to get caught doing something worthy of punishment. And although she loved causing trouble, she feared the inevitable discipline that followed. Fortunately, she had parents who loved the Lord and believed in godly discipline.

One day after getting herself into some serious trouble, Katherine trembled as her mom approached. However, instead of the much-deserved spanking that Katherine expected, her mom looked into her teary eyes and said, "Katherine, I grant you grace." Then her mom simply smiled, hugged her, and walked away! In the days that followed, Katherine received many well-deserved punishments for defiant behavior and wrong decisions. However, every once in a while, rather than doling out the punishment, her mom would say, "Katherine, I grant you grace." Each gift of grace brought great surprise and relief to the young girl.

When Katherine was older, her parents were able to recall her many escapades as a way of teaching her about the grace of God. Katherine was pleased to discover that the invitation of God's grace is extended to us, not just occasionally, but during every moment and every event of our lives!

Whenever some people think of God, they envision an angry figure with thunderbolts in His hand and judgment in His mind. But the next time you do something wrong and fear God's anger, I hope you hear clearly His loving voice saying, "I grant you grace."

Discussion Starters:

° Can you recall a time in your life when you were granted the gift of grace? How did you feel? How did you respond?

°° Paul says that "being justified by [God's] grace we would be made heirs according to the hope of eternal life." What does that tell you about the importance of grace?

°°° How good are you at granting grace to others? How can you get better at it?

Lifeline:

You can't do anything good to make God love you more than He already does. And you can't do anything bad to make Him love you less.

philemon

This shortest of Paul's letters is a passionate appeal to Philemon, a slaveholder whose slave Onesimus had stolen some valuables and run away. Paul had witnessed Onesimus's conversion to Christianity and appealed to Philemon to forgive and warmly accept the return of the fugitive slave. Paul's persuasive words illustrate a beautiful picture of the grace and mercy of our God. The book of Philemon is very relevant to us as well, because as Paul appeals on behalf of Onesimus, so Christ intercedes to make it possible for us to find reconciliation with our Master.

My thanks to Brett Causey for writing this devotion.

Active Faith

the **WORD** | Philemon 4-6

"I thank my God always, making mention of you in my prayers, because I hear of your love and of the faith which you have toward the Lord Jesus and toward all the saints; and I pray that the fellowship of your faith may become effective through the knowledge of every good thing which is in you for Christ's sake."

the Message

The Sisters of Charity were invited by the president of Mexico to open a home in Mexico City. The people they ministered to were extremely poor, but the requests of the poverty-stricken Mexicans surprised the sisters very much. The first thing they asked for was not clothes, medicine, or food. They only said, "Sisters, talk to us about God!"

Mother Teresa once picked up a small girl who was wandering the streets, lost and hungry. Mother Teresa offered her a piece of bread. The little girl started eating it, crumb by crumb. Mother Teresa told her, "Eat, eat the bread! Aren't you hungry?" The little girl looked up and said, "I am just afraid that when I run out of bread, I'll still be hungry."

We need to ask God to teach us how our faith can become more active. In this letter, Paul asked Philemon to live out his faith by forgiving Onesimus and accepting the slave as he would accept Paul himself. God might give us the opportunity to make faith more active by feeding a hungry little girl, listening to someone who desperately needs a friend, or even beginning a Bible study at school. As we reach out to other hurting people, it's as if we're helping Jesus Himself (Matthew 25:37-40).

Jesus comes to us in the tattered clothes of the poor, in the hunger of those who have no food, in the naked bodies of the ones who have no clothes, and in the lonely hearts of people who have no one to offer them love. We have placed our trust and faith in Jesus because He has given everything for us. But will we share our faith not only in words, but also in how we live? Will our faith become an active faith, reaching out to others because of our love for Jesus?

Discussion Starters:

• Has anyone ever loved you with the love of God? How did it make you feel?
•• Is your faith active? In what ways? What motivates you?
••• In what ways can your family live out your faith together?

Lifeline:

Remember that the love and forgiveness of Jesus cannot be earned. They are free gifts which we should desire to share with others.

hebrews

No one knows for sure who wrote the book of Hebrews, but in this fantastic book the author lays a convincing foundation for the faith of all Christians, assuring us that Jesus is indeed the Messiah, the Anointed One, the Expected One. As such, Jesus is worthy of our trust and faith, and our only hope for our salvation. To support his argument, the author uses 29 direct quotations from the Old Testament and 53 references to other Old Testament passages.

An emphasis is placed on the priesthood of Jesus. Jewish believers would understand this concept of Jesus being the "high priest" who escorts us into the presence of God, where we can "draw near with confidence to the throne of grace" (4:16).

This splendid book also uses numerous superlatives to describe the person and the work of Christ, such as "much better," "more excitement," and even "perfect." In this descriptive style, the author seeks to underline the idea that Jesus is indeed superior to any other person, angel, principality, or being in all creation.

Hebrews is a complex and thought-provoking book, and may be a challenge to comprehend on first reading. But as you return to the study of Hebrews throughout your lifetime, you will be rewarded as you discover more about the breadth and length and height and depth of Christ.

The Radiance of God's Glory

the WORD | Hebrews 1:3-4

"And [Jesus] is the radiance of [God's] glory and the exact representation of His nature, and upholds all things by the word of His power. When He had made purification of sins, He sat down at the right hand of the Majesty on high, having become as much better than the angels, as He has inherited a more excellent name than they."

the Message

To tour the Sistine Chapel in Rome is to see into the mind of perhaps the greatest painter of all time—Michelangelo. The ceiling of the chapel depicts the painter's vision of some of the great wonders and people of history: God, Creation, Jesus, the early saints of the faith, and so forth. Witnessing this masterpiece lingers in your mind for a lifetime.

To see a 1990s Duke basketball team is to see greatness among college basketball players, proven by their series of Final Four appearances and back-to-back national championships. Mike Krzyzewski, "the Maestro," is perhaps the greatest basketball coach since John Wooden, with the mind of a true genius! A Krzyzewski team flows across the court like a great artist's paint across a canvas.

To hear the Boston Philharmonic orchestra is to set your ears adrift in a musical paradise. You experience a sea of perfectly balanced melody, harmony, and percussion, all flowing like a Hawaiian wave onto the seashore of your mind.

To witness a sunset in Maui… a star-blazed sky from atop Mount Kilimanjaro …Niagara Falls beneath its perpetual multicolored rainbow…is to see the brush strokes of the Creator of the universe.

But more importantly, to look at Jesus is to see God. As we look into the eyes of a gentle, compassionate, 33-year-old man willfully hanging on a cross for the sins of a fallen world, we might not recognize the unfailing, almighty God. Yet Jesus, says the author of Hebrews, is the "exact representation of His nature."

It's been said often, but never with more accuracy: "Like Father, like Son."

Discussion Starters:

• What does it mean that Jesus is "the radiance of
God's glory and the exact representation of His nature"?
•• How does knowing Jesus teach us about the heart of God?
••• What are some specific characteristics of Jesus
that cause you to marvel at the nature of God?

Lifeline:

Jesus is a true representation of God. How accurate is the representation of Jesus that others see in you?

Ultimate Humility

the **WORD** | Hebrews 2:9-10

"But we do see Him who was made for a little while lower than the angels, namely, Jesus, because of the suffering of death crowned with glory and honor, so that by the grace of God He might taste death for everyone. For it was fitting for Him, for whom are all things, and through whom are all things, in bringing many sons to glory, to perfect the author of their salvation through sufferings."

the *Message*

As far as I'm concerned, snowboarding at blazing speed down freshly packed powder on a Colorado mountainside with my 17-year-old son is the ultimate father-son experience.

Upsetting a nationally ranked football team in a postseason bowl game before national television cameras and screaming fans has to be the ultimate sports experience in my memory.

Walking my daughter down the forest-green-carpeted wedding aisle amid white lace, white roses, and glistening candles, and placing her hand in the trustworthy grasp of her "knight in shining armor," is surely the ultimate relational experience we ever shared.

Gazing into my dear wife's sparkling brown eyes above our twenty fifth anniversary cake and reflecting on a quarter century of mutual respect, admiration, mountains climbed, dreams dreamed, and heartbeats melded together is definitely the ultimate marital experience (so far, at least).

But of all the ultimates, realized or imagined on this earth, none can ever begin to compare to the ultimate humility displayed by Jesus. He is the one to whom belong all things...the one in whom are hidden all the treasures of wisdom and knowledge...the one who holds all things together by His power...the one to whom God subjected everything in all creation...and the one to whom every knee shall one day bow. This man Jesus lowered Himself, humbled Himself, and sacrificed Himself for one reason: God would rather die for you than live without you!

That is ultimate love. That is ultimate selflessness. That is ultimate humility.

Discussion Starters:

• What emotions and thoughts do you feel
  when you think about the ultimate humility of Jesus?
•• What emotions and thoughts do you feel when
  you think about the ultimate love of Jesus?
••• How can you make your family stronger by demonstrating
similar humility to those whom you love the most?

Lifeline:

"Love one another, just as I have loved you" (John 15:12).

The Gift of Encouragement

the WORD | Hebrews 3:12-13

"Take care, brethren, that there not be in any one of you an evil, unbelieving heart that falls away from the living God. But encourage one another day after day, as long as it is still called 'Today,' so that none of you will be hardened by the deceitfulness of sin."

the Message

My friend Gene Stallings coached college and professional football for 20 years, winning an NFL championship, conference championships, bowl games, and coach of the year honors. But reflecting on his career, he told me the most amazing football season of his life was the year he and the Dallas Cowboys went to the Super Bowl with 13 rookies on the team. Nobody expected that kind of success. I asked Coach his secret, and he said bluntly, "We encouraged the players. It was a season when our coaching staff decided we were going to do everything we could do to make the players feel good about themselves."

If encouragement works with well-paid, adult, 300-pound defensive tackles, how much more with 12-year-old boys going through the pains of junior high? Or a mom who works her heart out all day, every day, as a "household executive"? Or a dad who pours out his energy during long weeks at the office to bring home the bacon and keep the bank account from drying up?

Encouragement is the powerful winch that pulls you out of the quicksand of doldrums, depression, or stages of perceived insignificance. It stands you on your tiptoes and puts a smile on your face.

"I'm so proud of you, Son!"

"Way to go, Dad!"

"Thanks, Mom! You're the best."

"Amazing job!"

"I'm impressed!"

"I cant help but love you!"

"I'm happy when you're around."

"I want to always remember how lucky I am to have you."

You get the idea. Now you take it from here. I know you can do it!

Discussion Starters:

• In what ways does encouragement enhance your life?

•• Whose encouragement do you need in order to walk closer with Christ?

••• How can encouragement keep you from falling into sin?

Lifeline:

I'm told it takes only 20 minutes to teach a pigeon to bowl. Every time he gets near the ball, you give him a grain of corn. Every time he touches it, give him two. With a little encouragement, he will learn in no time.

The Two-Edged Sword

the **WORD** | Hebrews 4:12

"For the word of God is living and active and sharper than any two-edged sword, and piercing as far as the division of soul and spirit, of both joints and marrow, and able to judge the thoughts and intentions of the heart."

the **Message**

My mom is in a class all her own! Never have I known a woman so consistent in her willingness to serve, her encouragement, and her readiness to ask with her big Texas smile, "What can I do for you?" On the other hand, my brother and I used to complain that she had eyes in the back of her head and ears like a deer in the forest. We called her "Sherlock" because she missed no detail, could tell *before* we tried something sneaky, and knew exactly what we were up to.

Mom's goal was simply to do whatever it took to serve her family and to raise good boys. (I know some days she has to wonder how she did!)

Mom was a wonderful model for the God at whom I would someday marvel. His Word points out my shortcomings. He corrects my faults. He strengthens my weaknesses. If I try to rationalize something I'm doing wrong, my daily Bible study quickly sets my wheels back on track. His guidelines are clear and simple: "Just be like My Son and do what He would do."

But that's not *all* God is to me. He is the all-seeing, trouble-preventing God I serve. In addition, He's a heavenly Father who gives me a shoulder to cry on, refuge in a storm, companionship in times of trouble, constant guidance during unsure times, and confident access in time of need.

With Jesus in my heart, the guidance of His Word is like a seeing-eye dog to a blind man. With Jesus as my Lord, I can go straight to God and open my heart to Him in prayer like picking up a direct phone line where there's never a busy signal.

God always tries to keep me from falling on my face. And even when I don't listen, He's always there to pick me up.

Discussion Starters:

* What do you think is the significance of God's Word being referred to as a *two-edged* sword?
** What does the phrase "draw near with confidence to the throne of grace" (Hebrews 4:16) mean to you?
*** What aspects of your relationship with God do you wish to develop more fully? Why?

Lifeline:

The guidance of Scripture and the privilege of prayer are like a two-way radio to and from the throne of God.

Training Wheels

the **WORD** | Hebrews 5:12, 14

"For though by this time you ought to be teachers, you have need again for someone to teach you the elementary principles of the oracles of God, and you have come to need milk and not solid food.... But solid food is for the mature, who because of practice have their senses trained to discern good and evil."

the Message

The unfinished plywood closets in my boyhood home contained all we wore and everything we owned. My two older brothers and I shared a simple tile-floored room. The closets Dad made gave us a little privacy and probably kept us from killing each other.

My favorite spot was a place on the end of my closet decorated with hand-drawn pencil lines, each marked carefully with the month, day, and year that the line was drawn. For these were the sacred lines that marked my growth (and my brothers') in inches from the floor, from the bottoms of our flat feet to the top of our short athletic haircuts.

Every time I would grow an inch or two, I would grab a pencil and run get Mom. She would make the official measurement, and I would subsequently burst out with proud excitement over my increase in stature. Equally exciting were the days I took the training wheels off my bike, and later when I got my driver's license and no longer needed Mom in the car to go to my girlfriend's house.

Stages of growth. They're the greatest! In today's passage, the author of Hebrews challenges his readers (including us) to consider some growth issues: How long have you been a Christian? How much have you grown? Do you still need a bottle? Are you still wearing diapers? Are you crawling on the floor, waving rattles? Do you still need training wheels? Or are you growing taller and forming some spiritual muscles by digging into God's Word daily, witnessing to friends, praying, integrating Christ-centered conversation into your friendships, and becoming a spiritual adult?

The key question at any age is not "How long have you been a Christian?" Much more important is your answer to "How much have you grown?"

Discussion Starters:

* How do you measure spiritual growth?
** If you were keeping a spiritual "growth chart," where would your "growth spurts" be?
*** In what ways would you like to "take the training wheels off" and grow spiritually over the next couple of months?

Lifeline:

Are you tired of "milk" and ready for some steak? Are you committed to setting some new records in your spiritual growth chart? Ready, set, grow!

Better Things

"For ground that drinks the rain which often falls on it and brings forth vegetation useful to those for whose sake it is also tilled, receives a blessing from God; but if it yields thorns and thistles, it is worthless and close to being cursed, and it ends up being burned. But, beloved, we are convinced of better things concerning you, and things that accompany salvation, though we are speaking in this way."

the **Message**

Sometimes it seems as though you're the only Christian in your school. If you go to parties, it seems everyone is drinking but you. You stay home when you don't feel comfortable attending the same movies as everyone else. You don't date much because you are saving your sexual life for your future spouse. And what's the payoff? Discouragement and loneliness.

Is it worth it? They are having so much fun! They seem unbelievably happy! What are you waiting for? Let me tell you.

They experience guilt by the truckload. They have hangovers. They get AIDS, herpes, and other sexually transmitted diseases. They have nothing to look forward to on their honeymoons. They get divorced. They have little if any self-respect. They aren't respected for their integrity. They aren't proud of themselves when they wake up in the morning.

You, however, have everything to look forward to. You understand purity and respect. You experience forgiveness for the mistakes you've made. You receive genuine love and can offer it to others. You are one in a million. You will hear God's voice saying, "Well done."

When you sow thistle seeds, you get thorns and briars within a month (if that's really what you want). When you plant apple seeds, you get green, leafy trees with precious red apples—but it will take eight to 10 years for the fruit to appear.

The next time you look at what they are doing and start to feel left out, keep looking to the future. The good choices you make today will surely be rewarded with better things in due time.

Discussion Starters:

* As others around you are growing "thorns and thistles," how do you feel? Why?
  ** What are some of the "better things" you've seen in the lives of people devoted to God?
    *** How can you ensure that you don't settle for less as you wait for the better things God has to offer?

Lifeline:

Look carefully around you and you will quickly see the truth of Galatians 6:7: "Do not be deceived, God is not mocked; for whatever a man sows, this he will also reap."

The Highest Priest

the WORD | Hebrews 7:26-28

"For it was fitting for us to have such a high priest, holy, innocent, undefiled, separated from sinners and exalted above the heavens; who does not need daily, like those high priests, to offer up sacrifices, first for His own sins and then for the sins of the people, because this He did once for all when He offered up Himself. For the Law appoints men as high priests who are weak, but the word of the oath, which came after the Law, appoints a Son, made perfect forever."

the Message

The role of church leader is indeed a varied one. Some wear coats and ties. Some appear in long, black robes. Some have black shirts with neatly pressed white, round collars. Some are in shirtsleeves. Some prefer flashy colors. They may have Ph.D.'s, doctorates in divinity, or no degree at all. They may be called bishops, cardinals, priests, pastors, preachers, or teachers.

But no matter what their title, position, or attire, they all have one thing in common: They are people. Mere human beings. They were all born, and they will all die. None is divine. None has a "secret entrance" to God that the rest of us don't know about. We all have the same opportunity to approach God directly on the avenue of faith, paved by the sacrificial blood of Jesus—the only, the supreme, the divine, the all-sufficient High Priest.

You might be Protestant, Catholic, evangelical, or charismatic. You might be American, African, Asian, European, or Chinese. No matter. You go to God the same way everyone else does—"in Jesus' name."

You don't have to have a church or a preacher to go directly to God (although such things are helpful in your ongoing spiritual growth). You don't need a prayer book or flowery words. You don't need to pay anyone. All you need is to go to God sincerely and reverently, with faith "in Jesus' name."

Jesus is our high priest. He is our intercessor to God. He is our guide to the throne of God Himself.

Discussion Starters:

• What is the role of your church leader? Which aspects of your spiritual growth is that person responsible for? Which are you responsible for?

•• What are some things that Jesus does for you that the high priest used to do for believers in God?

••• Why is Jesus more sufficient than any other high priest to connect you to God?

Lifeline:

Your preacher, priest, or pastor might get you to church, but only Jesus can get you to God.

The New Covenant

the **WORD** | Hebrews 8:8, 10, 12

"Behold, the days are coming, says the Lord, when I will effect a new covenant with the house of Israel and with the house of Judah.... I will put My laws into their minds, and I will write them on their hearts. And I will be their God, and they shall be My people.... For I will be merciful to their iniquities, and I will remember their sins no more."

the *Message*

In the Bible, the strongest agreement between two people wasn't a handshake, an oath, or even a written contract. The most unbreakable bonds were formed when two people, two tribes, or two nations made a covenant with each other. Historians tell us that the following guidelines frequently marked the establishment of a covenant.

1. The two parties exchanged coats to signify, "I am taking all your needs upon myself."

2. The two parties exchanged weapons to show, "If you ever have an enemy, he's mine too!"

3. The two covenant partners cut their palms or wrists and shook hands, mixing their blood. This indicated, "My life is yours and your life is mine."

4. The two rubbed dye into their wounds so the scar would always be noticeable— a sign that the covenant was binding forever.

5. The pair would then split an animal in half and walk between the parts, pledging to each other, "If I ever break this covenant, may God do this (or worse) to me." (See Genesis 15:7-21.)

6. The two would share a covenant meal of bread (symbolizing the body) and "the fruit of the vine" (symbolizing blood). This shared meal finalized the covenant. Now the two were one. From that point on, they were committed to living for each other.

When God made a covenant with Abraham, the Jewish nation became His chosen people. But when Jesus died on the cross, He established a new covenant between God and *all* people. His blood was shed. The scars in His hands are signs of His unbreakable agreement. And the Lord's Supper is a recurring reminder of this incredible, divine, eternal act of sacrificial love.

Discussion Starters:

• What right did Jesus have to make a covenant with God on your behalf?

•• The covenant wasn't finalized until *after* the covenant meal was shared. In what ways does an understanding of covenants affect your view of Communion?

••• Is your covenant with God a "done deal," or is there still something you need to do to make it official?

Lifeline:

Jesus has certainly come through with His part of the covenant. What are you doing for Him?

Once and For All

the WORD | Hebrews 9:27-28

"And inasmuch as it is appointed for men to die once and after this comes judgment, so Christ also, having been offered once to bear the sins of many, will appear a second time for salvation without reference to sin, to those who eagerly await Him."

the Message

The Jewish religion had a once-a-year ceremony when the high priest would go into the Holy of Holies in the tabernacle or temple—the one time he was allowed to enter this sacred room—for the sole purpose of placing the blood of a goat upon the cover of the Ark of the Covenant (the "mercy seat"). This offering to God for the sins of the people was good for only one year and was effective only for the Hebrew people the high priest represented.

Joseph Smith and Brigham Young taught that the blood of Jesus *partially* sufficed for the forgiveness of sins. But to complete their salvation, Mormons are expected to accept the teachings of Joseph Smith, conform to a lifestyle of strict religious practices, and commit to a lifetime of rigorous devotion to doing good works.

Other world religions offer a diversity of man-made salvation myths, such as returning to earth in different lives until you finally "get it right" and can move on to heaven.

Yet Scripture clearly teaches that Jesus provides a much better way to salvation. For one thing, His way is the *only* way to God. But in addition, His death on the cross was singularly sufficient to pay for sins—one sacrifice, one time, for all nations and all people who ever live.

All you have to do to take advantage of His incredible gift is to have faith, give Him your heart, and let His Spirit dwell within you. That seals it! You're His forever.

You're a child of God.

You're completely forgiven.

You want to please Him.

You want to tell others about Him.

Jesus died once for all. Just once. For all. You make one genuine commitment to serve Him as you invite Him to be your Lord and Savior. Just once. And believe me, it's for *good!*

Discussion Starters:

* Read Hebrews 9:24-28. What does this say about reincarnation?
  ** How does the passage explain Jesus' blood sacrifice for us?
  *** How does the passage clarify Jesus' statement that He is the only way to God?

Lifeline:

Jesus sacrificed Himself to provide us unity with God. As we sacrifice ourselves for others, we will experience unity in the family of God.

Two Beams of the Cross

"Let us hold fast the confession of our hope without wavering, for He who promised is faithful; and let us consider how to stimulate one another to love and good deeds, not forsaking our own assembling together, as is the habit of some, but encouraging one another; and all the more as you see the day drawing near."

the Message

Years ago Cooper saw a picture of Jesus hanging lifelessly on the cross. He was overwhelmed by emotional trauma and looked up at me with eyes full of tears. He asked hopefully, "Daddy, did God take away the pain?"

"No," I said softly, "God didn't take away the pain." I explained that Jesus' nerves shattered just like yours or mine would. He was a sinless human sacrifice, because no other substitute could restore our relationship with God that sin had destroyed.

That's what I think about when I see the vertical beam of the cross. It stands forever pointing skyward, triumphantly, toward God. Work done. Case closed. Sin paid. Sacrifice accomplished. Salvation purchased. Prayers answered.

Then, as I view the horizontal beam of the cross, I see where Jesus' hands were outstretched. I am reminded that you and I, out of hearts exploding with appreciation, have daily opportunities to reach out and demonstrate the love of Jesus to our parents, our kids, our spouses, our friends...even our enemies.

The agonizing reality of Jesus' work on the cross should create a tremor in your soul that shakes the stained-glass windows of your heart. The only possible response is an eternal sense of indescribable appreciation. And the only tangible way to show God how thankful you are is to show *others* and give Him the credit.

As the vertical beam of the cross reaches upward toward God's heart, so the horizontal beam reaches outward from the goodness of my heart to yours.

Discussion Starters:

• Which needs more work in your life: your "upreach" to God, or your outreach to others?
    •• How, specifically, can you show appreciation for
        Jesus' paying the price for your salvation?
        ••• How can you "stimulate one another to love and good deeds" this week?

Lifeline:

Express your gratitude for Jesus' sacrifice by being an encouragement to everyone around you.

The Essence of Faith

the WORD | Hebrews 11:1

"Now faith is the assurance of things hoped for, the conviction of things not seen."

the Message

By faith you believe in Jesus.

By faith you live for heaven.

By faith you carry your Bible to school.

By faith you save sex for marriage.

By faith you say your prayers at night.

By faith you keep your body pure from drugs and alcohol.

By faith you avoid all forms of pornography.

By faith you suffer ridicule for being a Christian.

By faith you witness to your friends.

By faith David told his drug buddies, "No more. I'm a Christian now." Then he told his girlfriend, "The next girl I touch will be my wife."

By faith Dora Tenenoff waits faithfully to be reunited with her missionary husband in heaven. He was captured in Colombia ten long years ago and according to New Tribes Mission, was killed in 1996.

By faith my dad writes my mom a love letter almost every morning. They've been happily married now for 68 years.

By faith my mom gladly cooks his meals, washes his clothes, and even removes his work boots after a long day.

By faith a teen listens to his parents' advice and calls when he's out later than expected so they won't worry.

By faith we can look forward to joining those already in God's "hall of fame" (Hebrews 11).

By faith we live forever in heaven.

Discussion Starters:

* Without referring to today's verse, how would you define *faith*?
** Complete this sentence five different ways: "By faith I…"
*** Read Hebrews 11 to see how other great people of God have demonstrated faith. What are some other contemporary ways you've witnessed people in your family serving God and each other by faith?

Lifeline:

What are you hoping for today? What things do you believe in that you haven't (yet) seen? Have faith!

Fan Support

the WORD | Hebrews 12:1-2a

"Therefore, since we have so great a cloud of witnesses surrounding us,…let us run with endurance the race that is set before us, fixing our eyes on Jesus, the author and per-fecter of faith."

the Message

Neither my eyes nor my feet will ever forget the walk into the great domed stadium in Houston for my first bowl game. The stadium was filled with screaming fans, many of whom had traveled a great distance to cheer us on as we played the giants of Oklahoma University. It was as if we could feel our fans pulling us across the goal line time after time as we accumulated 28 bloody, sweaty points—one more than "Goliath's" mere 27.

The author of Hebrews wants us to picture our lives as being on a playing field. Your Coach, Jesus Himself, provides the plays He wants you to run as you go to school, play sports, perform music, and go about your day. You have quite a playbook that includes purity, godliness, forgiveness, encouragement, kindness, diligence, and more.

On the other side of the field, Satan is also calling plays to thwart your progress for God. "Take a shortcut." "Tell a small lie." "Cheat on that exam." "Go ahead, lust a little." "You can skip Bible study today."

And some days the competition is close. You get confused, tired, and ready to quit. But you're on a playing field surrounded by supportive fans! Look up at the faithful Old Testament characters who anticipated the promised Messiah but didn't get to know Him. They desperately want you to know you can have "something better" (Hebrews 11:37-40). Then look at your friends and family members who love you dearly and want you to succeed in this game of life.

And finally, look at Jesus. Yes, He's your Coach, but He's also your biggest cheer-leader. He knows exactly what you're going through. Watch His lips move and hear His voice: "I did it, and so can you."

Discussion Starters:

- How does it feel to know that caring supporters are aware of your struggles in your "game of life"?
- The next time you're about to give up, how can you tap into the support of your number-one fan, Jesus Himself? What difference does His encouragement make?
- Review the "cloud of witnesses" in Hebrews 11. Which person might best understand what you're going through? Why?

Lifeline:

Jesus "endured the cross, despising the shame, and has sat down at the right hand of the throne of God" (Hebrews 12:2). After your hardest trials will come your most magnificent victories.

Undefiled

"Marriage is to be held in honor among all, and the marriage bed is to be undefiled; for fornicators and adulterers God will judge."

the *Message*

All I wanted was a soft drink, but the wrapper around the bottle also carried a promise: "Find love on Wednesday night on Fox TV."

Millions of teens and adults look for love on TV every night—with or without the reminders of soft drink companies. You can find pretty much whatever you're looking for: him and her, him and him, or her and her. The people are usually young, attractive, partially nude, and unmarried. The "love" is frequently sexual, inconsequential, wild, and free of worry, guilt, or shame.

Meanwhile, in real life, love is much harder to find. The promises on soft drink labels are coming up short. The words and actions that make the TV relationships seem so fulfilling are disappointingly empty. When I hear from real-life people who sacrifice their morals, Christian beliefs, and bodies for what they perceive to be love, their letters are frequently tear-stained. Somebody's not telling the truth! And millions of young people are feeling very real pain because of false promises. Do we really need to watch this stuff? Do we have to keep falling for every sensuous (yet senseless) ploy?

The steady truth of Scripture comes shining through the beguiling fog of falsehood with the reliability of the morning sunrise: "The marriage bed is to be undefiled."

If you're not married, sex with another person is wrong. It's a sin against God. It's a sin against you. It's a sin against him or her. It hurts; it takes away from a honeymoon; it destroys a pure relationship. It's true whether you're heterosexual, bisexual, homosexual, in junior high, in high school, in college, adult, Democrat, Republican, American, European, Antarctican, whatever, whoever, wherever.

God invented sex. He wrote the book on it. He wants your wedding, honeymoon, and marriage to be fantastic, enchanting, and never ending. So enjoy a good soft drink once in a while and watch TV occasionally. But don't let either sway you from God's firm and loving reminder, "The marriage bed is to be undefiled."

Discussion Starters:

* To what extent are your friends infatuated by TV "love"?
** Why are so many people hooked on TV romance? Why do many fall as a result?
*** What is God's provision if and when we sin in these areas? What, then, is our responsibility?

Lifeline:

Preparing for a great marriage begins today with a pure mind and a pure heart.

james

Although there are four men named James in the New Testament, careful study leads most scholars to believe that the author of this letter was James, son of Mary and Joseph, the half-brother of Jesus.

Scholars think that James wrote this book between A.D. 45 and 50, only 10 to 15 years after he dramatically converted to Christianity when his brother, Jesus, was resurrected from the dead.

This letter is what I call "grace on wheels." It explains the practical aspects of the Christian faith—what a believer does (through grace) after he or she has been saved (by grace). The book of James teaches that faith works! God's grace doesn't sit still. A person who is full of God's grace will give it back to others. As you study this book together, may your family find the tremendous joy in serving one another.

It's All Joy

the WORD | James 1:2-4

"Consider it all joy, my brethren, when you encounter various trials, knowing that the testing of your faith produces endurance. And let endurance have its perfect result, so that you may be perfect and complete, lacking in nothing."

the Message

My mom and dad dreamed and prayed that they would have three children someday. Their first baby was a boy named Frank. Tragically, due to complications during childbirth, Frank lived for just one hour. My parents were heartbroken. They felt as if God had mercilessly allowed their son to be taken from them.

Gradually, though, Mom and Dad realized that Frank belonged to God and that He had a plan for their pain. They learned that "in [God's] presence is fullness of joy" (Psalm 16:11). Slowly, they began to heal. As the years went by, my parents had two more boys. Then they had me—a third son.

I know that my life is part of God's plan. If Frank had lived, my parents wouldn't have had another child after my other two brothers were born, and I probably wouldn't be here today.

Our family has had many bumps and bruises. We've cried, and clung to God in prayer, but we've learned to find joy in all circumstances.

Life is full of trials. Your girlfriend dumps you. Your boss falsely accuses you of stealing money. Everyone was asked to the homecoming dance except you. Someone breaks into your car and takes your new stereo, twice. People make fun of you because you're a Christian.

When you feel the world is coming down on you, don't panic—pray. It may seem hard to believe, but God works through your pain. He gives endurance, hope, and eventually, joy.

My family knows. With one baby in heaven and three sons on earth, God has shown us that He is sovereign—*especially* in difficult times.

Discussion Starters:

* What's one trial you're experiencing? How can God turn it into a joyful experience?
** When trials come, your reaction makes you either bitter or better. What reaction could you have?
**** How do trials produce endurance? Why is endurance so important?

Lifeline:

Talk about the different trials you've faced as a family. What did you learn from them?

Tackling Temptation

the WORD | James 1:13-16

"Let no one say when he is tempted, 'I am being tempted by God'; for God cannot be tempted by evil, and He Himself does not tempt anyone. But each one is tempted when he is carried away and enticed by his own lust. Then when lust has conceived, it gives birth to sin; and when sin is accomplished, it brings forth death. Do not be deceived, my beloved brethren."

the Message

A while back, our TV set broke. Boy, did that upset me! (Yeah, right!) I'm so mad, I can't even find the phone number for the TV repairman. (Ha ha ha!) I'm so livid, I keep forgetting to get it fixed! (As if!)

Actually, that day was probably one of the best things that's ever happened in our home. I like to call TV "Temptation Vision." Every year, TV pipes more than 180,000 rapes, murders. and acts of violence, beer commercials, and sexual innuendoes into the minds of each family member in the average American home. No wonder we're tempted to argue, lust, fight, and drink.

These messages from the media—these temptations—have had sweeping effects, too. One out of five Americans has a sexually transmitted disease (STD), the number of teenagers with AIDS doubles every 14 months, and more college students die alcohol-related deaths than those who will go on to graduate school.[1]

Those are just some of the problems TV and the movies have helped to foster in our culture. What about materialism and eating disorders? Hollywood stars drip money. They have rock-hard, lean bodies and killer clothes to match. We get tempted to try to look like them, so we spend dollar after dollar and go on diet after diet, attempting to model ourselves after the stars. Unfortunately, we often end up with eating obsessions and shopaholic tendencies. And our focus leaves God and settles on ourselves.

Be careful about what you fill your mind with when you watch the screen. No one wants to end up with a drinking problem, an eating disorder, a violent temper, or an STD, but those Temptation Visions can affect you far more than you realize. As James said, "Do not be deceived."

Avoid the things that lure you away from God.

Discussion Starters:

• What do we mean when we pray, "Lead us not into temptation"?
•• Who tempts us? What part do we play in temptation?
••• Besides watching questionable TV shows and movies, how else do we expose ourselves to temptation?

Lifeline:

List some practical ways your family can help each other fight temptation.

Just Do It!

the WORD | James 1:22

"But prove yourselves doers of the word, and not merely hearers who delude themselves."

the Message

If James had worn tennis shoes back in the first century, I'll bet he would've worn Nikes. Why? James seems to push the same slogan: Just Do It.

Nike sells in excess of $3.6 billion worth of shoes and sports accessories annually.[2] Nike's advertisements say, in effect, "Don't talk about going jogging—get yourself outside and exercise now."

Nike's ads sell shoes, but James's slogan guides souls. His "Just Do It" passage is the heartbeat of his epistle. James said, "Don't just read about giving; put some money in a piggy bank for the less fortunate. Don't just talk about wanting a better prayer life; start praying more consistently. Don't just talk about that overstuffed closet; give some clothes away."

My son Cooper learned at an early age how hard it is to be a "doer of the Word." One evening, Cooper, then five years old, told me he wanted to memorize a Bible verse.

"Well, Cooper, how about Ephesians 6:1?" I said, hiding my smile.

Cooper soon found out the verse reads, "Children, obey your parents in the Lord, for this is right." He innocently smiled and said, "Daad! That verse isn't there; you just made that up."

It's easy to ignore certain verses and commands in the Bible, isn't it? But as James said, over and over, you've got to take action for Christ.

Discussion Starters:

• Why is it not enough to be just a "hearer of the Word"?

•• It has been rightly stated, "When all is said and done, there's a lot more said than done." Why does that truth present a problem for Christians?

••• We're saved by faith in Christ, but our works are still important. Why?

Lifeline:

In what ways can you and your family be better "doers of the Word"?

Up with the Underdog

"My brethren, do not hold your faith…with an attitude of personal favoritism. For if a man comes into your assembly with a gold ring and dressed in fine clothes…and you pay special attention…have you not made distinctions among yourselves, and become judges with evil motives?"

the **Message**

I've learned so much from my daddy that the encyclopedia couldn't contain it all. And 99 percent of what I've learned has been through his actions.

Dad never told me to love the underdog or those less fortunate, but I'll never forget watching him meet the garbage collectors at the back door of our house every Monday and Friday morning with a cup of hot coffee and a sweet roll for each worker, complete with a huge smile and a word of encouragement. When I was growing up, he often came home from work without his coat, shoes, or money because he'd met someone less fortunate who needed what he had. Even now, in church and at social gatherings, Dad automatically finds his way to the "lowest person on the totem pole." Those humble poor people are always Daddy's best friends.

You, too, are surrounded by the needy. The halls of junior high and high schools are filled with people who need love and support, like, for instance, that new girl with the shabby clothes who always sits by herself. Or the school mascot, the guy everyone loves to hate. Or Marshall, one of your childhood friends, the one your friends have nicknamed "Crater Face."

What do you do? Turn up your nose at them? Look past them in a crowd? Chime in with the insults?

Discussion Starters:

Why do we tend to push aside the less fortunate?

Why is it a sin to show partiality?

What is a Christian's responsibility toward the less fortunate?

Lifeline:

What opportunities do you have every day to help someone less fortunate? How can you show Christ's love to those needy people around you?

Faith that Works

"What use is it, my brethren, if someone says he has faith but he has no works? Can that faith save him? If a brother or sister is without clothing and in need of daily food, and one of you says to them, 'Go in peace, be warmed and be filled,' and yet you do not give them what is necessary for their body, what use is that? Even so faith, if it has no works, is dead, being by itself."

the *Message*

An old friend of mine, Mr. Plummer, ran a sawmill where I used to buy my lumber for building projects. He was in his mid-80s, living out the final days of his life in the historic Ozark mountains.

Whenever I dropped by to buy lumber, I'd stop and chat with Mr. Plummer. We spent hours visiting together. Once, I asked the savvy old character where he went to church. He raised his white, bushy eyebrows, stomped his worn, black boot, and scowled.

"I'll never go to any ol' church!" he said gruffly. "Thirty years ago, some folks from that church down the road bought some lumber from me and cheated me out of my money."

Mr. Plummer quickly changed the subject, but his words stuck with me. Soon after our talk, he passed away—not knowing Christ.

What use was that church and all their beautiful prayers and hymns if they didn't show an old lumberjack the love of Jesus?

What good are 16 Bibles in a home if they're not read?

What good is a big savings account if it's not used for people in need?

What good is a smile that's not shared?

What use is a hug or an "I love you" that's not given?

And what use is faith when it doesn't produce fruit?

Discussion Starters:

* What does faith look like when it's producing fruit?
** Why does James say faith is dead if it's by itself?
*** Whom do you know who connects his actions with his faith?

Lifeline:

Have you put your faith into action by loving a needy person? If so, describe the experience. If not, keep looking for opportunities to lend others a hand.

The Terrific, Terrible Tongue

the WORD | James 3:7-9

"For every species of beasts and birds, of reptiles and creatures of the sea, is tamed and has been tamed by the human race. But no one can tame the tongue; it is a restless evil and full of deadly poison. With it we bless our Lord and Father, and with it we curse men, who have been made in the likeness of God."

the Message

Human beings have gotten pretty good at harnessing nature.

My friend "Snake" actually trains rattlesnakes. He doesn't exactly turn snakes into play toys, but he subdues them and makes them pets.

Circus trainers tame lions, elephants, and bears.

My kids and I ride horses together, galloping across pastures and through the woods.

At our sports camps, the campers spend hours windsurfing. They love to catch the wind and skim speedily across the water.

It is impressive the way we've learned to control wild animals and the weather. But subduing a rattlesnake, training a wild beast, guiding a horse, and harnessing the wind take only time, patience, a bit on a horse's bridle, or a small rudder.

Our tongues are equally if not more powerful and destructive. Unfortunately, we don't focus our attention nearly enough on taming our tongues. We continually hurt one another with poorly chosen words.

Our words have the power to tear people down, but they can also be a great encouragement to others. Writing a love letter, saying "I'm proud of you," or complimenting a friend can bring sunshine to a cloudy day!

So what will it be? Gossip or encouragement? Cursing or enthusiasm? Negative comments or compliments? Sarcasm or praise?

The choice is yours.

Discussion Starters:

* Why is it more difficult to "tame the tongue" than to tame a lion?
** Why does the tongue work like a match that starts a forest fire?
*** When do you struggle most with taming your tongue? Why?
**** How can God help you guide your words?

Lifeline:

Try this exercise in your family: For every negative or cutting comment, give five compliments.

Are You a Wise Guy?

the **WORD** | James 3:13, 17

"Who among you is wise and understanding? Let him show by his good behavior his deeds in the gentleness of wisdom.... The wisdom from above is first pure, then peaceable, gentle, reasonable, full of mercy and good fruits, unwavering, without hypocrisy."

the *Message*

Do you value wisdom?

King Solomon sure did. His one request to God was for wisdom. Since Solomon's prayer was so noble and godly, God blessed him abundantly with both wisdom and wealth (see 2 Chronicles 1).

The Gospel author Luke thought wisdom was important, too. The other Gospel authors didn't mention Jesus' teenage years, but Luke noted that Jesus increased in wisdom (Luke 2:52). Luke didn't want us to overlook that significant detail.

Wisdom also enabled Ben Strong of Paducah, Kentucky, to act quickly and courageously. One school morning in December 1997, Strong and his high school student prayer group, the Agape Club, looked up to see a freshman student holding a semi-automatic handgun. The boy began shooting, killing three girls and injuring several others.

My friend Steven Curtis Chapman and I talked after he returned from the funeral, where he sang and offered an invitation to receive Jesus Christ. Steven said the number of killings could have been far worse if Ben, the group's leader, hadn't disarmed the gunman before he pulled out the rest of his weaponry. God gave Ben, a devout Christian and star football player, the wisdom and words to convince the boy to stop shooting. Little did Ben Strong know as he studied the Bible that God was preparing him for a life-saving talk with a classmate whose life had gone awry.[3]

Solomon outlined a few great truths about wisdom in Proverbs 2: The Lord gives it, and if you seek wisdom from God's Word, you will find it. Wisdom is a treasure to be sought after, and the person who finds it will be blessed.

The Bible devotes a lot of space to the subject of wisdom. Are you seeking God for it?

Discussion Starters:

* What is godly wisdom? How can we get it?
** Why is wisdom one of the greatest things you can ask God for?
*** What's the difference between being smart and being wise?

Lifeline:

Since wisdom comes from God's truths, commit to spending more time in His Word.

Whose Team Will You Join?

the **WORD** | James 4:4, 7-8

"You adulteresses, do you not know that friendship with the world is hostility toward God? Therefore whoever wishes to be a friend of the world makes himself an enemy of God.... Submit therefore to God. Resist the devil and he will flee from you. Draw near to God and He will draw near to you. Cleanse your hands, you sinners; and purify your hearts, you double-minded."

the **Message**

Michael Jordan and Shaquille O'Neal basketball cards get more valuable every year. Some Mickey Mantle baseball cards are worth hundreds, even thousands, of dollars today. An autograph from Joe Montana can generate huge amounts of cash from sports fans.

Those cards and autographs are expensive because enough people value them. People always want to be a part of the winning team.

But what about in life?

You may not always win your track meets or debate competitions, but if you're a Christian, your life will be eternally victorious. God is the winner. He always coaches the winning team. He never fails.

Satan, on the other hand, is a loser. When the devil fights God and His team, Satan gets defeated time and time again.

The devil often deceives people into thinking they're winning when they become friends with him. He gives temporary highs and fleeting satisfaction through partying, sex, power, and money. But Satan doesn't mention that the things you get from him will eventually destroy you.

You don't need to worry if you're on God's side, though. The Lord gives eternal, true happiness. If God lives in your heart, He'll help you deny the devil's temporary kicks and enable you to recognize counterfeit happiness.

Do you want to be a winner? Draw near to God. When you do, you'll find that He's already close beside you, guiding and coaching you every step of the way. No matter what the odds look like, God will always lead you to victory.

Discussion Starters:

• How is God like the coach of a winning team?
•• How is Satan like the coach of a losing team?
••• How do you draw near to God? How do you resist the devil? Be specific.

Lifeline:

Family members should be accountable to one another. If someone in your family seems to be "befriending" Satan in an area of his or her life, it's important to lovingly tell that person. But at the same time, be sure to acknowledge God's work in his or her life.

The Mysterious Lady

the **WORD** | James 4:11-12

"Do not speak against one another, brethren. He who speaks against a brother or judges his brother, speaks against the law and judges the law; but if you judge the law, you are not a doer of the law, but a judge of it. There is only one Lawgiver and Judge, the One who is able to save and to destroy; but who are you who judge your neighbor?"

the **Message**

Ruth Castillos always wore a bright red dress and dark sunglasses. Each Wednesday at 9:30 A.M., she'd meet a stocky, bearded man in front of the drugstore. Quietly, he would exchange a bottle of pills for her package of dollar bills. Then Ruth would quickly, mysteriously slip into her BMW and drive briskly away to her tiny house in the country.

Besides going to the drugstore each week, Ruth rarely left home.

She almost never had visitors, either. The only person who came to her house was a tall, handsome young man who stopped by each Friday afternoon—and stayed only an hour.

What do you think Ruth was doing? Drug dealing? Embezzling international funds? Holding hostages in her home?

Actually, Ruth was struggling to hold her life together. She had an eye disorder that made it difficult for her to see in daylight—forcing her to wear dark sunglasses. During the day, she went out only to see the pharmacist because her mom was terminally ill and needed medicine. Her mom was so sick that neither she nor Ruth could have any visitors. So the only person who came by was a young doctor who made house calls on Friday.

Ruth's life was so dark, she wore red to cheer herself up.

It's easy to jump to conclusions when you first hear about Ruth. I did. It's easy to judge when you don't know all the information. It's easy, but it's dangerous. Even if we do come to the right conclusions, we're still wrong to judge.

Don't try to do God's job. He's the only One who has any business judging people.

Discussion Starters:

* Why is it so dangerous to judge others? Why are we so quick to judge?
** What did you first think Ruth was up to? Why?
*** Who have you judged unfairly? Why did you jump to conclusions?

Lifeline:

How can we help each other refrain from judging and slandering others but also be discerning about who we choose as friends?

Rotting Riches

"Come now, you rich, weep and howl for your miseries which are coming upon you. Your riches have rotted and your garments have become moth-eaten. Your gold and your silver have rusted; and their rust will be a witness against you and will consume your flesh like fire. It is in the last days that you have stored up your treasure!"

the **Message**

My friend "ol' Norm" owns a large corporation. He has lots of money and a big house. Anyone would say that ol' Norm is a rich man.

Norm's a great steward of his money, though. He gives to 1,600 different ministries. He pays his employees well and prays diligently for everyone he knows. In his spare time, he does mission work in impoverished countries around the world. He loves his wife, kids, and grandkids. But above all, Norm enjoys spending time with God.

My teenage friend Madeleine started a clothing company a few years ago. Mady's been very successful and now makes about $100,000 a year. But since the beginning, she's given every cent away to needy kids around the world. Mady has always had a generous heart. Even as a child she would give 25 to 50 percent of her small allowance to her church to help alleviate world hunger.

Max, a dear 10-year-old I know, makes 25 cents a day by memorizing Bible verses. He puts each quarter into a piggy bank for poor inner-city kids.

Michael, an acquaintance of mine, inherited over $100 million when his father died. But he's selfish with his money and spends most of it on himself—his business and pleasures. Michael has lost more than 90 percent of his inheritance in the last 20 years, and if he doesn't become a better steward, he may lose it all. Even though right now he has virtually everything that money can buy, Michael's not happy. Most of the time, he looks nervous and stressed. In fact, I've never seen him smile.

Money won't make you happy, especially when you misuse or hoard it. But when you give it away—back to God—you'll be blessed with eternal riches.

Do you have the right attitude toward money?

Discussion Starters:

* When is money a bad thing?
** Jesus said that we cannot serve both God and money. In fact, He addressed the issue of wealth more than any other subject. Why?
*** How do you know when you're giving enough?

Lifeline:

As a family, how can you work together to give enough back to God and use your resources wisely?

Prayer Power

"Is anyone among you suffering? Then he must pray. Is anyone cheerful? He is to sing praises. Is anyone among you sick? Then he must call for the elders of the church and they are to pray over him, anointing him with oil in the name of the Lord; and the prayer offered in faith will restore the one who is sick, and the Lord will raise him up, and if he has committed sins they will be forgiven him. Therefore, confess your sins to one another, and pray for one another so that you may be healed. The effective prayer of a righteous man can accomplish much."

the Message

Eight thousand kids shivered like wet puppies as the early spring rain turned the outdoor youth rally into an event that would've made only Noah rejoice. As our staff tried to make a final "go/no-go" decision about whether to have the music concert in the outdoor arena, I stood with a group of unbelieving technicians who were huddled around cups of coffee.

"Should we call 'er off, Joe?" they teased.

"Not yet," I said. "Elijah was a man with a nature like ours, and he prayed earnestly that it would not rain; and it did not rain on the earth for three years and six months," I said, quoting from James 5:17.

I continued, "Fellows, God says, 'The effective prayer of a righteous man accomplishes much.' I'm going to pray that the rain stops."

"Yeah, but you're not Elijah!" the technicians scoffed.

But Elijah's God is my God, I thought. I walked to the sound stage and asked God to let us hold the concert. Within 60 seconds, the rain stopped. We had the rally. And, for the record, that event hasn't been rained out once in 17 years. (Rained on, but not out!)

Does it rain or stop raining every time I pray? No. Does everyone get instantly healed each time I pray? No. But I've seen God answer every prayer faithfully. He'll say either "yes," "no," "now," or "later."

An old Southern preacher summed prayer up by saying, "God may not be there when you want Him, but He'll always get there right on time."

God will be faithful to your requests. Do you believe that?

Discussion Starters:

 * Why do you think God created prayer?
 ** What prayer concerns do you have today?
 *** What prayers have you seen answered in your life recently?

Lifeline:

Pray for each other right now. Keep a log of each family member's prayer requests, and then update the log when the requests have been answered. Doing that will reveal how God is working in your family.

1 peter

If you read my books or hear me speak, you probably feel like you know Jamie Jo, my oldest daughter, as if she were one of your own best friends. Jamie has loved God since her earliest memory. She has a passion for the lost and a compassion for the poor. She is a wonderful friend-maker who sets a beautiful example for the rest of us. Jamie's soft, gentle heart and her love for God come through clearly in these devotionals for 1 Peter.

Peter was Jesus' most outspoken follower. His passion for knowing and following Jesus made him a "rock" in Scripture. His eloquence in this book assures you that these words weren't written by a mere fisherman on the shores of Galilee but by the Holy Spirit Himself, breathing into him the words of God.

Refined Like Gold

the WORD | 1 Peter 1:6-7

"You have been distressed by various trials, so that the proof of your faith, being more precious than gold which is perishable, even though tested by fire, may be found to result in praise and glory and honor at the revelation of Jesus Christ."

the Message

Gold is one of the most beautiful and precious elements found in the earth. And "in the earth" is a key distinction of gold. When gold is encased in rocks among the dirt, it looks nothing at all like the 24-carat metal we see in mall jewelry stores. It is dirty and impure.

Before gold becomes something you would want to wear around your finger or neck, it must be refined. Refining is a purification process involving heat, the application of acid, and/or other methods. The purpose is to start with gold-bearing ore and remove all the impurities, leaving gold in its purest form. While you might not look twice at a dirty rock containing gold ore, after the gold has been extracted and refined, it makes people "oooh" and "ahhh."

How would you like to make people "oooh" and "ahhh" about your golden character? What if someone thought you were as precious and priceless as gold? Someone does. The very reason Jesus allows us to undergo trials is to use them to purify us.

Even though we may have accepted Jesus' offer of salvation, our sinful impurities cling to us and aren't easily removed from our lives. But our sufferings make our impurities more evident. As we see them more clearly, we are able to deal with them. As we keep skimming and scraping off all our ungodly qualities, what's left is more pure and beautiful than before.

Refining fires may be intense, but they aren't ultimately destructive. Indeed, the heat is an essential part of the process to transform a glittery piece of rock into valuable jewelry to be treasured for generations. Genuine gold makes it through the heat. So do genuine Christians.

Discussion Starters:

- Have you identified any "purification" through recent trials?
  - Do you think it's possible to avoid trials in life? How do trials make us better people?
    - Can you think of positive and negative examples of how you've responded to "heat" in the past? How can you prepare to face future refining fires?

Lifeline:

If we endure the refining process with joy, just imagine what we may become.

Little Bible Man

the WORD | *1 Peter 1:14-16*

"As obedient children, do not be conformed to the former lusts which were yours in your ignorance, but like the Holy One who called you, be holy yourselves also in all your behavior; because it is written, 'You shall be holy, for I am holy.'"

the Message

When I was a kid, I ate dirt out of a potted plant by our staircase. A friend of mine was so jealous when his little brother was born that he shattered the sliding glass door with a baseball bat.

We all did silly things when we were kids, and now we can look back and laugh at the things we did that were immature or even wrong. One of my favorite stories is about my best friend. As a child, he never did anything wrong, although there was a "Little Bible Man" who kept getting him into trouble. For example, one night he wet the bed. When his parents asked him if he had done it, he innocently shook his head and said, "The Little Bible Man did it."

I think we all have our own versions of "Little Bible Man" whom we would like to take the blame for our wrongdoings. (Flip Wilson went to the other extreme to assign blame when he frequently proclaimed, "The devil made me do it!")

Today's passage urges us to be "obedient children" and "not be conformed to the former lusts which were yours in your ignorance." Peter is confirming what the apostle Paul wrote about doing away with "childish things" (1 Corinthians 13:11). So often we act in ignorance and then look for someone to blame. But if we would wait to hear the prompting of God *before* acting, we wouldn't need to lay blame on anyone else.

We need to keep in mind that childish stories are only funny when they're happening to children. Immaturity is amusing only in reference to kids with immature thoughts and actions. As adults, immaturity and childishness will only earn the scorn or pity of others. So it's time to start taking responsibility for ourselves. Let's leave behind the "Little Bible Man" as we become intelligent men and women who live according to the Bible.

Discussion Starters:

* What were some of the "childish things" of your past? Why is it important to put them away?
* What's the best way to make the transformation from childishness to holiness?
* What is one specific example of how you can act out of self-control and maturity today?

Lifeline:

Being children of God, we grow through the study of His Word and our constant communication with Him in prayer. He will then direct our steps out of childhood and into spiritual maturity.

Obedient Children

the **WORD** | *1 Peter 2:13-14*

"Submit yourselves for the Lord's sake to every human institution, whether to a king as the one in authority, or to governors as sent by him for the punishment of evildoers and the praise of those who do right."

the *Message*

I was raised in a godly home with parents who honored God and His Word. But can I tell you a secret? It sometimes grated on my human nature, and I occasionally harbored feelings of anger and rebellion in my soul.

For example, I wasn't allowed to do everything other kids did. I didn't get to go to certain movies. Potential parties and public gatherings were checked out before I could attend. Boys who asked me out were critiqued and inspected before they were given my parents' seal of approval.

As a result, I felt that my peers ridiculed me and I was discriminated against. I kept my pain and loneliness deep inside, and I was very unhappy much of the time. I resisted memorizing Bible verses, which my parents urged me and my siblings to do each day.

Yet I loved my parents and respected their teachings, so I complied with their wishes. Now, as I look back, I had a happy life. I was rewarded with God's gift of a wonderful husband who loves me as the girl he always desired in a wife. In fact, I recently thanked my dad publicly for the way he raised us kids. We reap blessings in our lives every day because of the path we walked while growing up.

As a teenager I was usually obedient, though many times reluctantly so. I hope you can learn early in life that obedience—whether to governments or parents—is God's design for His children. The sooner we can learn *willing* obedience, the sooner our lives will take a turn for the better.

Discussion Starters:

- What are a couple of areas where you resist being obedient to someone in authority?
- How do you respond when you pursue something you know is wrong and later regret it?
- What advice can you offer someone who is struggling to be obedient to God's Word?

Lifeline:

Look for signs of rebellion in your life and eliminate them. Try to appreciate the advice of authority figures, and find ways to use it to make yourself a better person.

The Ostrich Response

the WORD | 1 Peter 3:8-9

"To sum up, all of you be harmonious, sympathetic, brotherly, kindhearted, and humble in spirit; not returning evil for evil or insult for insult, but giving a blessing instead."

the Message

Give yourself a little test. For each of the following qualities or actions, rate yourself from 1 to 10. One is "I never get it right," 10 is "I always act that way."

QUALITY/ACTION	MY SCORE
Getting along with others	
Being sympathetic	
Being friendly	
Being kindhearted	
Being humble	
Ignoring the bad others do to you	
Letting insults bounce off you	
Wishing the best for others	

How'd you do? When I read today's verses, I want to hide my head in the sand.

Did you ever wish you could bite your tongue after blurting out something dumb, bitter, or hurtful, when it's too late to take it back? Do you ever insist on having the last word in an argument? Does something deep within drive you to get even when someone hurts, offends, or insults you?

If we don't quickly deal with personal resentment, it soon becomes a habit—an ongoing attitude! And few things are as unattractive as a person who is always vengeful and never gracious or kind.

It's time to take our heads out of the sand and take a good look at the things God has given us. Then we can tolerate the shortcomings of others and treat them as we wish to be treated.

Discussion Starters:

* What are you currently finding hardest to forgive? Are you willing to improve the situation?
** Which of the qualities listed in today's passage do you most need to work on?
*** What are the advantages of heeding Peter's instructions?

Lifeline:

When people annoy you, take my great-grandmother's advice: "Kill 'em with kindness."

Happily Hospitable

the **WORD** | *1 Peter 4:9-11*

"Be hospitable to one another without complaint. As each one has received a special gift, employ it in serving one another as good stewards of the manifold grace of God. Whoever speaks, is to do so as one who is speaking the utterances of God; whoever serves is to do so as one who is serving by the strength which God supplies; so that in all things God may be glorified through Jesus Christ, to whom belongs the glory and dominion forever and ever."

the **Message**

My grandmother is the most hospitable lady I have ever met, heard of, or even read about. My lifelong dream is to be as hospitable and unselfish as she is. I love going to visit her. Whether you are a grandchild, a friend, or even a complete stranger, she gives you the treatment of an honored guest.

Recently Gran'ma had been working hard all day and had settled into her chair to put her feet up and read a good book. Just then the doorbell rang and in came four grade-schoolers bringing her flowers and cookies. As exhausted as she was, Gran'ma got right up as if she had been expecting their visit for weeks and set out four glasses of lemonade and cookies. The children made themselves at home around her kitchen table. Gran'ma talked with them about their days and about school and their families. They were so happy to be "at home" in my grandmother's house that they ended up staying about an hour, just talking and eating. Then they thanked her and left, leaving their crumbs and dirty dishes behind. Gran'ma happily cleaned up after them and began cooking dinner for her husband. Her afternoon of relaxing and reading had been disturbed, but she was the only one who knew.

In Gran'ma I see that hospitality is not only a God-given gift, but also a talent that she works to develop. She serves with "the strength which God supplies," just as Peter instructs. Everyone who knows her firmly believes that my grandmother is the most accommodating hostess in history. I strongly agree.

Discussion Starters:

* Why do you think God gives people different spiritual gifts, such as hospitality, compassion, and leadership?
** What is a gift that God has given you? In what ways are you using it?
*** Who is someone who impresses you with his or her hospitality? What can you do this week to let that person know how much you appreciate him or her?

Lifeline:

If we serve each other using God's strength, then we will be serving each other constantly.

Look at Me!

the WORD | 1 Peter 5:6-7

"Therefore humble yourselves under the mighty hand of God, that He may exalt you at the proper time, casting all your anxiety on Him, because He cares for you."

the Message

Have you ever heard the expression "You gotta blow your own horn because no one is going to do it for you"? Do you agree?

Aren't there times when you just want to stand on top of your desk at school and yell, "Look at me! I'm a beautiful, talented, hardworking person who deserves better than you guys are treating me"? Don't you want to jump up on the bench and scream, "Hey, Coach! Look at me! I'm better than most of those guys out there! Why do I have to sit on this bench and shine the pine the whole game?" Do you ever just want to smack someone and say, "Quit acting like I'm invisible. Look at me"?

Most of us have such inclinations. Yet when we see other people who "toot their own horns," we don't usually like what we see.

Humility is one of the hardest attributes of God to acquire. Some people shout their accomplishments from the rooftops, probably to cover their inner insecurities. Others seem to have it all together, content in the knowledge that God loves them and without any pressing need for a "day in the sun." Still other quiet people continue to feel that inner "Look at me!" impulse, yet they live with the frustration of never seeming to get noticed. Sometimes I think it may be easier for people who excel at everything— sports, grades, popularity, etc.—to be humble. They can show a little humility now and then and still be in the limelight. Humility may come harder for "average" people.

Sometimes the best we can do is realize that God notices. He sees our beauty, talents, desires, and potential. After all, He put all those things within us, and we should continue to use them for Him. If people don't notice now, they will someday. And until then, we can dump all our anxiety and frustration on Him.

When you find it difficult to be humble, remember that Jesus has set an example for us.

Discussion Starters:

* Do you lean more toward "blowing your own horn" or being humble? Why?
** How can Jesus' example of humility motivate you to be more humble?
*** How can you show humility the next time you're confronted with the criticism and rejection of others, or when they ignore you completely?

Lifeline:

Don't forget that it is those who are gentle who "will inherit the earth" (Matthew 5:5).

2 peter

Peter wrote his second letter shortly before he was killed because of his faith in Jesus. He urgently encourages us to be ready and alert so we will not fall into the snare of indifference and false teaching at a time when we desperately need to walk in the light of Jesus. Peter reminds us of the promise and hope of eternity that we have, thanks to the death and resurrection of Jesus. With this reminder, we are warned to return to the true gospel, which comes only through Jesus Christ.

My thanks once again to Brett Causey for writing these devotionals.

Everything You Need?

"Grace and peace be multiplied to you in the knowledge of God and of Jesus our Lord; seeing that His divine power has granted to us everything pertaining to life and godliness, through the true knowledge of Him who called us by His own glory and excellence."

the **Message**

In the climax of *Rocky IV*, Rocky Balboa fights a Russian boxer to avenge the death of Apollo Creed. Their boxing match takes place in Moscow. Rocky not only faces an incredibly powerful opponent, but he also is surrounded by a hostile crowd. An entire country is pulling against him. The two fighters slug each other until they are both bruised, bleeding, cut, and exhausted. Can you relate? I can! Sometimes I feel like I cannot take another step because I hurt so much. I feel like the whole world is against me.

God's Word never promises that when we take up the cross of Christ, our problems will disappear. On the contrary, I believe the opposite is true. When you lift up a light in a dark world, the darkness opposes it. Scripture clearly expresses that God has an enemy who will do anything to turn us from the truth. Even though the enemy comes against us, One who is greater always stands with us in our trials and sufferings.

As Peter anticipated his execution, do you think he was fearful or felt alone? Probably so, yet he wrote a powerful message to us. He assures us that we have everything we need to serve, live, love, and grow in Jesus in order to become the people we were created to be. His joy and love for Jesus didn't waver during tough times. When his life might have seemed bleakest, he discovered that Jesus was all he needed.

Whenever your circumstances seem overwhelming, remember that Jesus has transformed you into a new creation. Refuse to give up. Trust that you have been given everything you need because you have been given Jesus!

Discussion Starters:

* What situations are you involved in where it seems as though the whole world is against you? What will it take for you to trust Jesus to deliver you from such situations?
  ** How can you prevent your joy and trust in Jesus from wavering when you encounter difficult times?
    *** Do you believe in a God who knows you personally and who makes miracles a reality? If so, how should you respond to Him?

Lifeline:

Reflect on an experience in the past that appeared to be hopeless but in which the Lord Jesus rescued you or delivered you—perhaps in an amazing way.

A New Definition of Everything

the WORD | 2 Peter 2:9

"The Lord knows how to rescue the godly from temptation, and to keep the unrighteous under punishment for the day of judgment."

the Message

I recently heard Mrs. Sun Ok Lee speak at the Voice of the Martyrs National Missions Conference. She is a frail, small Korean woman. Only a few years ago, she was imprisoned in a North Korean labor camp where she witnessed the executions of many people, including Christians. She said that before she knew Christ, she first heard hymns from the singing of the imprisoned Christians. Mrs. Lee could not understand why these Christians refused to deny the man they called Jesus. They were promised physical freedom for themselves and their families if they would turn from their faith and join the Communist party. When they refused to become slaves to communism, many of them were put to death.

Mrs. Lee was released from prison and fled to South Korea, where she received the Lord Jesus Christ as her personal Savior. With tears streaming down her face, she told us that now she understands why the Christians in prison chose to be executed rather than turn their backs on Jesus. She had realized that to be a Christian, we must be willing to give up everything to follow Him. Her testimony brings a whole new meaning to the concept of "everything."

I thank God for the strength and courage of those Korean believers because we are faced with the same decision as they were. No, our lives may not be in jeopardy, but our eternal souls are. Are we willing to compromise our faith to gain popularity, money, or success?

What are *you* being offered that replaces Jesus as the most important thing in your life? And are you brave enough to make the right choice?

Discussion Starters:

* Do you know anyone who has suffered for his or her faith in God? If so, how can you support that person?
  ** We serve a God who causes "all things to work together for good to those who love [Him], to those who are called according to His purpose" (Romans 8:28). How might the unpleasant circumstances of your life be used by Him?
    *** What are three things in your life that threaten to hinder your relationship with God? (Sports? Boyfriend or girlfriend? Work? Car?)

Lifeline:

Commit to pray every day this week for wisdom about the three things you have just listed.

When Time Runs Out

the WORD | 2 Peter 3:8-10

"With the Lord one day is like a thousand years, and a thousand years like one day. The Lord is not slow about His promise, as some count slowness, but is patient toward you, not wishing for any to perish but for all to come to repentance. But the day of the Lord will come like a thief."

the Message

In the 1996 AFC championship game, the Indianapolis Colts played the Pittsburgh Steelers to determine who would be in the Super Bowl against the NFC champion Dallas Cowboys. The game was well played and evenly matched. With only a few seconds remaining, the Colts were down by four points and had only enough time left for one play. Jim Harbaugh took the snap and dropped back to pass as five wide receivers sprinted toward the end zone almost 60 yards away. The final seconds ticked off the clock as he threw the ball. The ball hit one of the receivers directly in the hands but bounced out. As the receiver fell to the ground, he made another grab at the ball, but it again slipped through his fingers. No more time. The game was over. The Colts lost and the Steelers advanced to the Super Bowl.

In football the game is over when the clock ticks down to zero. In our Christian lives, the race is over when Jesus comes back. What an awesome day that will be for those of us who have trusted Him with our hearts. We will rejoice as we begin eternity with our Lord. Others may wish for more time, but it will be too late. Many will be devastated and utterly heartbroken because they had the opportunity to accept Jesus but chose not to believe.

God desires to have a relationship with you, but He will never force you into one. You must choose to believe in Him. The ball is in your hands. He eagerly awaits your decision. But choose quickly. The clock is ticking.

Discussion Starters:

* The Bible refers to a "book of life" in which Jesus has recorded the names of all those who have placed their faith in Him (Revelation 3:5; 20:12, 15). Is your name written in His book of life? How do you know?
* What, if anything, are you doing to strengthen your personal relationship with God?
* What do you hope to accomplish with your life before the clock runs out?

Lifeline:

If you knew this would be the last day God was going to give you before calling you home to heaven, what would you do? What is keeping you from doing those very things today?

epistles of john

John, Jesus' disciple, is usually credited with writing five New Testament books: the Gospel that bears his name, the book of Revelation, and these three letters that follow the epistles of Peter. John frequently identified himself in third person as "the disciple whom Jesus loved," and he has much to say about the undeniable importance of love in his three short letters.

In his first letter he makes it clear that "the one who does not love does not know God, for God is love" (1 John 4:8). In his second letter, John connects love with truth and warns of deceivers attempting to mislead God's people. John's third letter is addressed to three men: Gaius, whom John encouraged and affirmed; Diotrephes, whom he criticized and confronted; and Demetrius, whom he praised. It embraces love and truth as well, but also emphasizes the value of grace and compassion.

In this next group of devotions, you'll see more of the great heart for God possessed by my young friend Brett Causey.

The Choice Is Yours

the WORD | 1 John 1:5-7

"This is the message we have heard from Him and announce to you, that God is Light, and in Him there is no darkness at all. If we say that we have fellowship with Him and yet walk in the darkness, we lie and do not practice the truth; but if we walk in the Light as He Himself is in the Light, we have fellowship with one another, and the blood of Jesus His Son cleanses us from all sin."

the Message

Two years ago, I set off on a backpacking trip with my friend Bill. The trip began with a long and uneventful 11-hour drive. Although it was well after dark when we arrived, and both of us were inexperienced hikers, we decided to strap on our head lamps and hike the four miles up to where we were planning to camp the first night. We made it to our destination, but during the night an unexpected storm blew in with strong winds and pelting rains. The temperature dropped to about 25 degrees. The next morning we decided to end our trip early and head down the mountain. But because we had hiked up in the dark, we failed to recognize the right trail. We took a wrong turn and spent the next two days wandering almost 35 miles in the freezing rain all because we had made a decision to hike in the dark.

Each day you and I can choose to live with the guidance and direction of our Creator and Savior. Yet when we make our own plans, attempt to be in control, and disregard what He has for us, we choose to walk in darkness.

If we are not seeking the good and perfect plan God has for us (Jeremiah 29:11), we can easily start walking down a dark and destructive path. Jesus died a miserable death on the cross and arose from the dead so you and I may have the abundant life God offers. He is the Son of God who lights our paths. Let's choose to walk in the Light of our Father.

Discussion Starters:

- Why is it important to seek God's plan for your life for the decisions you make each day?
- Read Psalm 18:28. In what ways are you walking in darkness?
- How can we help each other walk in the light of Christ?

Lifeline:

What hard decisions are you facing today? What can your other family members do to help you make the best choices?

The Ultimate Example

the **WORD** | 1 John 2:6

"The one who says he abides in Him ought himself to walk in the same manner as He walked."

the *Message*

David was one of the better soccer players in the state of Alabama. He was also a Christian, a leader in his youth group, and active for God at his high school. Other students watched him because he didn't compromise his faith in Jesus.

David did have a bad temper, however, which surfaced while he played soccer. Because of his skill, opposing players often double- and triple-teamed him. In one game he was knocked down again and again, causing him to become increasingly frustrated and angry. David finally was knocked down one time too many and responded by punching out one of the other team's players. He received a red card, ejecting him from that game—and the next one. Later David was upset because he had let a lot of people down. Most importantly, he realized he had let Jesus down, so he decided to come up with a plan to control his temper.

During soccer games, he had the habit of wiping the sweat from his face with the collar of his shirt. He decided to put the letters WWJD inside his collar so that every time he wiped his face he would ask himself, *What would Jesus do?* As he was reminded to keep his focus on Jesus and reflect on how He would respond, David was better able to control his temper.

We often see WWJD on shirts and bracelets, but it is still easy to forget the power of Jesus' name and the example He has provided for us. That's why I like the alternative: WDJD, which stands for "What did Jesus do?" It's a reminder that Jesus gave up everything because He loves us. His was the ultimate example because He lived a perfect life. Jesus endured pain, suffering, insults, betrayals by His best friends, the crown of thorns, the nails, the cross…all because He loves us.

Discussion Starters:

• What do you find the most difficult thing(s) to give up
in order to follow Jesus? (Money? Activities? Friends?)
•• What can you do to focus more on His example for how to live your life?
••• What are some consequences you might
experience if you don't stay focused on Jesus?

Lifeline:

How can your family be a better example of how Jesus might live in your community?

Let's Not Kid Ourselves

the WORD | 1 John 3:16-18

"We know love by this, that He laid down His life for us; and we ought to lay down our lives for the brethren. But whoever has the world's goods, and sees his brother in need and closes his heart against him, how does the love of God abide in him? Little children, let us not love with word or with tongue, but in deed and truth."

the Message

Some people are easy to love. We like to hang around people who are kind and friendly. But how about those who are more difficult to love—the ones who may be rude, shy, sick, or poor? God doesn't tell us to show love just to those who are easy to love; He commands us to love everyone.

I guarantee we would all be in a big heap of trouble if Jesus loved only those who are easy to love. Let's not kid ourselves; we don't make it easy for Jesus to love us. In fact, if He hadn't died on the cross, most of us would never be convinced that He could love us. And even then, many of us still don't believe it.

Jesus has an incredible passion for the people we tend to overlook. Remember how He gave sight to the blind? Can you see His hand on the festering skin of the leper? Do you hear the compassion in His voice as He talked with the woman at the well? Yes, Jesus loves the people we never see because we choose not to see them. We're usually too busy trying to show love to those who are easy to love.

Mother Teresa said, "Because we cannot see Christ, we cannot express our love to Him; but our neighbors we can always see, and we can do for them what, if we saw Him, we would like to do for Christ."

And this is how we should love.

Discussion Starters:

- Who are the three people you have the hardest time loving?
- Do you really believe it is possible to love Jesus by loving others? How would you rate your love for Jesus, on a scale from 1 to 10 (1 = lousy, 10 = terrific), based solely on how you treat other people?
- Can you think of a time when one person's love made a significant difference in your life? Can you think of someone who needs to experience the love of Jesus expressed through you?

Lifeline:

How we live our lives is the most accurate reflection of what we believe. Today, create a game plan for how your family can do something nice for one of your neighbors.

Freedom

the **WORD** | 1 John 4:7-10

"Beloved, let us love one another, for love is from God; and everyone who loves is born of God and knows God. The one who does not love does not know God, for God is love. By this the love of God was manifested in us, that God has sent His only begotten Son into the world so that we might live through Him. In this is love, not that we loved God, but that He loved us and sent His Son to be the propitiation for our sins."

the **Message**

I was 17 years old when God really challenged me. At that point I knew a lot *about* God, but He wanted me to know *Him*. That's when I established a personal relationship with Jesus Christ. For the first time in my life I experienced love with no strings attached. His love for me didn't change according to how I performed on the baseball field or whether I made an A or a D in biology. He loves me because I am His, and He created me.

My high school years were definitely the most painful and toughest of my life. When I was a sophomore, my dad moved out. Yet it is during such times that God meets us right where we are. That's when God offered me His unconditional love and I chose to accept it.

During those years, I saw God's sacrificial love reflected in my mother's actions. After my parents divorced, my mom gave up many things she might have enjoyed so she could provide for my sisters and me. She gave without expecting much in return. Her sacrificial heart showed me God's love.

John 3:16 speaks powerfully of love so strong that God sacrificed His own Son so you and I can have the gift of eternity with Him. It was God's love that drew Peter from his fishing nets and Matthew from his position of prosperity and power to follow Jesus. After they met Him and experienced His love for others, their lives changed drastically. So can yours.

Discussion Starters:

* Do you believe God loves you unconditionally, or do you believe His love depends on your behavior? Give some specific examples.
** Has your life changed because of a personal encounter with Jesus? If so, in what ways?
*** How can you demonstrate sacrificial love in your family? In your friendships? In your school activities?

Lifeline:

The heart is the key to the Christian life. The truth of the gospel is intended to free us to love God and others with our whole hearts. Are you willing to offer your whole heart back to God?

Sweet Victory

the WORD | 1 John 5:4-5

"For whatever is born of God overcomes the world; and this is the victory that has over-come the world—our faith. Who is the one who overcomes the world, but he who believes that Jesus is the Son of God?"

the Message

It was the biggest football game of the year for both the Auburn Tigers and the Alabama Crimson Tide. The score was Alabama 17 and Auburn 15, with only 15 seconds remaining in the 1997 Iron Bowl. The ball was resting on the 23-yard line as Jaret Holmes, the Auburn kicker, trotted out to try for his fourth field goal of the game. With 93,000 fans going crazy, Jaret calmly booted a 40-yarder to win the game, 18-17. It was a sweet victory. Jaret later shared that this kick was one of the most incredible moments of his life.

Jaret Holmes had reason to celebrate. I remember him working hard in high school to recover from knee surgery. I can recall his many sessions of weightlifting and running wind sprints, the long hours of sweat and exhaustion. He eventually overcame his potentially career-ending injury, so his celebration was especially sweet.

Jaret is a Christian whose football talents have given him many opportunities to talk with others about Jesus. After speaking at a kicking camp, a couple of guys were very interested in knowing more about Jesus. Jaret was excited to share what Jesus had done in his life and to see God work in the lives of others. He said that all the field goals he had ever made could not compare to sharing Jesus with those two guys.

Romans 10:9 tells us that if we confess with our mouths that Jesus is Lord and believe in our hearts that God raised Him from the dead, we will be saved. If you choose to accept Jesus into your heart, you are going to heaven, where there will be no more tears, pain, or suffering. All the field goals and accomplishments of a lifetime can-not compare to seeing our Maker face-to-face. No victory will ever be sweeter.

Discussion Starters:

* Have you ever suffered an injury or been through an intense personal struggle? If so, how did it feel when you finally overcame the problem?
  ** The Bible says that we will all stand before God to be judged. Are you confident you will go to heaven? Why or why not?
  *** In addition to believing in Jesus, how else should you prepare for judgment day? (See 2 Corinthians 5:10.)

Lifeline:

Suppose a fellow student reads the verses at the top of this page and asks, "How does believing in Jesus help you to overcome the world?" How would you respond?

Hide and Seek

the WORD | 2 John 5-6

"Now I ask you…not as though I were writing to you a new commandment, but the one which we have had from the beginning, that we love one another. And this is love, that we walk according to His commandments."

the Message

I heard a true story of a medical missionary team that traveled to a remote village in Africa. The missionaries performed a simple operation and restored the sight of a man who had been blind since birth. After one day of celebration, the man disappeared. A week later the missionaries saw him returning, holding one end of a rope. Holding on to the other end were 30 blind men.

What an example of walking in love! The man was given sight and he immediately wanted to share the gift with those who couldn't see. It should also be our model for evangelism. You and I have received the greatest gift ever given. Are we driven by enthusiasm to share it with others? If we had the cure for AIDS, we would call a big press conference and tell the world. The love and forgiveness of Jesus is the "cure" to sin and death. Why aren't we more excited to spread the Good News?

As a child, you probably played hide-and-seek. One person who was "it" counted while everyone else ran to find a good place to hide. After a period of time the counter would shout, "Home free!" meaning it was safe for any remaining hiders to come in without being penalized.

This game is a perfect picture of how we can share our faith. Like Adam and Eve, many people tend to hide from God. They may be hiding in your schools, on your sports teams, in your neighborhood, and even in your own home. It's our job to look for these people and share with them the good news of Jesus. And the good news is that God has called "Home free!" He wants us to come to Him without fear of penalty. Everyone needs to hear about a God who passionately loves them.

Who's going to share Jesus with those sitting in class, on your school bus, or at the grocery store? That's right. *You're* "it."

Discussion Starters:

• Do you really believe that everyone needs Christ? Why?

•• Who are five people you talk to every day that to your knowledge don't have a personal relationship with Jesus?

••• In what practical ways can you show others God's love so they will want to know your motivation?

Lifeline:

You may be the clearest reflection of Christ that your friends ever see.

Delighting in Jesus

the WORD | 3 John 3-4

"For I was very glad when brethren came and testified to your truth, that is, how you are walking in truth. I have no greater joy than this, to hear of my children walking in the truth."

the Message

While attending a class at the Focus on the Family Institute, I stayed with a host family who clearly demonstrated the love of Jesus in the way they loved each other and me, their guest. Dwight and Laura Cloud confirmed my belief that the greatest gift two parents can give their children is to love each other.

While visiting Dwight at his office at Focus on the Family, he told me there was something I had to hear. He called home and got his youngest son, Cole, on the phone. Dwight handed me the receiver and Cole said, "Mr. Brett, I gave my heart to Jesus." Then Caleb, the older brother, picked up the phone and told me that he and a friend were talking about God, and Cole overheard them. Cole, being only three years old, didn't think he was old enough to be saved. Caleb replied that he wasn't too young— that if he told God he loved Him and asked to be saved, he *would* be. So right then and there, two five-year-olds prayed with a three-year-old, and Cole gave his heart to Jesus.

Psalm 37:4 says, "Delight yourself in the Lord; and He will give you the desires of your heart." Dwight and Laura delight in Jesus and have committed their hearts and family to Him. They would be the first to tell you they are not a perfect family. They encounter overwhelming struggles, challenges, and temptations as they attempt to live as godly parents and spouses. They experience the same frustrations as you and your family do, yet they deeply desire to remain in His will. I really believe that God is proud of His children Dwight and Laura Cloud for attempting to raise kids His way. I know I am.

Discussion Starters:

• In what ways do you delight in Jesus?
How does "walking in truth" show your love for Him?
•• What are the "desires of your heart" today?
••• Read Matthew 18:1-6. What is the importance of having childlike faith?

Lifeline:

How are you preparing your heart to be a godly friend to others? In what ways are you trying to be like Jesus?

jude

Jude, half brother to Jesus and brother to James, became a believer as an adult after the resurrection of Jesus. Jude's letter is a spiritual diagnosis of Christ's church. He presents an uncompromising warning and an unbending statement of faith. Jude encourages and challenges us to "contend earnestly for the faith" and to know the faith we profess so we can live out the true gospel. We are warned of many deceivers who will try to cause us to compromise our trust in Jesus. These godless men may even infiltrate our church bodies to create deceit and doubt. As you read Jude's powerful message, think about your own church. What is your church body's spiritual diagnosis?

Again, Brett Causey provides the insight in this devotional.

Shame for His Name

the WORD | Jude 4

"For certain persons have crept in unnoticed, those who were long beforehand marked out for this condemnation, ungodly persons who turn the grace of our God into licentiousness and deny our only Master and Lord, Jesus Christ."

the Message

Jude wrote about people who will call Christians names and hurl insults at our God and us. They will try every possible way to plant doubts in our minds. These people serve only themselves by pursuing lust, sex outside of marriage, and other evil desires. If you stand up unashamedly for your faith, consequences are inevitable.

You might be called names. You might be the last one chosen. Maybe you will be sitting at home on Saturday night while everyone else is out partying. You may not be asked to a school dance. Or perhaps you're an excellent employee yet never get a promotion at work.

When we place our faith in Jesus, our priorities shift from those of the world to His. Yes, choosing His way may be costly if we lose friends. But if we decide *not* to choose Jesus, the cost is higher—the loss of our souls.

We serve a God who will never forsake us. He does not abandon us to do battle by ourselves. He fights the war with us. He is our champion! We know He is who He says He is because of the change in our hearts and lives. When the world comes against us and we suffer because we're Christians, we need to remember that our faith cost Jesus His very life. Do not let Jesus' death be in vain! It is time for us to stand boldly for Christ!

Discussion Starters:

• Have you ever been ashamed to admit you were a Christian? If so, why? How could you act more boldly to demonstrate your love for Jesus?

•• Are you counting on Jesus' death on the cross for your salvation? Are you expecting Him to stand up for you on Judgment Day? If so, what are you currently doing to stand up for Him?

••• If a stranger observed you for a week, would he or she be quick to witness your faith in Christ? Why or why not?

Lifeline:

Read Jude 12-13. This is a description of people without God. Contrast the passage with verses 20-23, a description of people who depend on God. Which description do you desire to be true of you? How can you make sure it is true of you?

revelation

While most of Jesus' original 12 disciples died heroic martyrs' deaths, John was exiled to the tiny Mediterranean island of Patmos. During his latter years, God appeared to him with the prophecy of His final works on earth, which, written, became the book of Revelation.

This glorious and sometimes confusing book contains highly symbolic pictures describing the people and events surrounding the fall of humankind; the banishment of Satan; the second coming of Christ; His millennial, peaceful reign on earth; and the eternal home of all believers. These passages bring the assurance of our salvation, the encouragement we need to overcome all of Satan's ploys, and the hope of Christ's ultimate victory.

Tick-Tock

the **WORD** | Revelation 1:3

"Blessed is he who reads and those who hear the words of the prophecy, and heed the things which are written in it; for the time is near."

the Message

Angela wound her car around the narrow country road, excitedly anticipating her first trip home from college. She peered out the window, lost in memories. She couldn't wait to be talking with her parents, surrounded by the tick-tocking of the clocks that filled the house.

Angela had grown up listening to the sound of dozens of pendulum clocks that echoed throughout the house. Her parents had collected the antique timepieces while they were overseas in Frankfurt, Germany, during the Vietnam War. Every stately room resounded to the song of each clock's unique chime—some at the hour, some at the half hour, and with the great-grandfather clock in the entryway, every quarter hour as well.

She thought back to how her father would make the rounds once a week, winding the clocks and checking the accuracy of his beloved timepieces. The only time it was silent in the house was when the family left for vacation and the clocks ran down. It always struck Angela as rather odd that the sound of passing time could be so comforting.

Time is important, and it's constantly urging us forward. Our alarm clocks, watches, and even calendars remind us that time is precious—and short.

The Bible is like an alarm clock in some ways. The New Testament—and especially Revelation—always ticks away, pointing to Jesus' imminent return. Each word urges Christians forward, encouraging us to persevere, hold fast, and overcome.

We don't have an indefinite amount of time in our lives. Each day is significant. Each person we meet is important. And everything matters.

Jesus is coming back—soon. We shouldn't let one word of Scripture slip by us. We'll want to be ready when the final trumpet blows and the clock winds down for good.

Discussion Starters:

• Why do you think God didn't give a definite time for Jesus' return?
  •• What are some things you would do today if you knew Jesus was coming back tomorrow? Would you be ready for His return? Explain.
  ••• How can you make the most of each day?

Lifeline:

What are some practical ways your family can encourage one another to take advantage of today, especially if it turns out to be *the* day?

First Love

the WORD | Revelation 2:4-5

"But I have this against you, that you have left your first love. Therefore remember from where you have fallen, and repent and do the deeds you did at first; or else I am coming to you and will remove your lampstand out of its place—unless you repent."

the Message

The first love of Leah's life was Shane—a brawny, brown-faced, tempestuous Irish boy. Leah and Shane immediately fell in love the moment they gazed at each other across the park playground.

"What's yer name?" Shane asked Leah.

"Leah," she said, gazing shyly at him as she sat on a swing.

That meeting began their lovestruck friendship. And soon after, they decided to get married sometime in the future.

"I'll work on the highway crew, and you can stay home and take care of the family," Shane confidently told Leah.

"Okay. I'll put cookies in your lunch every day," Leah said, giggling.

The young lovebirds were inseparable. All day they played games, climbed trees, rode bikes, dug for buried treasure, and captured bad guys.

They talked about everything and made important decisions together.

Shane and Leah were in love. (As much as six-year-olds can be.)

The first time you fall in love—no matter what your age—it's unforgettable! In the Bible, God speaks of having a "first love." But He isn't talking about small schooltime crushes.

God says our first love should be for Him—*and He means business.*

That's the message God was trying to get across to the church at Ephesus—that He deserves to be loved above all things and all people. God should be more important in your life than your friends, activities, favorite things, and yes, even your family. God is to be your highest, most treasured, *forever* love.

Does your life reflect that God is your first love?

Discussion Starters:

* Who was your first love? How did you feel? How did you act?
  ** Is Jesus your first love now? Why or why not?
  *** What choices do you make that cause your love for God to grow cold?
  **** How can you keep your first love for Jesus Christ passionate and alive?

Lifeline:

Parents, when you first knew Christ, how was your faith "on fire" for Jesus? What did you do for Him? What have you done to maintain your love for Christ?

Passing Storm

"Do not fear what you are about to suffer. Behold, the devil is about to cast some of you into prison, so that you will be tested, and you will have tribulation for ten days. Be faithful until death, and I will give you the crown of life."

the Message

There's something romantic and delightfully scary about thunderstorm blackouts, especially when you're a kid. There's a certain giddy excitement about the darkness and the mad dash for candles and flashlights. But eventually the lights flicker and come back on, and the storm clouds roll away to reveal a vivid, rain-drenched world.

During World War II, thousands of British children sat in the flicker of candlelight in darkened London bunkers amidst the storm of war—but without giddy excitement. Air-raid sirens pierced the air, engines hummed, and booming explosions drew nearer each day. Parents and children alike huddled in fear, not knowing if the storm would pass them by or if the light of freedom and truth would be extinguished by Nazi Germany.

The storm of war was clouding their world.

You may not have experienced the terrors of war, but chances are you've weathered other storms—especially the trials of growing up.

I did. When I was in junior high, my best friend, Paul (the one who stole my eighth-grade girlfriend), made the varsity junior high football team, while I had to be a bench warmer on the "B team."

Another painful moment occurred when I was a junior in high school. Sue, a girl in typing class whom I'd asked to the movies, decided during fourth period on Friday that she didn't want to go..."Just because."

Some storms will be huge, and others will be small. But they're an inevitable, unavoidable part of life. The Bible doesn't say, "*If* you suffer." Instead, Revelation predicts, "You *will* suffer"—maybe even more than unbelievers. God tells us that during stormy times, we must persevere, have faith, and be courageous. No storm will last forever, but our faithful response to difficulty will have eternal significance.

And that's God's promise.

Discussion Starters:

* What "storms of life" are you experiencing right now?
    ** How are you responding? How do tough times affect your relationship with God? Do you become angry or confused with Him? Explain.
  *** How do God's promises bring comfort and understanding to our trials?

Lifeline:

Pray together for any family members who are going through storms.

The Snooze Button

the **WORD** | Revelation 3:2-3

"Wake up, and strengthen the things that remain, which were about to die; for I have not found your deeds completed in the sight of My God. So remember what you have received and heard; and keep it, and repent. Therefore if you do not wake up, I will come like a thief, and you will not know at what hour I will come to you."

the Message

Alarm clocks used to be so simple. They'd ring until you woke up, bounded out of bed, and shut them off. Alarms were simple but effective.

Then something happened. A mad scientist type, tinkering away in a laboratory somewhere, invented the "snooze button" and, in one swoop, changed the face of mornings and altered the wake-up ritual forever.

Some stalwart men and women still leaped out of bed at the first ring, ready to face the day. But thousands of sleepers rejected the old ways and embraced the new mechanism with delight. With the snooze button, they could retreat into the warmth of sleep for a few more minutes. All it took was a quick swipe of the hand to silence the clock's noisy protest and snooze until the last possible moment.

A few wise people sounded their warnings—in vain. "Mornings will be shattered," they said. "Precious time will be stolen forever."

But no one listened. They'd slept too long and were rushing around as fast as they could, scrambling to get to places on time.

The church at Sardis had been snoozing too long as well. The people had become spiritually sluggish, devoid of spiritual life and power.

"You snooze—you lose," God said (in effect) to the church. God's revelation to the people was supposed to be a wake-up call, reminding them to remember Him, to repent, and to change their ways.

God let the people of Sardis know they could be in for a rude awakening. "If you're not ready—if you're sleeping—I'll come back when you least expect Me," He warned.

Would He give the same urgent message to you?

Discussion Starters:

* What does it mean to be spiritually awake? Spiritually asleep?
** What kinds of "alarms" does God use to get our attention?
*** How do you hit the "snooze button" in your spiritual life?
What has God been calling you to wake up and do?

Lifeline:

Are you sleepy, wide awake, or in between? List some practical ways your family can encourage one another to stay wide awake spiritually.

Loving Discipline

"'Those whom I love, I reprove and discipline; therefore be zealous and repent."

the **Message**

Alison had a frightening temper. It was bad enough when she was a little girl, but once she crossed the hormone line of adolescence, she ruthlessly declared war on her entire family. And it didn't seem to matter that the other side had voted for peace.

Alison would throw some tremendously colorful tantrums, yelling and flinging books, pillows, and pans against the wall. Then she'd hurl her last comment into the air, stomp through the house, and pound her feet up the stairs to her bedroom. Furiously, she'd slam her bedroom door with such vengeance that the walls trembled.

Her dad had little patience with her tantrums. After a few gentle warnings, he took his creativity and hammer upstairs, knocked the hinge pins from her bedroom door, and carried the door to the basement for a rest from Alison's violent exertions. She quickly learned a lesson in self-control.

When my youngest son, Cooper, was about four, he threw a rock at his brother and connected perfectly with Brady's nose. Blood flew everywhere They both ran to the house—Brady in tears, Cooper in fear.

"Cooper," I interrogated, "what happened?"

"I hit Bwady with a wock," he said, his lip quivering.

"Well, I'm going to have to punish you for that," I said.

His big brown eyes filled with tears. "I can take it," Cooper said.

I had to turn around to hold back the laughter. It was tough to discipline him after hearing that comment, but I knew it was important.

Parents lovingly direct and shape their kids through encouragement and discipline, and God does the same thing with His children. He reproves us because He loves us! The Lord doesn't want us to be spoiled and selfish but mature in our faith, walking on the right path.

It isn't fun to be corrected—but the benefits we gain from receiving God's loving discipline will be everlasting.

Discussion Starters:

* What's the purpose of discipline?

What are the benefits? How does the Lord discipline us?

** Does God's discipline range in severity? What are some examples from God's Word? From your own life?

Lifeline:

Is God disciplining you in an area of your life? Take some time to pray for the strength to submit to God's authority today.

Virtual Reality

the WORD | Revelation 4:1-3

"After these things I looked, and behold, a door standing open in heaven, and the first voice which I had heard, like the sound of a trumpet speaking with me, said, 'Come up here, and I will show you what must take place after these things.' Immediately I was in the Spirit; and behold, a throne was standing in heaven, and One sitting on the throne. And He who was sitting was like a jasper stone and a sardius in appearance; and there was a rainbow around the throne, like an emerald in appearance."

the Message

As human beings, we have an unquenchable spirit of adventure and exploration inside us. We're always longing to turn a corner and unexpectedly tumble into another world through a black hole in outer space, the doorway of a wardrobe, or a rabbit hole.

Virtual reality creates technological rabbit holes that will allow you to tumble into three-dimensional computer worlds. Have you always wanted to explore outer space, discover new worlds, and battle alien enemies? With a pair of goggles and some pocket change, you'll be able to do all that and more. Virtual reality leads you to feel as if you're living inside a vision. Only once the time has run out and the goggles are off, the real world is always waiting outside.

The apostle John's adventure into his own "virtual reality" was incredibly different. He saw a real doorway in his dreams, and, through that opening, he saw unbelievable new worlds. It was the adventure of a lifetime and beyond, and it was real—real for life today and for the distant tomorrow. Nineteen hundred years have passed since John received his heavenly vision, but it's still as relevant now as it was then. The future times John saw seem a lot like the times in which we live today. His words of warning should speak soberly to our morally corrupt generation, which continuously turns its back on God.

But for those of us who strive to follow Him, God's words of hope and encouragement have never been as needed and welcome as they are today.

Discussion Starters:

* What does today's glimpse through John's doorway of revelation tell us about God? About heaven?
** What do you think eternal life is going to be like?
*** How does knowing you'll spend eternity with God in heaven affect the way you live now? Why?

Lifeline:

Many people want to ignore the realities of heaven and hell. How can you live in the present yet still be aware that your eternal life in heaven is of utmost significance?

Love, Dad

the WORD | Revelation 5:9-10

"And they sang a new song, saying, 'Worthy are You to take the book and to break its seals; for You were slain, and purchased for God with Your blood men from every tribe and tongue and people and nation. You have made them to be a kingdom and priests to our God; and they will reign upon the earth.'"

the Message

Sophie was terribly inept at handling her money. All through high school and college, her dad bailed her out of financial trouble or extended an extra "line of credit" if she was short for the month. Once, while she was in college, Sophie bounced so many checks that the return check fees were quadruple the face value of the checks.

Things got better after she closed her checking account, but then Sophie got herself into a couple thousand dollars of credit card debt. Once again, when Sophie's dad found out, he gave his daughter money.

Even when she got older and wanted to invest in a piece of furniture and had only half the amount, a check from Dad would show up in the mail. Sometimes Sophie paid him back, but more often than not, when her birthday, Christmas, or another convenient holiday rolled around, she would find the remainder of her debt listed inside a card with a small note that said, "Debt forgiven. Love, Dad."

Sophie's dad was generous to a fault. He should have made his daughter own up to her debts. Good parents know that if they don't make their kids "face the music" once in a while, their children will become emotionally insecure and morally crippled. But good parents will also find ways to help their kids just when they need it the most.

That's how our heavenly Father treats us. He sent His Son, Jesus, to pay our sin-debt with His blood. It doesn't matter how many mistakes we make or how bad they are—if we ask God for forgiveness, He will erase our sin-debts, once and for all.

Discussion Starters:

• What does today's scripture mean by saying that Jesus "purchased" us by His blood?
•• What does it mean to have a sin-debt?
••• How does God make us face up to our mistakes while, at the same time, forgiving us?

Lifeline:

How can your family encourage each other to forgive from the heart, no matter how large the other person's debt is? At the same time, how can you help one another own up to mistakes?

He's Got Plans for You

"When the Lamb broke the fifth seal, I saw underneath the altar the souls of those who had been slain because of the word of God, and because of the testimony which they had maintained; and they cried out with a loud voice, saying, 'How long, O Lord, holy and true, will You refrain from judging and avenging our blood on those who dwell on the earth?'...And they were told that they should rest for a little while longer, until the number of their fellow servants and their brethren who were to be killed even as they had been, would be completed also."

the **Message**

In *The Scarlet Pimpernel*, an adventure story set in the late 1700s, an English nobleman and his friends work during the French Revolution to save the lives of French noblemen and their families who have been sentenced to death. Using disguises and clever schemes, the Pimpernel and his band smuggle the innocent out of Paris and on to safety in England.

At one point in the story, it looks as though the Pimpernel is going to be captured by French soldiers. Posing as an old woman driving a farm wagon (in which a family he's helping is hiding), he passes through a Paris gate. All seems well. But a few minutes later, a troop of French cavalry rides through that same gate in hot pursuit.

A spirited chase follows. Soon the Frenchmen overtake the Pimpernel, forcing his wagon to a halt. It seems his luck is finally gone.

It turns out, however, that these soldiers are actually part of the Pimpernel's band! Once again, the Pimpernel was in control of the situation the whole time, even when all appearances seemed to the contrary.

In today's scripture, Christian martyrs impatiently ask God why He hasn't yet avenged their terrible deaths. His answer, while it's a little hard for us to understand, indicates that appearances to the contrary, He is very much in control of the situation. Even when His people are dying, it's all somehow a part of His sovereign plan. And in the end, things will work out exactly as He intended.

Because we know He loves us, and that ultimately He is always in control, we can find comfort and hope even in the worst of times.

Discussion Starters:

• Why do we so often struggle to trust God's plan in our lives?
•• Practically speaking, how can we learn to place all our hope in Christ?

Lifeline:

Often we can see God's hand in circumstances only after the difficulty has already passed. Have each family member describe a time in which he or she saw how God worked through a trial *after* the event was over.

The Fountain of Youth

the WORD | Revelation 7:16-17

" They will hunger no longer, nor thirst anymore; nor will the sun beat down on them, nor any heat; for the Lamb in the center of the throne will be their shepherd, and will guide them to springs of the water of life; and God will wipe every tear from their eyes."

the Message

The earth was still deeply shrouded in mystery. In the eyes of the masses, most still thought the world was flat, its vast oceans running off the edges. It was a time of great thought, reform, adventure—and superstition.

Around the beginning of the sixteenth century, the famous Spanish explorer Juan Ponce de León embarked on the high seas once again to search for the island of Bimini. The Spanish crown had a lot of faith in him; he had a remarkable track record for discoveries. In 1493, he had accompanied Christopher Columbus on his second voyage to America. Then in 1508, he discovered and settled in Puerto Rico.

Twenty years after he traveled with Columbus to the New World, Ponce de León sailed westward again, seeking to add rich new lands to Spain. But supposedly by royal decree, he was commanded to expend a great portion of his energy toward discovering the island of Bimini, home of the legendary fountain of youth.

The story had it that the fountain's waters would restore an old person's vitality and strength forever. To the Spanish crown and Ponce de León, one sip was worth any risk. It was the quest for eternal youth.

As Christians, we've got something even better than a fountain of youth. When we get to heaven, Jesus will give us a fountain of eternal life. There, we'll experience true, complete joy and everlasting life as we celebrate an eternal union with our heavenly Father.

People are constantly trying to extend their lives—through diets, exercise, vitamins, and medicine. There's nothing wrong with trying to live longer, healthier lives, but we should be concentrating on things that last—namely, our relationship with God, which will really lead us to the waters of life.

Discussion Starters:

• What are the "springs of the water of life" to which the Bible refers?

•• What are some modern-day quests to find a "fountain of youth"?

••• Today's passage in Revelation offers a glimpse through heaven's gates. What else do you think heaven will be like?

Lifeline:

Focus on your relationship with God. It's the only thing that'll last.

Woe, Woe, Woe!

the WORD | Revelation 8:13

"Then I looked, and I heard an eagle flying in midheaven, saying with a loud voice, 'Woe, woe, woe to those who dwell on the earth, because of the remaining blasts of the trumpet of the three angels who are about to sound!' "

the Message

For weeks Mindy, a 16-year-old Missouri teen, had dreamed of getting a phone call from Jake, the handsome running back on the high school football team. On Saturday morning, the phone rang.

"Want to go out tonight, Mindy?" Jake asked, his deep voice booming.

Mindy's heart pounded. She knew Jake's reputation with girls was shaky at best, but how could she pass up this opportunity? "Yeah! I'd love to," Mindy told him, ignoring the warning signal that went off in her head.

Jake picked her up and told Mindy they were going to a movie. But when they arrived at the theater, he said he didn't like any of the shows that were playing. "We'll go to the lake instead. Okay?" Jake told Mindy.

Another warning sounded in Mindy's head, but she said, "Uh, sure."

"Lots of my friends will be there having bonfires," Jake assured her.

But when they arrived at the lake, it was dark and desolate. Mindy's eyes grew large with worry, but Jake said they'd only sit and talk.

Again, the alarm sounded—louder this time but she agreed to stay.

Jake leaned over Mindy, and she shrank back. "Relax. It's just a kiss," he said. Another alarm rang in her head, but she kissed him back. Soon things heated up, and the kiss went much further than Mindy had intended.

Two months later, Mindy took a pregnancy test and realized her biggest fear had come true. She was carrying Jake's baby.

God fills our minds and His Word with warnings designed to lead us in the right direction. Mindy ignored God's warning voice and ended up pregnant. The book of Revelation depicts what will ultimately happen to those who don't heed God's warnings to turn back to Him. Someday, wayward people will undergo God's final, terrible judgment as described in Revelation 8. When it happens, they will wish they'd listened to God.

Pay attention to God's alarms. Don't let disaster creep up on you!

Discussion Starters:

* What warning signs have caused you to stop and think about something you were doing wrong?
** How does your commitment to Christ remove the fear from today's passage?

Lifeline:

Warnings given in the home help all of us avoid trumpets of disaster.

Whodunit?

"But in the days of the voice of the seventh angel, when he is about to sound, then the mystery of God is finished, as He preached to His servants the prophets."

the *Message*

Perry Mason always knew the answer. Of course, you had to wait through the entire episode for the suspense-filled courtroom conclusion before you finally knew "who-dunit." Perry Mason always had his mental machinery going full steam, and it was his calm logic that solved the mystery and made the criminals confess.

Among the ancient Greeks, mysteries were religious rites and ceremonies practiced by secret societies. Those who wanted to be a member of the societies (and who were selected) could be initiated and then would possess this special and coveted knowledge.

The mysteries of the Bible, however, can't be figured out on your own. And they can't be disclosed by other people. Only the Holy Spirit can reveal the secret things of God and enable us to understand some of the mysteries of His Word.

No matter how much we know, there'll always be things we won't be able to comprehend about God. Some issues just can't be resolved by human beings. So we can only do our best to explain the unexplainable—like, how the Trinity works or how Jesus can be both God and man. We can try to debate our nonbelieving friends over why a good, powerful God would allow evil in the world. But until the Lord reveals mysteries like these, we'll never know for sure if we've got it right.

The book of Revelation speaks of a time when all things will be made known. But until then, we've got to wait for the Holy Spirit to unveil the truth—and we must take the rest of it (what we don't understand) on faith.

Discussion Starters:

* Why can't we understand God's Word just by applying our own mental abilities or logically reasoning our way to an answer?
  What's the difference between having understanding and receiving revelation?
    ** What are some good ways to tackle the difficulties and questions you have about God's Word?
      *** What was one "unknown" the Holy Spirit revealed to His believers in the first-century church? (Hint: Look in the book of Acts.)

Lifeline:

Unless the Holy Spirit is working in an unbeliever's heart, most of the mysteries of the Bible won't seem logical or likely to him or her. If you have a pre-Christian friend, pray that God would make Himself known in your friend's heart, just as He reveals truth about Himself to you.

Anything but Boring

the WORD | Revelation 11:3-4

" 'And I will grant authority to my two witnesses, and they will prophesy for twelve hundred and sixty days, clothed in sackcloth.' These are the two olive trees and the two lampstands that stand before the Lord of the earth."

the Message

Robyn was no stranger to the church. As an infant, she had been consecrated at the marble baptismal of her family's church. As a child, she had sung the "Great Big Purple People Eater" song in Sunday school, gone on dozens of retreats at Camp Whatchamacallit, and daydreamed through a thousand sermons.

Then when she was 12, Robyn had to memorize the shorter catechism. It was the rite of passage into the ranks of church membership. Trembling and fearful, she recited them before the elders of the church.

She passed and became an official church member, but that wasn't important to her. To Robyn, everything about God was boring.

Her attitude soon changed. One night, Robyn's next-door neighbors invited her to their church down the street for a youth encounter weekend. Wanting to meet other kids her age, she went. She sat in the dark that night, electrified by the speaker and his message.

Filled with the Holy Spirit like the two witnesses in today's scripture, this speaker let life and laughter tumble out of him like a river. For the first time, Robyn saw someone who wasn't just talking about Jesus. The speaker was obviously someone who *knew* Jesus and lived by His power. Finally, she'd heard and met the gospel message—and it was anything but boring.

If you believe in Jesus, you *can* be a witness for Him. Once you accept Him into your heart, His Spirit lives in you. The Holy Spirit will give you the words to say and the courage to stand up for God.

Let your words and life reveal His power and vitality in you!

Discussion Starters:

• Who made a significant impact on your decision to follow Jesus Christ? Why was this person such a strong influence in your life?
•• Why is it so important to present the gospel to others?
••• What keeps you from witnessing for Jesus? How can you be a more effective witness?

Lifeline:

Have everyone in the family take turns presenting his or her testimony. Pretend this is the last opportunity to tell others about Jesus!

The Underdog

the **WORD** | Revelation 11:18

"And the nations were enraged, and Your wrath came, and the time came for the dead to be judged, and the time to reward to Your bond-servants the prophets and the saints and those who fear Your name, the small and the great, and to destroy those who destroy the earth."

the Message

People love the underdog. We cheer ourselves hoarse when a small, scrappy hometown team unexpectedly beats the strutting big-town players to win its way to the top of the heap. We roar with excitement when a bag-of-bones workhorse can outrun the finest racehorses in the world. We admire grit and verve and a stick-to-it heart. We have a passion for fairy tales come true—for Cinderella stories, which tell about those who go from rags to riches. It does us a world of good to see the humble and pure of heart win the day. We're *glad* David walloped Goliath. Our souls sing inside when we see great self-sacrifice, integrity, honesty, and justice.

Hurrah! The underdog overcame!

But did you ever think about the fact that Christians are the underdogs of this world?

We are. Both Jesus' words and the book of Revelation reveal that during the end times, we'll be treated as the lowest of the low. Christians will be persecuted, mocked, put through unbelievable trials, and even martyred because we claim Christ's name. But, as today's passage of scripture states, Christians will ultimately win. Nothing in all of creation will separate us from God's love (Romans 8:38-39). Eventually, God will judge everyone, and if we've accepted Him as our Savior, we'll be victorious.

It'll be an authentic rags-to-eternal-riches story.

Discussion Starters:

How can you hold on to the truth that one day all the injustices Christians face in this devil-dominated world will be reversed, and we'll reign victorious?

What do you think that day of judgment will be like? Which passages in Revelation add to your understanding?

A pebble hurled in faith can topple a giant any day. How can you fight back against society's worldly, anti-Christian "giant"?

Lifeline:

Which other people do you know who are despised and rejected by the world? How can your family better love those underdogs?

Grit Your Teeth

"And they overcame [the accuser] because of the blood of the Lamb and because of the word of their testimony, and they did not love their life even when faced with death."

the *Message*

The Kansas state motto proudly proclaims, *Ad astra per aspera*—"To the stars through hardship." It's a noble thought, but most people don't buy it. Sadly, most of us live by the world's motto, "Whoever has the most toys wins." If you have money and power, you've "made it." You've won.

Often it seems that those who have "made it"—the rich, popular, successful types— reach the stars just fine, without hardship. But a lot of times, those "successful" people are reaching for stars that will fade, not ones that will last forever.

Don't get discouraged if you feel as though you'll never succeed in the world's eyes. Your difficulties can actually be assets to your spiritual life. An old Spanish proverb says, "From a fallen tree, all make kindling." Hardship won't bring you any worldly good, but it can build character, strengthen family ties, and mature your faith.

Difficulty often brings spiritual gain.

But to find spiritual success, you must grit your teeth in the face of adversity and see obstacles as challenges, failures as opportunities. Sports psychologists call it mental toughness; God calls it faith.

The saints from Revelation had so much faith that they *lived* for eternal triumph. They didn't win in the world's eyes, but their spirits prevailed over "the accuser." These saints reached for the right stars—seeking to tell others about Jesus and please God in everything—and were willing to give up anything, even their lives, to gain heavenly victory.

It's not easy to place finding victory in God's eyes above winning on this earth. You need to have a long-term perspective, a ton of perseverance, and unshakable faith in God's promise of eternal glory.

Are you obsessed with obtaining what the world defines to be success? Which crown do you want? An earthly, flimsy Burger King crown or a solid, priceless one that lasts forever?

Discussion Starters:

* How can you focus solely on having eternal victory in Christ?
   ** What does it take to be successful and popular in your school, work place, or home? Do you place more importance on earthly "wins" or heavenly victories? Explain your answers.

Lifeline:

How can your family learn to keep a sense of humor when facing "failure"?

Bookmarked

the WORD | Revelation 13:16-17

"And he causes all, the small and the great, and the rich and the poor, and the free men and the slaves, to be given a mark on their right hand or on their forehead, and he provides that no one will be able to buy or to sell, except the one who has the mark, either the name of the beast or the number of his name."

the Message

Libraries have forged into the computer age, leaving behind a trail of index cards. The old card catalog indexes have been dumped for the neon glow of computer monitors that reference and cross-reference an array of newspapers, journals, films, music, microfiche, and books. The system then reveals important pieces of information about each item.

Library cards have followed suit. One swipe of the card's magnetic strip and the account appears on screen with a list of current information: which books the cardholder checked out, how many are overdue, how much the fine costs, and that person's personal history.

But not only libraries have become computerized. Almost all the merchandise we buy is marked with a bar code and scanned in a flash at the checkout counter. Entire inventories of nationwide chains like Wal-Mart are available to the company president via computer.

This computerized system has gotten so sophisticated that for tax and merchandising purposes, the government holds information on individuals and their bank accounts, too. These officials get the scoop on our lives through our social security numbers, bank card numbers, and personal identification numbers (PINs).

In the last 20 years, a significant marketing, banking, governing, and control system has been put into place. Now, I don't mean to be sensational, but I think this system will enable the future Antichrist to control all purchases and limit sales to those who bear his laser-tattooed mark on their hand or forehead. It's a terrifying thought, but don't be too concerned—the Bible already predicted this would happen.

As this system unfolds, keep reminding yourself that you belong to God. He'll be with you in all the days that lie ahead.

Discussion Starters:

* What does a mark signify?
  ** What are some spiritual marks of being a Christian? What physical symbols do Christians mark themselves with to represent their beliefs?
  *** If we were physically marked when we accepted Jesus, would it affect the way we acted or how we represented Him? Why or why not?

Lifeline:

Pray that you'll be so close to Jesus Christ that others will know you're a Christian—even without being physically marked.

The Golden Door

the **WORD** | Revelation 14:12-13

"Here is the perseverance of the saints who keep the commandments of God and their faith in Jesus. And I heard a voice from heaven, saying, 'Write, "Blessed are the dead who die in the Lord from now on!"' 'Yes,' says the Spirit, 'so that they may rest from their labors, for their deeds follow with them.'"

the **Message**

She was born in 1886. In portraits she stands alone, crowned and regal, with lamp in hand. Her father was Frédéric-Auguste Bartholdi, a Frenchman. But her birthplace was America, and in some American hearts, she still reigns. She is called the Mother of Exiles—the Statue of Liberty.

At her dedication, a sonnet by Emma Lazarus was inscribed on a plaque, which reads in part:

"Keep, ancient lands, your storied pomp!" cried she
With silent lips. "Give me your tired, your poor,
Your huddled masses yearning to breathe free,
The wretched refuse of your teeming shore.
Send these, the homeless, tempest-tossed to me,
I lift my lamp beside the golden door."

She holds her beacon 151 feet aloft to welcome refugees to the land of the free and the home of the brave. She welcomes them home.

Life can be wearisome, and growing up can be one of the most tiring aspects of life. It's hard work to be a Christian in a sometimes ugly, nonbelieving world. But when you feel like giving up, remember: This world is not where you belong.

One day, those of us who have yearned and dreamed and waited all our lives to reach the shores of God's kingdom will find our way to the golden door. The Prince of the Exiles, with lamp in hand, will welcome us home. As the book of Revelation states, we will "rest from our labors" because in Jesus Christ, we'll finally find peace, hope, and joy in our *true* home—heaven.

Discussion Starters:

* What does it mean to be an exile?
** Why do you think so many tens of thousands of families immigrated to the United States in the nineteenth century?
*** The Bible frequently says that a Christian's true home is heaven. What does that mean?
**** Why does Revelation say we will "rest from our labors"?

Lifeline:

Do you feel more "at home" living on earth than you should?

the **WORD** | *Revelation 15:3-4*

"And they sang, 'Great and marvelous are Your works, O Lord God, the Almighty; righteous and true are Your ways, King of the nations! Who will not fear, O Lord, and glorify Your name? For You alone are holy; for all the nations will come and worship before You, for Your righteous acts have been revealed.'"

the **Message**

I know it's hard to believe, but thousands of people think Elvis Presley is still alive. Some folks say they spotted him in New York City at Balducci's Grocery in Greenwich Village. Others claim that Elvis frequents the Piggly Wiggly in Manhattan, Kansas. It seems as if every week, the tabloids run a new article on yet another Elvis sighting.

Well, I say that if Elvis is alive (which is a mighty long shot), he's living "high on the hog" on profits from Graceland, his previous home and grave site. If you haven't been there, it's worth the trip to Memphis, Tennessee. At the time I'm writing this, tours leave every five minutes from 8:30 A.M. to 5:00 P.M. There are four tours available: $8.00 for Graceland mansion, $4.50 for the Elvis Car Museum, $4.25 to see his private airplanes, and $2.25 for Sincerely Elvis, a small museum that stores his personal items. You can also get a package deal to see all four museums for $16.00. Graceland does great business because there are a bazillion Elvis worshipers still around.

But Elvis isn't the only person who gets false glory. Many movie stars, musicians, supermodels, and multimillionaires bask in the riches, praise, and worship they get from countless numbers of people worldwide.

The glory these stars receive is fleeting, though—nothing compared to the worship Jesus will get when His people gather together to praise Him. That heavenly scene will be indescribable. Imagine seeing God in all His awesome power, holiness, and love. No teen idol or rock star will ever bring you the lasting joy and victory that come with praising God.

Who gets more of your attention? The stars who gaze from posters on your wall or the living God?

Discussion Starters:

- Why do people worship famous stars? What's the pitfall in worshiping the created rather than the Creator?
- What is worship? Why is it necessary to your faith?
- What are some of your favorite ways to worship God? Why?

Lifeline:

Plan a family worship service one Sunday. Include everyone's favorite ways to worship, whether it's through song, silence, or Scripture reading.

"That'll Be $109, Please"

the WORD | Revelation 16:5-7

"And I heard the angel of the waters saying, 'Righteous are You, who are and who were, O Holy One, because You judged these things; for they poured out the blood of saints and prophets, and You have given them blood to drink. They deserve it.' And I heard the altar saying, 'Yes, O Lord God, the Almighty, true and righteous are Your judgments.'"

the Message

Jessica sat in the Sumner County courthouse, her hands clasped firmly together to keep them from trembling. There was no backing out this time. She'd already pushed back her court date once to accommodate her travel schedule to and from college. Jessica was just hoping the judge would reduce the amount on her speeding ticket and waive the mark against her license. After all, it was her first speeding ticket. Hopefully she'd only have to pay a small fine and watch one of the "gore" films on reckless driving.

The judge called her up to the bench. He peered through his glasses at her, raised his white, bushy eyebrows, and sharply queried, "Guilty or not guilty?" Jessica meekly croaked out, "Guilty."

The bailiff escorted her out of the courtroom, and Jessica found herself handing $109 to the cashier. She drove the speed limit on her way home.

Because of our sin, we were destined to appear in a type of "divine courtroom." With weak knees and raspy voices, we came to God, begging His forgiveness. But unlike in a courtroom scene, we never had to worry whether God would forgive our sins. He wiped our record clean as soon as we humbly believed in Jesus.

God makes His truly amazing grace readily available to anyone who asks forgiveness for his or her sins. Sadly, though, not everyone accepts His offer. Today's passage in Revelation depicts those who not only rejected God's grace, but who also persecuted His prophets and saints. As this scripture shows, God's grace is abundant—but to those who repeatedly reject it, His final judgment will be severe.

Discussion Starters:

• Why does God graciously choose to forgive us?
•• Why is His punishment so severe in Revelation?
••• When have you experienced God's saving grace? Did you feel you deserved to be forgiven? Why or why not?

Lifeline:

Discuss together the meaning of grace. Talk about the difference between God's forgiveness and people's forgiveness. Remember—God forgives and *forgets*. If you accept His grace, you're clean in His sight.

He Will Overcome

the WORD | Revelation 17:14

"These will wage war against the Lamb, and the Lamb will overcome them, because He is Lord of lords and King of kings, and those who are with Him are the called and chosen and faithful."

the Message

It was 1836, and about 180 dirty, tired soldiers were stationed in the Alamo, a mission near San Antonio, Texas. The odds seemed hopeless. The men faced a Mexican army of thousands. The only things these Texans possessed were courage and determination.

Knowing the inevitable slaughter that lay ahead, Texas commander William B. Travis drew his sword and slashed a deep line in the southwest Texas sand. Each fighter who crossed the line knew he'd die if he stayed to fight. All but one made the gallant move.

The Texans believed that even death was not too high a price to pay for their sons', grandsons', and families' futures. And it wasn't. Though the Alamo fell, Texas later gained her freedom in the Battle of San Jacinto. In part because the freedom fighters possessed such courage, the people of Texas eventually enjoyed freedom and ensuing membership in the United States of America.

Do *you* know how to fight?

Now, more than a century later, the well-entrenched army of pornography, violence, drugs and alcohol, rape, and lewd movies and TV programs surrounds Christians as we fight to be free from Satan's ever-tightening grip on earth. If we're following Christ, we will step across the line and fight for God.

But the cost will be high.

Friends will laugh, girlfriends will turn their backs, and Saturday nights will be lonely as you battle for Christ. But hold on to this: Jesus will come back and redeem you. He'll reward your faithfulness to Him.

Today, Christians are sacrificing, suffering, and even dying for their faith. But Revelation states that someday—maybe soon—"the Lamb" will overcome Satan and his army, and the world's forces of darkness will be crushed.

Will you be strong and faithful enough to fight on God's side until He claims the victory?

Discussion Starters:

• Why must we as Christians be prepared to fight for our faith?
•• How can we get ready for spiritual battle?
••• How will you step across the line for God this week? Be specific.

Lifeline:

Though we live in the Alamo, we'll see the victory of San Jacinto!

Black Thursday

the **WORD** | Revelation 18:14-17

"The fruit you long for has gone from you, and all things that were luxurious and splendid have passed away from you and men will no longer find them. The merchants of these things, who became rich from her, will stand at a distance because of the fear of her torment, weeping and mourning, saying, 'Woe, woe, the great city, she who was clothed in fine linen and purple and scarlet, and adorned with gold and precious stones and pearls; for in one hour such great wealth has been laid waste!' "

the *Message*

In 1918, the United States emerged from World War I virtually untouched. Not only that, but most of western Europe was deeply in debt to her. As industry flourished and the 1920s roared in, a feverish attitude of prosperity and affluence swept the country. From mob bosses to shoe-shine boys, big spenders to conservative investors, people were speculating wildly in the stock market, looking to cash in on the boom. By late summer of 1929, millionaires were being made overnight as stock prices rose to unprecedented heights. But reality eventually hit the New York Stock Exchange.

On Thursday, October 24, 1929, an unprecedented 16 million shares traded hands, sending the stock market into an unstoppable decline. Wealthy financiers moved quickly to obtain large blocks of shares—hoping to abate the crisis. But the market crashed the following Tuesday, and when the dust had settled, $15 billion worth of stock value had vaporized. Vast fortunes and small savings alike were wiped out.

Thousands of people in the 1920s invested their money poorly. The Bible says millions more in the end times will foolishly invest their souls. They'll buy into the ungodliness of the world. At first, these misguided people will find wealth and power in their sinful investments. But as the book of Revelation says, in one hour their glory will lie in ruins.

Think before you buy into the temporary things the world has to offer. Instead, invest your time, money, and soul in God. He'll multiply your investments and give you something far more important than wealth—eternal life.

Discussion Starters:

* Why is your investment in Jesus in some ways a no-risk investment in the end?
** Why is it also costly to build a relationship with Him?
*** What spiritual investments are you making in your life?

Lifeline:

Read Matthew 16:24. What's the cost of discipleship? Be specific.

The Bride

the **WORD** | Revelation 19:7-9

" 'Let us rejoice and be glad and give the glory to Him, for the marriage of the Lamb has come and His bride has made herself ready.' It was given to her to clothe herself in fine linen, bright and clean; for the fine linen is the righteous acts of the saints. Then he said to me, 'Write, "Blessed are those who are invited to the marriage supper of the Lamb." ' And he said to me, 'These are true words of God.' "

the *Message*

It happened. My "little" girl Jamie (who is now 5'6" and 27 years old) made the most graceful walk of her life down the wedding aisle, into the arms of the only boy she ever loved. It was a dream come true. The beauty, excitement, and splendor that surrounded that awesome walk were indescribable.

Walking the road of purity wasn't always easy for Jamie, though.

One summer when she was in junior high, she and I and her little sister, Courtney, were driving to town. I was happily reminiscing about the wonderful summer we had shared and all the fun stuff we had done.

Or so I thought.

Jamie just stared out the window. After a few tense moments, she said, "My friends can see any movie they want, and I can't. They can go to all the parties, and I can't. You're mean. You don't let me do anything."

I pondered this, then said, "Jamie, my first job isn't to be your friend, but to be your dad. If you don't like me for the next few years, that's okay. Someday when you get married, I want you to be able to walk down the aisle as a pure young woman. Then I hope you'll say you love your dad." Jamie's dislike for me didn't last long. Soon after eighth grade, she realized she was making valuable sacrifices. On her wedding day, she had no regrets. Now, her honeymoon with her husband will last a lifetime.

Her story is wonderful, but it's a mere shadow of the real wedding walk that God's children will take when we see Christ face-to-face. You are Christ's bride. Make every effort to pursue purity and righteousness.

The sacrifice will be well worth it.

Discussion Starters:

• What do you think it will be like to meet Christ face-to-face?
•• Why does Jesus call us—His believers—His "bride"?
••• What sacrifices are you making in your life right now to live for Him?

Lifeline:

Look around your house. Is there anything that's getting in the way of your family's pursuit of righteousness for the wedding day? If so, toss it.

All Access

the WORD | Revelation 20:12-15

"And I saw the dead, the great and the small, standing before the throne, and books were opened; and another book was opened, which is the book of life; and the dead were judged from the things which were written in the books, according to their deeds. And the sea gave up the dead which were in it, and death and Hades gave up the dead which were in them; and they were judged every one of them according to their deeds. Then death and Hades were thrown into the lake of fire. This is the second death, the lake of fire. And if anyone's name was not found written in the book of life, he was thrown into the lake of fire."

the Message

As a camp director, I've had the privilege of befriending a lot of famous Christian artists. My kids love that part of my job.

"Dad! Can you get us backstage passes to the concert?" they plead. They know that since I'm friends with various artists, I can usually get them "all access" passes to see the stars after the show.

When that happens, my kids become the envy of all their friends, who know that there's no earthly way to get backstage and meet the musicians without a pass.

Not only have my kids been able to meet musicians, but my job once enabled them to get a similar "all access" pass into the Atlanta Braves' locker room. I'll never forget the wide-eyed look on my two sons' faces (then ages 8 and 10) as they sat in the room, listening while I addressed the Braves' chapel service. Brady's and Cooper's eyes got even wider when one of the star players walked over to them, shook their hands, and introduced himself.

Meeting the stars is exciting, but it's nothing compared to what it'll be like to "walk backstage" and hang with Jesus. Someday, every worldly superstar will yearn to have the pass you possess—the relationship you have with Christ, which puts your name in the book of life and allows you to enter heaven. Time is short. Don't wait to tell your friends about God.

Discussion Starters:

• How does God provide everyone the opportunity to have access to Him?
•• Why is absolute justice so important to God? Why can't everyone—or at least those who've led a good life—have their name in the book of life?

Lifeline:

If you knew how to get a backstage pass to meet your favorite star, you would probably tell your friends how they could get one, too. So why wouldn't you tell them how to get an "all access" pass into heaven?

No Pain

the WORD | Revelation 21:3-4

"And I heard a loud voice from the throne, saying, 'Behold, the tabernacle of God is among men, and He will dwell among them, and they shall be His people, and God Himself will be among them, and He will wipe away every tear from their eyes; and there will no longer be any death; there will no longer be any mourning, or crying, or pain; the first things have passed away.'"

the Message

Tim's funeral was one of the most difficult days of my life. *Why did it have to be Tim, God?* I kept asking the Lord.

My dear friend Tim was only 19. We laughed together, went fishing, and talked about the struggles of being a teenager. Tim smoked a little pot in high school and tried LSD once.

It was one time too many.

From that day on, Tim's mind became his enemy. He began having violent, haunting flashbacks. They must have been excruciating because soon after he experimented with LSD, Tim decided he couldn't bear life any longer. He grabbed his father's shotgun, loaded it, aimed it at his own head, and pulled the trigger. One thundering blast later, it was all over.

At the funeral, his druggie friends acted aloof and in control.

"I guess Tim couldn't handle it. We can," they said to me, scoffing.

What a waste, I thought. *What a pitiful waste. Why can't his friends learn from this? Why did Tim feel he had to take his life?*

Why is there so much pain in the world? Last spring, my friend Dennis and his baby were killed by a drunk driver. Rachel's husband left her after 22 years of marriage. Julia died of a rare heart disease just after her 16th birthday. And you've probably suffered as well.

Fortunately, this passage from Revelation offers hope. Scripture tells us the pain of this world is temporary. Someday, God will wipe all the tears from our faces. We'll be full of smiles and joy—all the time.

Be encouraged. God will fulfill that promise.

Discussion Starters:

* How does the world handle grief? Why should Christians handle death differently? Do they?
** What do you think causes God the most grief? Explain your answer.

Lifeline:

In this passage from Revelation, God offers one of many promises of hope to His people. Discuss: Where else in the Bible does God give His children encouraging promises? How did those biblical figures hold on to that hope?

Freiheit!

"There will no longer be any curse; and the throne of God and of the Lamb will be in it, and His bond servants will serve Him; they will see His face, and His name will be on their foreheads. And there will no longer be any night; and they will not have need of the light of a lamp nor the light of the sun, because the Lord God will illumine them; and they will reign forever and ever."

the **Message**

The infamous Berlin Wall was built in 1961 to stem the flood of refugees streaming from Communist East Berlin into the west after the Allies defeated Germany in World War II. But many people, hungry for freedom, still continued to risk their lives trying to cross the border.

Thirty years later, the world gasped in disbelief when democratic reform swept through the Eastern bloc countries, and the wall crumbled to deafening cries of *freiheit!* People everywhere cried out, "Free at last!"

You may not lack physical freedom, but as a fallen young man or woman, your soul is in bondage, longing to be freed from sin.

My friend "Ben" could tell you that. Ben, a talented young athlete I've been close to for the past four years, recently called to tell me he was fasting and praying that that particular day would be the day he would break free from the grip of pornography forever.

"Today," Ben said, "I no longer want to stop looking at those pictures. I will to quit. There's a big difference between willing to and just wanting to do something."

Ben's fight was too big for him to fight on his own. So he fasted and prayed. With God's help, Ben was released from his sin.

Although God has the power to free us from our sins, the reality is that we're still fallen people. We continue to mess up, think bad thoughts, lie, steal, and hurt God. Fortunately, though, the Bible tells us that one day all of God's children will be freed from sin forever. We will be united with the Lord and enjoy perfect communion with Him in heaven.

Discussion Starters:

* What did the Berlin Wall represent? How do you think it felt to live on the East (Communist) side of the wall?
** How does sin enslave us?
*** How does God give us freedom from sin each day? How will He give us ultimate freedom in heaven?

Lifeline:

Discuss some ways your family can minister to those who have lost their freedom (for example, prison inmates, hospital patients, or nursing home residents).

the 6-month challenge

Already beaten the 30-day challenge? Take this on.

We've chosen 172 Bible verses to give you a firm foundation of core New Testament scriptures. The challenge is to memorize one verse a week for six months. Of course, you could go one better and take two a week, or really hit the bull's eye with three verses a week. But give yourself six months to get familiar with the practice. We think you'll be glad you did. Like Psalm 119 says, when you're meditating on God's word, some amazing changes take place.

"For as [a man] thinks within himself, so he is."—Proverbs 23:7

Think about it: to know the Bible is to know God's thoughts. And if you know God's thoughts, you'll know (and be able to do) God's will. But if your mind is captured by trash, you'll think and do things that bring grief and regret. The things that capture your mind will stay with you.

For example, in second grade, I memorized a little poem, four lines long. It was about a mushroom and an oak tree. I'll never forget it. In fourth grade, I spent about an hour memorizing a few verses from the Sermon on the Mount—and it still comes to mind 40 years later! Regretfully, in high school, I heard a recording by a music group that rivals some of the street rap of today. Though I only heard it a few times, I still remember those raunchy lyrics.

the formula

There's no single, correct formula for memorizing Scripture. But it works *far* better when you do it together as a family. Here are a few ways to make it more effective:
1. Set a goal, pick a time to memorize together during the week, and stick to it!
2. Start by talking casually about the day. ("How was your day today?" "What was the highlight?" "Did anything unusual happen?" "What did you learn?" etc.)
3. After chatting, begin the Scripture memory and end with prayer.

Remember—it's about however you do it best. And above all, have fun.

1. Matthew 5:11-12

" 'Blessed are you when people insult you and persecute you, and falsely say all kinds of evil against you because of Me. Rejoice and be glad, for your reward in heaven is great, for in the same way they persecuted the prophets who were before you.' "

2. Matthew 5:16

" 'Let your light shine before men in such a way that they may see your good works, and glorify your Father who is in heaven.' "

3. Matthew 5:27-28

" 'You have heard that it was said, "You shall not commit adultery"; but I say to you that everyone who looks at a woman with lust for her has already committed adultery with her in his heart.' "

4. Matthew 6:22

" 'The lamp of the body is the eye; if therefore your eye is clear, your whole body will be full of light.' "

5. Matthew 6:23

" 'But if your eye is bad, your whole body will be full of darkness. If therefore the light that is in you is darkness, how great is the darkness!' "

6. Matthew 6:28-29

" 'And why are you worried about clothing? Observe how the lilies of the field grow; they do not toil nor do they spin, yet I say to you that not even Solomon in all his glory clothed himself like one of these.' "

7. Matthew 6:33

" 'But seek first His kingdom and His righteousness, and all these things will be added to you.' "

8. Matthew 7:2-3

" 'For in the way you judge, you will be judged; and by your standard of measure, it will be measured to you. Why do you look at the speck that is in your brother's eye, but do not notice the log that is in your own eye?' "

9. Matthew 7:13

" 'Enter through the narrow gate; for the gate is wide and the way is broad that leads to destruction, and there are many who enter through it.' "

10. Matthew 16:24-25

"Then Jesus said to His disciples, 'If anyone wishes to come after Me, he must deny himself, and take up his cross and follow Me. For whoever wishes to save his life will lose it; but whoever loses his life for My sake will find it.' "

11. Matthew 18:3

" '…Truly I say to you, unless you are converted and become like children, you will not enter the kingdom of heaven.' "

12. Matthew 18:12

" 'What do you think? If any man has a hundred sheep, and one of them has gone astray, does he not leave the ninety-nine on the mountains and go and search for the one that is straying?' "

13. Matthew 19:24

" 'Again I say to you, it is easier for a camel to go through the eye of a needle, than for a rich man to enter the kingdom of God.' "

14. Matthew 22:36-38

" 'Teacher, which is the great commandment in the Law?' And He said to him, 'You shall love the Lord your God with all your heart, and with all your soul, and with all your mind. This is the great and foremost commandment.' "

15. Matthew 22:39-40

" 'The second is like it, "You shall love your neighbor as yourself." On these two commandments depend the whole Law and the Prophets.' "

16. Matthew 24:44

" 'For this reason you also must be ready; for the Son of Man is coming at an hour when you do not think He will.' "

17. Matthew 25:40

" 'The King will answer and say to them, "Truly I say to you, to the extent that you did it to one of these brothers of Mine, even the least of them, you did it to Me.' "

18. Matthew 26:26-28

"Jesus took some bread...and said, 'Take, eat; this is My body.' And when He had taken a cup and given thanks, He gave it to them, saying, 'Drink from it, all of you; for this is My blood of the covenant, which is poured out for many for forgiveness of sins.' "

19. Mark 8:34

"And He summoned the crowd with His disciples, and said to them, 'If anyone wishes to come after Me, he must deny himself, and take up his cross and follow Me.' "

20. Mark 8:35

" 'For whoever wishes to save his life will lose it, but whoever loses his life for My sake and the gospel's will save it.' "

21. Mark 8:36-37

" 'For what does it profit a man to gain the whole world, and forfeit his soul? For what will a man give in exchange for his soul?' "

22. Mark 8:38

" 'For whoever is ashamed of Me and My words in this adulterous and sinful genera-tion, the Son of Man will also be ashamed of him when He comes in the glory of His Father with the holy angels.' "

23. Mark 9:42

" 'Whoever causes one of these little ones who believe to stumble, it would be better for him if, with a heavy millstone hung around his neck, he had been cast into the sea.' "

24. Mark 10:6-7

" 'But from the beginning of creation, God made them male and female. For this reason a man shall leave his father and mother.' "

25. Mark 10:8-9

" 'And the two shall become one flesh; so they are no longer two, but one flesh. What therefore God has joined together, let no man separate.' "

26. Mark 10:43-44

" 'But it is not this way among you, but whoever wishes to become great among you shall be your servant, and whoever wishes to be first among you shall be slave of all.' "

27. Mark 10:45

" 'For even the Son of Man did not come to be served, but to serve, and to give His life a ransom for many.' "

28. Mark 11:24

" 'Therefore I say to you, all things for which you pray and ask, believe that you have received them, and they will be granted you.' "

29. Mark 11:25

" 'Whenever you stand praying, forgive, if you have anything against anyone, so that your Father who is in heaven will also for-give you your transgressions.' "

30. Mark 12:30

"'And you shall love the Lord your God with all your heart, and with all your soul, and with all your mind, and with all your strength.'"

31. Mark 12:31

"The second is this, 'You shall love your neighbor as yourself.' There is no other commandment greater than these."

32. Mark 14:61

"Again the high priest was questioning Him, and saying to Him, 'Are You the Christ, the Son of the Blessed One?'"

33. Mark 14:62

"And Jesus said, 'I am; and you shall see the Son of Man sitting at the right hand of Power, and coming with the clouds of heaven.'"

34. Mark 16:15

"And He said to them, 'Go into all the world and preach the gospel to all creation.'"

35. Mark 16:16

"'He who has believed and has been baptized shall be saved; but he who has disbelieved shall be condemned.'"

36. Luke 2:52

"And Jesus kept increasing in wisdom and stature, and in favor with God and men."

37. Luke 6:31

"'Treat others the same way you want them to treat you.'"

38. Luke 6:38

"'Give, and it will be given to you. They will pour into your lap a good measure, pressed down, shaken together, and running over. For by your standard of measure it will be measured to you in return.'"

39. Luke 9:62

"But Jesus said to him, 'No one, after putting his hand to the plow and looking back, is fit for the kingdom of God.'"

40. Luke 11:9-10

"'So I say to you, ask, and it will be given to you; seek, and you will find; knock, and it will be opened to you. For everyone who asks, receives; and he who seeks, finds; and to him who knocks, it will be opened.'"

41. Luke 11:17

"But He knew their thoughts and said to them, 'Any kingdom divided against itself is laid waste; and a house divided against itself falls.'"

42. Luke 14:27

"'Whoever does not carry his own cross and come after Me cannot be My disciple.'"

43. Luke 14:28

"'For which one of you, when he wants to build a tower, does not first sit down and calculate the cost to see if he has enough to complete it?'"

44. Luke 15:7

"'I tell you that in the same way, there will be more joy in heaven over one sinner who repents than over ninety-nine righteous persons who need no repentance.'"

45. John 1:1-2

"In the beginning was the Word, and the Word was with God, and the Word was God. He was in the beginning with God."

46. John 1:3-4

"All things came into being through Him, and apart from Him nothing came into being that has come into being. In Him was life, and the life was the Light of men."

47. John 1:5
"The Light shines in the darkness, and the darkness did not comprehend it."

48. John 1:6-8
"There came a man sent from God, whose name was John. He came as a witness, to testify about the Light, so that all might believe through him. He was not the Light, but he came to testify about the Light."

49. John 1:9-10
"There was the true Light which, coming into the world, enlightens every man. He was in the world, and the world was made through Him, and the world did not know Him."

50. John 1:11-12
"He came to His own, and those who were His own did not receive Him. But as many as received Him, to them He gave the right to become children of God, even to those who believe in His name."

51. John 3:3
"Jesus answered and said to him, 'Truly, truly, I say to you, unless one is born again he cannot see the kingdom of God.'"

52. John 3:16
"'For God so loved the world, that He gave His only begotten Son, that whoever believes in Him shall not perish, but have eternal life.'"

53. John 6:35
"Jesus said to them, 'I am the bread of life; he who comes to Me will not hunger, and he who believes in Me will never thirst.'"

54. John 6:40
"'For this is the will of My Father, that everyone who beholds the Son and believes in Him will have eternal life, and I Myself will raise him up on the last day.'"

55. John 8:32
"'And you will know the truth, and the truth will make you free.'"

56. John 8:34, 36
"Jesus answered them, 'Truly, truly, I say to you, everyone who commits sin is the slave of sin.... So if the Son makes you free, you will be free indeed.'"

57. John 10:10
"'The thief comes only to steal and kill and destroy; I come that they may have life, and have it abundantly.'"

58. John 11:25
"Jesus said to her, 'I am the resurrection and the life; he who believes in Me will live even if he dies.'"

59. John 13:14
"'If I then, the Lord and the Teacher, washed your feet, you also ought to wash one another's feet.'"

60. John 14:2
"'In My Father's house are many dwelling places; if it were not so, I would have told you; for I go to prepare a place for you.'"

61. John 14:6
"Jesus said to him, 'I am the way, and the truth, and the life; no one comes to the Father but through Me.'"

62. John 14:13
"'Whatever you ask in My name, that will I do, so that the Father may be glorified in the Son.'"

63. John 14:16
"'I will ask the Father, and He will give you another Helper, that He may be with you forever.'"

64. John 14:17

" 'That is the Spirit of truth, whom the world cannot receive, because it does not see Him or know Him, but you know Him because He abides with you and will be in you.' "

65. John 14:18-19

" 'I will not leave you as orphans; I will come to you. After a little while the world will no longer see Me, but you will see Me; because I live, you will live also.' "

66. John 14:20

" 'In that day you will know that I am in My Father, and you in Me, and I in you.' "

67. John 14:21

" 'He who has My commandments and keeps them is the one who loves Me; and he who loves Me will be loved by My Father, and I will love him and will disclose Myself to him.' "

68. John 15:4

" 'Abide in Me, and I in you. As the branch cannot bear fruit of itself unless it abides in the vine, so neither can you unless you abide in Me.' "

69. John 15:5

" 'I am the vine, you are the branches; he who abides in Me and I in him, he bears much fruit, for apart from Me you can do nothing.' "

70. John 16:33

" 'These things I have spoken to you, so that in Me you may have peace. In the world you have tribulation, but take courage; I have overcome the world.' "

71. John 20:29

"Jesus said to him, 'Because you have seen Me, have you believed? Blessed are they who did not see, and yet believed.' "

72. Acts 1:8

" 'But you will receive power when the Holy Spirit has come upon you; and you shall be My witnesses both in Jerusalem, and in all Judea and Samaria, and even to the remotest part of the earth.' "

73. Romans 1:16-17

"For I am not ashamed of the gospel, for it is the power of God for salvation to every-one who believes, to the Jew first and also to the Greek. For in it the righteousness of God is revealed from faith to faith; as it is written, 'But the righteous man shall live by faith.' "

74. Romans 3:23

"For all have sinned and fall short of the glory of God."

75. Romans 5:1

"Therefore, having been justified by faith, we have peace with God through our Lord Jesus Christ."

76. Romans 5:3-4

"And not only this, but we also exult in our tribulations, knowing that tribulation brings about perseverance; and perseverance, proven character; and proven character, hope."

77. Romans 5:5

"And hope does not disappoint, because the love of God has been poured out within our hearts through the Holy Spirit who was given to us."

78. Romans 5:8

"But God demonstrates His own love toward us, in that while we were yet sinners, Christ died for us."

79. Romans 6:1-2

"What shall we say then? Are we to continue in sin so that grace may increase? May it never be! How shall we who died to sin still live in it?"

80. Romans 6:17

"But thanks be to God that though you were slaves of sin, you became obedient from the heart to that form of teaching to which you were committed."

81. Romans 6:23

"For the wages of sin is death, but the free gift of God is eternal life in Christ Jesus our Lord."

82. Romans 8:1

"Therefore there is now no condemnation for those who are in Christ Jesus."

83. Romans 8:6

"For the mind set on the flesh is death, but the mind set on the Spirit is life and peace."

84. Romans 8:14

"For all who are being led by the Spirit of God, these are sons of God."

85. Romans 8:31-32

"What then shall we say to these things? If God is for us, who is against us? He who did not spare His own Son, but delivered Him over for us all, how will He not also with Him freely give us all things?"

86. Romans 8:38-39

"For I am convinced that neither death, nor life, nor angels, nor principalities, nor things present, nor things to come, nor powers, nor height, nor depth, nor any other created thing, will be able to separate us from the love of God, which is in Christ Jesus our Lord."

87. Romans 10:9

"That if you confess with your mouth Jesus as Lord, and believe in your heart that God raised Him from the dead, you will be saved."

88. Romans 10:10

"For with the heart a person believes, resulting in righteousness, and with the mouth he confesses, resulting in salvation."

89. Romans 12:1

"Therefore I urge you, brethren, by the mercies of God, to present your bodies a living and holy sacrifice, acceptable to God, which is your spiritual service of worship."

90. Romans 12:2

"And do not be conformed to this world, but be transformed by the renewing of your mind, so that you may prove what the will of God is, that which is good and acceptable and perfect."

91. Romans 12:4-5

"For just as we have many members in one body and all the members do not have the same function, so we, who are many, are one body in Christ, and individually members one of another."

92. Romans 12:21

"Do not be overcome by evil, but overcome evil with good."

93. Romans 13:1

"Every person is to be in subjection to the governing authorities. For there is no authority except from God, and those which exist are established by God."

94. Romans 13:13

"Let us behave properly as in the day, not in carousing and drunkenness, not in sexual promiscuity and sensuality, not in strife and jealousy."

95. Romans 13:14

"But put on the Lord Jesus Christ, and make no provision for the flesh in regard to its lusts."

96. 1 Corinthians 2:2

"For I determined to know nothing among you except Jesus Christ, and Him crucified."

97. 1 Corinthians 6:18

"Flee immorality. Every other sin that a man commits is outside the body, but the immoral man sins against his own body."

98. 1 Corinthians 6:19

"Or do you not know that your body is a temple of the Holy Spirit who is in you, whom you have from God, and that you are not your own?"

99. 1 Corinthians 6:20

"For you have been bought with a price; therefore glorify God in your body."

100. 1 Corinthians 9:24

"Do you not know that those who run in a race all run, but only one receives the prize? Run in such a way that you may win."

101. 1 Corinthians 10:13

"No temptation has overtaken you but such as is common to man; and God is faithful, who will not allow you to be tempted beyond what you are able, but with the temptation will provide the way of escape also, so that you will be able to endure it."

102. 1 Corinthians 13:4

"Love is patient, love is kind and is not jealous; love does not brag and is not arrogant."

103. 1 Corinthians 13:5

"[Love] does not act unbecomingly; it does not seek its own, is not provoked, does not take into account a wrong suffered."

104. 1 Corinthians 13:6

"[Love] does not rejoice in unrighteousness, but rejoices with the truth."

105. 1 Corinthians 13:7-8a

"[Love] bears all things, believes all things, hopes all things, endures all things. Love never fails."

106. 2 Corinthians 1:3

"Blessed be the God and Father of our Lord Jesus Christ, the Father of mercies and God of all comfort."

107. 2 Corinthians 1:4

"[God] comforts us in all our affliction so that we will be able to comfort those who are in any affliction with the comfort with which we ourselves are comforted by God."

108. 2 Corinthians 5:21

"He made Him who knew no sin to be sin on our behalf, so that we might become the righteousness of God in Him."

109. 2 Corinthians 6:14

"Do not be bound together with unbelievers; for what partnership have righteousness and lawlessness, or what fellowship has light with darkness?"

110. 2 Corinthians 9:6

"Now this I say, he who sows sparingly will also reap sparingly, and he who sows bountifully will also reap bountifully."

111. 2 Corinthians 10:5

"We are destroying speculations and every lofty thing raised up against the knowledge of God, and we are taking every thought captive to the obedience of Christ."

112. 2 Corinthians 12:9

"And He has said to me, 'My grace is suffi-cient for you, for power is perfected in weakness.' Most gladly, therefore, I will rather boast about my weaknesses, so that the power of Christ may dwell in me."

113. Galatians 2:20

"I have been crucified with Christ; and it is no longer I who live, but Christ lives in me; and the life which I now live in the flesh I live by faith in the Son of God, who loved me and gave Himself up for me."

114. Galatians 5:22-23

"But the fruit of the Spirit is love, joy, peace, patience, kindness, goodness, faithfulness, gentleness, self-control; against such things there is no law."

115. Ephesians 2:8-9

"For by grace you have been saved through faith; and that not of yourselves, it is the gift of God; not as a result of works, so that no one may boast."

116. Ephesians 2:10

"For we are his workmanship, created in Christ Jesus for good works, which God prepared beforehand so that we would walk in them."

117. Ephesians 4:32

"Be kind to one another, tender-hearted, forgiving each other, just as God in Christ also has forgiven you."

118. Ephesians 5:3

"But immorality or any impurity or greed must not even be named among you, as is proper among saints."

119. Ephesians 5:4

"And there must be no filthiness and silly talk, or coarse jesting, which are not fitting, but rather giving of thanks."

120. Ephesians 6:1

"Children, obey your parents in the Lord, for this is right."

121. Ephesians 6:2-3

"Honor your father and mother (which is the first commandment with a promise), so that it may be well with you, and that you may live long on the earth."

122. Ephesians 6:13

"Therefore, take up the full armor of God, so that you will be able to resist in the evil day, and having done everything, to stand firm."

123. Philippians 1:21

"For to me, to live is Christ and to die is gain."

124. Philippians 2:2

"Make my joy complete by being of the same mind, maintaining the same love, united in spirit, intent on one purpose."

125. Philippians 2:3

"Do nothing from selfishness or empty con-ceit, but with humility of mind regard one another as more important than yourselves."

126. Philippians 2:4

"Do not merely look out for your own per-sonal interests, but also for the interests of others."

127. Philippians 3:13-14

"Brethren, I do not regard myself as having laid hold of it yet; but one thing I do: for-getting what lies behind and reaching for-ward to what lies ahead, I press on toward the goal for the prize of the upward call of God in Christ Jesus."

128. Philippians 4:13
"I can do all things through Him who strengthens me."

129. Colossians 1:15
"He is the image of the invisible God, the firstborn of all creation."

130. Colossians 2:9
"For in Him all the fullness of Deity dwells in bodily form."

131. Colossians 3:13
"Bearing with one another, and forgiving each other, whoever has a complaint against anyone; just as the Lord forgave you, so also should you."

132. 1 Thessalonians 4:3
"For this is the will of God, your sanctification; that is, that you abstain from sexual immorality."

133. 1 Thessalonians 5:21-22
"But examine everything carefully; hold fast to that which is good; abstain from every form of evil."

134. 1 Timothy 1:5
"But the goal of our instruction is love from a pure heart and a good conscience and a sincere faith."

135. 1 Timothy 2:3-4
"This is good and acceptable in the sight of God our Savior, who desires all men to be saved and to come to the knowledge of the truth."

136. 2 Timothy 1:7
"For God has not given us a spirit of timidity, but of power and love and discipline."

137. 2 Timothy 2:22
"Now flee from youthful lusts and pursue righteousness, faith, love and peace, with those who call on the Lord from a pure heart."

138. 2 Timothy 3:16
"All Scripture is inspired by God and profitable for teaching, for reproof, for correction, for training in righteousness."

139. 2 Timothy 3:17
"So that the man of God may be adequate, equipped for every good work."

140. Hebrews 10:24
"And let us consider how to stimulate one another to love and good deeds."

141. Hebrews 12:1
"Therefore, since we have so great a cloud of witnesses surrounding us, let us also lay aside every encumbrance and the sin which so easily entangles us, and let us run with endurance the race that is set before us…"

142. Hebrews 12:2
"Fixing our eyes on Jesus, the author and perfecter of faith, who for the joy set before Him endured the cross, despising the shame, and has sat down at the right hand of the throne of God."

143. Hebrews 13:4
"Marriage is to be held in honor among all, and the marriage bed is to be undefiled; for fornicators and adulterers God will judge."

144. James 1:2-3
"Consider it all joy, my brethren, when you encounter various trials, knowing that the testing of your faith produces endurance."

145. James 1:4
"And let endurance have its perfect result, so that you may be perfect and complete, lacking in nothing."

146. James 1:5

"But if any of you lacks wisdom, let him ask of God, who gives to all generously and without reproach, and it will be given to him."

147. James 1:6

"But he must ask in faith without any doubting, for the one who doubts is like the surf of the sea, driven and tossed by the wind."

148. James 1:7-8

"For that man ought not to expect that he will receive anything from the Lord, being a double-minded man, unstable in all his ways."

149. James 1:13

"Let no one say when he is tempted, 'I am being tempted by God'; for God cannot be tempted by evil, and He Himself does not tempt anyone."

150. James 1:14-15

"But each one is tempted when he is carried away and enticed by his own lust. Then when lust has conceived, it gives birth to sin; and when sin is accomplished, it brings forth death."

151. James 1:22

"But prove yourselves doers of the word, and not merely hearers who delude themselves."

152. James 1:25

"But one who looks intently at the perfect law, the law of liberty, and abides by it, not having become a forgetful hearer but an effectual doer, this man will be blessed in what he does."

153. James 2:15-16

"If a brother or sister is without clothing and in need of daily food, and one of you says to them, 'Go in peace, be warmed and be filled,' and yet you do not give them what is necessary for their body, what use is that?"

154. James 2:17

"Even so faith, if it has no works, is dead, being by itself."

155. James 3:2

"For we all stumble in many ways. If anyone does not stumble in what he says, he is a perfect man, able to bridle the whole body as well."

156. James 3:5a

"So also the tongue is a small part of the body, and yet it boasts of great things."

157. James 4:4

"You adulteresses, do you not know that friendship with the world is hostility toward God? Therefore whoever wishes to be a friend of the world makes himself an enemy of God."

158. James 4:7

"Submit therefore to God. Resist the devil and he will flee from you."

159. James 4:10

"Humble yourselves in the presence of the Lord, and He will exalt you."

160. James 5:16

"Therefore, confess your sins to one another, and pray for one another so that you may be healed. The effective prayer of a righteous man can accomplish much."

161. 1 Peter 2:2

"Like newborn babes, long for the pure milk of the word, that by it you may grow in respect to salvation."

162. 1 Peter 3:15

"But sanctify Christ as Lord in your hearts, always being ready to make a defense to everyone who asks you to give an account for the hope that is in you, yet with gentleness and reverence."

163. 2 Peter 1:5

"Now for this very reason also, applying all diligence, in your faith supply moral excellence, and in your moral excellence, knowledge…"

164. 2 Peter 1:6

"And in your knowledge, self-control, and in your self-control, perseverance, and in your perseverance, godliness.…"

165. 2 Peter 1:7

"And in your godliness, brotherly kindness, and in your brotherly kindness, love."

166. 2 Peter 1:8

"For if these qualities are yours and are increasing, they render you neither useless nor unfruitful in the true knowledge of our Lord Jesus Christ."

167. 1 John 1:9

"If we confess our sins, He is faithful and righteous to forgive us our sins and to cleanse us from all unrighteousness."

168. Revelation 3:15-16

" 'I know your deeds, that you are neither cold nor hot; I wish that you were cold or hot. So because you are lukewarm, and neither hot nor cold, I will spit you out of My mouth.' "

169. Revelation 3:20

" 'Behold, I stand at the door and knock; if anyone hears My voice and opens the door, I will come in to him and will dine with him, and he with Me.' "

170. Revelation 21:1-2

"Then I saw a new heaven and a new earth; for the first heaven and the first earth passed away, and there is no longer any sea. And I saw the holy city, new Jerusalem, coming down out of heaven from God, made ready as a bride adorned for her husband."

171. Revelation 21:3

"And I heard a loud voice from the throne, saying, 'Behold, the tabernacle of God is among men, and He will dwell among them, and they shall be His people, and God Himself will be among them.' "

172. Revelation 21:4

" 'And He will wipe away every tear from their eyes; and there will no longer be any death; there will no longer be any mourning, or crying, or pain; the first things have passed away.' "

notes

introduction

1. Joe White, *FaithTraining* (Wheaton, Ill.: Focus on the Family/Tyndale, 1994), p. 48.
2. Knight et al., "Alcohol abuse and dependence among U.S. college students," *Journal of Studies on Alcohol*, 2002 (www.collegedrinkingprevention.gov).
3. "Study Links Teen Promiscuity With Drugs, Alcohol," Anjetta McQueen, the Associated Press (www.cyi-stars.org/articles/TeenPromiscuity.htm).
4. Barna report: "Teenagers Embrace Religion but Are Not Excited About Christianity," January 10, 2000.
5. Ibid.

matthew

1. Brigham Young, *Journal of Discourses* (Salt Lake City: The Church of Jesus Christ of Latter-Day Saints, 1966), 1:50-51.
2. *Rolling Stone.*
3. *USA Today*, April 24, 1987, p. 1D.
4. *Dallas Morning News*, October 11, 1987.
5. *The New Research*, published by the Rockford Institute, November 1990, pp. 2-4
6. Peggy Anderson, *Great Quotes from Great Leaders* (Lombard, Ill.: Celebrating Excellence Publishing, 1990), p. 102.
7. Robert Wright, "Our Cheating Hearts," *Time,* August 15, 1994: p. 45.
8. William J. Federer, *America's God and Country* (Coppell, Tex.: Fame Publishing, 1994), p. 657.
9. Federer, p. 275.
10. Gideon Hausner, *Justice in Jerusalem* (New York: Harper & Row, 1966), pp. 354, 366, 446.
11. Joseph Smith, *The Pearl of Great Price* (Salt Lake City: The Church of Jesus Christ of Latter-Day Saints, 1952), 2:18-19.
12. Bruce R. McConkie, *Mormon Doctrine* (Salt Lake City: Bookcraft, 1979), pp. 238-39; Joseph Smith, Jr., *History of the Church* (Salt Lake City: The Church of Jesus Christ of Latter-Day Saints, n.d.), 6:310-12.
13. *Let God Be True* (Brooklyn: Watchtower Bible and Tract Society, 1946), p. 111.
14. *Encyclopaedia Britannica*, vol. 4, p. 294.
15. Topps baseball card, "Jim Abbott."
16. George Currie, *The Military Discipline of the Romans from the Founding of the City to the Close of the Republic.* An abstract of a thesis published under the auspices of the Graduate Council of Indiana University, 1928.
17. Josh McDowell, *Evidence That Demands a Verdict,* (San Bernardino, Calif.: Campus Crusade for Christ International, 1972), p. 217.
18. Ibid., p. 231.

luke

1. Charles Panati, *Book of Origins.*
2. Ibid.
3. *William Barclay's Commentary on Luke.*

john

1. Donald M. Bowman, "Number One Killer of Teenagers—Drunk Driving," *California Capitol Report*, December 1990. Mike Snider, "Alcohol Is Leading U. S. Drug Worry," *USA Today*, Tuesday, April 14, 1992, p. 1D. "It Is Time to Ban the Advertising of Alcohol from Broadcasting," *AFA Journal*, January 1990, p. 12. Andrea Stone and Conner Chance, "Courts Must Address Unborn's Rights," *USA Today*, February 2, 1990, p. 3A.
2. Josh McDowell, *Evidence That Demands a Verdict* (San Bernardino, Calif.: Here's Life, 1979-81).
3. Ibid.
4. Smith, *The Pearl of Great Price*, 2:18-19.
5. Joseph Smith, *Doctrines of Salvation* (Salt Lake City: Church of Jesus Christ of Latter-Day Saints, n.d.), pp. 189-90.
6. Shirley MacLaine, *Dancing in the Light* (New York: Bantam, 1985), p. 420.
7. Mary Baker Eddy, *Science and Health: With Key to the Scriptures* (Boston: Allison V. Stewart, 1906), 25:6-8.
8. *Make Sure of All Things* (Brooklyn: Watchtower Bible and Tract Society, 1953), p. 207; *Let God Be True*, pp. 33, 88.

acts

1. Dr. David Barrett, ed., *World Christian Encyclopedia*, 2nd ed. (Oxford University Press, 1998).
2. *Compass Direct*, September 26, 1997, p. 7.

romans

1. Nancy Leigh DeMoss, "Making It Personal," *Spirit of Revival* (September 1995), pp. 24-29.

james

1. Patricia Hersch, "Sexually Transmitted Diseases Are Ravaging Our Children," *American Health,* May 1991, p. 44; Hersch, "Teen Epidemic," *American Health* May 1991, pp. 42-45; Jeff Kleinhuizen, "Campus Drinking Targeted," *USA Today*, March 6, 1991, p. 1.
2. Nike annual sales for 1993, in *Moody's Industrial News Report* 65, 50, February 1, 1994, p. 3277.
3. Jonah Blank and Warren Cohen, "Prayer-Circle Murders," *U.S. News & World Report*, December 15, 1997, pp. 25-27.

Great Resources to Keep Teens on Track

Parents' Guide to the Spiritual Mentoring of Teens

A parent's greatest reward is adult children who know, love and serve the Lord. The teen years are critical to developing such character. They mark the changing relationship between you and your children as they begin making their faith more personal. This guide offers solid, proven advice and techniques that will enable you to succeed in the changing parent-teen relationship. It will also equip you to ignite a passion in your teens to become wholehearted disciples. Hardcover.

Movie Nights

Now, you can use some of Hollywood's best efforts to teach discernment to and reinforce godly values in your teenagers. *Movie Nights* converts 25 entertaining, thought-provoking films such as *Remember the Titans, Apollo 13, The Princess Bride, The Truman Show* and *Chariots of Fire* into dynamic opportunities to connect with your teens and help them critically evaluate the media they consume. Each section features discussion questions, activities, related Scriptures and more. Paperback.

Boom: A Guy's Guide to Growing Up

Where do teen guys go when they have questions about their life and the changes they're going through? In *Boom: A Guy's Guide To Growing Up*, all the issues facing today's guys are addressed and answered in this easy-to-read, engaging book. Honest and straightforward, *Boom* tackles physical changes, sexuality and dating, money management, spiritual growth and more. Paperback.

Bloom: A Girl's Guide to Growing Up

Teen girls have lots of questions about life. In *Bloom: A Girl's Guide To Growing Up*, their questions are addressed and answered with the straight-forward honesty teens expect and demand. From changing bodies, to dating and sex, to relationships, money and more, girls will find the answers they need. Paperback.

Look for these special books in your Christian bookstore. To request a copy, call 1-800-932-9123, fax 1-719-548-4654, e-mail sales@family.org or write to Focus on the Family, Sales Department, P.O. Box 15379, Colorado Springs, CO 80935-4654. Friends in Canada may write to Focus on the Family, PO Box 9800, Stn Terminal, Vancouver, BC V6B 4G3 or call 1-800-661-9800.

Visit our Web site (www.family.org) to learn more about the ministry or find out if there is a Focus on the Family office in your country.